W9-AET-096

The Everglades
p118

Miami
p38

**Florida Keys &
Key West**
p135

Transportation

**GETTING THERE
& AWAY**

Nearly all international travelers come to South Florida by air, while most US travelers prefer air or car. Getting to South Florida by bus is a distant third option and by train an even more distant fourth. Miami is a major international airline hub, particularly for American Airlines, and it's the first port of call for many flights from Latin America and the Caribbean. Airports come

ams is more of a termination of highways and rail lines, rather than a major landtransit interchange area. Flights, tours and rail tickets can be booked online at www.lonelyplanet.com /bookings.

Air

Unless you live on or near Florida, flying to the region and then renting a car is the most time-efficient option.

Airports & A

THIS EDITION WRITTEN AND RESEARCHED BY

Adam Karlin

welcome to Miami & the Keys

The Magic City

South Florida is a land of dreams. Miami is known as the Magic City. Whichever way you cut it, imagination and innovation are big here, manifesting themselves in art, architecture and festivals. You see it from the extravagance of Lincoln Rd to the ephemeral neon beauty of Ocean Dr; from the cloud-kissing skyline of downtown Miami to the shells of empty condos that bankrupted their speculators; from the pink castle walls of a Coral Gables mansion to the dark, sexy lounges of Overtown; and from the Fabergé-egg interior of the Vizcaya Museum to an experimental art piece in Midtown. Stay in Miami long enough and you might believe magic is real.

Arts & the Edge

In Miami proper and Miami Beach, the newest neighborhoods are the districts where the creative community is opening the best restaurants, bars and clubs (and here 'the newest' and 'the best' often go hand in hand). Sometimes this takes the form of massive public investment realized in architectural masterpieces such as the Adrienne Arsht Center and the New World Center, two impressive performing arts spaces that have spruced up Miami and Miami Beach respectively. Sometimes it takes the form of young artists using open houses, gallery nights and special studio shows to gentrify entire swathes of neighborhood. In both ways, greater Miami is growing, physically and culturally.

Beauty is the name of the game here. From fashion models to deco hotels, beach sunrises to a wetland ecosystem and alluring islands, South Florida is an aesthetic masterpiece.

(left) South Beach's Ocean Drive (p46)
(below) Skating and cycling at South Beach (p42)

Ah, Florida

If Miami is full of culture, fun and urban beauty, South Florida is full of natural beauty, especially the spectacular wetland ecosystem of the Everglades and the island jungles and waterways of the Keys. If you took America and shook it by its sides, all its eccentricities (and quite a few eccentrics) would tumble into the southeast corner pocket that is South Florida. What happens when these folks mix with the region's considerable immigrant population? Fun, diversity and the occasional chicken sacrifice to a *vodou* god. Miami is iconoclastic enough, but outside the city? In the Everglades you'll find alligator wrestlers and Bigfoot hunters sharing a beer at crab shacks where panthers prowl the backyard. Head out to the Keys and you'll meet drag queens working as insect exterminators and islands named No Name inhabited by miniature deer. All of this delightful sense of place is ensconced within considerable natural beauty: shimmering bays, serene tidal flats, fecund cypress groves, emerald islands scattered over a teal sea, and a bed of ancient-looking wetlands.

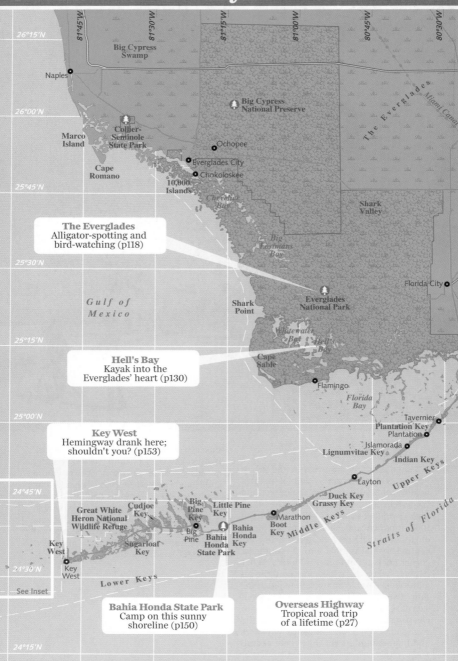

The Everglades
Alligator-spotting and
bird-watching (p118)

Hell's Bay
Kayak into the
Everglades' heart (p130)

Key West
Hemingway drank here;
shouldn't you? (p153)

Bahia Honda State Park
Camp on this sunny
shoreline (p150)

Overseas Highway
Tropical road trip
of a lifetime (p27)

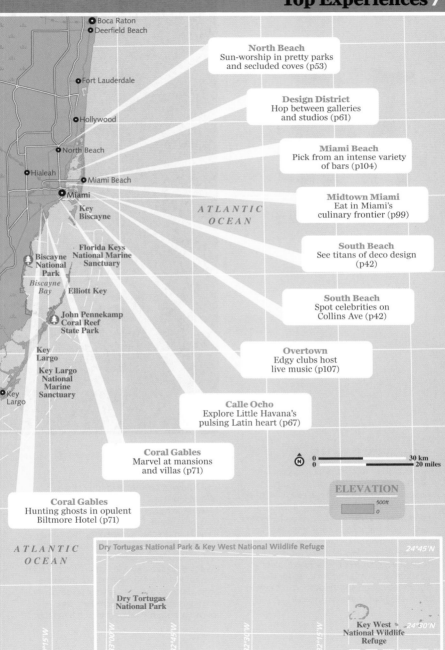

Boca Raton
Deerfield Beach

Fort Lauderdale

Hollywood

North Beach

Hialeah

Miami Beach

Miami

Key Biscayne

North Beach
Sun-worship in pretty parks
and secluded coves (p53)

Design District
Hop between galleries
and studios (p61)

Miami Beach
Pick from an intense variety
of bars (p104)

ATLANTIC
OCEAN

Midtown Miami
Eat in Miami's
culinary frontier (p99)

Florida Keys
National Marine
Sanctuary

Biscayne
National
Park

Biscayne
Bay   Elliott Key

South Beach
See titans of deco design
(p42)

South Beach
Spot celebrities on
Collins Ave (p42)

John Pennekamp
Coral Reef
State Park

Key
Largo

Key Largo
National
Marine
Sanctuary

Key
Largo

Overtown
Edgy clubs host
live music (p107)

Calle Ocho
Explore Little Havana's
pulsing Latin heart (p67)

Coral Gables
Marvel at mansions
and villas (p71)

0 ——————— 30 km
0 ——————— 20 miles

Coral Gables
Hunting ghosts in opulent
Biltmore Hotel (p71)

ELEVATION

500ft

0

ATLANTIC
OCEAN

Dry Tortugas National Park & Key West National Wildlife Refuge   24°45'N

Dry Tortugas
National Park

Key West
National Wildlife
Refuge   24°30'N

15 TOP EXPERIENCES

Miami Nightlife

1 Miami is a fun, good-looking city, and the best way to accept this truth is to head out on the town. In places like Midtown, Overtown and Coral Gables, you can find laid-back bars (p104) – even dives! – where clientele is glamorous, sexy and shiny, yet friendly and down to earth. Even the mega-clubs on Miami Beach, with their occasional restrictive red ropes and sky-high cover charges, are worth checking out for their sheer dedication and innovation in the field of creating bacchanalian excess.

Sun-Worshipping on North Beach

2 When people think of fun in the sun and Miami, their mental Rolodex often flips to two words: South Beach. And don't get us wrong! South Beach is stupendous. But if you're interested in escaping the crowds, the pressure to look fabulous and – again, people-spotting aside – a generally higher quality of beach, head to North Beach (p53). Places like Haulover Beach Park (p54) are pretty enough to serve as your screensaver, and if you really fancy a complete tan, there's a clothing-optional beach here, too.

Alligator-Spotting in the Everglades

3 South Florida loves to embrace the new in fashion, culinary trends and whatever the world thinks is hip. But look beneath the region's surface (literally) and you find a landscape and inhabitants who are ancient. How old? It doesn't get much more primeval than alligators, designed by nature to be perfect, leathery carnivores; predators whose engineering was so flawless, they haven't seen fit to change much since dinosaurs roamed. Spot dozens of gators from the boardwalks of the Royal Palm Visitor Center (p130).

Partying in Key West

4 Key West is many things: counterculture icon; southernmost tip of the continental USA; sun-drenched haven for the gay community. But let us never forget that for all these things, it is also, like it or not, a floating bar. Thousands of folks come here annually to cut loose. Join 'em! Start with a sunset over Mallory Square (p153), watch a dog on a tightrope and fire-eaters, then embark on the infamous 'Duvall Crawl' (p157) and get ready for the night of your life. Just don't plan much for the morning after.

Exploring Calle Ocho

5 *Ellos llaman a este barrio 'Little Havana' pero no son solo Cubanos los que viven aquí.* Sorry. We're just pointing out Little Havana (p67), nominal heart of Miami's Cuban community, is populated by more than Cubans. There are Spanish speakers from all over lining Calle Ocho, otherwise known as '8th St,' one of the most colorful, culturally vibrant thoroughfares in the country. It helps to speak some Spanish, but it doesn't matter if you don't. Just grab a cigar, a tall fruit juice and place your finger on Miami's multicultural pulse.

Gallery-Hopping the Design District

6 Miami's hippest residents pop into South Beach clubs occasionally, but for years the loci of cool-kid activity has been Midtown (the area north of Downtown that includes Wynwood and the Design District; p61), once a working-class 'hood. Many buildings are now galleries, studio spaces, art warehouses and sometimes all of the above. Every month these art outposts throw open their doors (p107). Wine flows. The artsy, literati-minded and just plain glamorous dance from gallery to gallery. And new frontiers in Miami cool are pushed.

Hunting the Biltmore's Ghosts

7 Miami doesn't lack for impressive buildings, and some say the grandest jewel in the city's crown is the Biltmore in Coral Gables (even the name rolls aristocratically off the tongue). Built in 1925, this hotel (p71) encapsulates the two initially disparate vibes of the Jazz Age: brilliant flashiness and elegant dignity. Today the well-to-do and the ghosts of guests past prowl the majestic grounds, and we don't just mean the Biltmore captures the essence of its heyday; some say spirits haunt the halls.

Celebrity-Sighting in South Beach

8 South Beach (p42) is all about glamour, in its original, Old English meaning: a spell. Magic. So many celebrities come to South Beach that their lifestyle rubs off on we mere mortals who chase them around, hoping to spot them strolling Lincoln Rd (p43; pictured below) or sipping a drink at the Shore Club (p87). There is a self-fulfilling magic to the paparazzi atmosphere of South Beach. Lose yourself in the swooning crowd, because as you search out celebrities and hang in their hot spots, you start feeling like one yourself.

RICHARD CUMMINS / LONELY PLANET IMAGES ©

ROUGH GUIDES / PHOTOLIBRARY ©

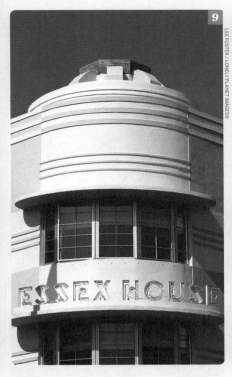

Checking Out Art-Deco Giants

9 Like all great cities, Miami and Miami Beach have a distinctive architectural style (p213). Actually, art deco isn't just distinctive in Miami. In places like South Beach (p42), it's definitive. The style is an early 20th-century expression of aesthetic that embodies seemingly contradictory impulses – modernity with nostalgia for the beaux arts; streamlining coupled with fantastic embellishment; subdued colors and riots of pastel. Whatever your take on deco may be, you'll be hard-pressed to find a better concentration of it outside of Miami and Miami Beach.

Eating Up Midtown Miami

10 Miami is a city that loves its indulgences, and the greatest of these is a fine meal. If you really want to play with your taste buds, come to Miami's culinary frontier: Midtown (Wynwood and surrounds; p99). In restaurants like Señora Martinez, Sustain and Michy's, you'll find the best in local ingredients – a rich banquet of decadence plucked from Florida's fields and oceans – prepared Miami-style, with plenty of tropical flair and fun.

Marveling at Coral Gables' Mansions

11 Coral Gables (p71) is called the City Beautiful with good reason. America in general and Miami in particular are often associated with gaudiness, but Coral Gables takes this cliché and turns it on its head. Yes, houses here are opulent, and some are admittedly over the top, but many are gorgeous executions of a Mediterranean-revival style that blends the best of Iberian villas, Moroccan *riads* and Roman pleasure domes. Coral Gables is Miami's House on the Hill; we highly recommend gawking.

STEPHEN MEESE / DREAMSTIME ©

RADIUS IMAGES / CORBIS ©

Kayaking Hell's Bay

12 Good old Glades boys who once lived in what is now one of America's most beautiful national parks dubbed one stretch of water 'Hell's Bay.' Why? The waterway, part of a complicated capillary network of Glades streams, was 'hell to get into, hell to get out of.' But it's also heavenly once inside, shaded and shadowed by a tunnel of vegetation that cools you while water runs past your paddles. Forget fearsome titles; kayaking Hell's Bay (p130) is one of the most romantic exploratory experiences in South Florida.

Camping on Bahia Honda

13 Everyone assumes the Florida Keys are ringed with beautiful beaches, but this is actually not the case. The Keys are mangrove islands, and as such their coasts are often a tangle of bracken and vegetation – pretty, but hardly a traditional beach. Not so at Bahia Honda (p150), where a pretty smear of buttery sand is spread along the coastline. Book early and you can camp here, waking to perfect saltwater breezes and the glimmer of a new day dancing on the nearby waves.

Exploring Nightlife North of Downtown

14 There's a feast for all seasons when it comes to partying north of downtown Miami. The bars, pubs and clubs here (p107), which stretch from rough Overtown to artsy Midtown to the long vistas of Biscayne Blvd, run a veritable gamut of styles: there are posh lounges where statuesque models in wedge heels sip chardonnay; gay dive bars where karaoke is often on the menu; studio spaces that have been converted into kickin' live-music venues; and quite a few eccentric examples that sample all of the above.

© 2011 DAN VIDAL

TAKE ME SPACE

Overseas Highway Road Trip

15 The Florida Keys are linked by Hwy 1, also known as the Overseas Hwy (p27). Heading over the road's many bridges and pulling over intermittently to admire the Gulf of Mexico or Florida Bay is simply one of the great pleasures of Florida travel. If you don't feel like driving, you can cycle much of the 127.5-mile route; most of the way is flat, shoulder lanes are established throughout, and more than 70 miles of the Florida Keys Overseas Heritage Trail (p142) are there for cyclists to enjoy.

ANDY NEWMAN / EPA / CORBIS ©

need to know

Currency
» US dollars ($)

Language
» English and Spanish

When to Go

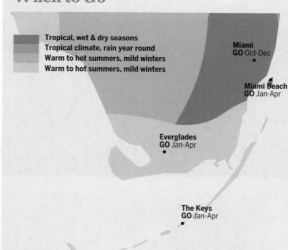

Tropical, wet & dry seasons
Tropical climate, rain year round
Warm to hot summers, mild winters
Warm to hot summers, mild winters

Miami
GO Oct-Dec

Miami Beach
GO Jan-Apr

Everglades
GO Jan-Apr

The Keys
GO Jan-Apr

Key West
GO Oct-Dec

Your Daily Budget

Budget less than
$100

» Hostel dorms around $25; cheap rooms $60 to $70

» Self-cater at grocery stores

» Walk and cycle – avoid cabs!

Midrange
$100-250

» Hotel rooms can be booked in advance for significant discounts

» Arts walks and gallery nights are fun, cheap night out options

» With mains running $15 to $25, eateries at the top end midrange are excellent value

Top End over
$250

» Cover at bigger nightclubs starts at $20

» Expect to pay at least $50 per person on mains at upscale restaurants

» Indulge in some room service!

High Season
(Jan–Mar)

» Winter weather in South Florida is dry, sunny and practically perfect.

» You'll need to book well in advance to line up rooms at this time.

» A preponderance of festivals equals lots of fun – and crowds.

Shoulder Season (Apr–May & Oct–Nov)

» The early end of spring resembles late winter; by May the weather gets humid.

» October is still hurricane season, but things dry off later in the month.

» Festival season gears up in late fall.

Low Season
(Jun–Sep)

» Sure, it's hot as hell, but sea breezes are cooling.

» Mosquitoes are at their worst, especially in the Everglades.

» Did we mention hurricanes? Fortunately there's good early-warning systems on hand.

Money

» Twenty-four-hour ATMs are widely available across Miami, the Keys and the towns that border the Everglades. Credit cards accepted at most businesses.

Visas

» Required for most foreign visitors unless eligible for the Visa Waiver Program (see p225)

Cell Phones

» Local SIM cards can be used in European or Australian phones. Other phones must be set to roaming.

Driving

» Drive on the right; steering wheel is on the left side of the car.

Websites

» **Art Circuits** (www .artcircuits.com) Gallery maps.

» **Everglades National Park** (www.nps.gov /ever) Maps and info.

» **Beached Miami** (www.beachedmiami .com) Arts website.

» **Miami Favs** (miami favs.tumblr.com) Love for everything Miami.

» **Miami Herald** (www .herald.com) News.

» **Florida Keys & Key West** (www.fla-keys .com) Keys visitor info.

» **Lonely Planet** (www .lonelyplanet.com/usa /miami) Destinations, hotel bookings, traveler forums and more.

Exchange Rates

Australia	A$1.06
Canada	C$1.04
Europe	€1.4
Japan	¥79
New Zealand	NZ$0.84
UK	£1.6

For current exchange rates see www.xe.com

Important Numbers

You need to dial the area code even for domestic calls, except emergency

Miami & the Keys/ Everglades Area Codes	☎305, 786/239
Police/Fire/ Medical Emergency	☎911
Miami Beach Patrol	☎305-673-7714
Hurricane Hotline	☎305-468-5400
Everglades National Park	☎305-242-7700

Arriving in Miami

» **Miami International Airport (MIA)**

Buses – The Airport Flyer goes between MIA and Miami Beach every 30 minutes
Train – Tri-Rail runs from MIA to routes downtown (see p117)
Taxi – Taxis to Lincoln Rd in Miami Beach are $32
Car – Major car-rental services are available right next to the main terminal
There's more information on getting to and from the Everglades (p119) and the Keys (p139)

Driving Directions in Miami

Remember: Miami and Miami Beach are two different cities separated by the blue waters of Biscayne Bay. Miami Beach is connected to Miami by five causeways; if you're heading to South Beach, take the MacArthur Causeway (A1A). You can also take the Venetian Causeway, which runs from NE 15th St – useful for getting to Lincoln Rd. The next causeway up, the Julia Tuttle Causeway, conveniently connects the beach to 41st St, the heart of Miami's Design District. The major north–south highway (I-95) connects Miami to Fort Lauderdale to the north. Driving on the highways is convenient in South Florida, and rental cars generally come equipped with Sun Pass transponders, devices that carry credit to get you through the region's many tolls. This charge is usually added to your rental fee; contact your rental agency and see www.sunpass.com for more information.

if you like...

Beaches

When many people think of Miami, they're really thinking of Miami Beach – that's how synonymous South Florida and beaches are. The coastline starts at the tip of South Beach and extends all the way up past over 100 blocks of cityscape. For a coast with nature's beauty instead of condos, head to North Beach, Crandon Park in Key Biscayne or the Bahia Honda State Park in the Florida Keys.

South Beach Normal folks come here – to sight models, celebrities and lifestyles of the fabulous (p42)

Bahia Honda State Park A windswept, serene spot that exemplifies the forested, sun-bleached beauty of the Keys (p150)

Crandon Park A gorgeous beach that mixes nature and fun on offshore Key Biscayne (p65)

Haulover Beach Park In North Beach, Haulover provides privacy, quiet – and birthday suits at the nude beach (p54)

Boardwalk Mid-Beach's boardwalk mixes up curious tourists with lovely sand, and black-coated Orthodox Jews – fabulously surreal (p53)

Nightlife

Is it any surprise that a region so famed for its sex appeal knows how to let loose and have a lot of fun come evening? Latin American sensuality, European hipness and the raw American ability to have fun mash up in some fantastic bars and clubs in Miami. The Keys abound with fun joints that attract tourists, fisherfolk and cheerfully insane pirates.

Midtown Miami's most innovative, interesting bars attract artists, the creative class and of course, the glam crowd (p106)

The Keys Key West gets the glory, but the other Keys have their own self-contained party scenes (p135)

Overtown Live music and hipsters mix it up with chichi decor and international DJs north of Downtown (p107)

Key West This island of eccentrics at the end of the rainbow does not lack for good times (p164)

South Beach Lovely local bars and lounges mix it up with a more red-rope scene of models and celebrities (p104)

Cuisine

South Florida is very much a magnet for immigrants, and as such it has an international palate, supplemented by a local bounty of tropical citrus and sea life. Many flavors are Latin American, but clouds of jet-setters demand – and receive – fusion cuisine from Europe and Asia. Heartier home cooking can be found in small towns around the Everglades, while the Keys balance native flavor and cosmopolitan tastes.

Little Havana Miami's Cuban community serves up some of the best Cuban cuisine outside actual Havana (p101)

Midtown Some of Miami's most original menus are served in some of its most beautiful eating spaces (p99)

North Beach It may not be as glamorous as South Beach, but there's great ethnic eateries up this way (p96)

Everglades Fried gator, fried frogs' legs, hot sauce and a cold beer – it's not haute, but it's damn delicious (p126)

Key West For an island of this size, there's a fantastic variety of food on offer (p163)

RICHARD I'ANSON / LONELY PLANET IMAGES ©

» Sunbathers on Miami's South Beach (p42)

Outdoor Activities

South Florida's tropical landscape is unique in the continental USA. From the mangrove islands of the Keys to gentle grasslands, beaches and palm hammock (forest) to the great wetland wilderness that is the Everglades, there's plenty of distinctive beauty here beyond clubs and models.

Everglades The 'River of Grass' is a uniquely beautiful ecosystem that can easily be the highlight of a visit to South Florida (p118)

Crane Point Museum On the island of Marathon, this outdoor museum is a great introduction to the ecology of the Florida Keys (p147)

Oleta River State Park Drive past the condos of North Miami Beach and slip into wilderness serenity on a canoe or kayak (p54)

Hell's Bay Canoe into the bracken heart of the marsh in this attractive series of small streams (p130)

10,000 Islands To truly appreciate the Zen of South Florida, camp in this lovely barrier archipelago (p128)

Music

Miami is arguably the greatest entrepôt in Latin America, a region that – forgive us the stereotype – likes its music. From samba to salsa to reggaeton, the rhythms of the Caribbean, Central and South America resound here, alongside Euro techno, indie rock, Haitian pop and local hip-hop. Needless to say, the beat is infectious.

The Stage Independent acts with an attitude, ranging from Orlando rockers to Overtown rappers (p108)

Green Parrot Local live bands regularly rock the scene at Key West's oldest, funkiest bar (p164)

Churchill's If you think Miami can't rock, out check the Mohawks at this hard-bitten British pub (p106)

Seven Seas Karaoke nights here are a fascinating tableau of Miami music, a mix of older Cubans, riot grrl rockers and artsy university students (p107)

Big Night in Little Haiti The monthly party at the Little Haiti Cultural Center is a Caribbean/Kreyol feast for the ears (p63)

Wildlife

The Everglades resemble footage from *Jurassic Park*. In the Keys some of the best sports fishing in the world takes advantage of a local piscatory population of tarpon, swordfish and marlin. In between are animal sanctuaries and underwater natural parks, scattered from Miami to the edges of the Everglades to the Keys.

Royal Palm Visitor Center Wander onto the boardwalk here and stare down hundreds of gators prowling the water (p130)

John Pennekamp Coral Reef State Park In the continental USA, diving simply doesn't get better (p139)

Big Pine Key Tiny deer – cute as all get-out – are the inhabitants of the largest island in the Keys (p150)

Biscayne National Park A national park that's almost entirely underwater, come to Biscayne to catch or spot fish (p132)

Everglades Outpost This animal sanctuary, by a committed band of do-gooders, is a must-see detour for Everglades visitors (p129)

» Robert Is Here farmers' market (p129)

Shopping

Miami unabashedly loves a bit of consumerism. Fashionistas flaunt Milanese levels of bling and sophistication thanks to a heavy European and Latin presence in Coral Gables and Miami Beach; more artsy labels and posh decor can be found in the Design District. Malls abound in Miami, but so do indie boutiques.

Books and Books The best independent bookstore in Miami is a bastion of good taste and great literature (p113)

Pepe Y Berta Slip by this Little Havana tailor and slip into the guayabera, Cuba's coolest shirt (p113)

Metta Boutique Get your karma balanced at this cute shop of sustainable, fair-trade gifts (p113)

Miami Mid Century Relive Miami's Golden Age of unbridled aesthetic cool with antiques and design pieces (p112)

C Madeleine's This is vintage clothing so beautiful it can rightfully be classified as classic couture (p113)

Arts

We give Miami credit for using the arts to stimulate urban revival. From events like Art Basel (23) to venues like the Adrienne Arsht Center to the intimate galleries of Wynwood, the arts have paved the way for much of Miami's renaissance. Artists also find inspiration amid the light and idiosyncrasies of crazy Key West.

Adrienne Arsht Center for the Performing Arts Resembling a series of seashells, the Arsht center is a performance space par excellence (p55)

New World Center Not to be outdone, Miami Beach's concert hall hosts both edgy art and mainstream productions (p43)

Studios of Key West A one-stop gallery-gazing spot for those into the artistic output of Key West (p158)

Cuba Ocho This Little Havana spot hosts visual and performing arts that showcase Miami's Cuban creativity (p68)

Wynwood Drop by on the second Saturday of each month for an open-house peek into Miami's best galleries (p107)

Architecture

Be it South Beach's classic deco hotels or the glittering crystal condos of North Beach, the pink villas of Coral Gables or the Caribbean-colonial stately homes of Key West, South Florida does not lack for architecture that sets her apart as a region unlike any other in the USA.

Art Deco Historic District South Beach's heart is clustered with hotels, promenades and other prime examples of the art-deco movement (p42)

Freedom Tower Downtown Miami is known for skyscrapers, and this classic tower was one of the first (p60)

Coral Gables The mansions of Coral Gables run the gamut, from Mediterranean wedding cakes to neo-Arabic palaces (p71)

Key West There's a shady joy to strolling under the eaves of Key West's French-Caribbean and Spanish-revival homes (p153)

Vizcaya This fairy-tale estate is the most opulent, over-the-top jewel in Miami's considerably sparkly architectural crown (p68)

If you like...the circus, try to attend a class at the South Florida Circus Arts School, where your flying-trapeze fantasies become a reality (p79)

Quirky Florida

Sometimes we think Florida needs a new state motto: 'Florida is a delightfully weird state'. There are lots of eccentrics that get attracted to this part of the world. Be it for weather, gators, hedonism – we're not sure, but what follows are some of our favorites from the 'Only in Florida' category.

Everglades International Hostel The backyard of this fantastic hostel resembles the trippy art of '60s psychedelic album sleeves (p129)

Skunk Ape Research Headquarters It's a reptile zoo-'museum' dedicated to hunting the Everglades' Bigfoot. Why aren't you here yet? (p125)

Coral Castle A palace that a Latvian hewed from coral that doubles as a monument to lost love? Why not? (p128)

Robbie's Marina Like an aquatic petting zoo, except the pets are enormous monster tarpon fish (p142)

Florida Keys History of Diving Museum PADI people, check out possibly the most complete collection of diving paraphernalia in the USA (p143)

Old Florida

'Old Florida' is a term associated with nostalgia for a simpler, more rural, less developed Florida. The Old Florida ideal is a bit of an invented affectation, but the term is also a byword for ecofriendly, preservation-minded attractions that are well worth your time.

Robert Is Here At this farmers' market, taste the bounty of the region – sometimes shipped direct to your home (p129)

Turtle Hospital At this Keys institution, visitors can see injured and sick sea turtles cared for by a dedicated staff of volunteers (p147)

Rod & Gun Club Lodge Smooth paneled wood, spirits at the bar and photos from hunting and fishing trips of the past (p127)

Florida Keys Wild Bird Rehabilitation Center This sanctuary for injured avian animals has long been an attraction in the Keys (p140)

No Name Key This quiet island boasts miniature deer and some of the best pizza in the Keys (p151)

Multicultural Encounters

The Keys are a crossroads of the Caribbean, while Miami is one of the most immigrant-rich cities in the country. Diversity is more than a buzzword here – it's the cloth that the social fabric of South Florida is cut from. These sites speak to the tropical cosmopolitan nature of this region.

Viernes Culturales Little Havana transforms into a Cuban street party on the last Friday of the month (p68)

Goombay Festival In late October, Key West explodes into a celebration of Bahaman music, food and dance (p161)

Little Haiti Cultural Center Pick up a beaded purse from Port-au-Prince or original art by young Haitian Americans (p63)

Miccosukee Village In the Everglades, learn about the folkways of Florida's indigenous inhabitants (p124)

Arthur Godfrey Road Also known as 41st St, this Miami Beach road is the heart of this city's sizable Jewish population (p54)

month by month

Top Events

1. **Art Basel Miami Beach**, December
2. **Winter Music Conference**, March
3. **Sweatstock**, May
4. **Hemingway Days**, July
5. **Fantasy Fest**, October

January

The beginning of the new year also happens to be the height of the tourist season in these parts. Expect fair weather, crowds, higher prices than usual and a slew of special events.

Orange Bowl

Hordes of football fans descend on Miami for the Super Bowl of college football, the infamous Orange Bowl (www.orangebowl .org). The entire city gets a youthful-demographic shot in the arm, while team rivalries simmer in sports bars.

Key West Literary Seminar

Key West has long been a haven for writers escaping the real world, and its expat authors have turned the annual Key West Literary Seminar (http://keywestlit eraryseminar.org/lit) into one of the premier festivals of letters in the USA.

Art Deco Weekend

This weekend fair (www .artdecoweekend.com) of everything art deco (Miami's signature style) features guided tours of the city's many clusters of deco structures, concerts, classic-auto shows, sidewalk cafes, and vendors of arts and antiques. Held in mid-January.

Miami Jewish Film Festival

This international film festival (www.miamijewishfilm festival.com) gets a large amount of attention outside of Miami, and is a great chance to cinematically *kibitz* (chat) with one of the biggest Jewish communities in the USA.

February

The last hurrah for northerners needing to escape the harsh winter, February brings arts festivals, street parties and excellent wildlife-viewing in the Everglades.

Coconut Grove Arts Festival

One of the most prestigious festivals (www.coconut groveartsfest.com) of its kind in a city that doesn't lack for an artistic calendar, this late-February fair features more than 300 artists from across the globe.

Original Miami Beach Antique Show

This show (www.original miamibeachantiqueshow .com) is sort of like unearthing a combination attic of all the world's quirky, cool stuff crossed with an archaeology dig, attracting some 800 dealers from over 20 countries.

South Beach Wine & Food Festival

A festival (www.sobefest .com) of fine dining and sipping that has become a fixture of South Florida's social calendar. Expect star-studded brunches, dinners and barbecues. Your best time of year to brush shoulders with a celebrity chef by a mile.

March

Spring arrives, bringing warmer weather, world-class golf and outdoor tennis festivals, and St Patrick's Day. Expect some Spring Breakers to behave badly on the beach.

Winter Music Conference

Party promoters, DJs, producers and revelers come from around the globe to hear new artists, catch up on technology and party the nights away. If you've any interest in electronic music, it'd be criminal to miss WMC (www.wmcon .com).

 ### Miami International Film Festival

The Miami International Film Festival (www.miami filmfestival.com), sponsored by Miami-Dade College, is a two-week festival show-casing documentaries and features from all over the world. Spanish-language films are an important component of the event.

South Beach Comedy Festival

We're not going to say March is the happiest month in Miami, but during the South Beach Comedy Festival (www .southbeachcomedyfestival .com) it's hard to leave town without a smile, as excellent talent performs stand-up in venues across the city.

 ### Miami Fashion Week

Vogue, darling. Models are like fish in the ocean in Miami during most of the year, but they're simply ubiquitous during Miami Fashion Week (www.miami fashionweek.com), when designers descend on the city and catwalks become disconcertingly commonplace.

 # April

Welcome to shoulder season, lower prices, balmier temperatures and some choice events. This is Miami's best transition period between winter crowds and summer swelter.

Billboard Latin Music Awards

This prestigious awards show (www.billboard events.com/billboard events/latin/index.jsp) in late April draws top indus-try execs, star performers and a slew of Latin-music fans. Live music sets by Latin performers from across the world frequently accompany the ceremony.

Robert Frost Poetry Festival

Key West celebrates one of the many poet laureates that have called the island home with the Robert Frost Poetry Festival (www .robertfrostpoetryfestival. com). The festival is meant to coincide with National Poetry Month.

Miami Gay & Lesbian Film Festival

Held in late April to early May, this annual fes-tival (www.mglff.com) is screened at various South Beach theaters. Lesbian, Gay, Bisexual and Transgen-der (LGBT) visitors will find fun events bracketing the event, generally of a more cerebral bent than is normal for Miami's scene.

May

Spring in South Florida can either mean pleasantly subdued heat or sweaty soup. This is when mosquito season begins in earnest in the Everglades.

 ### Sweatstock

Every year, Sweat Records (www.sweatrecords miami.com), one of the best record shops in town, puts on a festival aimed at locals with headline acts perform-ing indie rock, punk and electronica. Visiting will throw you into the Miami music scene.

Miami Museum Month

This event pretty much makes the entire month of May a good time to visit. Mu-seum month (www.miami museummonth.com) is an excellent chance to experi-ence happy hours, special exhibitions and unique lectures in some of the best museums in the city.

June

This is when the real baking heat and wet humidity begins in Miami, and the events calendar tends to tone down a little as a result.

 ### Goombay Festival Coconut Grove

Bahamas Mama. One of a few Goombay festivals held in South Florida, this mas-sive fest, held on the first week of June, celebrates Ba-hamian culture in Coconut Grove. Expect music, street food and *lots* of dancing (www.goombayfestival coconutgrove.com).

July

OK – not only is it hot, it's hurricane season. Yay! But seriously, this is a good time to visit. Crowds are low and locals are frankly friendlier and more accessible to tourists.

 Independence Day

July 4 features an excellent fireworks and laser show with live music that draws more than 100,000 people to breezy Bayfront Park. The pyrotechnics light up the sky above Biscayne Bay in an oddly romantic way.

 Hemingway Days

One of Key West's more (in)famous annual rituals is Hemingway Days, a party that celebrates all things Hemingway (our way of saying: expect drinking, if not game hunting). The highlight is the yearly running of the Ernest-look-crowd.

August

August is the sweltering deepest dip in the low tourist season. Many visitors head to the Keys, where cooling sea winds are a regular phenomenon.

 Miami Spice

Top restaurants around Miami participate in Miami Spice's Food Month (Ilovemiamispice.com), offering prix-fixe meals to lure folks out of the air-con.

For most tourists, this is an easier festival to appreciate than the celebrity-focused South Beach Wine & Food Festival.

September

The weather is still steamy, and autumn brings back college students – expect lots of revelry in the university 'hoods like Coconut Grove and Coral Gables.

⭐ **International Ballet Festival of Miami**

While much of Miami's arts calendar is given over to modern visual art and music, the International Ballet Festival of Miami (www .internationalballetfestival .org) is the main event for the city's considerably active patrons of classical dance.

🏃 **Great Grove Bed Race**

Between the pajama pub crawl and drag racing beds through Coconut Grove, the Great Grove Bed Race (www.thegreatgrovebedrace .com), held around Labor Day Weekend (the first weekend in September), is one of Miami's wackier celebrations.

 Womenfest

This fest (www .womenfest.com) gives ladies the chance to seize the large LGBT spotlight in Key West. This is the premier event for the island's lesbian population, attracting thousands of lesbian visitors from around the world for a Sapphic good time.

October

As hurricane season ends and the weather gets properly pleasant again, Key West takes over the events calendar with two raucous street celebrations.

⭐ **Fantasy Fest**

Held in late October, Fantasy Fest (www.fantasy fest.net) is by far the highlight of the Keys social calendar. The body paint, glitter, feathers and crazy floats come out, inhibitions are left at home, and a seriously decadent Roman bacchanal is had by all.

👁 **Goombay Key West**

In the heart of Bahama Village, one of the most vibrant Caribbean neighborhoods in the country, the Bahamanian Goombay Festival (www .goombay-keywest.org) serves up music, food, singing and dancing during the same insane week as Fantasy Fest.

November

Tourist season kicks off at the end of the month, bringing more crowds and cooler days. Festival time starts in earnest with the White Party.

⭐ **White Party**

If you're gay, love music, excess and naughty fun and aren't at the White Party (www.whiteparty.net), there's a problem. This week-long extravaganza draws thousands of gay men and women for nonstop partying at clubs and venues all over town.

Miami Book Fair International

Occurring in mid- to late November, the Miami Book Fair International (www .miamibookfair.com) is among the most important and well-attended book fairs in the USA. Hundreds of nationally known writers join hundreds of publishers; Latin American authors form a considerably strong contingent.

December

Tourist season is in full swing, with northerners booking rooms well in advance so they can bask in sunshine and be here for holiday festivities.

Art Basel Miami Beach

One of the seminal international art shows in the world, Art Basel (www .artbaselmiamibeach.com) can reasonably claim responsibility for putting Miami Beach on the map of the international jet-setter crowd. Gallery showcases, public installations and parties appear throughout Miami and Miami Beach.

King Mango Strut

Held each year just after Christmas, this quirky 24-year-old Coconut Grove parade (www.kingman gostrut.org) is a politically charged, fun fair that began as a spoof on current events and the now-defunct Orange Bowl Parade.

Art Miami

Held in January or December, Art Miami (www .art-miami.com) is a massive fair that displays modern and contemporary works from more than 100 galleries and international artists. It may not have Basel's big name, but the talent is still very impressive.

itineraries

Whether you've got six days or 60, these itineraries provide a starting point for the trip of a lifetime. Want more inspiration? Head online to lonelyplanet. com/thorntree to chat with other travelers

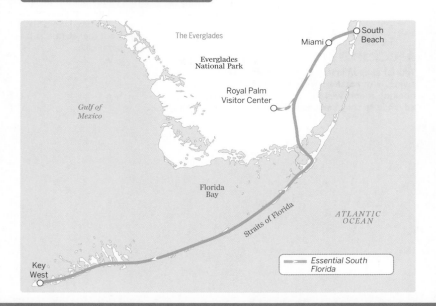

10 Days
Essential South Florida

We'd recommend starting your trip in **South Beach**, Miami, which encapsulates the best and worst of what South Florida has to offer. Take hotels like the Delano, Tides and the Shore Club, places that capture both the sheer aesthetic innovation and off-putting exclusivity of the South Beach experience. Enjoy the people watching on Lincoln Rd and a tour of the Art Deco Historic District.

Using South Beach as a base, spend the next few days exploring some of Miami's neighborhoods, including the Latin flavor of **Little Havana**, the Euro-style cafes and mansions of **Coral Gables** and the art galleries, excellent food and bumping nightlife around **Wynwood** and the **Design District**.

Four or five days is a good amount of time to get a feel for Miami. Spend the remainder of your time embarking on either our Overseas Highway Road Trip or the Everglades National Park trips following, making sure to spend at least a day and a night in **Key West** and visit the **Royal Palm Visitor Center** in the Everglades.

Five Days
Miami: Downtown to South Miami

On this trip you'll get to experience some of the best of Miami's ethnic enclaves, hobnob in some of its wealthiest neighborhoods and witness firsthand the opulent magic that gives this city the nickname 'The Magic City'.

Start in Downtown, a glittering fist of steel and glass that shadows rough alleyways and cheap international flea markets. Take a long ride on the free Metromover, hopping on and off to see the excellent **HistoryMiami** museum and the gorgeous **Adrienne Arsht Center for the Performing Arts**. Have a stroll along the **Miami River**, taking in the sunset and romantic seediness (try not to walk too far from the Metromover station, for safety's sake). At night, have a beer at **Tobacco Road** before doing as the locals do with a Colombian hot dog at **La Moon**.

The next day, head to Coral Gables, making sure not to miss the **Biltmore Hotel**, the **Venetian Pool** (possibly the loveliest public pool in the USA) and a shopping stroll down Miracle Mile. If that isn't opulent enough, see what happens when Mediterranean revival, Baroque stylings and money get mashed together at the **Vizcaya Museum & Gardens**. Afterwards, top off a visit to these elegant manses with dinner at one of the best restaurants in Miami in – no kidding – a gas station at **El Carajo**.

On the third day, head to Little Havana and have a stroll down **Calle Ocho**, making sure to watch the dominoes at Máximo Gómez Park. Have a Cuban lunch, browse the local cigar shops, then pop over to Coconut Grove, where the hippies of yesterday have been utterly replaced with the yuppies of today. Well, there's still some good karmic vibe under the banyan trees in the form of stores like the **Metta Boutique**.

Spend your last day exploring Key Biscayne, enjoying beaches, sunbathing and bliss in areas like **Crandon Park**. Before you leave, guzzle a beer and pick at some smoked fish and fascinating stories on the couches of **Jimbo's** on Virginia Key, a sort of bar-squatter camp filled with old pirates and fishermen, where the manatees sometimes swim right up to the adjacent docks.

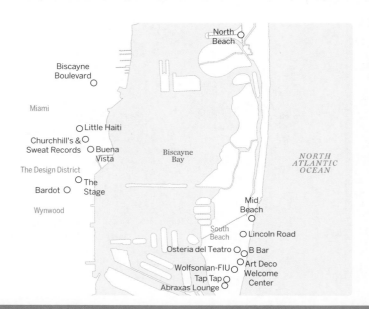

Miami: Miami Beach & North Miami

Start your trip in South Beach and use this region and its excellent hotels as your base. Make sure you visit the **Wolfsonian-FIU** design museum to get background on the surrounding art deco. Head for **Lincoln Road** to people-watch and browse the trendy shops; afterwards, you'd be remiss to not take a tour with the lovely folks at the **Art Deco Welcome Center**. For a nice dinner try **Osteria del Teatro** (classy Italian) or **Tap Tap** (psychedelic Haitian). When you're ready to hit the town (and the rails), we suggest early cocktails at **B Bar** and some beers at the **Abraxas Lounge**.

The next day, check out **Little Haiti**. This is one of the most colorful, recognizably 'foreign' neighborhoods in Miami, and it can be edgy at night, but by day you're fine to explore. A half mile south of here you'll find **Sweat Records** and **Churchill's**; the former is one of Miami's best music shops, while the latter is a down and dirty British punk pub.

You can easily make a day out of visiting Little Haiti, so the next morning go to the trendy **Design District** and the art galleries and studio spaces of **Wynwood**. Taken together, these neighborhoods constitute Midtown Miami, the most self-consciously artsy-creative section of the city. The Design District is a compact area that's easy to walk around and good for shopping (assuming you're loaded; these ain't starving artists, apparently). If you're hungry, head to one of the new restaurants flowering just north of here in shady **Buena Vista** or along **Biscayne Boulevard**. At night, clubs like **Bardot** and venues like **The Stage** are great spots to wet your whistle, watch DJs and live music and get your dance on.

After a few days of exploring Midtown and South Beach, head north along Collins Ave to **Mid-Beach** and **North Beach**. To get here you'll pass through the Condo Canyons – rows and rows of glittering residential skyscrapers, all testament to the power of real estate in Miami. In Mid-Beach, near the north end of South Beach, you'll find an excellent boardwalk if you feel like strolling near the sand.

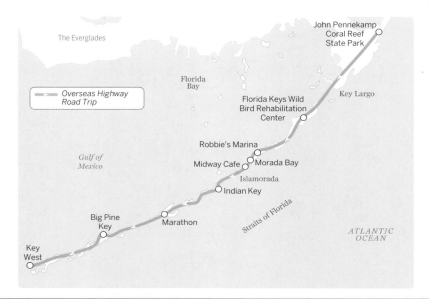

Three Days
Overseas Highway Road Trip

> The Overseas Highway (Hwy 1) runs from the tip of the Florida mainland all the way to the famed Mile Marker 0: Key West, the end of the road and the end of America. As you tick the mile markers down, you'll be treated to some of Florida's oddest attractions and the ever-inspiring view of Florida Bay on one side, the Gulf of Mexico on the other.

Well, OK, you'll get to that view, but first you have to go through the Upper Keys, larger islands that block the view of the water via big fields of scrub pine and mangroves. On northerly Key Largo, check out the diving options at **John Pennekamp Coral Reef State Park**, or visit the injured birds at the **Florida Keys Wild Bird Rehabilitation Center**. After a day's activities among fish or birds, tear into some lunch at the lovely Key Largo Conch House.

It'd be good to sleep in Islamorada on your first day in the Keys – if you can afford it, splurge at excellent **Morada Bay**. Wake up the next morning and feed the enormous tarpon at **Robbie's Marina**, and if you're feeling fit, hire a kayak and paddle out to **Indian Key**. When you're done you'll likely be feeling a little sapped, so make sure you caffeinate yourself at the excellent **Midway Cafe**.

By midday you'll easily have arrived at **Marathon**, geographic center of the Keys. If you're curious about the unique ecological background of the Keys and fancy a walk in the woods, head to the Crane Point Museum; if sea turtles happen to be your thing, a visit to the good doctors at the sanctuary Turtle Hospital may be in order. Eat dinner over the water at Keys Fisheries, then grab a beer at Hurricane.

Wake up and cross the Seven-Mile Bridge onto **Big Pine Key**, where tiny Key deer prance alongside the road.

Another hour's drive south and you're in **Key West**. Truly, this island deserves its own itinerary – just make sure you don't miss the sunset show in Mallory Sq, the six-toed cats at Hemingway's House and a night out at the infamous Green Parrot, the mother of all Keys bars.

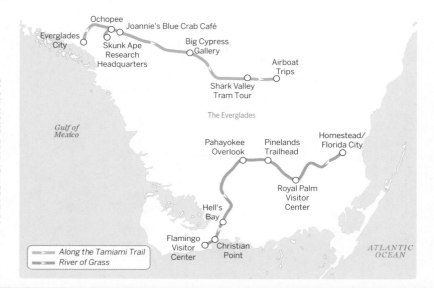

Two Days
Along the Tamiami Trail

This route takes you into the heart of what many consider the stereotypical Everglades: airboat tours through waterlogged wetlands, cypress swamps crawling with gators; with a stay in a fishing village.

Go west on Tamiami Trail (US 41) past the **airboat tours** to the entrance to Shark Valley. Take the well-regarded **Shark Valley Tram Tour** or rent a bicycle from the front kiosk and ride back on an asphalt path (the same one used by the tram) that curves into the swamp. You're almost guaranteed a glimpse of alligators and wading birds.

Push on to **Everglades City** (the other sights on the Tamiami Trail can be revisited on the return trip to Miami), a warm hamlet that once made its custom smuggling into the swamps but today is more tied to the tourism trade.

The next day head back toward Miami. Stop at the **Skunk Ape Research Headquarters**, a delightfully weird zoo, gift shop and Bigfoot hunting camp; have lunch at the excellent **Joannie's Blue Crab Café**; check out the country's smallest post office in **Ochopee**; and stop by the **Big Cypress Gallery**, which contains some of the finest photos of the beauty of the Glades.

Two Days
River of Grass

This route into the Everglades takes in vistas of long prairies and cypress domes.

Drive south from Miami to Homestead/Florida City (adjoining towns), and pull over by the **Coral Castle**, a maudlin monument to unrequited love. You'll then be just outside Everglades National Park, where you'll find **Robert Is Here**, a fantastic farmer's market–produce stand–petting zoo. Continue on to the **Everglades Outpost**, an animal hospital for exotic critters.

Push west to see some of the most impressive points within the park, including the **Royal Palm Visitor Center**, where walkways lead over dark waterways prowled by enormous alligators; the **Pinelands Trail**, which takes you through a grove of skeleton-thin swamp pine; and **Pahayokee Overlook**, with views over the Zen quiet of the greater Glades.

Head back to Florida City and spend the night in the fantastic **Everglades Hostel**.

The next morning head back into the Glades and push further south – there's great kayaking and canoeing at **Hell's Bay**, good low country over the windswept mud flats at **Christian Point** and boating in Florida Bay at the **Flamingo Visitor Center**.

Travel with Children

Best Regions for Kids

Coconut Grove
Big malls, mainstream cuisine and a pedestrian-friendly center.

Everglades
The National Park exhibits are all kid-friendly. And there's big alligators. Kids love alligators.

Florida Keys
Active families with older kids will adore the snorkeling, diving, fishing, boating and all-around no-worries vibe.

Key Biscayne
An enormous, central park basically devoted to kids is surrounded by child-friendly nature trails and public beaches.

Coral Gables
More malls, midrange restaurants that are happy to host children, and the fairy-tale Venetian Pool.

Miami Beach
Lincoln Rd, South Pointe Park, Ocean Drive Neon and the sandy beach will keep your kids grinning.

South Florida doesn't possess the reputation that child-friendly-travel Orlando has, but sheesh, where does? This region still knows how to care for your young ones. South Florida has a plethora of parks, nature trails, megamalls, beaches, zoos and family-friendly hotels and restaurants to keep your young ones happy on holiday. With the obvious exception of our nightlife listings, Miami's seedier neighborhoods and a few high-end restaurants (and OK, the nude beach at Haulover State Park), there are no places listed in this book we would consider unfriendly to children, although some are naturally more friendly than others.

Miami & the Keys for Kids

There is a plethora of kid-themed activities in Miami. Just remember: this is Florida, and every tourist town in Florida has already anticipated the needs of every age in your family. With increasing skill and refinement, nearly every Florida museum, zoo, attraction, restaurant and hotel aims to please traveling families of all stripes.

Your only real trouble is deciding what to do. Florida offers so much for kids and families that planning can be tough. Simple itineraries can suddenly become a frantic dawn-to-dusk race to pack it all in. We can't even fit everything in this book.

Eating Out

Most midrange Florida restaurants have a dedicated kids' menu, along with high chairs, crayons for coloring, and changing tables in restrooms. Even cheap ethnic eateries – a delicious, ubiquitous constant in the Miami dining scene – are good at accommodating children. Nearly every restaurant, even high-end ones, is happy to make a kid meal by request. As a rule, families with infants or toddlers will get better service earlier in the dinner hour (by 6pm). Some higher-end restaurants may look askance at young diners; simply ask when making reservations.

Animal Parks

Some foreign visitors come to South Florida expecting Disney World and Universal Studios to be just outside Miami (they're a few hours away). South Florida isn't any kind of theme-park contender, but what this region does possess, in oddly high numbers, are animal parks. Some of these are grassroots volunteer outfits that rescue injured beasts, like the Turtle Hospital and Bird Sanctuary in the Keys. Others more closely resemble hybrid zoo-theme parks, like Monkey Island and Jungle Island in Miami. All these locations are a hit with kids, although you can expect more specifically child-oriented infrastructure and exhibits in the Miami examples.

Beaches

The prototypical Florida family beach is fronted by or near very active, crowded commercial centers with lots of water sports and activities, tourist shops, grocery stores and midrange eats and sleeps. Admittedly, the region's most popular beach, South Beach, is a bit more sophisticated and snooty. But c'mon – this is still Florida. Lots of families hang out on the southern end of South Beach. Mid-Beach and North Beach are also more traditionally family-oriented, as are the beaches on Key Biscayne. The Keys actually lack for beaches, even if they are islands, but Bahia Honda State Park on Bahia Honda Key is safe, reasonably nature-focused while still fun in a beach-y way, and there's a kid-oriented small science center on-site. Sombrero Beach on Marathon is near a playground and good food options.

Museums & Attractions

Miami and the Keys holds its own in the Stuff Kids Love stakes. Besides all of that animal life both in the Everglades National Park and outside of it is decades worth of Only in America kitsch. Harder to define 'sites' like the Coral Castle in Homestead wow kids if only for their unique weirdness. The visitor centers of the area's many parks all have child-friendly interactive exhibits. Many of the art museums we review may seem like a funny place to take your young ones, and it's true that some won't jive with your kids, although the more cerebral ones may appreciate the trip. But museums like HistoryMiami and the Bass Museum directly and indirectly sneak learning right into a child's day.

Getting into Nature

So much of your time here is spent in air-conditioning, but don't overlook unpackaged nature. Florida is exceedingly flat, so rivers and trails are ideal for short legs and little arms. Raised boardwalks through alligator-filled swamps make perfect pint-size adventures. Placid rivers and intercoastal bays are custom made for first-time paddlers, adult or child. Never snorkeled a coral reef or surfed? Florida has gentle places to learn. Book a sea-life cruise, a manatee swim, a nesting sea turtle watch or a glass-bottom boat tour. At Oleta River State Park and most every state park we review in the Keys, there's family-accessible kayaking and boating.

Children's Highlights

Beaches & Parks

» South Pointe Park – Ice-cream stands, soft grass and plans to install a water feature.

» Mid-Beach Boardwalk – Fronts a family-friendly stretch of sand.

» Arch Creek Park – Has nature walks *and* ghost walks.

» Crandon Park – Pretty Key Biscayne spot with sand and nature trails.

» Bill Baggs Cape Florida State Recreation Area – Picnic tables front a pretty sweep of beach.

» Biscayne Community Center & Village Green Park – Playgrounds, sports fields and a packed kids' activities schedule.

» Barnacle Historic State Park – Outdoor paths and frequent family-friendly outdoor concerts.

» Fruit & Spice Park – Pretty trails wind past freshly fallen fruit.

» Biscayne National Underwater Park – Glass-bottom boat tours, snorkeling over epic reefs.

» John Pennekamp Coral Reef State Park – Same great coral reefs, by snorkel or glass-bottom boat tour.

» Harry Harris Park – In Key Largo, this small park is one of the best in the Keys for kids, with a playground and excellent swimming.

» Sombrero Beach Park – Sugar-soft sand lines calm water on one side, playground facilities are on the other.

Animal Encounters

» Metrozoo – In Miami, it's extensive and wide-ranging with all the big-ticket species.

» Marjory Stoneman Douglas Biscayne Nature Center – On Key Biscayne, kid-friendly intro to subtropical South Florida, great hands-on programs.

» Monkey Jungle – In Miami, the tagline 'Where humans are caged and monkeys run wild' says it all. Unforgettable.

» Jungle Island – In Miami, tropical birds and exotic species like the liger, a tiger-and-lion crossbreed.

» Everglades Outpost – This volunteer-run animal sanctuary is essentially a great small zoo.

» Miami Seaquarium – On Key Biscayne, one of the state's biggies; various swim-with-the-fishes programs.

» Shark Valley – In the Everglades, bike or take a tram tour along Shark Valley's paved road; wading birds and alligators are practically guaranteed.

» Royal Palm Visitor Center – Take a boardwalk trail over some of the Everglades' most beautiful wetland landscapes.

» Everglades City – Visit Everglades City and Flamingo visitor centers for family-friendly

kayaking and boating, with a chance of seeing dolphins.

» National Key Deer Refuge – On Big Pine Key, kids love spotting these cute-as-Bambi minideer.

» Florida Keys Wild Bird Rehabilitation Center – On Key Largo, injured birdlife is sheltered along several windy paths.

» Turtle Hospital – In Marathon, turtles get tender loving care from a staff of dedicated volunteers. Visitors welcome (and appreciated).

» Crane Point Museum – In Marathon, excellent alfresco introduction to the ecology of the Keys.

Miscellaneous

» Metromover – See the city from the sky via this free elevated train.

» Miami-Dade Public Library – Fantastic flagship library for Miami.

» Vizcaya Museum & Gardens – Older children will appreciate the whimsy of this fairy-tale mansion.

» Venetian Pool – One of the most beautiful public pools in the country.

» Coral Castle – Kids may not appreciate the kitsch, but they still love the weirdness of this odd structure.

» Robert Is Here – The Everglades' favorite farmers' market has a petting zoo and fresh juice.

» Miccosukee Village – On Tamiami Trail in the Everglades, this Native American village has culture shows and alligator wrestling.

» Jacob's Aquatic Center – Small water park and plenty of kiddie pools.

» Robbie's Marina – In Islamorada, a sort of 'working' harbor-aquatic petting zoo.

FLORIDA-THEMED BOOKS FOR KIDS

Get reading-age kids in a Florida mood with these great books.

» *Hoot* (2002) by Carl Hiaasen: Hiaasen's same zany characters, snappy plot twists and environmental message, but PG-rated. If you like it, pick up *Flush* (2005) and *Scat* (2009).

» *Because of Winn-Dixie* (2000) by Kate DiCamillo: heart-warming coming-of-age tale about a 10-year-old girl adjusting to her new life in Florida.

» *The Yearling* (1938) by Marjorie Kinnan Rawlings: Pulitzer prize–winning literary classic about a boy who adopts an orphaned fawn in Florida's backwoods.

» *The Treasure of Amelia Island* (2008) by MC Finotti: historical fiction that re-creates Spanish-ruled Florida through the eyes of an 11-year-old.

» *Bad Latitude* (2008) by David Ebright: unabashed pirate adventure for tween boys, with a dash of historical realism.

» Mallory Square – A carnival for the crowds that pops off on any evening as the sun sets.

Museums

» Miami Children's Museum – Huge and extensive role-playing environments.

» HistoryMiami – Bookish kids will appreciate the thoughtful exhibitions.

» Miami Museum of Science & Planetarium – A bit old and dated, but still fun and child-oriented.

» Gold Coast Railroad Museum – Little train-spotters will get their fix here.

» Florida Keys Eco-Discovery Center – In Key West, fantastic, entertaining displays pull together Florida Keys ecology.

Planning

If you're a parent, you already know that luck favors the prepared. But in Florida's crazy-crowded, overbooked high-season tourist spots, planning can make all the difference. Before you come, plot your trip like a four-star general: make reservations for every place you might go. Then, arrive, relax and go with the flow.

What to Bring

If you forget something, don't sweat it. Just bring yourself, your kids and any of their can't-sleep-without items. Florida can supply the rest, from diapers to clothes to sunscreen to boogie boards.

That said, here are some things to consider.

☐ For sleeping, a pack-and-play/portacot for infants and/or an inflatable mattress for older kids can be handy, especially if you're road-tripping or sticking to amenity-poor, budget-range motels.

☐ Bring light rain gear and umbrellas; it *will* rain at some point.

☐ Bring water sandals, for beach, water parks, and play fountains.

☐ Bring sunscreen (a daily necessity) and mosquito repellent.

☐ Prepare a simple first-aid kit; when an unexpected cut or fever strikes is not the moment to run to the drugstore.

Accommodations

The vast majority of Florida hotels stand ready to aid families: they have cribs (often pack-and-plays) and rollaway beds (some charge extra); they have refrigerators and microwaves; and they have adjoining rooms and suites. Make sure to enquire about all of the above when you book. Large hotels and resorts can go toe-to-toe with condos for amenities: including partial or full kitchens, laundry facilities, pools and barbecues, and various activities. Properties in this book catering specifically to families are marked by a family icon (🏃).

High-end boutique hotels in Miami Beach and adult-oriented B&Bs in the Keys may discourage young kids, but they aren't allowed to discriminate and ban them. If you're unsure, ask, and they'll tell you what minimum age they prefer. In general, we believe the best Miami neighborhoods to stay with kids are South Beach (yes, it may be a mad party scene, but these are simply the best hotels in town), North Beach, Coconut Grove and Coral Gables. In any of these places you shouldn't have trouble bringing kids, with the exception of South Beach's priciest hotels, which are generally looking to attract a celebrity-party crowd as opposed to families. In the Keys, Marathon, Islamorada and Key Largo all have good family-style motels and B&Bs.

Travel Advice & Baby Gear

If you prefer to pack light, several services offer baby-gear rental (high chairs, strollers, car seats etc), while others sell infant supplies (diapers, wipes, formula, baby food etc), all delivered to your hotel; book one to two weeks in advance. These and other websites also provide family-centered travel advice. Most of the information here relates to Miami.

RULES OF THE ROAD

Florida car-seat laws require that children under three must be in a car seat, and children under five in at least a booster seat (unless they are over 80lb and 4ft 9in tall, allowing seat belts to be positioned properly). Rental-car companies are legally required to provide child seats, but *only if you reserve them in advance;* they typically charge $10 to $15 extra. You can also rent them from baby-gear-rental companies.

DATE NIGHT

Traveling with kids doesn't necessarily mean doing *everything* as a family. Want a romantic night on the town? Several child-care services offer in-hotel babysitting by certified sitters; a few run their own drop-off centers. Rates vary based on the number of children, and typically they require a four-hour minimum (plus a $10 travel surcharge). Hourly rates generally range from $14 to $20. Keep in mind these services generally apply to Miami; in the Keys you may have to ask the folks at your hotel front desk about local babysitting options, although larger resorts should have sitter staff in-house.

» **Kid's Nite Out** (www.kidsniteout.com)

» **Sittercity** (www.sittercity.com)

» **Sunshine Babysitting** (www.sunshinebabysitting.com) Statewide.

Baby's Away (www.babysawayrentals.com) Rents baby gear.

Traveling Baby Company (www.traveling babyco.com) Rents baby gear.

Babies Travel Lite (www.babiestravellite.com) Sells baby supplies for delivery; also offers general and Florida-specific family-travel advice.

Jet Set Babies (www.jetsetbabies.com) Sells baby supplies, plus general infant travel advice.

Travel for Kids (www.travelforkids.com) Florida-specific family travel; helpful planning advice.

Family Vacation Critics (www.familyvaca tioncritics.com) Trip Advisor–owned; parent-reviewed hotels, sights and travel.

Go City Kids (http://gocitykids.parentscon nect.com) Nickelodeon-sponsored family travel in Miami, Orlando and Tampa.

regions at a glance

Miami is the urban heart of this region, filled with the best dining, nightlife and shopping – plus, of course, some very fine beaches. In the past, travelers gravitated to Miami Beach over Miami, but today the city on the mainland can give the beach a run for its money when it comes to culture (and it's always been a bit more cosmopolitan). The Everglades are a wet wilderness filled with some of the best wildlife-spotting in Florida, pools, rivers and lakes that constrict and expand with the moon and tides, and nearby funky roadside attractions. The islands of the Florida Keys are particularly good for idiosyncratic attractions, tasty dining, fun bars, tolerance and diversity, as exemplified by Key West.

Miami

Food ✓✓✓
Nightlife ✓✓✓
Architecture ✓✓✓

Edible Exploration

Be it Colombian hot dogs with plum sauce or Thai-Japanese fusion cafes, the shabbiest Central American shack doling out carne asada and Italian *osterias* prepping truffles and pasta, this city has a taste for cheap ethnic eateries and their budgetary evolution into high-end, four-star restaurants.

Club Kids

With a large Latin population, warm tropical evenings, several universities and (in some places) income to burn, Miami doesn't like to turn in early. Bump shoulders with students from the University of Miami in Coconut Grove, or dance to indie pop and trip-hop in the clubs that adjoin Midtown and Overtown.

Deco Decor

In North Beach, the Miami Modern movement is keenly felt in the shadows of enormous condos. In South Beach, deco rules the day. Take a few hours to wander the Art Deco Historic District, one of the most distinctive pockets of architectural preservation in the USA.

p38

The Everglades

Wildlife ✓✓✓
Quirkiness ✓✓✓
Camping ✓✓✓

Gator-gawking

Wildlife-viewing is good in the Glades any time of year, but if you visit in the winter dry season, you'll see a Jurassic Park landscape of prehistoric reptiles plus an avian rainbow of wading birds.

Only in Florida

From a blue-crab shack across the street from the USA's smallest post office, to a giant Coral Castle located next to a sanctuary that houses armadillos, timber wolves and tigers, the Everglades attracts America's eccentrics.

Kayaking & Camping

There is something simply magical about paddling a kayak or canoe over sheets of sunrise-dappled water, be it slow marsh tinkle or the wide teal expanses of Florida Bay. This is how mornings were made to be spent.

p118

Florida Keys & Key West

Environment ✓✓
Arts ✓✓
Food ✓✓

Mangroves & Hammocks

The Keys are an ecological anomaly in the USA, a series of mangrove islands that conceal hammocks, or contained groves, of palm, pine and tropical hardwoods found nowhere else in the country (and in some cases, the world).

Authors & Artists

Thanks largely to its historical toleration of the homosexual community, the Keys (especially Key West) have long been an artist colony. Authors, from Hemingway to Frost, have been attracted to the island and its piratical, creative cast as well.

Fish & Mango Salsa

Folks here are mad for fishing and the natural culinary accompaniment to said hobby. If the fish you eat here isn't fresh, there's something wrong. Land food exists as well, of course, accompanied by tropical garnishes and famous Key lime pie.

p135

❯ **Every listing is recommended by our authors, and their favourite places are listed first**

❯ **Look out for these icons:**

TOP CHOICE Our author's top recommendation

A green or sustainable option

FREE No payment required

See the Index for a full list of destinations covered in this book.

On the Road

Miami

Includes »

Best Places to Eat

» Señora Martinez (p99)
» Osteria Del Teatro (p94)
» Tap Tap (p93)
» Michy's (p100)
» Steve's Pizza (p96)

Best Places to Sleep

» The Standard (p86)
» Shore Club (p87)
» Circa 39 (p90)
» Pelican Hotel (p84)
» Hotel St Augustine (p84)

Why Go?

Miami is so many things, but to most visitors, it's mainly glamour, condensed into urban form.

They're right. The archaic definition of 'glamour' is a kind of spell that mystifies a victim. Well, they call Miami the Magic City. And it is mystifying. In its beauty, certainly: the clack of a model's high heels on Lincoln Rd, the teal sweep of Biscayne Bay, flowing cool into the wide South Florida sky; the blood-orange fire of the sunset, setting the Downtown skyline aflame.

Then there's less-conventional beauty: a Haitian dance party in the ghetto attended by University of Miami literature students, or a Venezuelan singing Metallica *en español* in a Coral Gables karaoke bar, or the passing *shalom/buenas días* traded between Orthodox Jews and Cuban exiles.

Miami is so many things. All glamorous, in every sense of the word. You could spend a fun lifetime trying to escape her spell.

When to Go

Miami

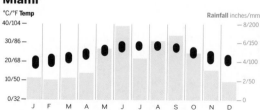

Jan–Mar Warm and dry, with lots of tourists; snowbirds from the northeast and Europeans.

Apr–Jun Not as muggy as deep summer, but lusher and greener than winter.

Jul–Oct Prices plummet. When it's not as hot as an oven, there's storms: it's hurricane season.

History

It's always been the weather that's attracted Miami's two most prominent species: developers and tourists. But it wasn't the sun per se that got people moving here – it was an ice storm. The great Florida freeze of 1895 wiped out the state's citrus industry; at the same time, widowed Julia Tuttle bought out parcels of land that would become modern Miami, and Henry Flagler was building his Florida East Coast Railroad. Tuttle offered to split her land with Flagler if he extended the railway to Miami, but the train man didn't pay her any heed until north Florida froze over and Tuttle sent him an 'I-told-you-so' message: an orange blossom clipped from her Miami garden.

The rest is a history of boom, bust, dreamers and opportunists. Generally, Miami has grown in leaps and bounds following major world events and natural disasters. Hurricanes (particularly the deadly Great Miami Hurricane of 1926) have wiped away the town, but it just keeps bouncing

and building back better than before. In the late 19th and early 20th centuries, Miami earned a reputation for attracting design and city-planning mavericks such as George Merrick, who fashioned the artful Mediterranean village of Coral Gables, and James Deering, designer of the fairy-tale Vizcaya mansion.

Miami Beach blossomed in the early 20th century when Jewish developers recognized the potential American Riviera in their midst. Those hoteliers started building resorts that were branded with a distinctive art-deco facade by daring architects willing to buck the more staid aesthetics of the northeast. The world wars brought soldiers who were stationed at nearby naval facilities, many of whom liked the sun and decided to stay. Latin American and Caribbean revolutions introduced immigrants from the other direction, most famously from Cuba. Cuban immigrants arrived in two waves: first, the anti-Castro types of the '60s, and those looking for a better life since the

MIAMI IN...

Two Days

There's more to Miami than South Beach, but we're assuming you're starting – and sleeping – here. Have breakfast at **Puerto Sagua** (p93) and, gorged, waddle to the **Wolfsonian-FIU** (p42) to get some background on the surrounding art-deco architecture. Now stroll around **Lincoln Road** (p43), hotel-spot on Collins Ave or check out South Beach's most flamboyant structures, like the **Delano Hotel** (p88), **Tides** (p88) and the **Shore Club** (p87).

Get in some beach time and as evening sets in consider an excellent deco district tour with the **Art Deco Welcome Center** (p115). For a nice dinner try **Osteria del Teatro** (p94) or **Tap Tap** (p93). When you're ready to hit the town (and the rails), we suggest early cocktails at **B Bar** (p104).

The next day potter around either of the excellent ethnic enclaves of **Little Haiti** (p61) or **Little Havana** (p67) before dining in the trendy **Design District** (p61). End your trip rocking out in one of Midtown's excellent venues, like **Bardot** (p107) or **Electric Pickle** (p106).

Four Days

Follow the two-day itinerary and visit whichever one of the 'Littles' (Haiti or Havana) you missed the first time round. If you can, visit Coral Gables, making sure not to miss the **Biltmore Hotel** (p71), the **Venetian Pool** (p71) and a shopping stroll down Miracle Mile. If all that isn't opulent enough for you, see what happens when Mediterranean revival, baroque stylings and a lot of money gets mashed together at the **Vizcaya Museum & Gardens** (p68). Top off a visit to these elegant manses with dinner at one of the best restaurants in Miami in, no kidding, a gas station at **El Carajo** (p102).

On day four, head downtown and take a long ride on the free **Metromover** (p117), hopping on and off to see the excellent **HistoryMiami** (p58) and the gorgeous **Adrienne Arsht Center for the Performing Arts** (p55). Have your last meal at **Michy's** (p100) on emergent N Biscayne Blvd and please, before you leave, guzzle a beer and pick at some smoked fish on the couches of **Jimbo's** (p66).

Miami Highlights

1 Catch a show in South Beach at the incredible **New World Center** (p43)

2 Go out for drinks and a stumble through Wynwood and the Design District on an **art walks gallery night** (p107)

3 Cigar smoke, dominoes and guayaberas (linen dress shirts); say *bienvenido a* Little Havana in **Máximo Gómez Park** (p67)

4 Take a free tour of downtown Miami via the old-school **Metromover** (p117)

5 Smoked fish, beer, La-Z-Boys and a mangrove swamp – aw, yeah – get to **Jimbo's** (p66)

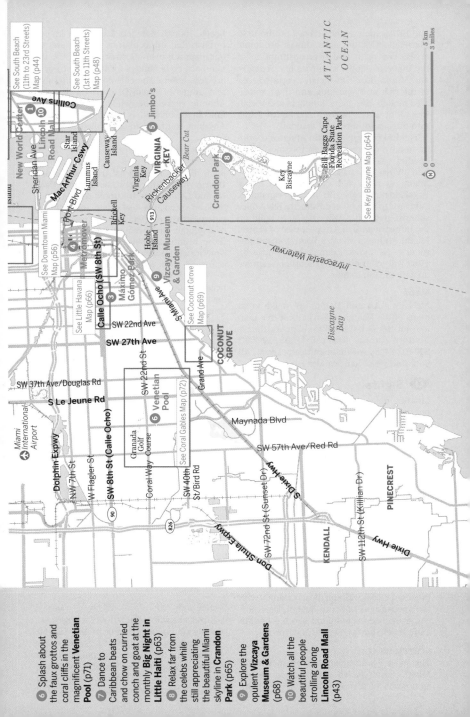

6 Splash about the faux grottos and coral cliffs in the magnificent **Venetian Pool** (p71)

7 Dance to Caribbean beats and chow on curried conch and goat at the monthly **Big Night in Little Haiti** (p63)

8 Relax far from the celebs while still appreciating the beautiful Miami skyline in **Crandon Park** (p65)

9 Explore the opulent **Vizcaya Museum & Gardens** (p68)

10 Watch all the beautiful people strolling along **Lincoln Road Mall** (p43)

late 1970s, such as the arrivals on the 1980 Mariel Boatlift during a Cuban economic crisis. The glam and overconsumption of the 1980s, as shown in movies like *Scarface* and *Miami Beach,* attracted a certain breed of the rich and beautiful, and their associated models, designers, hoteliers and socialites, all of whom transformed South Beach into the beautiful beast it is today.

Political changes in Latin America continue to have repercussions in this most Latin of cities – as former mayor Manny Diaz once said, 'When Venezuela or Argentina sneezes, Miami catches a cold.' Current mayor Tomas Regalado now deals with his town expanding outwards to Kendall and Palmetto Bay – once suburbs, now city – while trying to build up the infrastructure and appearance of central Miami. Midtown Miami – Wynwood and surrounds – is a good example of this growth. Time will tell if other neighborhoods spruce up with the same shine.

Maps

McNally, AAA and Dolph's all make great maps of the Miami area. The best free map is from the **Greater Miami Convention & Visitors Bureau** (Map p56; ☎305-539-3000, 800-933-8448; www.miamiandbeaches.com; 701 Brickell Ave; ☺8:30am-5pm Mon-Fri).

◉ Sights

Miami's major sights aren't concentrated in one neighborhood; there is something for everyone just about everywhere. The most frequently visited area is South Beach, home to hot nightlife, beautiful beaches and art-deco hotels, but you'll find historic sites and museums downtown, art galleries in Wynwood and the Design District, old-fashioned hotels and eateries in Mid-Beach (in Miami Beach), more beaches on Key Biscayne, and peaceful neighborhood attractions in Coral Gables and Coconut Grove.

Water and income – canals, bays and bank accounts – are the geographic and social boundaries that divide Miami. Of course, the great water that divides here is Biscayne Bay, holding the city of Miami apart from its preening sibling Miami Beach (along with the fine feathers of South Beach). Don't forget, as many do, that Miami Beach is not Miami's beach, but its own distinct town.

SOUTH BEACH

The most iconic neighborhood in Greater Miami, South Beach encompasses the region south of 21st St in the city of Miami Beach, though hoteliers have been known to push that up as high as 40th St and on our maps it is below 23rd St. Collins Ave, the main artery, is famous for its long string of art-deco hotels. The chic outdoor cafes and restaurants of Ocean Dr overlook the wide Atlantic shorefront, while pedestrian-only Lincoln Road Mall is a shopper's heaven. Anything south of 5th St is called 'SoFi.'

⟨TOP CHOICE⟩ Art Deco Historic District
NEIGHBORHOOD

South Beach's heart is its Art Deco Historic District, from 18th St and south along Ocean Dr and Collins Ave. It's ironic that in a city built on speculative real estate, the main engine of urban renewal was the preservation of a unique architectural heritage. See, all those beautiful hotels, with their tropical-Americana facades, scream 'Miami.' They screamed it so loud when they were preserved they gave this city a brand, and this neighborhood a new lease on life. Back in the day, South Beach was a ghetto of vagrants, druggies and retirees. Then it became one of the largest areas in the USA on the National Register of Historic Places, and then it attracted models, photographers, hoteliers, chefs and...well, today it's a pastel medina of cruisers, Euro-fashionistas, the occasionally glimpsed celebrity, and tourists from Middle America.

Your first stop here should be the **Art Deco Welcome Center** (Map p44; ☎305-531-3484; 1200 Ocean Dr; ☺9:30am-7pm daily). To be honest, it's a bit of a tatty gift shop, but it's located in the old beach-patrol headquarters, one of the best deco buildings out there. You can book some excellent $20 guided walking tours (plus audio and private tours), which are some of the best introductions to the layout and history of South Beach on offer. Tours depart at 10:30am daily, except on Thursday when they leave at 6:30pm. No advance reservations required; just show up and smile. Call ahead for information on walking tours of Lincoln Rd (p43) and Collins Park, the area that encompasses upper South Beach.

Wolfsonian-FIU
MUSEUM

(Map p48; www.wolfsonian.org; 1001 Washington Ave; adult/student, senior & child under 12yr $5/3.50; ☺11am-9pm Thu, 11am-6pm Fri & Sat, noon-5pm Sun) Visit this excellent design museum early in your stay to put the aesthetics of Miami Beach into fascinating context. It's one thing to see how wealth, leisure and the pursuit of beauty manifests in Miami Beach, it's another to understand the roots and shadings of local artistic movements. By chronicling the interior evolution of everyday life, the Wolfsonian reveals how these trends were architecturally manifested in SoBe's exterior deco. Which reminds us of the Wolfsonian's own noteworthy facade. Remember the Gothic-futurist apartment complex-cum-temple of evil in *Ghostbusters*? Well, this imposing structure, with its grandiose 'frozen fountain' and lion-head-studded grand elevator, could serve as a stand-in for that set.

Lincoln Road Mall   ROAD

Calling Lincoln Rd a mall, which many do, is like calling Big Ben a clock: it's technically accurate but misses the point. Yes, you can shop, and shop very well here. But this outdoor pedestrian thoroughfare between Alton Rd and Washington Ave is really about seeing and being seen; there are times when Lincoln feels less like a road and more like a runway. We wouldn't be surprised if you developed a slight crick in your neck from whipping around to check out all the fabulously gorgeous creatures that call 'the road' their natural environment. Carl Fisher, the father of Miami Beach, envisioned the road as a '5th Ave of the South'. Morris Lapidus, one of the founders of the loopy, neo-Baroque Miami-Beach style, designed much of the mall, including several shady overhangs and waterfall structures, traffic barriers that look like the marbles a giant might play with, plus the wonderfully deco **Colony Theatre** (p110) and the currently empty **Lincoln Theatre** (541 Lincoln Rd). There's also an excellent **farmers' market** (⊙9am-6pm Sun) and the **Antique & Collectible Market** (⊙9am-5pm, every 2nd Sun Oct-May; www.antiquecollectiblemarket.com), both held along Lincoln.

1111 Lincoln Rd

(Map p44; www.1111lincolnroad.com) The West Side of Lincoln Rd is anchored by what may be the most impressive parking garage you'll ever lay eyes on, a geometric pastiche of sharp angles, winding corridors and incongruous corners that looks like a lucid fantasy dreamed up by Pythagoras after a long night out. In fact, the building was designed by Swiss architecture firm Herzog & de Meuron, who describe the structure as 'all muscle without cloth'.

ArtCenter/South Florida

(Map p44; www.artcentersf.org; 924 Lincoln Rd) Established in 1984 by a small but forward-thinking group of artists, this compound is the creative heart of South Beach. In addition to some 52 artists' studios (many of which are open to the public), ArtCenter offers an exciting lineup of classes and lectures. The residences are reserved for artists who do not have major exposure, so this is a good place to spot up-and-coming talent. Monthly rotating exhibitions keep the presentation fresh and pretty avant-garde.

Miami Beach Community Church

(Map p44; www.mb-communitychurch.org; 1620 Drexel Ave) In rather sharp and refreshing contrast to all the uber-modern structures muscling their way into the art-deco design of South Beach, the community church puts one in mind of an old Spanish mission – humble, modest and elegantly understated in an area where overstatement is the general philosophy. Fourteen stained-glass windows line the relatively simple interior, while the exterior is built to resemble coral stone in a Spanish Revival style.

New World Center   CULTURAL BUILDING

(Map p44; ☑305-673-3330; www.nws.edu; 500 17th St) Miami has a penchant for sumptuous performing-arts venues and the New World Center is certainly competing with the Arsht Center (p55) for most-impressive concert hall in the city. The New World Center, designed by Frank Gehry, rises majestically out of a manicured lawn just above Lincoln Rd, looking somewhat like a tissue box (note the 'fluttering' stone waves that pop out of the exterior) from the year 3000 with a glass facade. The grounds form a 2½-acre public

HAVE YOUR SAY

Found a fantastic restaurant that you're longing to share with the world? Disagree with our recommendations? Or just want to talk about your most recent trip?

Whatever your reason, head to lonelyplanet.com, where you can post a review, ask or answer a question on the Thorn Tree forum, comment on a blog, or share your photos and tips on Groups. Or you can simply spend time chatting with like-minded travelers. So go on, have your say.

South Beach (11th to 23rd Streets)

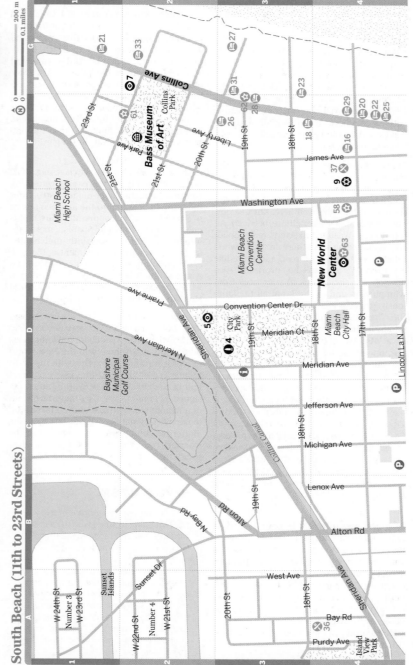

45

MIAMI

ATLANTIC OCEAN

South Beach

Art Deco Historic District

A1A

Lincoln Rd

16th St

15th St

14th La

Ocean Dr

The Promenade

10

Lummus Park

24

39
34
15

17

30

12th St

Ocean Ct

Collins Ave

32
13

43

45

56
53
41

14

54

42

Collins Ct

60

52

8

19

11

Washington Ave

Old City Hall

11th St

65
47

12

68
38

Drexel Ave

3

50

Drexel Ave

13th St

14th St

6

49

59

70

Pennsylvania Ave

Española Way

12th St

See South Beach (1st to 11th Streets) Map (p48)

55

Euclid Ave

64
69 44 40

Lincoln Rd Mall

16th St

15th St

14th Pl

Meridian Ave

2

Meridian Ave

48
67

Jefferson Ave

Jefferson Ave

Courtyard

66

46

Flamingo Park

MIAMI BEACH

35

Michigan Ave

Lincoln La S

57

Lenox Ave

14th St

13th St

12th St

11th St

51

Sun Trust Bank

1

907

Alton Rd

14th Ct

13th Tce

Alton Ct

Alton Ct

Alton La

Lincoln Rd

15th Tce

15th St

West Ave

Flamingo Way

14th Tce

Bay Rd

park; performances inside the center are projected to those outside via a 7000-sq-ft projection wall (like you're in the classiest drive-in movie theater in the universe). Inside, the folded layers of white walls feel somewhere between organic and origami. The venue is the home of the acclaimed New World Symphony (p112); to get inside you generally need tickets to a show, but if you call ahead you may be able to organize a free guided walking tour of the interior, a program that was just beginning at the time of research.

Ocean Drive   ROAD

(Map p48; runs from 1st to 11th St) Yar, here be the belly of the South Beach beast. It's just a road, right? No, it's the great cruising strip of Miami; an endless parade of classic cars, testosterone-sweating young men, peacock-like young women, street performers, vendors, those guys who yell unintelligible crap at everyone, celebrities pretending to be tourists, tourists who want to play celebrity, beautiful people, ugly people, people people

and the best ribbon of art-deco preservation on the beach. Say 'Miami.' That image in your head? Probably Ocean Drive.

South Pointe Park   PARK

(Map p48; 1 Washington Ave; ☉sunrise-10pm) The very southern tip of Miami Beach has been converted into a lovely park, replete with manicured grass for lounging; views over a remarkably teal and fresh ocean; a restaurant; a refreshment stand; warm, scrubbed-stone walkways; and lots of folks who want to enjoy the great weather and views sans the South Beach strutting. That said, we saw two model photo shoots go off here in under an hour, so it's not all casual relaxation.

A1A   ROAD

'Beachfront Avenue!' The A1A causeway, coupled with the Rickenbacker Causeway in Key Biscayne, is one of the great bridges in America, linking Miami and Miami Beach via the glittering turquoise of Biscayne Bay. To drive this road in a convertible or with the windows down, with a setting sun behind you, enormous cruise ships to the side, the palms swaying in the ocean breeze and, let's just say 'Your Love' by the Outfield on the radio, is basically the essence of Miami.

Bass Museum of Art   MUSEUM
(Map p44; www.bassmuseum.org; 2121 Park Ave; adult/student & senior $8/6; ☺noon-5pm Wed-Sun) The best art museum in Miami Beach has a playfully futuristic facade, a crisp interplay of lines and bright, white wall space – like an Orthodox church on a space-age Greek isle. All designed, by the way, in 1930 by Russell Pancoast (grandson of John A Collins, who lent his name to Collins Ave). The collection isn't shabby either: permanent highlights range from 16th-century European religious works to northern European and Renaissance paintings. The Bass forms one point of the **Collins Park Cultural Center** triangle, which also includes the three-story **Miami City Ballet** and the lovingly inviting **Miami Beach Regional Library**, which is a great place for free wi-fi.

Española Way Promenade   PROMENADE
(Map p44; btwn 14th & 15th Sts) Española Way is an 'authentic' Spanish promenade...in the Florida theme-park spirit of authenticity. Oh, whatever; it's a lovely, terra-cotta and cobbled arcade of rose-pink and Spanish-cream architecture, perfect for browsing art (it was an arts colony in the 1920s and today houses the studios of several local artists), window-shopping, people-watching and cafe-sipping. A craft market operates here on weekend afternoons.

Jewish Museum of Florida   MUSEUM
(Map p48; www.jewishmuseum.com; 301 Washington Ave; adult/student & senior $6/5, Sat admission free; ☺10am-5pm Tue-Sun, closed Jewish holidays) Housed in a 1936 Orthodox synagogue that served Miami's first congregation, this small museum chronicles the rather large contribution Jews have made to the state of Florida, especially this corner of Florida. After all, it could be said that while Cubans made Miami, Jews made Miami Beach, both physically (in a developer's sense) and culturally (in an 'anyone is welcome' attitude of tolerance). Yet there were times when Jews were barred from the American Riviera they carved out of the sand, and this museum tells that story, along with some amusing anecdotes (like seashell Purim dresses). The mainstay is

MIAMI

South Beach (1st to 11th Streets)

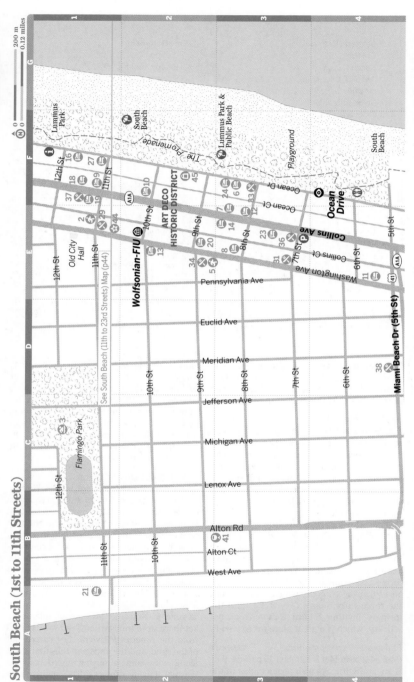

200 m
0.12 miles

Lummus Park

South Beach

Lummus Park & Public Beach

The Promenade

Playground

South Beach

12th St

Ocean Drive

Ocean Dr

Ocean Ct

Collins Ave

Ocean Ct

Collins Ct

Washington Ave

ART DECO HISTORIC DISTRICT

Wolfsonian-FIU

10th St

9th St

8th St

7th St

6th St

5th St

Miami Beach Dr (5th St)

Old City Hall

12th St

11th St

10th St

Pennsylvania Ave

Euclid Ave

Meridian Ave

Jefferson Ave

Michigan Ave

Lenox Ave

Alton Rd

Alton Ct

West Ave

Flamingo Park

See South Beach (11th to 23rd Streets) Map (p44)

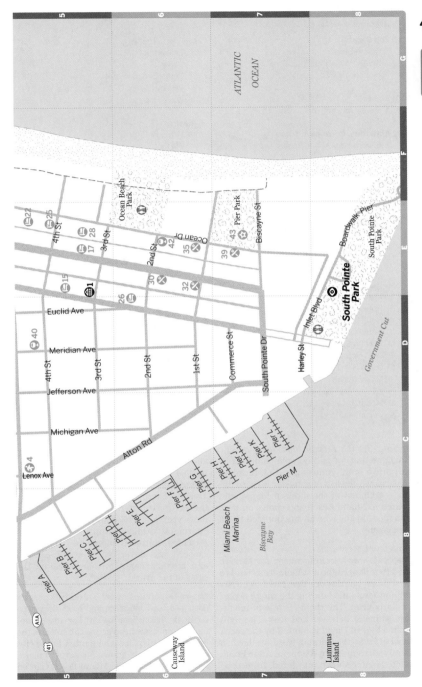

South Beach (1st to 11th Streets)

Mosaic: Jewish Life in Florida, a mosaic (imagine that) of photographs and historical bric-a-brac. Amusingly, the museum makes a whitewash of gangster Meyer Lansky – architect of the modern Mafia, who retired to Miami Beach and comes off here as a nice old guy who always donated to his synagogue.

Holocaust Memorial   MEMORIAL
(Map p44; www.holocaustmmb.org; cnr Meridian Ave & Dade Blvd) Holocaust memorials tend to be somber, but this one dedicated to the six million Jews killed during the *shoah* is particularly grim. The theme is one of relentless sadness, betrayal and loss. The light from a Star of David is blotted by the racist label of *Jude* (the German word for 'Jew'); a family surrounded by a hopeful Anne Frank quote is later shown murdered, framed by

another Frank quote on the death of ideals and dreams. The memorial was created in 1984 through the efforts of Miami Beach Holocaust survivors and sculptor Kenneth Treister. There are several key pieces, with the *Sculpture of Love and Anguish* the most visible to passers-by. The sculpture's enormous, oxidized bronze arm bears an Auschwitz tattooed number – chosen because it was never issued at the camp – and terrified camp prisoners scaling the sides of the arm.

Miami Beach Botanical Garden   GARDEN
(Map p44; www.mbgarden.org; 2000 Convention Center Dr; ⊙9am-5pm Tue-Sat) For more contemplation space head across the street to the botanical garden, a secret garden in the city. This lush but little-known 4½ acres of plantings is operated by the Miami Beach Garden

Conservancy, and is an oasis of palm trees, flowering hibiscus trees and glassy ponds.

The Promenade   PROMENADE
(Map p44; Ocean Ave) This beach promenade, a wavy ribbon sandwiched between the beach and Ocean Dr, extends from 5th St to 15th St. A popular location for photo shoots, especially during crowd-free early mornings, it's also a breezy, palm-tree-lined conduit for in-line skaters, cyclists, volleyball players (there's a net at 11th St), dog walkers, yahoos, locals and tourists. The beach that it edges, called Lummus Park, sports six floridly colored lifeguard stands. There's a public bathroom at 11th St; heads up, the sinks are a popular place for homeless bathing.

Post Office   HISTORIC BUILDING
(Map p44; 1300 Washington Ave) Make it a point to mail a postcard from this 1937 deco gem of a post office, the very first South Beach renovation project tackled by preservationists in the '70s. This Depression moderne building in the 'stripped classic' style was constructed under President Roosevelt's reign and funded by the Works Progress Administration (WPA) initiative, which supported artists who were out of work during the Great Depression. On the exterior, note the bald eagle and the turret with iron railings, and inside, a large wall mural of Florida's Seminole Wars.

Temple Emanu El   RELIGIOUS
(Map p44; Washington Ave at 17th St) An art-deco temple? Not exactly, but the smooth, bubbly dome and sleek, almost aerodynamic profile

WORTH A TRIP

THE CAMPTON

If you're walking around Miami Beach enjoying the eye candy of all the beautiful people, hotels and restaurants, make a small detour to 1451 Washington St to see the old roots of South Beach. The **Campton** is a small residential condo complex (you may recognize it as the place where Jim Carrey lived in *Ace Ventura: Pet Detective*) occupied by older folks leading regular lives in one of the most unique neighborhoods in Florida. The condos themselves, with their swooping curves and shady, semicircular buttresses, are gems of art-deco design. This is what South Beach used to be, a collection of fading architectural treasures occupied by quiet retirees, before it became an international playground. The Campton is a residential building, so don't just wander in, but feel free to admire the exterior of the buildings.

of this Conservative synagogue, established in 1938, fits right in on SoBe's deco parade of moderne this and streamline that. Sabbath services are on Friday at 6:30pm and on Saturday at 8:45am.

World Erotic Art Museum   MUSEUM
(Map p44; WEAM; www.weam.com; 1205 Washington Ave; adult/student/senior $15/13.50/14, over 18yr only; ⊙11am-10pm, to midnight Fri & Sat) In

---

THE CORAL CASTLE OF MANY NAMES

On a street full of fairly opulent buildings, 1114 Ocean Drive, a cream-colored Mediterranean revival castle built of hewn coral and exposed timber that should rightly be the center set piece of a *Pirates of the Caribbean* movie, stands out. The three-story palace, built in the 1930s, was modeled after the Governor's House in Santo Domingo, where Christopher Columbus' son once laid his head. For years it was known as the **Amsterdam Palace** – until one day, in the early 1980s, it caught the eye of a certain fashion designer named Gianni Versace. Versace bought the property, renamed it the **Versace Mansion** and promptly locked horns with local preservationists after announcing plans to tear down a neighboring hotel so he could build a pool. After a battle, the moneyed designer won – but also struck a deal that would allow for law changes, saving more than 200 other historic hotels in the process.

None of it mattered in 1997, when stalker Andrew Cunanan gunned Versace down in front of the beloved mansion. For years after, the house was known as **Casa Casuarina** and operated as a members-only club. Currently it is the site of the grand **Villa by Barton G Hotel** (p86). Ironically, the death of a European fashion guru here has attracted lots of, well, European fashion gurus. Tourists still shuffle by, armed with morbid curiosity and a thirst for celebrity-related photos of any kind.

MIAMI

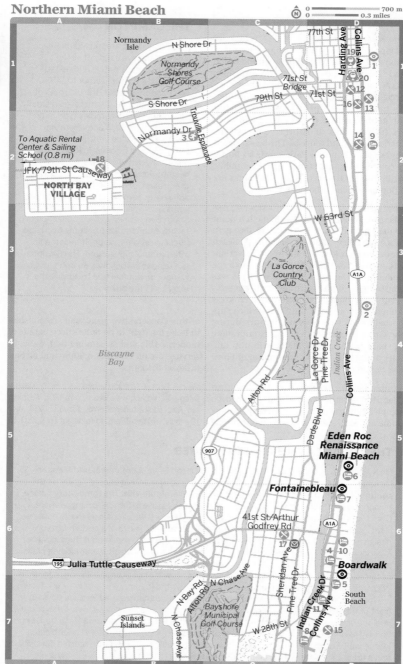

Northern Miami Beach

a neighborhood where no behavior is too shocking, the World Erotic Art Museum screams, 'Hey! We have a giant golden penis!' We'll sound like nerds if we analyze the historical merits of an old lady's smut collection (the museum was founded by 70-year-old Naomi Wilzig, who turned her 5000-piece private erotica collection into a South Beach attraction in 2005), but here goes. WEAM's exhibits are a lot more seriously minded than its marketing material, which definitely tries to rope in anyone interested in the smutty. The collection is actually full of fascinating erotica through the ages, from ancient sex manuals to Victorian peep-show photos, to centuries of sex toys to, yes, a big golden phallus by the exit.

Maps refer to the area above South Beach as Miami Beach, but locals use the jargon Mid-Beach (around the 40th streets) and North Beach (70th St and above). Communities like Surfside, Bal Harbour, Sunny Isles and Aventura are further north and can be included in spirit. Indian Creek waterway separates the luxury hotels and high-rise condos from the residential districts in the west. Keep in mind the separate city of North Miami Beach (as opposed to the *region* of Northern Miami Beach) is not, technically, on the spit of land known as Miami Beach – it's on the mainland. Confused? So are most residents.

MIAMI SIGHTS

Fontainebleau   HISTORIC BUILDING
(Map p52; www.fontainebleau.com; 4441 Collins Ave) As you proceed north on Collins, the condos and apartment building grow in grandeur and embellishment until you enter an area nicknamed Millionaire's Row. The most fantastic jewel in this glittering crown is the Fontainebleau hotel. You may remember the old lobby from the final scene from *Scarface,* where Al Pacino snorts a small hill of cocaine and guns down a small army of Colombians. This iconic 1954 leviathan is a brainchild of the great Miami Beach architect Morris Lapidus and has undergone many renovations; in some ways, it is utterly different from its original form, but it retains that early glamour. Note the spectacular trompe l'oeil mural on the southern exterior, designed by Richard Haas and painted over an eight-week period by Edwin Abreu.

**Eden Roc Renaissance
Miami Beach**   HISTORIC BUILDING
(Map p52; www.edenrocmiami.com; 4525 Collins Ave) The Eden Roc Resort was the second groundbreaking resort from Morris Lapidus, and it's a fine example of the architecture known as MiMo (Miami Modern). It was the hangout for the 1960s Rat Pack – Sammy Davis Jr, Dean Martin, Frank Sinatra and crew. Extensive renovation has eclipsed some of Lapidus' style; the Ocean Tower, for example, is a completely new addition. But with that said, the building is still an iconic piece of Miami Beach architecture, and an exemplar of the brash beauty of Millionaire's Row.

Boardwalk   BEACH
(Map p52; 21st St to 46th St) What's trendy in beachwear this season? Seventeenth-century Polish gabardine coats, apparently. There are plenty of skimpily dressed hotties on the Mid-Beach boardwalk, but there are

THE FULL MOON DRUM CIRCLE

If there's a full moon, check out the beach between 79th and 85th street – a big, boisterous **drum circle** is held here that doubles as a full-moon party. The beat tends to start between 8:30pm and 9:30pm, and can run well into the wee hours. That said, drinking (and the consumption of other substances) is technically illegal on the beach, and police have broken up the event before. Still, it tends to be a pretty fun party that shouldn't be missed if you're in the area and want to see an incredible moonset. Check www.miamidrums.com for more information.

also Orthodox Jews going about their business in the midst of gay joggers, strolling tourists and sunbathers. Nearby are numerous condo buildings occupied by middle-class Latinos and Jews, who walk their dogs and play with their kids here, giving the entire place a laid-back, real-world vibe that contrasts with the nonstop glamour of South Beach.

Arthur Godfrey Road (41st Street)   ROAD
(Map p52; 41st St) It's no *shtetl,* but Arthur Godfrey Rd is a popular thoroughfare for the Jewish population of Miami Beach, and possibly the best place in Florida to enjoy a good reuben sandwich (and the only place outside Tel Aviv with kosher sushi houses). Just as Jews have shaped Miami Beach, so has the beach shaped its Jews: you can eat lox *y arroz con moros* (salmon with rice and beans) and while the Orthodox men don *yarmulkes* and the women wear head-scarves, they've all got nice tans and drive flashy SUVs.

Normandy Isle & Ocean Terrace   NEIGHBORHOOD
(Map p52; 71st St west of Collins Ave) A few years ago Normandy Isle was dubbed Little Argentina, and it's still one of the best places outside Mendoza to people-watch with a *cortada* (Argentine espresso) before digging into traditional pasta and steak dishes. But today the Argentines compete with their neighbors the Uruguayans, their rivals the Brazilians, and even a big crop of Colombians, for first place in the Normandy Isle ethnic-enclave stakes. Not that there's tension; this is as prosperous and pleasant as

Miami gets. On Saturday mornings the small village green hosts a lovely farmers' market. Just across Collins Ave is Ocean Tce, which evokes an old-Miami main street (note the colorfully tiled facade of Walgreens) with oceanfront cafes, MiMo apartment buildings and a strong Argentine flavor.

Haulover Beach Park   PARK
(www.miamidade.gov/parks/parks/haulover_park .asp; 10800 Collins Ave; per car $4; ☺sunrise-sunset) Where are all those tanned men in gold chains and Speedos going? That would be the clothing-optional beach in this 40-acre park hidden from condos, highway and prying eyes by vegetation. There's more to do here than get in the buff, though; most of the beach is 'normal' (there's even a dog park) and is one of the nicer spots for sand in the area (also note the colorful deco-ish shower 'cones'). The park is located on Collins Ave about 4.5 miles north of 71st St.

Oleta River State Park   PARK
(www.floridastateparks.org/oletariver; 3400 NE 163rd St; per person $2, per car $6; ☺8am-sunset) Tequesta people were boating the Oleta River estuary as early as 500 BC, so you're just following in a long tradition if you canoe or kayak in this park. At almost 1000 acres, this is the largest urban park in the state and one of the best places in Miami to escape the maddening throng. Boat out to the local mangrove island, watch the eagles fly by, or just chill on the pretension-free beach. On-site **Blue Moon Outdoor Center** (☎305-957-3040; www.bluemoonmiami.com) offers single kayaks ($18 per 1½ hours, $25 per three hours), tandem kayaks ($25.50 per 1½ hours, $40 per three hours) and bike rental ($18 per 1½ hours, $25 per three hours). The park is off 163rd St NE/FL-826 in Sunny Isles, about 8 miles north of North Miami Beach.

Arch Creek Park   PARK
(www.miamidade.gov/parks/parks/arch_creek .asp; 1855 NE 135 St; ☺9am-5pm Wed-Sun) This compact-and-cute park, located near Oleta River, encompasses a cozy habitat of tropical hardwood species that surrounds a pretty, natural limestone bridge. Naturalists can lead you on kid-friendly ecotours of the area, which includes a lovely butterfly garden, or visitors can peruse a small but well-stocked museum of Native American and pioneer artifacts. Call ahead to book into ghost tours (also fun for the kids), held on Wednesdays and Saturdays. The park is just off North

Biscayne Blvd, 7 miles north of the Design District.

DOWNTOWN MIAMI

Downtown Miami is the city's international financial and banking center, but also boasts new condos and high-rise luxury hotels in the area known as Brickell (or 'the Brick'), which includes the very posh Brickell Key. The lazy, gritty Miami River divides Downtown into north and south. Many of Miami's homeless gather here at night (and sometimes by day).

TOP CHOICE **Adrienne Arsht Center for the Performing Arts** CULTURAL BUILDING
(Map p56; www.arshtcenter.com; 1300 N Biscayne Blvd) The largest performing-arts center in Florida (and second largest, by area, in the USA) is Miami's beautiful, beloved baby. It is also a major component of Downtown's urban equivalent of a facelift and several regimens of Botox. Designed by Cesar Pelli (the man who brought you Kuala Lumpur's Petronas Towers), the center has two main components: the Ziff Ballet Opera House and Knight Concert Hall, which span both sides of Biscayne Blvd. The venues are connected by a thin, elegant pedestrian bridge, while inside the theaters there's a sense of ocean and land sculpted by wind; the rounded balconies rise up in spirals that resemble a sliced-open seashell. If you have the chance, catch a show here (see p110); the interior alone is easily a highlight of any Miami trip.

Bayfront Park PARK
(Map p56; www.bayfrontparkmiami.com; 301 N Biscayne Blvd) Few American parks can claim to front such a lovely stretch of turquoise (Biscayne Bay), but Miamians are lucky like that. Lots of office workers catch quick naps under the palms at a little beach that does you the favor of setting out 'sit and chill' chairs. Notable park features are two performance venues: the **Klipsch Amphitheater**, which boasts excellent views over Biscayne Bay, is a good spot for live-music shows, while the smaller 200-seat (lawn seating can accommodate 800 more) **Tina Hills Pavilion** hosts free springtime performances. Look north for the **JFK Torch of Friendship**, and a fountain recognizing the accomplishments of longtime US congressman Claude Pepper. There's a huge variety of activities here, including yoga classes, trapeze classes and, we hear, flying-trapeze yoga classes (seriously); check out the Activities section of this chapter for details (p80).

Sculptures

Noted artist and landscape architect Isamu Noguchi redesigned much of Bayfront Park in the 1980s and dotted the grounds with three sculptures. In the southwest corner is the **Challenger Memorial**, a monument designed for the astronauts killed in the 1986 space-shuttle explosion built to resemble both the twisting helix of a human DNA chain and the shuttle itself. The **Light Tower** is a 40ft, somewhat abstract allusion to Japanese lanterns and moonlight over Miami. Our favorite is the **Mantra Slide**, a twisting spiral of marble that doubles as a playground piece for the kids.

American Airlines Arena CULTURAL BUILDING
(Map p56; www.aaarena.com; 601 N Biscayne Blvd) Just north of the park, and resembling a massive spaceship that perpetually hovers at the edge of Biscayne Bay, this arena has been the home of the Miami Heat basketball team since 2000. The Waterfront Theater, Florida's largest, is housed inside; throughout the year it hosts concerts, Broadway

DOWNTOWN'S INTERNATIONAL BAZAARS

Downtown Miami has a reputation for being a bit rough around the edges. We think this is a bit undeserved; the area is dodgy at night but safe by day, if a little down-at-heel. Part of this ratty atmosphere is due to large amounts of cheap, knock-off electronics, fashion and jewelry shops that cluster in half-abandoned malls and shopping arcades. These stores are almost all run by immigrants, from West Africa, East Asia, South America and the Middle East (did we cover all the directions?). While we doubt you need cheap consumer goods of dubious origin, we do think it's fun to check out one of these markets, like the **777 International Mall** (145 E Flagler St). This may be as close as you'll get to the messy, shouting, sweaty and exciting bazaars of the developing world, where folks yell at you to seal a deal and haggling is often an option. It's not as pretty as shopping in Miami Beach or the Design District, but it's a fascinating slice of this city's life.

Downtown Miami

400 m
0.3 miles

A1A

MacArthur Causeway

41

Herald Plaza

Omni

Biscayne Blvd

Adrienne Arsht Center for the Performing Arts

Bicentennial Park

Bicentennial Park

Intracoastal Waterway

Port Blvd

Lummus Island

Bayside Marketplace

Marina

14

8

7

Bayfront Park

38

1

Biscayne Blvd

41

5

Freedom Tower

College North

College/Bayside

1st St

NE 1st St

NE 2nd Ave

Park West

11th St

School Board

NE 14th St

NE 13th St

NE 12th St

NE 10th St

NE 9th St

NE 8th St

NE 7th St

NE 6th St

NE 5th St

NE 4th St

NE 3rd St

NE 2nd St

SE 1st Ave

12

N Miami Ave

35

3

31

34

30

36

37

395

NW 1st Ave

Overtown

Arena/State Plaza

Government Center

Government Center

Metromover

NW 1st Ave

NW 1st Ct

9

NW 2nd Ave

NW 3rd St

NW 2nd St

Greyhound Station (Downtown)

95th St

NW 3rd Ct

Gibson Park

North-South Expwy

NW 12th St

Lummus Park

Miami River

20

24

NW 4th Ave

NW 9th St

NW 8th St

NW 5th Ave

NW 6th Ave

NW 7th St

NW 10th St

Reeves Park

NW 6th St

NW 5th St

NW 4th St

SW N River Dr

SW 8th River Dr

NW 3rd St

NW 2nd St

Culmer

NW 7th Ave

NW 7th Ave

NW 10th Ave

SW 6th Ave

SW 7th St

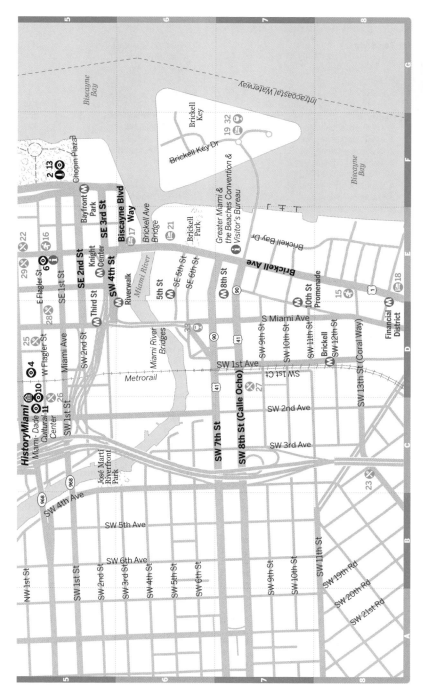

Downtown Miami

performances and the like. A giant airplane is painted on top of the arena; you may spot it (it looks like the shadow of a plane from afar) when you fly out of the city, or if you're Superman.

HistoryMiami   MUSEUM
(Map p56; www.historymiami.org; 101 W Flagler St; adult/child 6-12 yr/senior $8/5/7, combined ticket to MAM $10; ☺10am-5pm Tue-Fri, noon-5pm Sat & Sun) South Florida – a land of escaped slaves, guerilla Native Americans, gangsters, land grabbers, pirates, tourists, drug dealers and alligators – has a special history, and it takes a special kind of museum to capture that narrative. This place, located in the **Miami-Dade Cultural Center**, does just that, weaving together the stories of the region's successive waves of population, from

Native Americans to Nicaraguans. It's interesting for kids and manages to explain the story of Miami's many demographic groups while still feeling tightly focused. Get off the Metromover at the Government Center stop.

**Brickell Avenue Bridge &
Brickell Key**   ISLAND
(Map p56; Brickell Ave) Crossing the Miami River, the lovely Brickell Avenue Bridge between SE 4th St and SE 5th St was made wider and higher several years ago, which was convenient for the speedboat-driving drug runners being chased by Drug Enforcement Administration agents on the day of the bridge's grand reopening! Note the 17ft bronze statue by Cuban-born sculptor Manuel Carbonell of a Tequesta warrior and his family, which sits atop the towering Pillar

of History column. Walking here is the best way to get a sense of the sculptures and will allow you to avoid one of the most confusing traffic patterns in Miami. Brickell Key looks more like a floating porcupine with glass towers for quills than an island. To live the life of Miami glitterati, come here, pretend you belong, and head into a patrician hangout like the Mandarin Oriental Hotel Miami, where the lobby and intimate lounges afford sweeping views of Biscayne Bay.

Metromover TRAIN
(Map p56; www.miamidade.gov/transit/mover.asp) This elevated, electric monorail is hardly big enough to serve the mass-transit needs of the city, and has become something of a tourist attraction. Whatever its virtues as a commuting tool, the Metromover is a really great (and free!) way to see central Miami from a height (which helps, given the skyscraper-canyon nature of Downtown). Because it's gratis, Metromover has a reputation as a hangout for the homeless, but at the time of research a fair few folks were using it to commute as well, a number the media reported was climbing due to the price of gas.

Miami River RIVER
(Map p56) For a taste of a seedy Old Florida that reeks of Humphrey Bogart in shirtsleeves and a fedora, come to the lazy, sultry and still kinda spicy Miami River. Much of the shore feels abandoned, and is lined with makeshift warehouses, where you-can-only-imagine-what is loaded and unloaded onto small tugboats bound for you-can-only-imagine-where. Fisherfolk float in with their daily catch, fancy yachts 'slumming it' dock at restaurants, nonconformists hang out on their houseboats and all in all, it just seems like a matter of time before the music from *Buena Vista Social Club* starts drifting over the scene.

Gusman Center for the Performing Arts CULTURAL BUILDING
(Map p56; www.gusmancenter.org; 174 E Flagler St) The Arsht Center is modernly pretty, but the Olympia Theater at the Gusman Center for the Performing Arts is vintage-classic beautiful. You know how the kids at Hogwarts can see the sky through their dining-hall roof? Well the Olympia re-creates the whole effect sans Dumbledore, using 246 twinkling stars and clouds cast over an indigo-deep, sensual shade of a ceiling, frosted with classical Greek sculpture and Vienna Opera House–style embellishment. The theater

first opened in 1925; today the lobby serves as the Downtown Miami Welcome Center (p115), doling out helpful visitor information and organizing tours of the historic district; at night you can still catch theater and music performances (p110).

Miami Art Museum MUSEUM
(Map p56; MAM; www.miamiartmuseum.org; 101 W Flagler St; adult/child under 12 yr & students/senior $8/free/4, 2nd Sat of month free, combined ticket to HistoryMiami $10; ⊙10am-5pm Tue-Fri, noon-5pm Sat & Sun) Located within the Miami-Dade Cultural Center, this museum is ensconced in spectacular Philip Johnson–designed digs. Without having a permanent collection, its fine rotating exhibits concentrate on post-WWII international art. MAM is scheduled to move a new waterfront location at Bicentennial Park in 2013; check the website for details on the impressive design schematics for the new digs. The museum is open late (noon to 9pm) on the third Thursday of the month.

Miami-Dade Public Library LIBRARY
(Map p56; www.mdpls.org; 101 W Flagler St; ⊙9am-6pm Mon-Wed & Fri, 9am-9pm Thu, 1-5pm Sun) The main branch of the Miami-Dade library system is a lovely escape from Downtown's bustle. To learn more about Florida (especially

---

RESURRECTING THE LYRIC

Hallowed names Duke Ellington and Ella Fitzgerald once walked across the stage of the **Lyric Theater** (Map p56; 819 NW 2nd Ave), a major stop on the 'Chitlin' Circuit' – the black live-entertainment trail of preintegration USA. But as years passed both the theater and the neighborhood it served, Overtown, fell into disuse. Then the **Black Archives History & Research Center of South Florida** (p115) kicked in $1.5 million for renovations and overhauled everything. The phoenix reopened its doors in 1999 to general appreciation, but at the time of research the theater's doors were closed due to accusations of fraud and financial mismanagement against contractors renovating the building. We expect this situation to be cleared by the time you read this, when hopefully the Lyric will be hosting performances that match the glamour of its heyday.

DON'T MISS

LITTLE HAITI

If you haven't been to Port-au-Prince, then Little Haiti (La Petite Haïti), one of the most evocative neighborhoods in Miami, is the next best thing. Young men in tank tops listen to Francophone rap, while broad-necked women wearing bright wraps gossip in front of the *botanicas* – which, by the way, are not selling plants. A *botanica* here is a *vodou* shop. The neighborhood is one of Miami's poorest and it's not advisable to walk around here alone after dark, but by day or if visiting the Little Haiti Cultural Center (p63) you'll be fine.

Botanicas are perhaps the most 'foreign' sight in Little Haiti. Storefronts promise to help in matters of love, work and sometimes 'immigration services,' but trust us, there are no marriage counselors or INS guys in here. As you enter you'll probably get a funny look, but be courteous, curious and respectful and you should be welcomed. Before you browse, forget stereotypes about pins and dolls. Like many traditional religions, *vodou* recognizes supernatural forces in everyday objects, and powers that are both distinct from and part of one overarching deity. Ergo, you'll see shrines to Jesus next to altars to traditional *vodou* deities. Notice the large statues of what look like people; these actually represent *loa* (pronounced lwa), intermediary spirits that form a pantheon below God in the *vodou* religious hierarchy. Drop a coin into a *loa* offering bowl before you leave, especially to Papa Legba, spirit of crossroads and, by our reckoning, travelers. Two good *botanicas* are **Vierge Miracle & St Phillipe** (Map p62; 5910 NE 2nd Ave) and **3×3 Santa Barbara Botanica** (Map p62; 5700 NE 2nd Ave).

For a more cerebral taste of Haitian culture, peruse the shelves at **Libreri Mapou** (Map p62; www.librerimapou.com; 5919 NE 2nd Ave), bursting with thousands of titles (including periodicals) in English, French and Creole, as well as crafts and recorded music.

South Florida), take a browse through the extensive Florida Department, or ask to see the Romer Collection, an archive of some 17,500 photos and prints that chronicle the history of the city from its early years to the 1950s.

Freedom Tower   HISTORIC BUILDING
(Map p56; 600 Biscayne Blvd) Designed by the New York architectural firm of Shultz & Weaver in 1925, this tower is one of two surviving towers modeled after the Giralda bell tower in Spain's Cathedral of Seville (the second is at the Biltmore Hotel in Coral Gables). The 'Ellis Island of the South,' it served as an immigration processing center for almost half a million Cuban refugees in the 1960s. Placed on the National Register of Historic Places in 1979, it was also home to the *Miami Daily News* for 32 years.

Old US Post Office   HISTORIC BUILDING
(Map p56; 100 NE 1st Ave; 9am-5pm Mon-Fri) Constructed in 1912, this post office and county courthouse served as the first federal building in Miami. The building, which features a low-pitched roof, elaborate doors and carved entryways, was purchased in 1937 to serve as the country's first savings and loan (funny, considering S&Ls helped build Miami

in the 1980s). Check out Denman Fink's 1940 mural *Law Guides Florida Progress* in the main courtroom on the 2nd floor.

Cisneros Fontanal Arts Foundation   MUSEUM
(Map p56; CIFO; 305-455-3380; www.cifo.org; 1018 N Miami Ave; 10am-4pm Thu-Sun) The arts foundation is one of the best spots in Miami to catch the work of contemporary Latin American artists, and has an impressive showroom to boot. Even the exterior blends postindustrial rawness with a lurking, natural ambience, offset by the extensive use of Bisazza tiles to create an overarching tropical motif. Similar to the Arsht Center, CIFO was built near the rattier edge of Downtown with the intention of revitalizing this semi-blighted area with fresh arts spaces. The opening hours only apply during exhibition showings, although informal tours can be arranged if you call ahead.

Dade County Courthouse   HISTORIC BUILDING
(Map p56; 73 W Flagler St) If you end up on trial here, at least you'll get a free tour of one of the most imposing courthouses in the USA. When Miami outgrew its first courthouse it moved legal proceedings to this neoclassical icon, built between 1925 and 1929 for $4 million. It's a very...appropriate building:

if structures were people, the courthouse would definitely be a judge. Some trivia: back in the day, the top nine floors served as a 'secure' prison, from which more than 70 prisoners escaped.

WYNWOOD, DESIGN DISTRICT & LITTLE HAITI

Now rebranded as 'Midtown', Wynwood and the Design District are Miami's official arts neighborhoods, plus the focal points of new art, food and nightlife in Greater Miami. This area still abuts some of the city's poorer 'hoods, and if you come here via city streets instead of the highway you'll see the rough edges that once characterized the vicinity. The Midtown mall is the area's natural center of gravity. Wynwood is the place for dedicated art galleries, while the small collection of posh retail outlets in the Design District are filled with things as beautiful as any canvas. Between the Italian-designed chairs, Russian Romanov-era cabinets and Dale Chihuly-esque chandeliers, the Design District tends to be expensive (we're talking thousands for a single item), although there are some relative bargains to be found if you look.

Unlike Wynwood, the Design District is pretty compact and walkable. Little Haiti is not to be missed and sits above the Design District. In between the two lies the leafy, lovely residential neighborhood of Buena Vista, where restaurants, bars, gay hot spots and gentrification are rapidly spreading.

Rubell Family Art Collection   MUSEUM
(Map p62; www.rfc.museum; 95 NW 29th St, Wynwood; adult/student & under 18yr $10/5; ⊙10am-6pm Wed-Sat Dec-Aug) The Rubell family – specifically, the niece and nephew of the late Steve, better known as Ian Schrager's Studio 54 partner – operates some top-end hotels in Miami Beach, but they've also amassed an impressive contemporary art collection that spans the last 30 years. The most admirable quality of this collection is its commitment to not just displaying one or two of its artists' pieces; the museum's aim is to showcase a contributor's entire career.

FINDING ART IN WYNWOOD

There is a plethora of art galleries in Wynwood, with new spaces opening on what sometimes feels like a weekly basis. The stomping grounds of 'Wypsters' (Wynwood hipsters, those who enjoy, staff and provide content for the neighborhood's galleries) shift month by month as 'guerilla' galleries, new murals, graffiti, cafes, restaurants and studio spaces spread across Midtown. In general, art galleries can be found in a square bound by NW 20th and NW 37th streets to the south and north, and N Miami Ave and NW 3rd Ave to the east and west. It's difficult for us to recommend one specific set of galleries given the diversity of what's on offer, but the following are some of our favorites.

» **Artopia** (Map p62; ☑305-374-8882; 1753 NE 2nd Ave) Proves the extents for Wynwood we mention above are flexible – Artopia is physically in Overtown, but culturally part of the gallery circuit. This was the old studio space of the late, renowned self-taught artist Purvis Young, who grew up near the studio. His folk-arty works and similar pieces are often displayed, as are pieces by up-and-coming artists local or otherwise. Call for opening hours.

» **PanAmerican Art Projects** (Map p62; ☑305-573-2400; www.panamericanart.com; 2450 NW 2nd Ave; ⊙9:30am-5:30pm Tue-Fri, noon-5:30pm Sat) Despite the name, PanAmerican also showcases work from European and Chinese artists. But much of what is on display comes from fine artists representing Latin America, the Caribbean and the USA.

» **Art Modern Gallery** (Map p62; www.artmoderngallery.com; 175 NW 23rd St; ⊙noon-4:30pm Mon-Sat) Curators here unsurprisingly focus on modern, contemporary and pop art drawn from both domestic and international talent.

» **Curator's Voice Art Projects** (Map p62; www.curatorsvoiceartprojects.com; 2509 NW 2nd Ave; ⊙9:30am-5:30pm Mon-Fri, from noon Sat) Another large, elegant showing space that prides itself on displaying some of the most avant-garde work in Wynwood.

There are literally dozens of other galleries to check out; a nice way of seeing them and getting some drinking is attending the famous **Wynwood Art Walks** (see p107). Check out websites like www.beachedmiami.com and www.miamiartguide.com for more information.

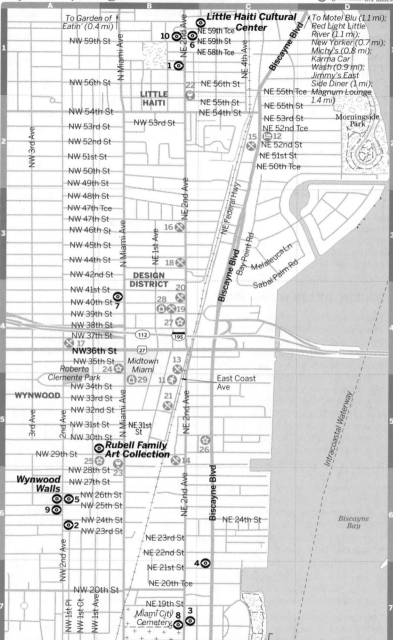

MIAMI

To Garden of
Eatin' (0.4 mi)

Little Haiti Cultural Center

To Motel Blu (1.1 mi);
Red Light Little
River (1.1 mi);
New Yorker (0.7 mi);
Michy's (0.8 mi);
Karma Car
Wash (0.9 mi);
Jimmy's East
Side Diner (1 mi);
Magnum Lounge
1.4 mi)

10
6
1

22

LITTLE
HAITI

NW 59th St
NE 59th Tce
NE 59th St
NE 58th Tce

NW 56th St

NE 56th St

NW 54th St
NW 53rd St

NE 55th Tce
NE 55th St
NE 54th St

NE 55th Tce
NE 55th St
NE 53rd St
NE 52nd Tce

Morningside
Park

NW 53rd St
NW 52nd St
NW 51st St
NW 50th St
NW 49th St
NW 48th St
NW 47th Tce
NW 47th St
NW 46th St
NW 45th St
NW 44th St
NW 42nd St
NW 41st St
NW 40th St
NW 39th St
NW 38th St
NW 37th St
NW 36th St
NW 35th St
NW 34th St
NW 33rd St
NW 32nd St
NW 31st St
NW 30th St
NW 29th St
NW 28th St
NW 27th St
NW 26th St
NW 25th St
NW 24th St
NW 23rd St
NW 20th St

15
12

NE 52nd St
NE 51st St
NE 50th Tce

16

18

**DESIGN
DISTRICT**

20
28
19
27

7

17

NW 36th St

24

Midtown
Miami

13

27

Roberto
Clemente Park

WYNWOOD

29
11
21

East Coast
Ave

NE 31st
St

**Rubell Family
Art Collection**

25
23

14

26

**Wynwood
Walls**

5
9
2

NE 23rd St
NE 22nd St
NE 21st St
NE 20th Tce

4

NE 24th St

Biscayne
Bay

NW 19th St
Miami City
Cemetery

8 3

Biscayne Blvd

NE 4th Ave

N Miami Ave

NE 2nd Ave

NE 1st Ave

NE 2nd Ave

NE Federal Hwy

Biscayne Blvd

Bay Point Rd

Melaleuca Ln

Sabal Palm Rd

NE 2nd Ave

Biscayne Blvd

NW 3rd Ave

NW 2nd Ave

3rd Ave

2nd Ave

NW 1st Pl
NW 1st Ct
NW 1st Ave

Intracoastal Waterway

112
195

Little Haiti Cultural Center　　　GALLERY
(Map p62; www.miamigov.com/lhculturalcenter; 212 NE 59th Tce; ◎9am-5pm, plus evenings during events) Miami has the largest community of Ayisyens (Haitians) in the world outside Haiti, and this is the place to learn about their story. The cultural center is a study in playful island designs and motifs that houses a small but vibrant art gallery, crafts center and activities space – dance classes, drama productions and similar events are held here year-round. The best time to visit is for the Big Night in Little Haiti (www.bignightlittlehaiti.com), a street party held on the third Friday of every month from 6pm to 10pm. The celebration is rife with music, mouth-watering Caribbean food and beer, and is one of the safest, easiest ways of accessing the culture of Haiti outside of that island.

Wynwood Walls　　　PUBLIC ART
(Map p62; www.thewynwoodwalls.com; NW 2nd Ave btwn 25th & 26th St; ◎noon-8pm Wed-Sat) Not a gallery per se, Wynwood Walls is a collection of murals and paintings laid out over an open courtyard in the heart of Wynwood. What's on offer tends to change with the coming and going of major arts events like Art Basel (one of the US's major annual art shows); when we visited the centerpiece was a fantastic portrait of Aung San Suu Kyi by artist Shepard Fairey.

Miami City Cemetery　　　CEMETERY
(Map p62; 1800 NE 2nd Ave; ◎7am-3:30pm Mon-Fri, 8am-4:30pm Sat & Sun) This quiet graveyard, the final resting place of some of Miami-Dade's most important citizens, is a sort of narrative of the history of the Magic City cast in bone, dirt and stone. The dichotomy of the past and modernity gets a nice visual representation in the form of looming condos shadowing the last abode of the Magic City's late, great ones. More than 9000 graves are divided into separate white, black and Jewish sections. Buried here are mayors, veterans (including about 90 Confederate soldiers) and the godmother of South Florida, Julia Tuttle, who purchased the first orange groves that attracted settlers to the area.

Living Room　　　PUBLIC ART
(Map p62; cnr NW 40th St & N Miami Ave) Just to remind you that you're entering the Design District is a big, honking, public art installation of, yep, a living room – just the sort of thing you're supposed to shop for while you're here. Actually this Living Room, by

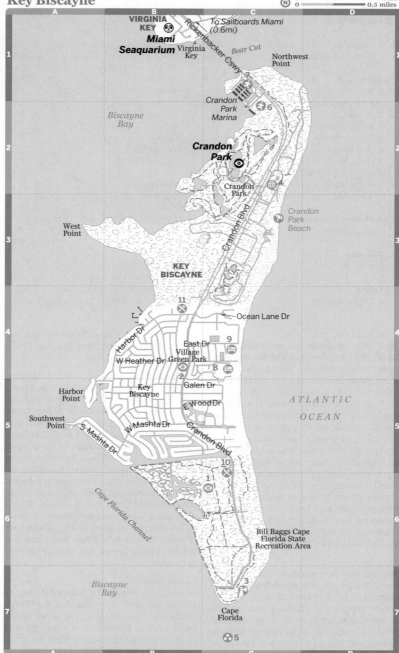

N
0 — 1 km
0 — 0.5 miles

VIRGINIA
KEY
Miami
Seaquarium   Virginia
Key

Rickenbacker Cswy

*To Sailboards Miami
(0.6mi)*

Bear Cut

Northwest
Point

*Crandon
Park
Marina*

6

*Biscayne
Bay*

*Crandon
Park*

Crandon
Park

Crandon Blvd

*Crandon
Park
Beach*

West
Point

**KEY
BISCAYNE**

11

Ocean Lane Dr

Harbor Dr

East Dr
Village
Green Park

9

W Heather Dr

8

2   Galen Dr

Key
Biscayne

E Wood Dr

Harbor
Point

ATLANTIC

OCEAN

Southwest
Point

S. Mashta Dr

W Mashta Dr

Crandon Blvd

10

Cape Florida Channel

1

Bill Baggs Cape
Florida State
Recreation Area

*Biscayne
Bay*

3

Cape
Florida

5

Argentine husband-and-wife team Roberto Behar and Rosario Marquardt, is an 'urban intervention' meant to be a criticism of the disappearance of public space, but we think it serves as a nice metaphor for the Design District as a whole: a contemporary interior plopped into the middle of urban decay.

Bacardi Building   ARCHITECTURE
(Map p62; 2100 Biscayne Blvd; admission free; ⊙9am-3:30pm Mon-Fri) You don't need to down 151 to appreciate the striking Miami headquarters of the world's largest family-owned spirits company, Bacardi. The main event is a beautifully decorated tower that looks like the mosaic pattern of a tropical bathhouse on steroids. There used to be a small art gallery and museum inside dedicated to the famously anti-Castro Bacardis (think about what 'Cuba Libre' actually means the next time you order one) but it was indefinitely closed at time of research.

KEY BISCAYNE

The scenic drive along the Rickenbacker Causeway leads first to small Virginia Key, then over to Key Biscayne, an island that's just 7 miles long with unrivalled views of the Miami skyline. As you drive over the causeway, note the small public beaches, picnic areas and fishing spots arranged around on its margins. The road turns into Crandon Blvd, the key's only real main road, which runs to the Cape Florida Lighthouse at the island's southernmost tip.

Miami Seaquarium   AQUARIUM
(Map p64; www.miamiseaquarium.com; 4400 Rickenbacker Causeway; adult/child $39/30, parking $8; ⊙9:30am-6pm) This 38-acre marine-life park excels in preserving, protecting and educating about aquatic creatures, and was one of the country's first places dedicated to sea life. There are dozens of shows and exhibits, including a tropical reef; the Shark Channel, with feeding presentations; and Discovery Bay, a natural mangrove habitat that serves as a refuge for rehabilitating rescued sea turtles. Check out the Pacific white-sided dolphins or West Indian manatees being nursed back to health; some are released. Frequent shows put gorgeous animals on display, including a massive killer whale, some precious dolphins and sea lions. The Seaquarium's newly opened Dolphin Harbor is an especially fun venue for watching marine mammals play and show off; it also offers swim-with-the-cetacean fun via its Encounter (adult/child five to nine years $139/99), Odyssey ($199) and, for total dolphin-lovers only, Trainer for a Day ($495). Note that children under five cannot participate in the Encounter, people under 5ft 2in cannot participate in the Odyssey and children under three cannot enter the observation area. Read about the pros and cons of swimming with dolphins (see p146) before committing to these programs. Last entry is at 4:30pm.

Crandon Park   PARK
(Map p64; www.miamidade.gov/parks/parks/crandon_beach.asp; 6747 Crandon Blvd; per car $5; ⊙sunrise-sunset) This 1200-acre park boasts Crandon Park Beach, a glorious but crowded beach that stretches for 3 miles. Much of the park consists of a dense coastal hammock (hardwood forest) and mangrove swamps. Pretty cabanas at the south end of the park can be rented by the day for $37.45. The 2-mile-long beach here is clean, uncluttered with tourists, faces a lovely sweep of teal goodness and is regularly named one of the best beaches in the USA.

Marjory Stoneman Douglas Biscayne Nature Center
(Map p64; www.biscaynenaturecenter.org; Crandon Park, 6767 Crandon Blvd; admission free; ⊙10am-4pm) Marjory Stoneman Douglas was a beloved environmental crusader (see p126)

JIMBO'S

It's the simple things that make life worth living, and sometimes their simplicity is even more elegant in the face of life's complexity. To wit: come to **Jimbo's** (Map p64; www.jimbosplace.com; Duck Lake Rd; ☉sunrise-sunset) in Virginia Key. In a city of unfettered development, this bar...no, shrimp shack...no, smoked-fish house...no, 24-hour trailer park bonfire...well, whatever. A series of dilapidated river shacks and a boccie court has been, for decades, its own version of everything that once was right in Florida. Of course, even here the vibe is a little artificial; all those rotting fish houses were set pieces for the 1980 horror movie *Island Claws*. Other flicks filmed here include *Ace Ventura: Pet Detective*, *True Lies* and the cinematic masterpiece, *Porky's 2*. But today the shacks have been claimed as the set pieces of the Jimbo show. Oh – the last time we were here, we went swimming off the dock and a manatee popped up. A manatee! To find Jimbo's, go to the end of Arthur Lamb Jr Rd.

and a worthy namesake of this child-friendly nature center. The structure is a perfect introduction and exploration of the continental USA's own subtropical ecosystem: South Florida. There are weekend hikes and nature lessons that let kids wade into the water with nets and try to catch sea horses, sponges and other marine life (released after a short lesson); check the website for a full breakdown of the many activities on offer, most of which cost $12 per person.

Bill Baggs Cape Florida State Park   PARK
(Map p64; www.floridastateparks.org/capeflorida; 1200 S Crandon Blvd; per car $8, pedestrian $2; ☉8am-sunset) If you don't make it to the Florida Keys, come to this park for a taste of their unique island ecosystems. The 494-acre space is a tangled clot of tropical fauna and dark mangroves – look for the 'snorkel' roots that provide air for half-submerged mangrove trees – all interconnected by sandy trails and wooden boardwalks,

and surrounded by miles of pale ocean. A concession shack rents kayaks, bikes, in-line skates, beach chairs and umbrellas.

Cape Florida Lighthouse
At the state recreation area's southernmost tip, the 1845 brick lighthouse is the oldest structure in Florida (it replaced another lighthouse that was severely damaged in 1836 by during the Second Seminole War). Free tours run at 10am and 1pm Monday to Thursday.

FREE **Biscayne Community Center & Village Green Park**   PARK
(Map p64; ☎305-365-8900; www.keybiscayne.fl.gov/pr; Village Green Way, off Crandon Blvd; ☉Community Center 6am-10pm Mon-Fri, 8am-8pm Sat & Sun; ⊕) An unmissable park for kids: there's a swimming pool, jungle gyms, an activity room with a playset out of a child's happiest fantasies and an

Little Havana

African baobab tree that's over a century old and teeming with tropical birdlife. Did we mention it's free?

Stiltsville
HISTORIC BUILDINGS

(Map p64; www.stiltsville.org) This collection of seven houses that stand on pilings out in Biscayne Bay has been around since the early '30s. You can view them, way out in the distance, from the southern shore of the Bill Baggs park, or take a **boat tour** (☎305-379-5119; www.islandqueencruises.com /stiltsville.htm; tours $49) out there with the illustrious historian Dr Paul George. In 2003, the nonprofit Stiltsville Trust was set up by the National Parks Service to rehabilitate the buildings into as-yet-unknown facilities; proposals include a National Parks Service visitor center, artist-in-residence colony or community center. Not much work seems to have progressed towards this idea, but if you'd like more information, check www .stiltsvilletrust.org.

LITTLE HAVANA
Little Havana's main thoroughfare, Calle Ocho (SW 8th St), doesn't just cut through the heart of the neighborhood; it is the heart of the neighborhood. In a lot of ways, this is every immigrant enclave in the USA – full of restaurants, mom-and-pop convenience shops and phonecard kiosks. Admittedly, the Cubaness of Little Havana is slightly exaggerated for visitors, and many of the Latin immigrants here are actually from Central America. With that said, this is an atmospheric place with a soul that's rooted outside the USA. Be on the lookout for the Cuban Walk of Fame, a series of sidewalk-implanted stars emblazoned with the names of Cuban celebrities that runs up and down much of 8th St.

TOP CHOICE Máximo Gómez Park
PARK

(Map p66; SW 8th St at SW 15th Ave; ⊙9am-6pm) Little Havana's most evocative reminder of Old Cuba is Máximo Gómez Park, or 'Domino Park,' where the sound of elderly men trash-talking over games of chess is harmonized by the quick clak-clak of slapping dominoes. The jarring backtrack, plus the heavy smell of cigars and a sunrise-bright mural of the 1993 Summit of the Americas, combine to make Máximo Gómez one of the most sensory sites in Miami.

Cuban Memorials
MONUMENTS

(Map p66) The two blocks of SW 13th Ave south of Calle Ocho contain a series of monuments to Cuban and Cuban-American heroes, including those that died in the Cuban War of Independence and anti-Castro conflicts. The memorials include the **Eternal Torch in Honor of the 2506th Brigade** for the exiles who died during the Bay of Pigs

Little Havana

Invasion; a huge **Cuba brass relief** depicting a map of Cuba, dedicated to the 'ideals of people who will never forget the pledge of making their Fatherland free'; a **José Martí memorial**; and a **Madonna statue**, which is supposedly illuminated by a shaft of holy light every afternoon. Bursting out of the island in the center of the boulevard is a massive ceiba tree, revered by followers of Santeria. The tree is an unofficial reminder of the poorer *Marielitos* (those who fled Cuba in the 1980 Mariel Boatlift) and successive waves of desperate-for-work Cubans, many of whom are *santeros* (Santeria practitioners) who have come to Miami since the 1980s.

Just away from the main drag are a fountain and monument, collectively entitled **La Plaza de la Cubanidad** (Map p66; cnr W Flagler St & NW 17th Ave), which is a tribute both to the Cuban provinces and to the people who were drowned in 1994 while trying to leave Cuba on a ship, *13 de Marzo,* which was sunk by Castro's forces just off the coast.

Cuba Ocho   GALLERY
(Map p66; www.cubaocho.com; 1465 SW 8th St; ⊙9am-6pm) The jewel of the Little Havana Art District, Cuba Ocho functions as a community center, art gallery and research outpost for all things Cuban. The interior resembles a cool old Havana cigar bar, yet the walls are decked out in artwork that references both the classical past of Cuban art and its avant-garde future. Frequent live music, film, drama performances, readings and other events go off every week. The center opens during the evening for these events; check online for more information.

FREE **Bay of Pigs Museum & Library**   LIBRARY
(Map p66; 1821 SW 9th St; ⊙10am-5pm Mon-Fri) This small museum is more of a memorial to the 2506th Brigade, otherwise known as the crew of the ill-fated Bay of Pigs Invasion. Whatever your thoughts on Fidel Castro and Cuban-Americans, pay a visit here to flesh out one side of this contentious story. You'll likely chat with survivors of the Bay of Pigs, who like to hang out here surrounded by pictures of comrades who never made it back to the USA.

Tower Theater   HISTORIC BUILDING
(Map p66; www.mdc.edu/culture/tower.htm; 1508 SW 8th St) This renovated 1926 landmark theater has a proud deco facade and a newly done interior, thanks to support from the Miami-Dade Community College. In its heyday, it was the center of Little Havana social life, and via the films it showed served as a bridge between immigrant society and American pop culture. Today the space frequently shows independent and Spanish-language films (sometimes both) and hosts varied art exhibitions in the lobby.

COCONUT GROVE

Coconut Grove, which attracts a mix of old hippies, middle-class and mall-going Miami and college students, unfolds along S Bayshore Dr as it hugs the shoreline. US Hwy 1 (S Dixie Hwy) acts as the northern boundary for the Grove.

TOP CHOICE **Vizcaya Museum & Gardens**   HISTORIC BUILDING
(www.miamidade.gov/vizcaya; 3251 S Miami Ave; adult/child $12/5; ⊙museum 9:30am-4:30pm Wed-Mon) They call Miami the Magic City, and if it is, this Italian villa, the housing equivalent of a Fabergé egg, is its most fairy-tale residence. In 1916, industrialist James Deering started a long and storied Miami tradition by making a ton of money and building some ridiculously grandiose digs. He employed 1000 people (then 10% of the local population) for four years to fulfill his desire for a pad that looked centuries old. He was so obsessed with creating an atmosphere of old money that he had the house stuffed with 15th- to

---

VIERNES CULTURALES (CULTURAL FRIDAYS)

The Little Havana Arts District may not be Wynwood, but it does constitute an energetic little strip of galleries and studios (concentrated on 8th St between SW 15th Ave & SW 17th Ave) that house some of the best Latin American art in Miami. Rather than pop into each gallery, look around and feel pressure to buy, why not visit on the last Friday of each month for **Viernes Culturales** (www.viernesculturales.org). No wine-sipping art walk this; Cultural Fridays in Little Havana are like little carnival seasons, with music, old men in *guayaberas* (Cuban dress shirts) crooning to the stars and more booty-shaking than brie. Although there is also brie, and plenty of time to appreciate local art as all the Little Havana galleries throw open their doors.

19th-century furniture, tapestries, paintings and decorative arts; had a monogram fashioned for himself; and even had paintings of fake ancestors commissioned. The 30-acre grounds are full of splendid gardens and Florentine gazebos, and both the house and gardens are used for the display of rotating contemporary-art exhibitions. It's located between Downtown and Coconut Grove, roughly where SW 32nd Rd intersects with Dixie Hwy and S Miami Ave.

Barnacle Historic State Park PARK
(Map p69; www.floridastateparks.org/thebarnacle; 3485 Main Hwy; admission $2, house tours $3; ⏰park 9am-4pm Fri-Mon, house tours 10am, 11:30am, 1pm, 2:30pm Fri-Mon) In the center of the village is the 1891, 5-acre pioneer residence of Ralph Monroe, Miami's first

Coconut Grove

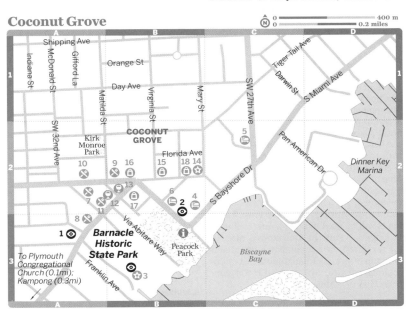

Coconut Grove

honorable snowbird. The house is open for guided tours, led by folks who are quite knowledgeable and enthusiastic about the park – which is, by the way, a lovely, shady oasis for strolling. Barnacle hosts frequent (and lovely) moonlight concerts, from jazz to classical. A little way down Main Hwy, on the other side of the road, there's a small Buddhist temple shaded by large groves of banyan trees, which gives it an authentically Southeast Asian feel (although it's a Tibetan Buddhist temple, so perhaps not).

Miami Museum of Science & Planetarium
MUSEUM

(www.miamisci.org; 3280 S Miami Ave; adult/child, student & senior $15/11; ☉10am-6pm) The Miami Museum of Science is a dedicated if small institution with exhibits ranging from weather phenomena to creepy crawlies, coral reefs and vital-microbe displays. The planetarium hosts space lessons and telescope-viewing sessions, as well as old-school laser shows with trippy flashes set to the music of the Beatles and Pink Floyd. That said, at the time of research the old Museum of Science was getting a bit too old. Help has come in the form of a $35 million gift from local philanthropists Patricia and Phillip Frost. Those funds will be used to build a new facility in Bicentential Park in Downtown, next to the (expected) new grounds for the Miami Museum of Art. It's located northeast of Coconut Grove, near SW 32nd Rd if you're on Dixie Hwy or S Miami Ave.

Kampong
HISTORIC SITE, GARDENS

(Map p69; ☎305-442-7169; 4013 Douglas Rd; www.ntbg.org/gardens/kampong.php; ☉tours by appointment only 10am-2pm Mon-Fri) If you speak Malay or Indonesian, then yes, this Kampong is named for the Bahasa word for village. David Fairchild, Indiana Jones of the botanical world and founder of Fairchild Tropical Gardens (p74), came up with the title, undoubtedly after a long Javanese jaunt. This was where the adventurer would rest in-between journeys in search of beautiful and economically viable plant life. Today it's listed on the National Register of Historic Places and the lovely grounds serve as a classroom for the National Tropical Botanical Garden. Free self-guided tours (allow at least an hour) are available by appointment, as are $20 two-hour guided tours. It's located in southwest Coconut Grove; if you're following the grid, Douglas Rd is also SW 37th Ave.

Arts Precinct
GALLERY

Coconut Grove, like many of Miami's neighborhoods, has been making a big deal of promoting its homegrown art galleries. You can walk among them, concentrated near CocoWalk and Streets of Mayfair malls (with a few exceptions), on the first Saturday night (from 7pm) of every month; the Coconut Grove Art Walk is decidedly the most family friendly of Miami's many neighborhood art walks.

AC Fine Art
GALLERY

(www.acfineartsite.com; 2911 Grand Ave; ☉10am-6pm) One our favorite galleries, AC Fine Art specializes in limited editions and originals (!) of masters like Dalí, Picasso, Lautrec, Warhol, Basquiat and Lichtenstein.

Plymouth Congregational Church
CHURCH

(Map p69; www.plymouthmiami.com; 3400 Devon Rd; ☉8:30am-4:30pm Mon-Fri) This 1917 coral church is striking, from its solid masonry to a hand-carved door from a Pyrenees monastery, which looks like it should be kicked in by Antonio Banderas carrying a guitar case full of explosives and Salma Hayek on his arm. Architecturally, this is one of the finest Spanish Mission–style churches in a city that does not lack for examples of the genre.

Ermita de la Caridad
MONUMENT

(☎305-854-2404; www.ermitadelacaridad.org; 3609 S Miami Ave) The Catholic diocese purchased some of the bayfront land from Deering's Villa Vizcaya estate and built a shrine here for its displaced Cuban parishioners. Symbolizing a beacon, it faces the homeland, exactly 290 miles due south. There is

---

EVA MUNROE'S GRAVE

Tucked into a small gated area near the Coconut Grove Library (Map p69; 2875 McFarlane Rd), you'll find the humble headstone of one Ms Eva Amelia Hewitt Munroe. Eva, who was born in New Jersey in 1856 and died in Miami in 1882, lies in the oldest American grave in Miami-Dade County (a sad addendum: local African American settlers died before Eva, but their deaths were never officially recorded). Eva's husband Ralph entered a deep depression, which he tried to alleviate by building the **Barnacle** (p69), now one of the oldest historic homes in the area.

RESURRECTING THE COCONUT GROVE PLAYHOUSE

Miami's oldest theater is the Coconut Grove Playhouse, which sits at 3500 Main Hwy in the heart of the Grove (Map p69). Back in the day this was a grand dame of a building, with a snazzy marquee and celebrity vibe balanced by a good deal of artsy cred; Samuel Beckett's *Waiting for Godot* had its US premiere here in 1956 (the show was apparently a disaster). Sadly, the theater was shut down during its 50th-anniversary season due to major debt issues and still sits, today, like a sad shell over Main Hwy. Now the theater's board, in conjunction with Miami-Dade's Department of Cultural Affairs, is trying to resurrect the theater; at the time of research, backing for the project was shuttling between several nonprofits.

also a mural that depicts Cuban history. After visiting Vizcaya or the science museum, consider picnicking at this quiet sanctuary on the water's edge.

CORAL GABLES

The lovely city of Coral Gables, filled with Mediterranean-style buildings, is bordered by Calle Ocho to the north, Sunset Dr to the south, Ponce de León Blvd to the east and Red Rd to the west. The main campus of the University of Miami is located just south of the enormous Coral Gables Biltmore Golf Course and the main pedestrian drag is Miracle Mile – heaven for the shopping obsessed.

Biltmore Hotel   HISTORIC BUILDING
(Map p72; www.biltmorehotel.com; 1200 Anastasia Ave) In the most opulent neighborhood of one of the showiest cities in the world, the Biltmore peers down her nose and says, 'hrmph'. It's one of the greatest of the grand hotels of the American Jazz Age, and if this joint were a fictional character from a novel, it'd be, without question, Jay Gatsby. Al Capone had a speakeasy on-site, and the Capone Suite is still haunted by the spirit of Fats Walsh, who was murdered here (for more ghost details, join in the weekly storytelling in the lobby, 7pm Thursday). Back

in the day, imported gondolas transported celebrity guests like Judy Garland and the Vanderbilts around because, of course, there was a private canal system out the back. It's gone now, but the largest hotel pool in the continental USA, which resembles a sultan's water garden from *One Thousand & One Nights*, is still here. The lobby is the real kicker: grand, gorgeous, yet surprisingly not gaudy, it's like a child's fantasy of an Arabian castle crossed with a Medici villa.

Lowe Art Museum   MUSEUM
(www.lowemuseum.org; 1301 Stanford Dr; adult/student $10/5; ☺10am-4pm Tue-Sat, from noon Sun) Your love of the Lowe, located on the campus of the University of Miami, depends on your taste in art. If you're into modern and contemporary works, it's good. If you're into the art and archaeology of cultures from Asia, Africa and the South Pacific, it's great. And if you're into pre-Columbian and Meso-American art, it's simply fantastic; the artifacts are stunning and thoughtfully strung out along an easy-to-follow narrative thread. That isn't to discount the lovely permanent collection of Renaissance and baroque art, Western sculpture from the 18th to 20th centuries, and paintings by Gauguin, Picasso and Monet – they're also gorgeous. To get here, look for the entrance to the University of Miami at Stanford Dr off Dixie Hwy.

Venetian Pool   HISTORIC SITE
(Map p72; www.coralgablesvenetianpool.com; 2701 De Soto Blvd; adult/child $11/7.35; ☺10am-4:30pm; ⊛) Just imagine: it's 1923, tons of rock have been quarried for one of the most beautiful neighborhoods in Miami, but now an ugly gash sits in the middle of the village. What to do? How about pump the irregular hole full of water, mosaic and tile up the whole affair, and make it look like a Roman emperor's aquatic playground? Result: one of the few pools listed on the National Register of Historic Places, a wonderland of coral rock caves, cascading waterfalls, a palm-fringed island and Venetian-style moorings. Take a swim and follow in the footsteps (finsteps?) of stars like Esther Williams and Johnny 'Tarzan' Weissmuller. Opening hours vary depending on the season, so check the website for details.

Merrick House   HISTORIC BUILDING
(Map p72; ☎305-460-5361; 907 Coral Way; adult/child/senior $5/1/3; ☺tours 1pm, 2pm & 3pm Sun & Wed) It's fun to imagine this simple homestead, with its little hints of Med-style, as the

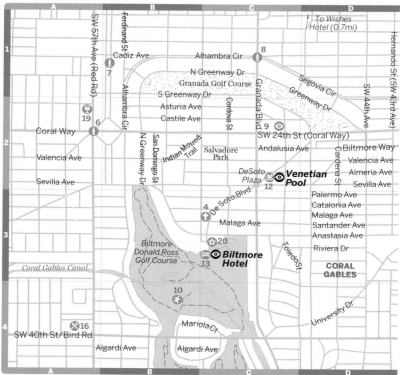

core of what would eventually become the gaudy Gables. When George Merrick's father purchased this plot, site unseen, for $1100, it was all dirt, rock and guavas. The property is now used for meetings and receptions, and you can tour both the house and its pretty organic garden. The modest family residence looks as it did in 1925, outfitted with family photos, furniture and artwork.

Entrances & Watertower   LANDMARKS
(Map p72) Coral Gables designer George Merrick planned a series of elaborate entry gates to the city, but the real-estate bust meant that projects went unfinished. Among the completed gates worth seeing, which resemble the entrance pavilions to grand Andalucian estates, are the **Country Club Prado**; the **Douglas Entrance**; the **Granada Entrance** (cnr Alhambra Circle & Granada Blvd); the **Alhambra Entrance** (cnr Alhambra Circle & Douglas Rd) and the **Coral Way Entrance** (cnr Red Rd & Coral Way). The **Alhambra Watertower**

(Alhambra Circle), where Greenway Ct and Ferdinand St meet Alhambra Circle, resembles a Moorish lighthouse.

Coral Gables City Hall   HISTORIC BUILDING
(Map p72; 405 Biltmore Way) This grand building has housed boring city-commission meetings since it opened in 1928. It's impressive from any angle, certainly befitting its importance as a central government building. Check out Denman Fink's *Four Seasons* ceiling painting in the tower, as well as his framed, untitled painting of the underwater world on the 2nd-floor landing. There's a small farmers' market on-site from 8am to 1pm, January to March.

Coral Gables Congregational Church   CHURCH
(Map p72; www.coralgablescongregational.org; 3010 De Soto Blvd) George Merrick's father was a New England Congregational minister, so perhaps that accounts for him donating the

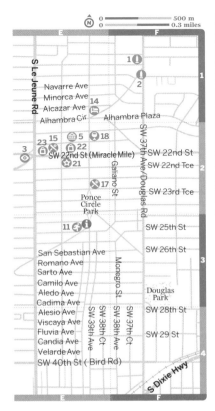

land for the city's first church. Built in 1924 as a replica of a church in Costa Rica, the yellow-walled, red-roofed exterior is as far removed from New England as...well, Miami. The interior is graced with a beautiful sanctuary and the grounds are landscaped with stately palms.

Coral Gables Museum   MUSEUM
(Map p72; www.coralgablesmuseum.org; 285 Aragon Ave) Set to open by the time you read this (although delays have slowed the project in the past), this museum, based on its sample exhibition, should be a well-plotted introduction to the oddball narrative of the founding and growth of the City Beautiful (Coral Gables). The collection will include historical artifacts and mementos from succeeding generations in this tight-knit, eccentric little village. The main building is the old Gables police and fire station, itself a lovely architectural blend of Gables' Mediterranean revival and a more Miami Beach–esque, muscular Depression-moderne style.

GREATER MIAMI – NORTH
Museum of Contemporary Art   MUSEUM
(MoCA; www.mocanomi.org; 770 NE 125th St; adult/ student & senior $5/3; ⊗11am-5pm Tue & Thu-Sat,

1-9pm Wed, noon-5pm Sun) Located up in North Miami, a rapidly evolving neighborhood and real-estate magnet for hipsters who have tired of the South Beach scene, the Museum of Contemporary Art has long been a reason to hike up to this stretch of Miami. Its galleries feature excellent rotating exhibitions of contemporary art by local, national and international artists. Open late on the last Friday of every month (7pm to 10pm) for a jazz concert.

Ancient Spanish Monastery CHURCH
(☑305-945-1461; www.spanishmonastery.com; 16711 W Dixie Hwy; ☺10am-4pm Mon-Sat, 11am-4pm Sun) The Episcopal Church of St Bernard de Clairvaux is a stunning early-Gothic and Romanesque building. Constructed in 1141 in Segovia, Spain, it was converted to a granary 700 years later, and eventually bought by newspaper tycoon William Randolph Hearst. He had it dismantled and shipped to the USA in more than 10,000 crates, intending to reconstruct it at his sprawling California estate. But construction was never approved by the government, and the stones sat in boxes until 1954, when a group of Miami developers purchased the dismantled monastery from Hearst and reassembled it. Now it's a lovely, popular (especially for weddings, so call before going) oasis and allegedly the oldest building in the western hemisphere. Church services are held at 8am, 10:30am and noon on Sunday, and a healing service is held at 10am on Wednesday. You can get here easily via North Biscayne Blvd; it's about 10 miles north of the Design District.

Hialeah Park PARK
(www.hialeahparkracing.com; 2200 E 4th Ave; ☺9am-5pm Mon-Fri) Hialeah is more Havanan than Little Havana (more than 90% of the population speak Spanish as a first language), and the symbol and center of this working-class Cuban community is this grand but endangered former racetrack. Seabiscuit and Seattle Slew once raced here, but in 2001 this gem was in danger of being paved over. A public campaign ensued to preserve the park; in 2008, the song 'Save Hialeah Park' by Los Primeros, a Hialeah-based Latin boy band, became a major local hit. Thanks to the passage of a controversial gambling and gaming bill, the park was saved from destruction. Today a walk through the grounds is recommended, if only to gaze at the grand staircases and pastel-painted concourse, and imagine the thunder of racing hooves. Look for the caps, boots and saddle carved into the window below the administration building, and the oft-photographed central fountain. You can get here by heading west on NW 79th St, just north of Little Haiti.

GREATER MIAMI – SOUTH

Fairchild Tropical Garden GARDENS
(www.fairchildgarden.org; 10901 Old Cutler Rd; adult/child/senior $25/12/18; ☺9:30am-4:30pm) If you need to escape Miami's madness, consider a green day in the country's largest tropical botanical garden. A butterfly grove, jungle biospheres, and gentle vistas of marsh and keys habitats, plus frequent art installations from folks like Roy Lichtenstein, are all stunning. In addition to easy-to-follow, self-guided walking tours, a free 40-minute tram tours the entire park on the hour from 10am to

HIBISCUS, PALM & STAR ISLANDS

Floating off the edge of the A1A, in the heart of Biscayne Bay (and posh exclusivity), Hibiscus Island, Palm Island and Star Island are little floating Primrose Hills. There aren't many famous people living here – just wealthy ones – although Star Island is home to Gloria Estefan and for a short time Al Capone lived (and died) on Palm Island. In the 1970s and '80s a mansion on Star Island was the headquarters of the Ethiopian Zion Coptic Church (EZCC; www.ethiopianzioncopticchurch.org), a Rastafari sect eventually convicted of smuggling large amount of marijuana into the US. That incident prompted a media circus that focused on both the indictments and neighborly disputes between the long-haired, bearded white Rastas and their aristocratic Star Island neighbors, who complained about the fog of cannabis smoke constantly emanating from the EZCC's compound.

Today the drives for the islands are guarded by a security booth, but the roads are public, so if you ask politely and don't look sketchy, you can get in. Star Island is little more than one elliptical road lined with royal palms, sculpted ficus hedges and fancy gates guarding houses you can't see.

3pm. Located 5 miles south of Coral Gables; Old Cutler Rd is accessible via SW 57th Ave.

Charles Deering Estate LANDMARK
(www.deeringestate.org; 16701 SW 72nd Ave; adult/child under 14yr $12/7; ☉10am-5pm) The Deering estate is sort of 'Vizcaya lite', which makes sense as it was built by Charles, brother of James Deering (of Vizcaya fame). The 150-acre grounds are awash with tropical growth, an animal-fossil pit of bones dating back 50,000 years and the prehistoric remains of Native Americans who lived here 2000 years ago. There's a free tour of the grounds included in admission, and the estate often hosts jazz evenings under the stars. Last tickets sold at 4pm.

Metrozoo ZOO
(www.miamimetrozoo.com; 12400 SW 152nd St; adult/child $16/12; ☉9:30am-5:30pm) Miami's tropical weather makes strolling around the Metrozoo almost feel like a day in the wild. Look for Asian and African elephants, rare and regal Bengal tigers prowling an evocative Hindu temple, pygmy hippos, Andean condors, a pack of hyenas, cute koalas, colobus monkeys, black rhinoceroses and a pair of Komodo dragons from Indonesia. Keep your eyes peeled for informative zookeeper talks in front of some exhibits. For a quick overview (and because the zoo is so big), hop on the Safari Monorail; it departs every 20 minutes. There's a glut of grounds tours available, and kids will love feeding the Samburu giraffes ($2). Last admission at 4pm.

Jungle Island ZOO
(www.jungleisland.com; 1111 Parrot Jungle Trail, off MacArthur Causeway, Watson Island; adult/child/senior $33/25/31; ☉10am-5pm, to 6pm Sat & Sun) Jungle Island, packed with tropical birds, alligators, orangutans, chimps, lemurs, a (wait for it, *Napoleon Dynamite* fans) liger (a cross between a lion and a tiger) and a Noah's Ark of other animals, is a ton of fun. It's one of those places kids (justifiably) beg to go, so just give up and prepare for some bright-feathered, bird-poopie-scented fun in this artificial, self-contained jungle. The waterfront facility, lushly landscaped and using a minimum of pesticides, is pretty impressive, thanks in part to the flamingos, macaws, cockatoos and other parrots, flying about in outdoor aviaries. The Cape Penguin colony is especially cute.

Monkey Jungle ZOO
(www.monkeyjungle.com; 14805 SW 216th St; adult/child/senior $30/24/28; ☉9:30am-5pm) The

Monkey Jungle brochures have a tag line: 'Where humans are caged and monkeys run free.' And, indeed, you'll be walking through screened-in trails, with primates swinging freely, screeching and chattering all around you. It's incredibly fun, and just a bit odorous, especially on warm days (well, most days). In 1933, animal behaviorist Joseph du Mond released six monkeys into the wild. Today, their descendants live here with orangutans, chimpanzees and lowland gorilla. The big show of the day takes place at feeding time, when crab-eating monkeys and Southeast Asian macaques dive into the pool for fruit and other treats. There's also a lovely aviary for clouds of beautiful rescued parrots. Last admission at 4pm.

Pinecrest Gardens PARK
(www.pinecrest-fl.gov/gardens; 11000 SW 57th Ave; adult/child $3/2; ☉9am-5pm fall & winter, to 6pm spring & summer) When Parrot Jungle (now Jungle Island) flew the coop for the big city, the village of Pinecrest, which is the community that hosted the Jungle's former location, purchased the lovely property in order to keep it as a municipal park. It's now a quiet oasis with some of the best tropical gardens this side of the Gulf of Mexico; biomes include cypress hammocks, tropical hammocks, banana groves, rubber trees and a gorgeous centerpiece banyan tree. Outdoor movies and jazz concerts are held here, and in all this is a total gem that is utterly off the tourism trail.

Fruit & Spice Park PARK
(www.fruitandspicepark.org; 24801 SW 187th Ave; adult/child $8/2; ☉9am-5pm) Set just on the edge of the Everglades, this 35-acre tropical public park grows all those great tropical fruits you usually have to contract dysentery to enjoy. The park is divided into 'continents' (Africa, Asia etc) and admission to the pretty grounds includes a free tour; you can't pick the fruit, but you can eat anything that falls to the ground. If you're coming down this far, you may want to consider taking a day trip into Everglades National Park (p119).

Gold Coast Railroad Museum MUSEUM
(www.gcrm.org; 12450 SW 152nd St; adult/child 3-11yr $6/4; ☉10am-4pm Mon-Fri, from 11am Sat & Sun) Primarily of interest to serious train buffs, this museum was set up in the 1950s by the Miami Railroad Historical Society. It displays more than 30 antique railway cars, including the Ferdinand Magellan presidential car, where President Harry Truman famously brandished a newspaper with the erroneous

headline 'Dewey Defeats Truman.' On weekends the museum offers 20-minute rides on old cabooses ($6), standard gauge cabs ($12) and, for kids, on a small 'link' train ($2.50). It's advised you call ahead to make an appointment to ride. It's located about 13 miles southwest of Coral Gables near the Miami Zoo.

Miami Children's Museum   CHILDREN'S MUSEUM
(www.miamichildrensmuseum.org; 980 MacArthur Causeway, Watson Island; admission $15; ☺10am-6pm) This museum, located between South Beach and downtown Miami, isn't exactly a museum. It feels more like an uberplayhouse, with areas for kids to practice all sorts of adult activities – banking and food shopping, caring for pets, reporting scoops as a TV news anchor in a studio, and acting as a local cop or firefighter. Be forewarned, this place is a zoo on rainy days.

Matheson Hammock Park   PARK
(www.miamidade.gov/parks/parks/matheson _beach.asp; 9610 Old Cutler Rd; per car $5; ☺sunrise-sunset) This 100-acre county park is the city's oldest and one of its most scenic. It offers good swimming for children in an enclosed tidal pool, lots of hungry raccoons, dense mangrove swamps and (pretty rare) crocodile-spotting.

Wings Over Miami   MUSEUM
(www.wingsovermiami.com; Kendall-Tamiami Executive Airport, 14710 SW 128th St; adult/child under 12yr/senior $10/6/7; ☺10am-5pm Wed-Sat, from noon Sun) Plane-spotters will be delighted by this Kendall-Tamiami Executive Airport museum, which chronicles the history of aviation. Highlights include a propeller collection, J47 jet engine, a Soviet bomber from Smolensk and the nose section of a B-29 called *Fertile Myrtle,* the same type of aircraft used to drop atomic bombs on Hiroshima and Nagasaki. An impressive exhibit on the Tuskegee Airmen features videos of the African American pilots telling their own stories. Historic bombers and other aircraft drop in for occasional visits, so you can never be sure what you'll see.

🏃 Activities
Biking
🏞 **Miami-Dade County Parks & Recreation Department**   CYCLING
(☎305-755-7800; www.miamidade.gov/parksmaster plan/bike_trails_map.asp) Leads frequent eco-bike tours through parklands and along waterfront paths, and offers a list of traffic-free

cycling paths on its website. For less strenuous rides, try the side roads of South Beach or the shady streets of Coral Gables and Coconut Grove. Some good trails:

Old Cutler Bike Path Starts at the end of Sunset Dr in Coral Gables and leads through Coconut Grove to Matheson Hammock Park and Fairchild Tropical Garden.

Rickenbacker Causeway This route takes you up and over the bridge to Key Biscayne for an excellent workout combined with gorgeous water views.

Oleta River State Park (3400 NE 163rd St) Has a challenging dirt trail with hills for off-road adventures.

Bowling
Bowlmor Lanes   BOWLING
(www.bowlmor.com/miami; 11401 NW 12th St; ☺4pm-1am Mon-Thu, noon-3am Fri, 11am-3am Sat, 11am-1am Sun) In the Dolphin Mall, this is a good example of what happens when Miami's talent for glitz and glamour (they post pics of Lindsay Lohan bowling here on the website) meets some humble 10-pins.

Lucky Strike   BOWLING
(www.bowluckystrike.com; 1691 Michigan Ave; ☺11:30am-1am Mon-Thu, to 2am Fri, 11am-2am Sat, 11am-1am Sun) Just off Lincoln Rd, this is Miami Beach's answer to high-end bowling, full of house and hip-hop music, electric-bright cocktails and beautiful club kids.

Day Spas
As you may have guessed, Miami offers plenty of places to get pampered. Some of the most luxurious spas in town are found at high-end hotels, where you can expect to pay $300 to $400 for a massage and/or acupressure, and $200 for a body wrap. Notable spas:

Spa at Viceroy   SPA
(Map p56; ☎305-503-0369; www.viceroyhotel sandresorts.com; 485 Brickell Ave)
Philippe Starck–designed with an enormous gym, a cardio theater and (wow) a floating library.

Spa Internazionale   SPA
(☎800-537-3708; www.fisherislandclub.com; Inn at Fisher Island) The most exclusive spa in the city, with a huge range of massage, yoga and body treatments, shouldn't be missed if you're staying on private Fisher Island.

Spa at the Setai   SPA
(Map p44; ☎305-520-6900; www.setai.com/the spa; 101 20th St) A silky Balinese haven in one of South Beach's most beautiful hotels.

Just because you enjoy a good back rub doesn't mean you need to go to some glitzy spa where they constantly play soft house music on a repetitive loop. Right? Why not head to a favorite 'hot' spot among folks who want a spa experience without the glamour, the **Russian & Turkish Baths** (Map p52; ☑305-867-8316; www.russianandturkishbaths.com; 5445 Collins Ave; ☺noon-midnight). Enter this little labyrinth of *banyas* (steam rooms) and there's a plethora of spa choices. You can be casually beaten with oak-leaf brooms (for $40) called *venik* in a lava-hot spa (it's actually really relaxing...well, interesting anyway). There's Dead Sea salt and mud exfoliation ($50), plus, the on-site cafe serves delicious borscht, blintzes, dark bread with smoked fish and of course, beer. The crowd is interesting too: hipsters, older Jews, model types, Europeans and folks from Russia and former Soviet states, some of whom look like, um, entirely legitimate businessmen and we're leaving it at that.

Diving & Snorkeling

Head to the Keys or **Biscayne National Park** (p132), in the southeastern corner of Dade county. Operators in Miami:

Divers Paradise　　　　　　DIVING
(Map p64; ☑305-361-3483; www.keydivers .com; 4000 Crandon Blvd; dive trip $60) In Key Biscayne, one of the area's most reliable outfits.

South Beach Divers　　　　DIVING
(Map p48; ☑305-531-6110; www.southbeach divers.com; 850 Washington Ave, South Beach; dive trip $100) Runs regular excursions to Key Largo and around Miami, plus offers three-day classes.

Fishing

Places to drop a line:

South Pointe Park (Map p48)

Rickenbacker Causeway (Map p64)

Key Biscayne Beach (Map p64)

Fishing charters are commonplace but expensive; expect to pay at least $1000 for a day of sport fishing:

Yacht Charters Miami (☑305-490-0049; www.yachtchartersinmiami.com)

Ace Blue Waters Charters (Map p56; ☑305-373-5016; www.fishingmiami.net; Bayside Marketplace, 401 Biscayne Blvd, Downtown Miami)

Kelley Fleet (☑305-945-3801; www.miami beachfishing.com; Haulover Beach Park, 10800 Collins Ave, Bal Harbour).

Golf

At high-end resorts, expect to pay between $150 and $350 to tee off, depending on the season and time of day (it's more expensive in winter and daylight hours).

Biltmore Donald Ross Golf Course　GOLF
(Map p72; ☑305-460-5364; www.biltmorehotel .com/golf; 1210 Anastasia Ave, Coral Gables) Designed by the golfer of that name and boasts the immaculate company of the Biltmore Hotel.

Doral Golf Course　　　　　　GOLF
(☑305-592-2000; www.doralresort.com; 4400 NW 87th Ave) Very highly rated, which may explain why it's difficult to get in and also why it once hosted the PGA Ford Championship.

Crandon Golf Course　　　　GOLF
(Map p64; ☑305-361-9129; 6700 Crandon Blvd, Key Biscayne; daylight Dec-Apr $140, twilight May-Nov $30) Overlooks the bay from its perch on Key Biscayne.

Haulover Golf Course　　　　GOLF
(Map p52; ☑305-940-6719; 10800 Collins Ave, Bal Harbour; $21-43) A nine-hole, par-three course that's great for beginners.

CRICKET – IT'S A PITCH

Cricket in South Florida? Oh yes. Really? There's a huge West Indian and Jamaican community in South Florida, plus a very sizable British expat population. As such cricket is actually quite popular in these parts. The **South Florida Cricket Alliance** (☑954-805-2922; www.southfloridacricket.com) is one of the largest cricket clubs in the US, the **Cricket Council of the USA** (www.cricketcouncilusa.com) is based in Boca Raton, and the first dedicated cricket pitch in the country opened in Lauderhill (where the population is 25% West Indian), north of Fort Lauderdale, in 2008. Contact any of the above if you'd like to watch a test or join a team.

Art-Deco Miami Beach
Walking Tour

❯ Start at the ➊ **Art Deco Welcome Center**, at the corner of Ocean Dr and 10th St (named Barbara Capitman Way here after the founder of the Miami Design Preservation League). Step in for a permanent exhibit on art-deco style, then head out and go north along Ocean Dr; between 12th St and 14th St you'll see three examples of deco hotels: the ➋ **Leslie**, a boxy shape with eyebrows (cantilevered sun shades) wrapped around the side of the building; the ➌ **Carlyle**, featured in the film *The Birdcage* and boasting modernistic styling; and the graceful ➍ **Cardozo Hotel**, built by Henry Hohauser, owned by Gloria Estefan and featuring sleek, rounded edges. At 14th St, peek inside the sun-drenched ➎ **Winter Haven Hotel** to see its fabulous floors of ubiquitous terrazzo, made of stone chips set in mortar that is polished when dry. Turn left and head down 14th St to Washington Ave and the ➏ **US Post Office**, at 13th St. It's a curvy block of white deco in the stripped classical style. Step inside to admire the wall mural, domed ceiling and marble stamp tables. Stop for lunch at the ➐ **11th Street Diner**, a gleaming aluminum Pullman car that was imported in 1992 from Wilkes-Barre, Pennsylvania. Get a window seat and gaze across the avenue to the corner of 10th St and the stunningly restored ➑ **Hotel Astor**, designed in 1936 by T Hunter Henderson. After your meal, walk half a block east to the imposing ➒ **Wolfsonian-FIU**, an excellent museum of design, formerly the Washington Storage Company. Wealthy snowbirds of the '30s safely stashed their pricey belongings before heading back up north. Continue walking Washington Ave and turn left on 7th St and then continue north along Collins Ave to the ➓ **Hotel**, featuring an interior and roof deck by Todd Oldham. L Murray Dixon designed the hotel as the Tiffany Hotel, with a proud deco spire, in 1939. Turn right on 9th St and go two blocks to Ocean Dr, where you'll spy nonstop deco beauties, such as the 1935 ⑪ **Edison Hotel**, another beautiful creation of deco legend Henry Hohauser.

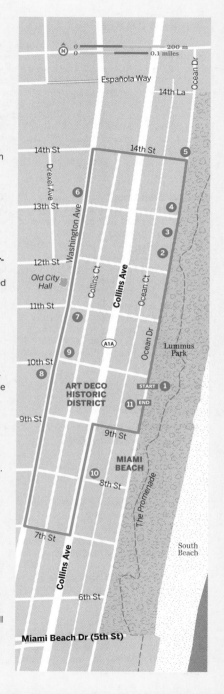

In-Line Skating

Serious crowds have turned promenades into obstacle courses for anyone crazy enough to strap on some blades. Leave the crowded strips to experts and try the ocean side of Ocean Ave, or Lincoln Rd before the shoppers descend.

Rent your wheels from **Fritz's Skate Shop** (Map p44; ☑305-532-1954; www.fritzs miamibeach.com; 1620 Washington Ave; ⊙10am-10pm), which also offers free lessons on Sunday at 10:30am – just about the only time there's ever room on the mall any more.

Kayaking & Windsurfing

Kayaking through mangroves, one of the coolest ecosystems on Earth, is magical: all those slender roots kiss the water while the ocean breeze cools your flanks. Try these places:

Haulover Beach Park (10800 Collins Ave)

Bill Baggs Cape Florida State Park (Map p64; www.floridastateparks.org/capeflorida; 1200 S Crandon Blvd)

Oleta River State Park (3400 NE 163rd St)

You can rent gear from the following:

Blue Moon Miami   WATER SPORTS
(☑305-957-3040; www.bluemoonmiami.com) Offers single kayaks ($18 per 1½ hours, $25 per three hours), tandem kayaks ($25.50 per 1½ hours, $40 per three hours) and bike rental ($18 per 1½ hours, $25 per three hours).

Sailboards Miami   WATER SPORTS
(☑305-361-7245; www.windsurfingmiami.com; 1 Rickenbacker Causeway; per hr s/tandem $15/20) Also rents kayaks. You can purchase 10 hours' worth of kayaking for $90. This is also a good spot to rent (and learn how to operate) windsurfing gear (lessons from $35, gear per hour $30).

Aquatic Rental Center and Sailing School   WATER SPORTS
(off Map p52; ☑305-751-7514, evening 305-279-7424; 1275 NE 79th St; sailboats per 2hr/3hr/4hr/day $85/125/150/225) If you're a bona-fide seaworthy sailor, this place will rent you a sailboat. If you're not, it can teach you how to operate one (sailing courses $400, $500 for two people).

Rodeo

Rodeo in South Florida? You just have to head a little way out of Miami. Check the below websites or call ahead for specific rodeo

SOUTH FLORIDA CIRCUS ARTS SCHOOL

Admit it: you always wanted to fly on the trapeze, clamber out of the clown car, tame a lion. Well, we can't really help you with those last two activities, but if you want to learn some circus-worthy acrobatics, contortion and flexibility skills, come to the **South Florida Circus Arts School** (SFCAS ☑954-540-1344; www.sfcas.com; 15161 NE 21st Ave) in North Miami, off North Biscayne Blvd, about 8 miles north of the Design District. SFCAS claims to be the only institution of its kind offering all-levels accessible education in the skills of the circus. It's a ton of fun and pretty unique; classes include aerial fitness, trapeze skills and the extremely popular flying yoga course (just try it), with fees ranging from $15 to $75 for an hour of instruction. See you in the center ring…

times. If the idea of performing animals and spurs in the same arena makes you ill at ease, you may want to avoid local rodeos.

Bergeron Rodeo Grounds   RODEO
(☑954-680-3555; www.davie-fl.gov/gen/daviefl _spclprjcts/bergeronrodeo; 4271 Davie Rd, Fort Lauderdale) In Davie, about 20 miles north of downtown Miami.

Homestead Rodeo   RODEO
(☑305-247-3515; www.facebook.com/pages /Homestead-Rodeo/277924761912; 1034 NE 8th St, Homestead) In Homestead, about an hour south of Downtown.

Running

Running is quite popular, and the beach is very good for jogging, as it's flat, wide and hard-packed (apparently with amazingly hot joggers). A great resource for races, special events and other locations is the **Miami Runners Club** (☑305-255-1500; www.miami runnersclub.com).

Some good places for a run include the **Flamingo Park** track, located east of Alton Rd between 11th St and 12th St, for serious runners; **Promenade** in South Beach for its style; the **boardwalk** on Mid-Beach for great people-watching and scenery; and **South Bayshore Drive** in Coconut Grove for its shady banyan trees.

Surfing

Miami is not a good place for surfing. The Bahamas block swells, making the water very calm; many will tell you it's best to head about 100 miles north to Jupiter or Palm Beach to catch decent waves (not big waves, just surf consistent enough to hold a board upright). Plus, Miami surfers have worse reputations than Miami drivers when it comes to aggressive, territorial behavior. If you want to ride waves here, the best surfing is just north of **South Pointe Park** (Map p48), where you can sometimes find 2ft to 5ft waves and a nice, sandy bottom. Unfortunately it's usually closer to 2ft than 5ft, it can get a little mushy (so longboards are the way to go), and it's swamped with weekend swimmers and surfers. Conditions are better further north, near **Haulover Beach Park** (10800 Collins Ave, Bal Harbour) or anywhere north of 70th St, like **Sunny Isles Beach** (Sunny Isles Causeway). Check in with **Island Water Sports** (305-944-0104; www.iwsmiami.com; 16231 Biscayne Blvd) for gear, **SoBe Surf** (786-216-7703; www.sobesurf.com) for lessons (private instructors will meet with you somewhere on the beach) and www.dadecosurf.com for general information.

Swimming

All of the following pools have lap lanes, but call the Venetian beforehand, as their lap hours change often.

Venetian Pool (p71)

Flamingo Park Swimming Pool (Map p48; 305-673-7750; 999 11th St, South Beach; adult/child $10/6; laps 6:45-9am & 7-9pm)

Normandy Isle Park & Pool (Map p52; 305-673-7750; 7030 Trouville Esplanade; adult/child $10/6; laps 6:45-9am & 7-9pm)

Yoga

The beach is definitely not the only place to salute the sun in Miami. All of the following studios offer a large range of classes; bring your own mats.

Green Monkey Yoga (Map p62; 305-669-5959; www.greenmonkey.net; 3301 NE 1st Ave, Miami; classes from $20) Midtown, also has branches in South Beach and South Miami.

Brickell Hot Yoga (Map p56; 305-856-1387; www.brickellyoga.com; 301 SW 17th Rd, Brickell; 1/5/10-class pass $19/85/160) Downtown.

Prana Yoga Center (Map p72; 305-567-9812; www.pranayogamiami.com; 247 Malaga Ave, Coral Gables; 1/2/5-class pass $18/34/50) In Coral Gables.

MIAMI FOR CHILDREN

Well really, it's Florida, folks; your kids will be catered to. Many of the attractions run toward animal experiences, starting with the **Miami Seaquarium** (p65), which boasts a large collection of crocodiles, dolphins and sea lions and a killer whale, most of which perform. Next comes the **Metrozoo** (p75), a 740-acre zoo with plenty of natural habitats (thank you, tropical weather). Should your little ones like colorful animal shows, the outdoors and the smell of animal poo in all its myriad varieties, Miami shall not disappoint. **Monkey Jungle** (p75) acts as a habitat for endangered species and is everything you'd expect: screeching primates, covered pathways and a grand finale show of crab monkeys diving for fruit. **Jungle Island** (p75), on the other hand, tends to entertain with brilliant bird shows. Next door is the new **Miami Children's Museum** (p76), an indoor playland where youngsters can try out the roles of TV anchor, banker and supermarket customer, among others. Coral Gables draws the water-wise to its way-fun, lagoonlike **Venetian Pool** (p71). For a more educational experience, let your kids explore the **Marjorie Stoneman Douglas Environmental Center** (p65) on Key Biscayne. Coconut Grove is probably the most child-friendly neighborhood in Miami, with its malls, easy-to-digest (on every level) mainstream dining and thanks to events put on at places like **Barnacle Historic State Park** (p69).

Child Care

When it's time to head out for some adult time, check with your hotel, as many offer child-care services – any larger resort worth its salt should be able to provide child-care services. Or call the local **Nanny Poppinz** (305-607-1170; www.nannypoppinz.com). For more information, advice and anecdotes, read Lonely Planet's *Travel with Children*.

Bikram Yoga Miami Beach (Map p48; 305-448-3332; www.bikramyogamiami.com; 235 11th St, Miami Beach; per day/week $25/50) South Beach.

There's a lovely 'yoga by the sea' course offered at the **Barnacle Historic State Park** (p69; classes 6-7:15pm Mon & Wed; per class $13) in Coconut Grove. If you don't feel like breaking out your wallet, try the free yoga classes at **Bayfront Park** (p55; classes 6-7:15pm Mon & Wed, 9-10:15am Sat), held outdoors at Tina Hills Pavilion, at the south end of the park, three times a week.

Tours

Art Deco Welcome Center WALKING
(Map p48; 305-531-3484; 1001 Ocean Dr, South Beach; guided tour per adult/child/senior $20/free/15; tours 10:30am Fri-Wed, 6:30pm Thu) Tells the stories and history behind the art-deco buildings in South Beach, either with a lively guide from the Miami Design Preservation League, or a well-presented recording and map for self-guided walks (try the guides). Tours last 90 minutes.

Dr Paul George WALKING
(305-375-1621; www.historymiami.org/tours/walking-tours; tours $25-42) For great historical perspective, call the lively Dr George, a historian for HistoryMiami (p58). George leads several popular tours – including those that focus on Stiltsville, Miami crime, Little Havana and Coral Gables at twilight – between September and late June; hours vary. Dr George also offers private tours by appointment.

Miami Food Tours WALKING
(Map p56; 800-838-3006; www.miamifoodtours .com; 429 Lennox Ave; adult/child $45/30; tours 11am-2pm Mon-Sat) You'll be visiting five of South Beach's best restaurants, but hey, it's a walking tour – you're burning calories, right?

Urban Tour Host WALKING
(Map p56; 305-416-6868; www.miamicultural tours.com; 25 SE 2nd Ave, ste 1048; tours from $20) Has a rich program of custom tours that provide face-to-face interaction in all of Miami's neighborhoods. A deluxe city tour includes Coral Gables, South Beach, downtown Miami and Coconut Grove.

Captain Jimmy's Fiesta Cruises BOAT
(Map p56; 305-371-3033; www.fiestacruises .com; 401 Biscayne Blvd; adult/child from $17/10) Fun, fantastic boat tours coordinated by a small, family-run operation. Try the

tarpon-feeding extravaganza (tarpon are basically very big fish) for $20.

Eco-adventure Bike Tours BICYCLE
(305-365-3018; www.miamidade.gov/ecoadven tures; from $28) The Dade County parks system leads excellent bike tours through peaceful areas of Miami and Miami Beach, including along beaches, on Key Biscayne and into the Everglades.

Island Queen BOAT
(Map p56; 305-379-5119; www.islandqueen cruises.com; 401 Biscayne Blvd; adult/child from $26/18) Boat tours of Millionaire's Row, the Miami River and Stiltsville, among other locations.

HMC Helicopters HELICOPTER
(305-233-8788; www.hmchelicopters.com; Watson Island; flights $89-250) Runs scenic helicopter jaunts over the skyscrapers of Downtown and the waters of Biscayne Bay and Government Cut.

Miami Nice Tours BUS
(305-949-9180; www.miaminicetours.com; 17030 Collins Ave; $25-99) Has a wide range of guided bus excursions to the Everglades, the Keys and Fort Lauderdale, as well as trips around Miami.

Festivals & Events

There's something special happening year-round in Miami, with well-touted events bringing in niche groups from serious DJs (Winter Music Conference) to obsessed foodies (Miami Spice Restaurant Month). Addresses are given where there is a fixed festival location.

January

The beginning of the new year also happens to be the height of the tourist season in these parts. Expect fair weather, crowds of visitors, higher prices than usual and a slew of special events. New Year's Eve brings fireworks and festivals to South Beach and downtown Miami's bayfront.

Orange Bowl FOOTBALL
(www.orangebowl.org; Sun Life Stadium, 2269 Dan Marino Blvd, Miami Gardens) Hordes of football fans descend on Miami for the Super Bowl of college football.

Art Deco Weekend CULTURAL
(www.artdecoweekend.com; Ocean Dr btwn 1st St & 23rd St) This weekend fair featuring guided tours, concerts, classic-auto shows, sidewalk cafes, arts and antiques is held in mid-January.

NORTHERN CAPITAL OF THE LATIN WORLD

Miami may technically be part of the USA, but it's widely touted as the 'capital of the Americas' and the 'center of the New World.' That's a coup when it comes to marketing Miami to the rest of the world, and especially to the USA, where Latinos are now the largest minority. Miami's pan-Latin mixture makes it more ethnically diverse than any Latin American city. At the turn of the 21st century, the western suburbs of Hialeah and Hialeah Gardens were numbers two and one respectively on the list of US areas where Spanish is spoken as a first language (over 90% of the population).

How did this happen? Many of Miami's Latinos arrived in this geographically convenient city as political refugees – Cubans fleeing Castro starting around the '60s, Venezuelans fleeing President Hugo Chávez (or his predecessors), Brazilians and Argentines running from economic woes, Mexicans and Guatemalans arriving to find work. And gringos, long fascinated with Latin American flavors, can now visit Miami to get a taste of the pan-Latin stew without having to leave the country.

This has all led to the growth of Latin American businesses in Miami, which has boosted the local economy. Miami is the US headquarters of many Latin companies, including Lan Chile, a Chilean airline; Televisa, a Mexican TV conglomerate; and Embraer, a Brazilian aircraft manufacturer. Miami is also home to Telemundo, one of the biggest Spanish-language broadcasters in the US, as well as MTV Networks Latin America and the Latin branch of the Universal Music Group. Miami is the host city of the annual Billboard Latin Music Conference & Awards.

Cubans have a strong influence on local and international politics in Miami. Conservative exile groups have often been characterized as extreme, many refusing to visit Cuba while Castro remains in power. A newer generation, however – often referred to as the 'YUCAs' (Young Urban Cuban Americans) – are more willing to see both sides of issues in Cuba.

While many of the subtleties may escape you as a visitor, one thing is obvious: the Latino influence, which you can experience by seeking it out or waiting for it to fall in your lap. Whether you're dining out, listening to live music, overhearing Spanish conversations, visiting Little Havana or Little Buenos Aires, or simply sipping a chilled mojito at the edge of your hotel pool, the Latin American energy is palpable, beautiful and everywhere you go.

Miami Jewish Film Festival   FILM
(www.miamijewishfilmfestival.com; 4200 Biscayne Blvd) A great chance to cinematically *kvetch* with one of the biggest Jewish communities in the USA.

February

The last hurrah for northerners needing to escape the harsh winter, February brings arts festivals and street parties, as well as warm days and cool nights.

Coconut Grove Arts Festival   CULTURAL
(www.coconutgroveartsfest.com; Biscayne Blvd btwn NE 1st St & 5th St, Coconut Grove) One of the most prestigious arts festivals in the country, this late-February fair features more than 300 artists.

Original Miami Beach Antiques Show   ANTIQUES
(www.originalmiamibeachantiqueshow.com; Miami Beach Convention Center) One of the largest events of its kind in the USA, with over 800 dealers from more than 20 countries.

South Beach Wine & Food Festival   FOOD
(www.sobefest.com) A festival of fine dining and sipping to promote South Florida's culinary image. Expect star-studded brunches, dinners and barbecues.

March

Spring arrives, bringing warmer weather, world-class golf and tennis, outdoor festivals and St Patrick's Day. Expect some Spring Breakers to behave badly on the beach.

Miami International Film Festival   FILM
(www.miamifilmfestival.com) This event, sponsored by Miami-Dade College, is a two-week festival showcasing documentaries and features from all over the world.

South Beach Comedy Festival   COMEDY
(www.southbeachcomedyfestival.com) Some of the best comedic talent in the world does stand-up in venues across the city.

Miami Fashion Week   FASHION
(www.miamifashionweek.com; Miami Beach Convention Center) Models are as abundant

as fish in the ocean as designers descend on the city and catwalks become ubiquitous.

Winter Music Conference · MUSIC
(www.wmcon.com) Party promoters, DJs, producers and revelers come from around the globe to hear new artists, catch up on technology and party the nights away.

April

Welcome to the shoulder season, bringing quieter days, lower prices, balmier temperatures and a few choice events.

Billboard Latin Music Awards · MUSIC
(www.billboardevents.com) This prestigious awards show in late April draws top industry execs, star performers and a slew of Latin music fans.

Miami Gay & Lesbian Film Festival · FILM
(www.mglff.com) Held in late April to early May, this annual event features shorts, feature films and documentaries screened at various South Beach theaters.

May & June

May and June boast increased heat, fewer visitors and several cultural events.

Sweatstock · MUSIC
(www.sweatrecordsmiami.com) Sweat Records puts on an annual music festival aimed at locals, with headline acts performing indie rock, punk and electronica.

Goombay Festival · CULTURAL
(Grand Ave, Coconut Grove) A massive festival, held on the first week of June, which celebrates Bahamian culture.

Miami Museum Month · CULTURAL
(www.miamimuseummonth.com) An excellent chance to see and hang out in some of the best museums in the city in the midst of happy hours, special exhibitions and lectures.

July & August

The most beastly, humidity-drenched days are during these months, when locals either vacation elsewhere or spend their days melting on the beach.

Independence Day Celebration · HOLIDAY
(Bayfront Park, downtown Miami) July 4 is marked with excellent fireworks, a laser show and live music that draw more than 100,000 people to breezy Bayfront Park.

Miami Spice Restaurant Month · FOOD
(www.ilovemiamispice.com) Top restaurants around Miami offer prix-fixe lunches and dinners to try to lure folks out during the heat wave.

September & October

The days and nights are still steamy and the start of school brings back college students.

International Ballet Festival · DANCE
(www.internationalballetfestival.org) Some of the most important ballet talent in the world performs at venues across the city.

The Great Grove Bed Race · RACE
(www.thegreatgrovebedrace.com) Between the pajama pub crawl and drag-racing beds through Coconut Grove, this is one of Miami's wackier celebrations.

November

Tourist season kicks off at the end of the month, bringing more crowds and slightly cooler days.

Miami Book Fair International · CULTURAL
(www.miamibookfair.com; 401 NE 2nd Ave) Occurring in mid- to late November, this is among the most important and well-attended book fairs in the USA. Hundreds of nationally known writers join hundreds of publishers and hundreds of thousands of visitors.

White Party · MUSIC
(www.whiteparty.net) If you're gay and not here, there's a problem. This weeklong extravaganza draws more than 15,000 gay men and women for nonstop partying at clubs and venues all over town.

December

Tourist season is in full swing, with northerners booking rooms so they can bask in the sunshine and be here for holiday festivities.

Art Miami · ART
(www.art-miami.com) Held in January or December, this massive fair displays modern and contemporary works from more than 100 galleries and international artists.

Art Basel Miami Beach · ART
(www.artbaselmiamibeach.com) One of the most important international art shows in the world, with works from more than 150 galleries and a slew of trendy parties.

King Mango Strut · PARADE
(www.kingmangostrut.org; Main Ave & Grand Ave, Coconut Grove) Held each year just after Christmas since 1982, this quirky Coconut Grove parade is a politically charged, fun freak that began as a spoof on current events and the now-defunct Orange Bowl Parade.

🛏 Sleeping

It's in this category, more than any other, where all the hype surrounding Miami, and particularly South Beach, is justified. What sets South Beach apart – what defines it as a travel destination – is the deco district, and the deco district's backbone is hotels. This is one of the largest concentrations of boutique hotels in the country. And the Beach's glam only grows with every new accommodation lauded by the travel glossies, which brings the designers, which brings the fashionistas, which brings the models, which brings the tourists, which brings the chefs and...well, you get the idea.

South Beach hotels are some of the most expensive in Florida. Also, if you opt for hotel parking, expect to be charged $25 to $40 a day for the privilege. It may be easier to park in the large public garages scattered all around South Beach.

SOUTH BEACH (1ST TO 11TH STREETS)

TOP CHOICE Pelican Hotel   BOUTIQUE HOTEL $$$

(Map p48; ☎305-673-3373; www.pelicanhotel.com; 826 Ocean Dr; r $225-345, ste from $1500; ❄🔊) When the owners of Diesel jeans purchased the Pelican in 1999, they started scouring garage sales for just the right ingredients to fuel a mad experiment: 30 themed rooms that come off like a fantasy-suite hotel dipped in hip. From the cowboy-hipster chic of 'High Corral, OK Chaparral' to the jungly electric tiger stripes of 'Me Tarzan, You Vain,' all the rooms are completely different (although all have beautiful recycled-oak floors), fun and even come with their own 'suggested soundtrack'.

TOP CHOICE Hotel St Augustine   BOUTIQUE HOTEL $$

(Map p48; ☎305-532-0570; www.hotelstaugustine .com; 347 Washington Ave; r $180-280; Ⓟ❄🔊) Wood that's blonder than Barbie and a crisp-and-clean deco theme combine to create one of SoFi's most elegant yet stunningly modern sleeps. Color schemes blend beige, caramel, white and cream – the sense is the hues are flowing into one eye-smoothing palette. The familiar, warm service is the cherry on top for this hip-and-homey standout, although the soothing lighting and glass showers – that turn into personal steam rooms at the flick of a switch – are pretty appealing too.

TOP CHOICE Sense South Beach   BOUTIQUE HOTEL $$$

(Map p48; ☎305-538-5529; www.sensesobe.com; 400 Ocean Dr; r $240-280; Ⓟ❄🔊🏊👫) The Sense is fantastically atmospheric – smooth white walls disappearing behind melting blue views of South Beach, wooden paneling arranged around lovely sharp angles that feel inviting, rather than imposing, and rooms that contrast whites and dark grays into straight duochromatic cool. Pop art hangings and slender furnishings round out the MacBook-esque air. The staff are extremely helpful – warm even – which is eminently refreshing.

Lords Hotel   BOUTIQUE HOTEL $$

(Map p48; ☎877-448-4754; www.lordsouthbeach .com; 1120 Collins Ave; r $120-240, ste $330-540; Ⓟ❄🔊) The epicenter of South Beach's gay scene is this cream puff of a hotel, with rooms decked out in lemony yellow and whites offset by graphic and pop art. A giant polar bear stands to greet you in the lobby, while out the back the boys gather around a pool and prepare to party. As hip as the Lords is, it doesn't affect any attitude; you'll be at ease here, unless you sit the wrong way on the weird studded chairs situated around the bar.

Hotel Victor   BOUTIQUE HOTEL $$$

(Map p48; ☎305-428-1234; www.hotelvictorsouth beach.com; 1144 Ocean Dr; r $370-820; Ⓟ❄🔊🏊) The Victor wins – the 'hot design' stakes, that is. And the 'fishtanks full of jellyfish' competition. And the 'damn that room is fly' pageant too. Designed by L Murray Dixon in 1938, the redone Victor was opened in 2005 to much acclaim; these days, Shaquille O'Neal is famous for throwing parties in the $6000-a-night penthouse.

Kent Hotel   BOUTIQUE HOTEL $$

(Map p48; ☎305-604-5068; www.thekenthotel.com; 1131 Collins Ave; r $79-220; Ⓟ❄🔊) Young party types will probably get a kick out of this lobby, filled with fuchsia and electric-orange geometric furniture plus bright Lucite toy blocks, which makes for an aggressively playful welcome. The special Lucite Suite is almost entirely constructed of the see-through material, giving it an icy playground feel. Take refuge in a side garden with Indonesian-style tables, bamboo and hammocks. One of the beach's better deals.

Hotel Astor   BOUTIQUE HOTEL $$

(Map p48; ☎305-531-8081; www.hotelastor.com; 956 Washington Ave; r $140-290; Ⓟ❄🔊🏊) They lay the retro-punk on thick in the Astor lobby, glamorizing and exaggerating the Age of Transportation into a hip caricature of itself:

a gigantic industrial fan blows over a ceiling studded with psychedelic 'lamp balls,' all suspended over a fanciful daydream of an old-school pilots' club. The earth-toned rooms are relaxing, and the small pool gets covered at night to make room for clubgoers who bop on the back-patio lounge.

Fashionhaus BOUTIQUE HOTEL **$$**
(Map p48; ☎305-673-2550; www.fashionhaushotel.com; 534 Washington Ave; r $130-250; P❄📶🏊) The Fashionhaus doesn't just sound like a Berlin avant-garde theater; it kinda feels like one, with its smooth geometric furnishings, 48 individualized rooms decked out in original artwork – from abstract expressionism to washed out photography – and its general blending of comfort, technology and design. Popular with Europeans, fashionistas, artists (and European fashionista artists) and those who just want to emulate that lifestyle.

Hotel BOUTIQUE HOTEL **$$$**
(Map p48; ☎305-531-2222; 801 Collins Ave; www.thehotelofsouthbeach.com; r $260-425; P❄📶🏊) This place is stylin' – and why shouldn't it be, when Todd Oldham designed the boldly beautiful rooms? The themed palette of 'sand, sea and sky' adds a dash of eye candy to the furnishings, as do the mosaic doorknobs and brushed-steel sinks. The Hotel boasts one of the best rooftop pools in South Beach, overshadowed only by a lovely deco spire (which says 'Tiffany,' because that was the name of this place before the blue-box jewelry chain threatened a lawsuit).

Chesterfield Hotel BOUTIQUE HOTEL **$$**
(Map p48; ☎305-531-5831; www.thechesterfieldhotel.com; 855 Collins Ave; r $140-220, ste $280-520; P❄📶) Hip-hop gets jiggy with zebra-stripes on the curtains and cushions in the small lobby, which turns into the site of one of the hoppin'-est happy hours on Collins when the sun goes down. Leave a tip for the giant African statue while you're draining that mojito. Rooms mix up dark wood furniture overlaid with bright-white beds and vaguely tropical colors swathed throughout.

Clinton Hotel BOUTIQUE HOTEL **$$**
(Map p48; ☎305-938-4040; www.clintonsouthbeach.com; 825 Washington Ave; r $140-396; P❄📶🏊) Washington Ave is the quietest of the three main drags in SoBe, but the Clinton doesn't mind. This joint knows it would be the hottest girl in the most crowded party, with her blue velveteen banquettes and ubercontemporary metal ceiling fans. The tiny sunporches in the Zen rooms are perfect for breakfast or an evening cocktail.

Essex House Hotel BOUTIQUE HOTEL **$$**
(Map p48; ☎305-534-2700, 800-553-7739; www.essexhotel.com; 1001 Collins Ave; r $154-204, ste $354-404; ❄📶🏊) When you gaze at this lobby, one of the best-preserved interiors in the deco district, you're getting a glimpse of South Beach's glorious gangster heyday. Beyond that the Essex has helpful staff, rooms furnished with soft, subdued colors and a side veranda filled with rattan furnishings that's a particularly pleasant people-watching perch.

Hotel Shelley BOUTIQUE HOTEL **$$**
(Map p48; ☎305-531-3341; www.hotelshelley.com; 844 Collins Ave; r $120-260; ❄📶) Gossamer curtains, a lively lounge and a sublimely relaxing violet-and-blue color scheme combines with orblike lamps that look like bunched-up glass spider webs. The rooms are as affordably stylish as the rest of the offerings in the South Beach Group selection of hotels (see www.southbeachgroup.com).

Dream South Beach BOUTIQUE HOTEL **$$$**
(Map p48; ☎305-673-4747; www.dreamsouthbeach.com; 1111 Collins Ave; r $190-240, ste $300-570; P❄📶) How to explain the Dream? From the outside it looks like an ice-cube box of clean white lines, but come inside and it feels like a cross between the interior of an Indian palace, an electric-blue tube of toothpaste and one of those hip European ice hotels – not the construction material, mind, but the way it seems to resemble a glittering arctic palace plucked from, well, your dreams. The rooftop bar is a perfect place to kick back and pretend you're some kind of film-industry mogul, before returning to your room and pretending to be a futuristic Mughal.

Miami Beach International Travelers Hostel HOSTEL **$**
(Map p48; ☎305-534-0268; www.hostelmiamibeach.com; 236 9th St; dm from $25, r from $29; ❄@📶) The rooms are a tad worn, but security is good, the staff friendly and the lobby cheerful (at night it sort of resembles a club). Half the 100 rooms are private; the others are four-bed dorms, all clean and even vaguely deco-ish. Strictly speaking, to get a room you'll need an out-of-state university ID, HI card and a US or foreign passport with a recent entry stamp or an onward

ticket, but these rules are only enforced when it's crowded. There's a good social vibe throughout.

South Beach Hostel
HOSTEL **$**

(Map p48; ☑305-534-6669; www.thesouthbeach hostel.com; 235 Washington Ave; dm from $23, r from $60; ✴@🛜) On a quiet end of SoFi (the area south of 5th St, South Beach), this hostel has a happening common area and spartan rooms. It may not be too flashy, but the staff are friendly and the on-site bar (open to 5am) seems to stay busy. The property is split between six-bed dorms and private rooms; regarding the latter, couples are probably better off in midrange hotel rooms elsewhere, which are probably twice as nice for the same price.

The Villa by Barton G
RESORT **$$$**

(Map p48; ☑305-576-8003; www.thevillabybar tong.com; 1116 Ocean Dr; r from $900; P✴🛜≋) Formerly the Versace Mansion, it has been turned into one of South Beach's most upscale resorts by Barton G, replete with a mosaic pool plucked from Ancient Rome, marble bathrooms, linen spun from angel's hair and rooms that resemble the guest wing of a minor South American oligarch's personal compound.

Mondrian
RESORT **$$$**

(Map p48; ☑305-514-1500; www.mondrian-miami .com; 1100 West Ave; r $250-500, ste $550-750; P✴🛜≋) Morgan Hotel Group hired Dutch design star Marcel Wanders (whose name they'll drop till it falls through the floor) to basically crank it up to 11 at the Mondrian. The theme is inspired by *Alice in Wonderland* (if it had been penned by Crockett from *Miami Vice*) – columns carved like giant table legs, chandelier showerheads, imported Delft tiles with beach scenes instead of windmills, and magic walls with morphing celebrity faces (perhaps because the morphing nature of celebrity is what fuels South Beach's glamour?). Oh, and there's a private island (naturally).

Casa Grande Hotel
BOUTIQUE HOTEL **$$$**

(Map p48; ☑866-420-2272; www.casagrandesuit ehotel.com; 834 Ocean Dr; r $315-575; P✴🛜≋) Fall colors and a splash of bright citrus start the show in the lobby, but the main event is the snow-white elegance of the 35 so-chic rooms, each one an ultramodern Scandinavian designer's dream – although we've got to say the big, marble Virgin Mary in the room we visited was way out of place. We do

like the flowers on the pillow, though – nice touch, guys.

Wave Hotel
BOUTIQUE HOTEL **$$**

(Map p48; ☑305-673-0401, 800-501-0401; www .wavehotel.com; 350 Ocean Dr; r $100-250; P✴🛜) Dark-blue, plush molded furniture and curving, cool lines give the lobby a sense of tidal momentum. There's a space-race theme (as in '50s Sputnik-era retro chic) going on in the rooms; you have to love the lamps, which look like cartoon bubble helmets from *Buck Rogers*. Book early enough and you can get a room here for an absolute steal.

Ocean Five Hotel
BOUTIQUE HOTEL **$$**

(Map p48; ☑305-532-7093; www.oceanfive.com; 436 Ocean Dr; r/ste from $130/200; P✴🛜) This boutique hotel is all pumpkin-bright; deco dressed up on the outside, with cozy, quiet rooms that reveal a maritime-meets-vintage theme on the inside, with a dash of Old West ambience on top. Think mermaid murals on pale stucco walls. There are no balconies here, but the attached restaurant is a warm, friendly spot to have a drink and a fine Italian meal before strolling up Ocean Dr.

Ohana Hostel
HOSTEL **$**

(Map p48; ☑305-534-2650; 750 Collins Ave; dm from $33; ✴@🛜) Rooms are kept sparkly clean, an international crowd chills in the lounge, and all is basically well in this corner of the budget-travel world.

Jazz on South Beach
HOSTEL **$**

(Map p48; ☑305-672-2137; www.jazzhostels.com /jazzsouthbeach; 321 Collins Ave; ✴@🛜) A nice addition to the expanding SoBe backpacker scene. The hip vibe attracts lots of scenesters and club kids.

SOUTH BEACH (11TH TO 23RD STREETS)

TOP CHOICE The Standard
BOUTIQUE HOTEL **$$$**

(☑305-673-1717; www.standardhotels.com/miami; 40 Island Ave; r $170-280, ste from $480; P✴🛜≋) Look for the upside-down 'Standard' sign on the old Lido building on Belle Island (between South Beach and downtown Miami) and you'll find the Standard – which is anything but. This excellent boutique blends hipster funk with South Beach sex, and the result is a '50s motel gone glam. There are organic wooden floors, raised white beds, and gossamer curtains, which open onto a courtyard of earthly delights, including a heated hammam (Turkish bath). The crowd, which feels like the Delano kids with a bit more maturity, gathers to flirt and gawk.

Shuttles ferry guests to the Sagamore every 30 minutes, so you're never too isolated from the scene – unless you want to be, and given the grace of this place, we'd totally understand why. Show up on Sunday afternoons for the coolest outdoor bingo-bar-barbecue experience in the city.

TOP CHOICE Shore Club
BOUTIQUE HOTEL $$$
(Map p44; ☎305-695-3100; www.shoreclub.com; 1901 Collins Ave; r $270-470, ste from $1400; P✳@☀) Imagine a Zen ink-brush painting; what's beautiful isn't what's there, but what gets left out. If you could turn that sort of art into a hotel room, it might look like the stripped-down yet serene digs of the Shore Club. Yeah, yeah: it has the 400-thread-count Egyptian cotton sheets, Mexican sandstone floors etc; a lot of hotels in SoBe lay claim to similar luxury lists. What the Shore Club does like no other hotel is arrange these elements into a greater whole that's impressive in its understatement; the aesthetic is compelling because it comes across as an afterthought.

Cardozo Hotel
BOUTIQUE HOTEL $$$
(Map p44; ☎305-535-6500, 800-782-6500; www.cardozohotel.com; 1300 Ocean Dr; r $220-290, ste $320-460; P✳☀) The Cardozo and its neighbor, the Carlyle, were the first deco hotels saved by the Miami Design Preservation League, and in the case of the Cardozo, we think they saved the best first. Owner Gloria Estefan, whose videos are looped on flat-screen mini-TVs in the lobby, likely agrees. It's the combination of the usual contemporary sexiness (white walls, hardwood floors, high-thread-count sheets) and playful embellishments: leopard-print details, handmade furniture and a general sense that, yes, you are cool if you stay here, but you don't have to flaunt it. Oh – remember the 'hair gel' scene in *There's Something About Mary*? Filmed here.

Sagamore
BOUTIQUE HOTEL $$$
(Map p44; ☎305-535-8088; www.sagamorehotel.com; 1671 Collins Ave; r $260-320, ste $400-680; P✳@☀) Spencer Tunick got 600 people to pose nude in massive structured photo shoots sent all around the Sagamore in 2007. Nude art installation – that's hot, but also expected at this hotel-cum-exhibition space, which likes to blur the boundaries between interior decor, art and conventional hotel aesthetics. Almost every space within this hotel, from the lobbies to the rooms, doubles

as an art gallery thanks to a talented curator and an impressive roster of contributing artists.

Cadet
BOUTIQUE HOTEL $$
(Map p44; ☎305-672-6688; www.cadethotel.com; 1701 James Ave; r $170-280, ste $340-530; P✳☀) The Cadet wins our award for most creative embellishments in its rooms. From paper lanterns hanging from ceilings to furry throw rugs; from clamshell designs encapsulating large mirrors to classical Asian furniture and, as always, a great art-deco facade, this spot has the aesthetics right. Check out the shaded veranda at the back, lifted from a fantasy idea of what a plantation should feel like.

Betsy Hotel
BOUTIQUE HOTEL $$$
(Map p44; ☎305-531-6100; www.thebetsyhotel.com; 1440 Ocean Dr; r from $330; P✳☀☀) The Betsy's 63 rooms present a sort of blend of Caribbean plantation and modern Ikea store; pastel and tropical color schemes blot into the usual South Beach monochrome white, which makes for an elegant but friendly vibe. The exterior suggests much the same spirit, but given the elite set this hotel attracts, areas like the lobby and the pool feel more exclusive and self-assured. The shutter-style doors that frame the windows within the rooms are a nice touch, as are the walnut floors and bath mirrors with inbuilt LCD TVs.

Townhouse Hotel
BOUTIQUE HOTEL $$
(Map p44; ☎305-534-3800; www.townhousehotel.com; 150 20th St at Collins Ave; r $145-195, ste from $350; ✳☀☀) You'd think the Townhouse was designed by the guy who styled the iPod but no, it was Jonathan Morr and India Mahdavi who fashioned a cool white lobby and igloo-like rooms with random scarlet accents and a breezy, white rooftop lounge. Who needs mints on pillows when the Townhouse provides beach balls?

Setai
BOUTIQUE HOTEL $$$
(Map p44; ☎305-520-6000; www.setai.com; 101 20th St; ste $900-6000; P✳☀☀⚓) There's a *linga* in the lobby – nothing says high-end luxury like a Hindu phallus. It's all part of the aesthetic at Miami's most expensive sleep, where a well-realized theme mixes Southeast Asian temple architecture, Chinese furniture, contemporary luxury and an overarching Anywhere Asia concept. Each floor is staffed by teams of 24-hour butlers, while rooms are decked out in chocolate

teak wood, clean lines, and Chinese and Khmer embellishments. Note: the studio is small for four figures. Service is outstanding and surprisingly down-to-earth, and the Setai, hip as it is, is quite family-friendly.

W Hotel
RESORT $$$

(Map p44; ☎305-938-3000; www.starwoodhotels .com; 2201 Collins Ave; r $460-510, ste $660-1100; P✳️🛜🏊) There's an astounding variety of rooms available at the South Beach outpost of the famous W chain, which brings the whole W-brand mix of luxury, hipness and overblown cool to Miami Beach in a big way. The 'spectacular studios' balance long panels of reflective glass with cool tablets of *cippolino* marble; the Oasis suite lets in so much light you'd think the sun had risen in your room; the Penthouse may as well be the setting of an MTV video (and given the sort of celebrities who stay here, that assessment might not be far off). The attendant bars, restaurants, clubs and pool built into this complex are some of the most well regarded on the beach.

Delano Hotel
BOUTIQUE HOTEL $$$

(Map p44; ☎305-672-2000; www.delano-hotel .com; 1685 Collins Ave; r $380-540, ste $885-1400; P✳️🛜🏊) The Delano opened in the 1990s and immediately started ruling the South Beach roost. If there's a quintessential 'I'm too sexy for this song' South Beach moment, it's when you walk into the Delano's lobby, which has all the excess of an overbudgeted theater set. 'Magic mirrors' in the halls disclose weather info, tide charts and inspirational quotes. The pool area resembles the courtyard of a Disney princess' palace and includes a giant chess set; there are floor-to-ridiculously-high-ceiling curtains in the two-story waterfront rooms; and the bedouin tent cabanas are outfitted with flat-screen TVs. Rooms are almost painfully white and bright; all long, smooth lines, reflective surfaces and sexy, modern, luxurious amenities.

Gansevoort South
RESORT $$$

(Map p44; ☎866-932-6694; www.gansevoortmiam ibeach.com; 2377 Collins Ave; r $300-500, ste from $550; P✳️🛜🏊) The Gansevoort has been aggressively pushing the glamour bar higher and higher in South Beach, which is a quite an accomplishment given neighbors like the W, Delano and Shore Club. Nonetheless the Gansevoort delivers, from its lobby where a small shark swims through a fuchsia-backlit aquarium, to one of the best rooftop pools

in Miami, to rooms that drip luxury but are surprisingly understated (if still posh).

Aqua Hotel
BOUTIQUE HOTEL $$

(Map p44; ☎305-538-4361; www.aquamiami .com; 1530 Collins Ave; r $150-180, ste from $200; P✳️🛜🏊) A front desk made of shiny surfboard sets the mellow tone at this former motel – the old, family kind where the rooms are set around a pool. That old-school vibe barely survives under the soft glare of aqua spotlights and an alfresco lounging area, popular with the mostly gay clientele. The sleekness of the rooms is offset by quirky furniture, like a sumptuous chair made of spotted cowhide.

Tides
BOUTIQUE HOTEL $$$

(Map p44; ☎305-604-5070, 800-439-4095; www .tidessouthbeach.com; 1220 Ocean Dr; r $320-625, ste $1000-4000; P✳️🛜🏊) The 50 oceanfronting rooms are icy cool, with their jumbled vintage, ocean organic and indie vibe. The pure-white bedding is overlaid by beige, tan and shell, and offset with cream accents. Rooms come with telescopes for planetary (or Hollywood) stargazing, and the lobby, bedecked with nautical embellishments, looks like a modern sea god's palace. You can't miss this place; it's one of the biggest buildings fronting Ocean Dr.

Clay Hotel & Miami Beach International Hostel
HOSTEL $

(Map p44; ☎305-534-2988, 800-379-2529; www .clayhotel.com; 1438 Washington Ave; dm $25-29, r $60-120; ✳️@🛜) How many HI hostels are located in a 100-year-old Spanish-style villa? The Clay has clean and comfortable rooms, from single-sex, four- to eight-bed dorms to decent private rooms, many of which are located in a medinalike maze of adjacent buildings. Staff are harassed due to sheer volume, but are friendly and helpful. This is yet another Miami place where Al Capone got some shut-eye.

Cavalier Hotel
BOUTIQUE HOTEL $$

(Map p44; ☎305-531-3555, 800-688-7678; www .cavaliermiami.com; 1320 Ocean Dr; r $129-155, ste $229; P✳️🛜) The exterior is a rare Ocean Dr example of the Mayan/Incan inspiration that graced some deco facades (look for Meso-American details like the step pattern on the sides of the building). Inside? The Cavalier sacrifices ultrahip for Old Florida casualness, which is refreshing. We love the earthy touches in the rooms, like batik fabrics in tones of brown and beige.

MIAMI'S BEST HOTEL POOLS

Miami has some of the most beautiful hotel pools in the world, and they're more about seeing and being seen than swimming. Most of these pools double as bars, lounges or even clubs. Some hotels have a guests-only policy when it comes to hanging out at the pool, but if you buy a drink at the poolside bar you should be fine.

» **Delano Hotel** (p88)
» **Shore Club** (p87)
» **Gansevoort South** (p88)
» **Epic Hotel** (p91)
» **Biltmore Hotel** (p71)
» **Raleigh Hotel** (p89)
» **Fontainebleau** (p90)

Beachcomber Hotel   HOTEL $$
(Map p44; ☎305-531-3755, 888-305-4683; www
.beachcombermiami.com; 1340 Collins Ave; r $89-
189; ❄@) Green takes center stage at this
deco classic, with a green-banana-colored
facade, a soothing mint-green lobby, green-
flecked terrazzo floor, sea-foam-green couches and a chartreuse bar, all floating beneath
sleek aluminum ceiling fans. The rooms,
while not quite as seductive as the entrance,
are basic, cozy and clean.

Winter Haven Hotel   BOUTIQUE HOTEL $$
(Map p44; ☎305-531-5571; www.winterhavenhotel
sobe.com; 1400 Ocean Dr; r $149-259; P❄☀≋)
Al Capone used to stay here; maybe he liked
the deco ceiling lamps in the lobby, with
their sharp, retro sci-fi lines and grand-
Gothic proportions, and the oddly placed
oriental mirrors (which have nothing to do
with art deco whatsoever). A young but laid-
back crowd hangs at the Haven, which sits
on the pretty-people end of Ocean Dr. The
rooms, with their dark-wood accents and
ice-white bedspreads, are a bit warmer than
your average South Beach digs.

Surfcomber   HOTEL $$$
(Map p44; ☎305-532-7715; www.surfcomber.com;
1717 Collins Ave; r $310-560; P❄☀≋) Simply
one of the best classical deco structures in
Miami, the Surfcomber is (sh) actually owned
by Doubletree. Well, more power to 'em; the
chain has renovated this property into
an immaculate state. Note the movement-

suggestive lines on the exterior and semicircular, shade-providing 'eyebrows' that jut
out of the windows. Also especially note the
lobby – the rounded, aeronautical feel of the
space suggests you're entering a 1930s airline lounge but no, you're just going to your
room. Parking is $39 per day.

Royal Palm Hotel   HOTEL $$$
(Map p44; ☎305-604-5700; www.royalpalmmiami
beach.com; 1545 Collins Ave; r $169-369, ste $299-
689; P❄☀≋) Even the trolleys here have a
touch of curvy deco flair, to say nothing of
the chunky staircase and mezzanine, which
are the best South Beach examples of the
building-as-cruise-liner deco theme. Note
the porthole windows, wire railings and general sense of oceanic space; you can almost
hear waves slapping the side of the building.
There's a glut of pop art by Romero Britto
in the lobby (and even a Britto-themed restaurant); rooms are full of sharp, square-ish
angles and modern furnishings.

National Hotel   HOTEL $$
(Map p44; ☎305-532-2311; www.nationalhotel
.com; 1677 Collins Ave; r $240-420, ste from $450;
P❄☀≋) The National is an old-school
deco icon, with its bell-tower–like cap and
slim yet muscular facade. Inside the hotel
itself you'll find off-white rooms fashioned
to fit more traditional, as opposed to uber-
modern, tastes – a departure from the South
Beach norm. The lobby and halls are riots of
geometric design, while outside a lovely in-
finity pool beckons guests and visitors. The
decadent cabana suites are exercises in luxury, offering unfettered access to said pool,
private terraces and on-site tropical gardens.

Raleigh Hotel   BOUTIQUE HOTEL $$$
(Map p44; ☎305-534-6300, 800-848-1775; www
.raleighhotel.com; 1775 Collins Ave; r $360-470, ste
$560-740; P❄☀≋) While everyone else was
trying to get all modern, the Raleigh pains-
takingly tried to restore itself to prewar
glory. It succeeded in a big way. Celebrity
hotelier André Balazs has managed to capture a tobacco-and-dark-wood men's club
ambience and old-school elegance while
simultaneously sneaking in modern design
elements and amenities. Have a swim in the
stunning pool; Hollywood actress Esther
Williams used to.

Catalina Hotel   BOUTIQUE HOTEL $$
(Map p44; ☎305-672-4554; www.catalinahotel
.com; 1732 Collins Ave; r $160-250; P❄☀≋) The
Catalina is a lovely example of midrange

deco style. Not too flashy, like the uber-resorts further up Collins, yet also not too ratty like many of the cheaper properties in the area, this is a great middle of the road option that nonetheless knows how to lay on the luxury should the need present itself. The back pool, concealed behind the main building's crisp white facade, is particularly attractive and shaded by a large grove of tropical trees.

Tropics Hotel & Hostel HOTEL $
(Map p44; ☑305-531-0361; www.tropicshotel.com; 1550 Collins Ave; dm $27, r from $59; ❄✉) The surprisingly nice Tropics (which looks a bit tacky from the outside) sports a big swimming pool and a patio area that seems consistently packed with chatting travelers. The clean four-bed dorms have attached bathrooms; private rooms are basic and serviceable.

Santa Barbara HOSTEL $
(Map p44; ☑305-538-4411; www.miami-santa-barbara.hostel.com; 230 20th St; dm from $22, r from $55; ❄@🛜) This hostel is located in a classical old deco apartment building. The rooms are all clean and well-tended, although the eight-bed dorms can get a little cramped. The rooms front a large courtyard that becomes a default social area for guests, making this place feel like *Melrose Place* for backpackers.

NORTHERN MIAMI BEACH

TOP CHOICE **Circa 39** BOUTIQUE HOTEL $
(Map p52; ☑305-538-3900; www.circa39.com; 3900 Collins Ave; r $90-150; ❄@✉) If you love South Beach style but loathe South Beach attitude, Circa has got your back. The lobby, with its multicolored light board, molded furniture and wacky embellishments, is one of the funkiest in Miami. The hallways are low-lit under sexy red lamps and the icy-blue-and-white rooms are hip enough for the most exclusive scenesters (although Circa frowns on folk who act like snobs). Be you a family, a gay person or just someone who loves laid-back fun, this hotel welcomes all. The buy-in-advance web rates are phenomenal – you can find deals here for under $80.

Indian Creek Hotel BOUTIQUE HOTEL $
(Map p52; ☑305-531-2727; www.indiancreekhotel.com; 2727 Indian Creek Dr; from r $90; ❄🛜✉) Get your room key – attached to a plastic alligator – and walk through the old Miami lobby, spruced up with souvenir-stand schlock, to your comfortable, earthy-warm

digs. Or wander out to the surprisingly modern pool, where happy, sexy people are ready to have a good time. Mix in friendly staff and an easy stroll to the boardwalk, and you've got a classic boutique hotel.

Red South Beach BOUTIQUE HOTEL $$
(Map p52; ☑800-528-0823; www.redsouthbeach.com; 3010 Collins Ave; r $130-200; ❄🛜✉) Red is indeed the name of the game, from the cushions on the sleek chairs in the lobby to the flashes dancing around the marble pool to deep, blood-crimson headboards and walls wrapping you in warm sexiness in the small but beautiful guest rooms. The Red is excellent value for money and come evening the pool-bar complex is a great place to unwind and meet fellow guests.

Fontainebleau RESORT $$$
(Map p52; ☑800-548-8886; www.fontainebleau.com; 4441 Collins Ave; r $369-461, ste $551-861; ℗❄🛜✉) The 1200-room Fontainebleau opened in 1954, when it became a celeb-sunning spot. Numerous renovations have added beachside cabanas, seven tennis courts, a grand ballroom, a shopping mall and a fabulous swimming pool. The rooms have a midcentury-modern vibe and are surprisingly bright and cheerful – we expected more hard-edged attempts to be cool, but the sunny disposition of these chambers is a welcome surprise.

Eden Roc Renaissance RESORT $$$
(Map p52; ☑305-531-0000, 800-327-8337; www.edenrocmiami.com; 4525 Collins Ave; r from $310, ste from $430; ℗❄🛜✉) The Roc's immense inner lobby draws inspiration from the Rat Pack glory days of Miami Beach cool, and rooms in the New Ocean Tower boast lovely views over the Intracoastal Waterway. All the digs here have smooth, modern embellishments and amenities ranging from MP3 players to HDTV, ergonomic furniture and turn-down service, among others.

Daddy O Hotel BOUTIQUE HOTEL $$
(☑305-868-4141; www.daddyohotel.com; 9660 E Bay Harbor Dr; r $150-260; ℗❄🛜) The Daddy O is a cheerful, hip option that looks, from the outside, like a large B&B that's been fashioned for MTV and Apple employees. This vibe continues in the lobby and the rooms: cool, clean lines offset by bright, bouncy colors, plus a nice list of amenities: flat-screen TVs, custom wardrobes, free wi-fi and the rest. It's located about 3 miles north of North Miami Beach.

Claridge Hotel
HOTEL $$

(Map p52; 305-604-8485, 888-422-9111; www
.claridgefl.com; 3500 Collins Ave; r $120-215;
❀@☎) This 1928 Mediterranean-style pal-
ace feels like a (Americanized) Tuscan villa,
with a honey-stone courtyard enclosing a
sparkling pool, framed by palms, frescoed
walls and gleaming stone floors. The sooth-
ing, old-world rooms are set off by rich earth
tones and staff are eager to please.

Mimosa
BOUTIQUE HOTEL $$

(Map p52; 305-867-5000; www.themimosa
.com; 6525 Collins Ave; r from $210; ❀☎☎) The
Mimosa is decked out in mid-20th-century
modern furniture, offset by deco embellishment like portico-style mirrors, dark-and-
light room color schemes and a tangerine-
and-cream lobby with a citrus-bright vibe.
The pool is smallish, but overlooks a lovely
stretch of the Atlantic Ocean.

Palms South Beach
HOTEL $$$

(Map p52; 305-534-0505; www.thepalmshotel
.com; 3025 Collins Ave; r $140-289, ste $320-550;
P❀@☎) The lobby of the Palms manages
to be imposing and comfortable all at once;
the soaring ceiling, cooled by slow-spinning
giant rattan fans, makes for a colonial-villa-
on-convention-center-steroids vibe. Upstairs
the rooms are perfectly fine, a mix of pastel
colors and comfortable, if slightly bland, fur-
nishings.

DOWNTOWN MIAMI

Miami River Inn
B&B $$

(Map p56; 305-325-0045, 800-468-3589;
www.miamiriverinn.com; 119 SW South River Dr;
$99-300; P❀☎) Cute mom-and-pop B&Bs
stuffed full of antique furniture, pretty-as-
lace gardens and a general 'Aw, thanks for
breakfast' vibe are comparatively rare in Miami. The River Inn, listed on the National
Register of Historic Places, bucks this trend,
with charming New England-style rooms,
friendly service and one of the best libraries of Miami literature in the city. In a place
where every hotel can feel like a loud experiment in graphic design, this relaxing watercolor invites you onto the back porch.

Epic
HOTEL $$$

(Map p56; 305-424-5226; www.epichotel.com;
270 Biscayne Blvd; r $250-510; P❀☎☎) Epic in-
deed! This massive Kimpton hotel is one of
the more attractive options downtown and
it possesses a coolness cred that could match
any spot on Miami Beach. Of particular note
is the outdoor pool and sun deck, which

overlooks a gorgeous sweep of Brickell and
the surrounding condo canyons. The rooms
are outfitted in designer-chic furnishings
and some have similarly beautiful views of
greater Miami-Dade. There's an on-site spa
and bar that gives this spot a bit of youthful
energy that's lacking in other corporate-style
downtown hotels.

Mandarin Oriental Miami
HOTEL $$$

(Map p56; 305-913-8288, 866-888-6780; www
.mandarinoriental.com/miami; 500 Brickell Key Dr; r
$480-750, ste from $900; P❀☎☎) The Mandarin shimmers on Brickell Key, which is actually annoying – you're a little isolated from
the city out here. Not that it matters; there's
a luxurious world within a world inside this
exclusive compound, from swank restaurants to a private beach and skyline views
that look back at Miami from the far side of
Biscayne Bay. Rooms are good in a luxury-
chain kind of way, but nothing sets them
apart from other sleeps in this price range.

Four Seasons Miami
HOTEL $$$

(Map p56; 305-358-3535, 305-381-3381; www
.fourseasons.com/miami; 1435 Brickell Ave; r $350-
580, ste $750-1500; P❀☎☎) The marble com-
mon areas double as art galleries, a massive
spa caters to corporate types and there are
sweeping, could-have-been-a-panning-shot-
from-*Miami-Vice* views over Biscayne Bay
in some rooms. The 7th-floor terrace bar, Ba-
hia, is pure mojito-laced, Latin-loved swank-
iness, especially on Thursdays and Fridays
from 6pm to 8pm, when ladies drink free.

KEY BISCAYNE

Silver Sands Beach Resort
RESORT $$

(Map p64; 305-361-5441; www.silversandsbeach
resort.com; 301 Ocean Dr; r $169-189, cottages
$279-349; P❀☎) Silver Sands: aren't you
cute, with your one-story, stucco tropical
tweeness? How this little, Old Florida–style
independent resort has survived amid the
corporate competition is beyond us, but
it's definitely a warm, homey spot for those
seeking some intimate, individual attention
– to say nothing of the sunny courtyard, garden area and outdoor pool.

Ritz-Carlton Key Biscayne
RESORT $$$

(Map p64; 305-365-4500; www.ritzcarlton.com;
455 Grand Bay Dr; r from $330, ste $1200-3000;
P❀☎☎❀) Many Ritz-Carlton outposts
feel a little cookie-cuttered, but the Key Bis-
cayne outpost of the empire is pretty unique.
There's the magnificent lobby, vaulted by
four giant columns lifted from a Cecil B

MIMO ON BIBO

That cute little phrase means "Miami Modern on Biscayne Boulevard", and refers to the architectural style of buildings on north Biscayne Blvd past 55th Street. Specifically, there are some great roadside motels here with lovely, Rat Pack–era '50s neon beckoning visitors in. This area was neglected for a long time, and some of these spots are seedy (when we asked one owner why she advertised rooms for only $25, she smiled and said, '*Por hora*' – by the hour). But north BiBo is also one of Miami's rapidly gentrifying areas, and savvy motel owners are cleaning up their act and looking to attract the hipsters, artists and gay population flocking to the area. There's already exciting food here (see p100). Now the lodgings are getting stimulating too. All these hotels provide South Beach comfort at half the price.

» **New Yorker** (off Map p62; ☑305-759-5823; www.hotelnewyorkermiami.com; 6500 Biscayne Blvd; r $75-130; P✴☎☎) This hotel has been around since the 1950s and it shows – in a good way. If you could turn a classic Cadillac into a hotel with a modern interior and hipster cred, then bam, there's the New Yorker in a nutshell. Staff are friendly and rooms – done up with pop art, geometric designs and solid colors – would make Andy Warhol proud.

» **Motel Blu** (off Map p62; ☑877-784-6835; www.motelblumiami.com; 7700 Biscayne Blvd; r $52-150; P✴☎☎) Situated above Miami's Little River, the Blu may not look like much from the outside, but inside you'll find freshly-done-up rooms with a host of modern amenities. Rooms are comfortable and have a soothing lime-and-lemon interior.

» **Motel Bianco** (Map p62; ☑305-751-8696; www.motelbianco.com; 5255 Biscayne Blvd; r $80-110; P✴☎) The Bianco situates several orange-and-milky-white rooms around a glittery courtyard where coffee is served and guests can get to know each other. Contemporary art designs swirl through the larger rooms and wicker furniture abounds throughout.

DeMille set – hell, the whole hotel is lifted from a DeMille set. Tinkling fountains, the view of the bay and the marble grandeur speak less of a chain hotel and more of early-20th-century glamour. Rooms and amenities are predictably excellent.

COCONUT GROVE

Mutiny Hotel　　　　　HOTEL $$$
(Map p69; ☑305-441-2100, 866-417-0640; www.providenceresorts.com/mutiny-hotel; 2951 S Bayshore Dr; ste $190-390; P✴☎☎) This small, luxury bayfront hotel, with 120 one- and two-bedroom suites featuring balconies, boasts an indulgent staff, high-end bedding, gracious appointments, fine amenities and a small heated pool. Although it's on a busy street, you won't hear the traffic once inside. The property boasts fine views over the water.

Ritz-Carlton Coconut Grove　　RESORT $$$
(Map p69; ☑305-644-4680; www.ritzcarlton.com; 3300 SW 27th Ave; r & ste $270-399; P✴☎☎☎☎) Another member of the Ritz-Carlton organization in Miami, this one overlooks the bay, has immaculate rooms and offers butlers for every need, from shopping and web-surfing to dog-walking and bathing. The massive spa is stupendous.

**Sonesta Hotel & Suites
Coconut Grove**　　　　　HOTEL $$
(Map p69; ☑305-529-2828; www.sonesta.com/coconutgrove; 2889 McFarlane Rd; r $140-400, ste $210-660; P✴☎☎☎) The Coco Grove outpost of this luxury chain of hotels has decked its rooms out in almost all white with a splash of color (South Beach style). The amenities, from flat-screen TVs to mini-kitchenettes, add a layer of luxury to this surprisingly hip big-box. Make your way to the top of the building to enjoy a wonderful outdoor deck pool.

Grove Isle Club & Resort　　RESORT $$$
(☑305-858-8300, 800-884-7683; www.groveisle.com; 4 Grove Isle Dr; r $250-529, ste $389-879; P✴☎☎☎) One of those 'I've got my own little island' type places, Grove Island is off the coast of Coconut Grove. This stunning boutique hotel has colonial elegance, lush tropical gardens, its own jogging track, decadent pool, sunset views over Biscayne Bay, amenities galore and the cachet of staying in your own floating temple of exclusivity.

CORAL GABLES

TOP CHOICE **Biltmore Hotel** HOTEL $$$

(Map p72; ☑305-913-3158, 800-727-1926; www
.biltmorehotel.com; 1200 Anastasia Ave; r $240-
400, ste from $1200; P❋🖥🌊🐕🐾) Though the
Biltmore's standard rooms can be small, a
stay here is a chance to sleep in one of the
great laps of US luxury. The grounds are so
palatial it would take a solid week to explore
everything the Biltmore has to offer – we
highly recommend reading a book in the
Romanesque/Arabian-nights opulent lobby,
sunning underneath enormous columns
and taking a dip in the largest hotel pool in
the continental USA.

Hotel St Michel HOTEL $$

(Map p72; ☑305-444-1666; www.hotelstmichel
.com; 162 Alcazar Ave; r $125-220; P❋🖥🐾) The
Michel is more Metropole than Miami, and
we mean that as a compliment. The old-
world wooden fixtures, refined sense of
tweedy style and dinner-jacket ambience
don't get in the way of friendly service. The
lovely restaurant and cool bar-lounge are as
elegant as the hotel they occupy.

Wishes MOTEL $

(Map p72; ☑305-566-9871; 4700 SW 8th St; r from
$60; P❋🖥) The Wishes is a cute motel lo-
cated in a strong of seedy flophouses; while
the neighbors may not look the best, Wishes
itself is excellent. The rooms are surprisingly
large and comfortable, clean if a little dark,
with TVs and good hot water. Their main
draw is they're on offer for quite a bargain.

GREATER MIAMI

Inn at the Fisher Island Club RESORT $$$

(☑305-535-6060, 800-537-3708; www.fisherisland
club.com; r $600-2250; ❋🖥🌊) If you're not
Jeb Bush (who lives here), the only way to
glimpse Fisher Island is to stay at this luxu-
rious resort. Whether in 'simple' rooms or
Vanderbilt-era cottages, your money will be
well spent: one of the best-rated spas in the
country is here, as well as eight restaurants
(this seems like overkill given the size of the
island) and enough royal perks to please a
pharaoh.

✖ Eating

Miami is a major immigrant entrepôt and
a place that loves showing off its wealth.
Thus you get a good mix of cheap ethnic
eateries and high-quality top-end cuisine
here. There's admittedly a lot of dross too,
especially on Miami Beach, where people
can overcharge tourists and get away with
it. The best new spots for dining are in the
Wynwood, Midtown and Design District
area, a trend started by the famed Michelle
Bernstein; Coral Gables is also an estab-
lished foodie hot spot. Note that new hotels
often try to market themselves with new res-
taurants and big-name celebrity chefs.

SOUTH BEACH (1ST TO 11TH STREETS)

TOP CHOICE **Tap Tap** HAITIAN $$

(Map p48; ☑305-672-2898; www.taptaprestaurant
.com; 819 5th St; ⏰noon-11pm Mon-
Thu, to midnight Fri & Sat) In Haiti, tap-taps are
brightly colored pickup trucks turned public taxis, and their tropi-psychedelic paint
scheme inspires the decor at this excellent
Haitian eatery. No Manhattan-style South
Beach Lounge, this – here you dine under
bright murals of Papa Legba, guardian of the
dead, emerging from a Port-au-Prince cemetery. Meals are a happy marriage of West African, French and Caribbean: spicy pumpkin
soup, snapper in a scotch-bonnet lime sauce,
curried goat and charcoal-grilled Turks and
Caicos conch. Make sure you try the *mayi
moulen*, a signature side of cornmeal smoth-
ered in a rich bean sauce – bloody delicious!
If you need some liquid courage, shoot
some Barbancourt rum, available in several
grades (all strong).

Grazie ITALIAN $$$

(Map p48; ☑305-673-1312; www.grazieitalian
cuisine.com; 702 Washington Ave; mains $19-34;
⏰noon-3pm Mon-Fri, 6pm-midnight daily) Thanks
indeed; Grazie is top class and comfort-
ably old-school Northern Italian. There's a
distinct lack of gorgeous, clueless waitstaff
and unwise menu experimentation. Instead
there's attentive service, solid and delicious
mains, and extremely decent prices given
the quality of the dining and high-end na-
ture of the location. The porcini risotto is
simple in construction yet deeply complex
in execution – one of the best Italian dishes
on the beach.

Puerto Sagua CUBAN $

(Map p48; ☑305-673-1115; 700 Collins Ave; mains
$6-17; ⏰7:30am-2am) There's a secret colony
of older working-class Cubans and construc-
tion workers hidden among South Beach's
sex-and-flash, and evidently, they eat here
(next to a Benetton). Puerto Sagua challenges
the US diner with this reminder: Cubans can
greasy-spoon with the best of them. Portions
of favorites such as *picadillo* (spiced ground

beef with rice, beans and plantains) are stupidly enormous. The Cuban coffee here is not for the faint of heart – strong stuff.

11th Street Diner
DINER $

(Map p48; www.eleventhstreetdiner.com; 1065 Washington Ave; mains $8-15; ☺24hr) You've seen the art-deco landmarks. Now eat in one: a Pullman-car diner trucked down from Wilkes-Barre, Pennsylvania, as sure a slice of Americana as a *Leave It to Beaver* marathon. If you've been drinking all night, we'll split a three-egg omelet with you and the other drunkies at 6am – if there's a diner where you can replicate Edward Hopper's *Nighthawks,* it's here.

Pizza Rustica
PIZZERIA $

(Map p48; www.pizza-rustica.com; 863 Washington Ave; slices $3-5; ☺11am-3am Sun-Thu, 11am-6am Fri & Sat) South Beach's favorite pizza place has several locations to satisfy the demand for crusty Roman-style slices topped with an array of exotic offerings. A slice is a meal unto itself and goes down a treat when you need something to soak up the beer.

Taverna Opa
GREEK $$

(Map p48; ☎305-673-6730; www.tavernaoparest aurant.com; 36 Ocean Dr; mains $11-29; ☺4pm-midnight, to 1am weekends) Cross Coyote Ugly Saloon with a big fat Greek wedding and you get this tourist-oriented restaurant and ouzo fest, where the meze are decent and the vibe resembles something like a Hellenic frat party. Seriously, who knew feta, lamb and bachelorette parties went together? By the end of the night, table dancing is pretty much mandatory, and this may be the only Greek dining experience you have that ends with a sloppy make-out session.

Spiga
ITALIAN $$

(Map p48; ☎305-534-0079; www.spigarestaurant .com; Impala Hotel, 1228 Collins Ave; mains $15-26; ☺6pm-midnight) This romantic nook is a perfect place to bring your partner and gaze longingly at one another over candlelight, before you both snap out of it and start digging into excellent traditional Italian such as lamb in olive oil and rosemary, and baby clams over linguine.

Big Pink
DINER $

(Map p48; ☎305-532-4700; 157 Collins Ave; mains $11-23; ☺8am-midnight Sun-Wed, to 2am Thu, to 5am weekends) Big Pink does American comfort food with a joie de vivre and a dash of whimsy. We're more impressed with the lunch offerings than the dinner options; in the former, pulled Carolina pork holds the table next to a nicely done reuben. In the evening, expect seared tuna and roasted ribeye. The interior is somewhere between a '50s sock hop and a South Beach club; expect to be seated at a long communal table.

Nemo
FUSION $$$

(Map p48; ☎305-532-4550; www.nemorestaurant .com; 100 Collins Ave; mains $29-44; ☺noon-3pm & 6:30pm-midnight Mon-Sat, 11am-3pm & 6:30pm-midnight Sun) Raw bars and warm, copper sconces are a good sign; the nudge into greatness comes when Asian elegance graces Latin-American exuberance. Fish with chimichurri sauce and kiss-the-grill nori-dusted tuna are a few jewels plucked from this fusion gem mine.

Prime 112
STEAKHOUSE $$$

(Map p48; ☎305-532-8112; www.prime112.com; 112 Ocean Dr; mains $29-68; ☺noon-3pm Mon-Fri, 5:30pm-midnight Sun-Thu, to 1am weekends) Sometimes, you need a steak: well aged, juicy, marbled with the right bit of fat, served in a spot where the walls sweat testosterone, the bar serves Manhattans and the hostesses are models. Chuck the above into Miami Beach's oldest inn – the beautiful 1915 Browns Hotel – and there's Prime 112. Prime can definitely be said to attract celebrities; one night in 2008 it is rumored Enrique Iglesias, Anna Kournikova, Alonzo Mourning, LL Cool J, Mike Piazza and the King of Jordan all ate here...on the same night. On that note, don't come dressed in shorts and sandals. The steak, incidentally, is very good, although the service can leave something to be desired – some wait staff are lovely, but others behave with unwarranted pretension (hey, our money is as good as LL Cool J's).

News Cafe
AMERICAN $

(Map p48; www.newscafe.com; 800 Ocean Dr; mains $7-17; ☺24hr) News Cafe is an Ocean Dr landmark that attracts thousands of travelers. We find the food to be pretty uninspiring, but the people-watching is good, so take a perch, eat some over-the-average but not-too-special food and enjoy the anthropological study that is South Beach as she Rollerblades, salsas and otherwise shambles by.

SOUTH BEACH (11TH TO 23RD STREETS)

TOP CHOICE ⟩ **Osteria del Teatro**
ITALIAN $$

(Map p44; ☎305-538-7850; www.osteriadelteatro miami.com; 1443 Washington Ave; mains $16-31;

⊗6-11pm Mon-Thu, to 1am weekends) There are few things to swear by but the specials board of Osteria, one of the oldest and best Italian restaurants in Greater Miami, ought to be one. When you get here, let the gracious Italian waiters seat you, coddle you and then basically order for you off the board. They never pick wrong.

Burger & Beer Joint   BURGERS $
(Map p44; ☑305-531-1200; www.bnbjoint.com; 450 Lincoln Rd; mains $5.50-9; ⊗11:30am-midnight; ✍) Gourmet burgers. Microbrew beer. Clearly, the folks at B&B did their marketing research. Because who doesn't love both? Oh yes, vegetarians, you're catered to as well; the 'Dear Prudence', a mix of portobello, red pepper, walnut pesto and zucchini fries will keep herbivores happy. Oh, there's a turkey and stuffing burger with gravy served *between turkey patties,* an ahi tuna burger, a patty of wagyu beef with foie gras...you get the idea. Did we mention the microbrew beer?

Jerry's Famous Deli   DELI $$
(Map p44; ☑305-532-8030; www.jerrysfamousdeli.com; 1450 Collins Ave; mains $9-17; ⊗24hr) Important: Jerry's delivers. Why? Because when you've gorged on the pastrami on rye, turkey clubs and other mile-high sandwiches at this enormous Jewish deli (housed in what used to be the Warsaw nightclub), you'll be craving more of the above 24/7.

Casa Tua   ITALIAN $$$
(Map p44; ☑305-673-1010; www.casatualifestyle.com/restaurant; 1700 James Ave; mains $23-58; ⊗11:30am-3pm Mon-Fri, 6:30-11pm daily) Casa Tua is way too cool to have a sign out front. You'll know it by the oh-so-fabulous crowd streaming in, the hovering limos and what you can see of the beautiful building itself (much of it hidden behind a high hedge). If you manage to get a table in the magnificent, 1925 Mediterranean-style villa, you can linger over delicious prosciutto, Dover sole, risotto with lobster and veal cheeks.

Grillfish   SEAFOOD $$
(Map p44; ☑305-538-9908; www.grillfish.com; 1444 Collins Ave; mains $13-28; ⊗11:30am-11pm, to 12:30pm weekends) Sometimes it's all in a name. They grill here. They grill fish. They could call it 'Grillfish Awesome' because that's what this simple yet elegant restaurant, with its cutely mismatched plates and church-pew benches, serves: fresh seafood, done artfully, simply and joyfully.

Mr Chow   CHINESE $$$
(Map p44; ☑305-695-1695; www.mrchow.com; 2201 Collins Ave; mains $30-45; ⊗6pm-midnight) Located in the W Hotel, Mr Chow takes Chinese-American comfort food to gourmet heights. The setting is almost intimidatingly cool, with dangling moderne-style chandeliers and an enormous bar plucked out of *Sex and the City,* yet service is friendly and the food lovely: velvet chicken served with diced chilies; stinky, spicy tofu; squid sautéed with asparagus.

Van Dyke Cafe   FUSION $$
(Map p44; ☑305-534-3600; www.thevandykecafe.com; 846 Lincoln Rd; mains $10.50-26; ⊗8am-2am) One of Lincoln Rd's most touristed spots, the Van Dyke is an institution akin to the News Cafe, serving adequate food in a primo spot for people-watching. It's usually packed and takes over half the sidewalk. Service is friendly and efficient, and you get free preening models with your burgers and eggplant Parmigiana. There's excellent nightly jazz upstairs.

Guru   INDIAN $$
(Map p44; ☑305-534-3996; www.gurufood.com; 232 12th St; mains $15-23; ⊗noon-11:30pm) A sexy, soft-lit interior of blood reds and black wood sets the stage for this Indian eatery, where local ingredients like lobster swim into the korma. Goan fish curry goes down a treat but the service often seems rushed and the kitchen can be inconsistent. Try coming at lunchtime for the *thali* special, an assemble-your-own meal extravaganza that's a steal at $9.

Balans   FUSION $$
(Map p44; ☑305-534-9191; www.balans.co.uk; 1022 Lincoln Rd; mains $13-36; ⊗8am-midnight) Kensington, Chiswick...South Beach? Oi, give this Brit-owned fusion favorite a go. Where else do veal saltimbocca and lamb *jalfrezi* share a menu? After you down the signature lobster club, you'll agree tired stereotypes about English cooking need to be reconsidered.

Nexxt Cafe   FUSION $$
(Map p44; ☑305-532-6643; 700 Lincoln Rd; mains $7-23; ⊗11:30am-11pm Mon-Thu, to midnight weekends, 11am-11pm Sun) There's a lot of cafes arranged around Lincoln Rd that offer good people-watching along one of Miami Beach's most fashionable stretches. Many of these spots are of questionable quality. Nexxt is the best of the bunch, with a huge menu that jumps between turkey chili, gourmet

BUILDING A CUBAN SANDWICH

The traditional Cuban sandwich, also known as a *sandwich mixto*, is not some slapdash creation. It's a craft best left to the experts – but here's some insight on how they do it. Correct bread is crucial – it should be Cuban white bread: fresh, soft and easy to press. The insides (both sides) should be buttered and layered (in the following order) with sliced pickles, slices of roast Cuban pork, ham (preferably sweet-cured ham) and baby Swiss cheese. Then it all gets pressed in a hot *plancha* (sandwich press) until the cheese melts. Mmmm.

burgers and low-cal salads the size of your face. Speaking of which, the menu is simply enormous, and though nothing is really excellent, everything is pretty good.

Yuca   LATIN $$$

(Map p44; ☑305-532-9822; www.yuca.com; 501 Lincoln Rd; mains $22-42; ☺noon-11:30pm) This was one of the first Nuevo Latino hot spots in Miami and it's still going strong, even if locals say it has lost a little luster over the years. The Yuca *rellena* (a mild chili stuffed with truffle-laced mushroom *picadillo*) and the tender guava ribs still make our mouth water.

Gelateria Parmalat   ICE CREAM $

(Map p44; 670 Lincoln Rd; mains $3.85-8; ☺9am-midnight Sun-Thu, to 1:30am Fri & Sat) It's hot. You've been walking all day. You need ice cream, stat. Why hello, tamarind-and-passionfruit homemade gelato! This is an excellent spot for creamy, pillowy waves of European-style frozen goodness, and based on the crowds it's the favorite ice cream on South Beach.

Pasha's   MEDITERRANEAN $

(Map p44; ☑305-673-3919; www.pashas.com; 900 Lincoln Rd; meals $4-12; ☺8am-midnight, to 1am weekends) Pasha's is a serious self-promoter judging by this place, a sleek, two-level, healthy fast-food emporium that has its name everywhere you look. No matter; the food at Pasha's rocks. Have some delicious *labneh* (thick yogurt), a plate of hummus and grilled chicken served over rice. Pasha's has started expanding as a chain and now has locations across Miami.

Flamingo Restaurant   NICARAGUAN $

(Map p44; ☑305-673-4302; 1454 Washington Ave; mains $2.50-7; ☺7am-9pm Mon-Sat) This tiny Nicaraguan storefront-cafe serves the behind-the-scenes laborers who make South Beach function. You will very likely be the only tourist eating here. Workers devour hen soup, pepper chicken and cheap breakfasts prepared by a meticulous husband-and-wife team.

Paul   BAKERY $

(Map p44; 450 Lincoln Rd; mains $5.50-9; ☺8:30am-8pm; ☑) Paul sells itself as a 'Maison de Qualite', which in other words means you can get some very fine bread here, the sort of crusty-outside and pillow-soft-inside bread you associate with a Parisian *boulangerie*. Gourmet sandwiches and light pastries make for a refreshing Lincoln Rd lunch stop.

Front Porch Cafe   AMERICAN $$

(Map p44; www.frontporchoceandrive.com; 1418 Ocean Dr; mains $10-18; ☺7am-11pm) A blue-and-white escape from the madness of the cruising scene, the Porch has been serving excellent salads, sandwiches and the like since 1990 (eons by South Beach standards). Weekend brunch is justifiably mobbed; the big omelets are delicious, as are the fat pancakes and strong coffees.

NORTHERN MIAMI BEACH

▲ Steve's Pizza   PIZZA $
TOP CHOICE

(☑305-233-4561; www.stevespizzas.net; 18063 Dixie Hwy; pizzas from $10; ☺10:30am-11pm, to midnight weekends, 11am-11pm Sun) So many pizza chains compete for the attention of tourists in South Beach, but ask a Miami Beach local where to get the best pizza and they'll tell you about Steve's. This is New York–style pizza, thin crust and handmade with care and good ingredients. New branches of Steve's are opening elsewhere in Miami, all in decidedly nontouristy areas, which preserves that feeling of authenticity.

Indomania   INDONESIAN $$

(Map p52; ☑305-535-6332; www.indomaniarestaurant.com; 131 26th St; mains $17-28; ☺6pm-10:30pm Tue-Sun) There's a lot of watered-down Asian cuisine in Miami; Indomania bucks this trend with an authentic (and welcome) execution of dishes from the largest country in Southeast Asia. Dishes reflect Indonesia's diversity, ranging from chicken in coconut curry to snapper grilled in banana leaves to gut-busting rijsttafel, a sort of buffet of small, tapas-style dishes that reflects the culinary character of particular Indonesian regions. Indomania is delicious, unique and decidedly off the tourist trail, and the service is enthusiastically friendly to boot.

Roasters' n Toasters   DELI $
(Map p52; www.roastersntoasters.com; 525 Arthur Godfrey Rd; mains $8-16; ⊙6:30am-3:30pm) Miami Beach has one of the largest Jewish populations in the US, so people here expect a lot out of their delis. Given the crowds and the satisfied smiles of customers, Roasters' n Toasters meets the demanding standards of its target demographic thanks to juicy deli meat, fresh bread, crispy bagels and warm latkes. Sliders (mini-sandwiches) are served on Jewish challah bread, an innovation that's as charming as it is tasty.

Cafe Prima Pasta   ARGENTINE $$
(Map p52; ☑305-867-0106; www.primapasta .com; 414 71st St; mains $13-24; ⊙5pm-midnight Mon-Sat, from 4pm Sun) We're not sure what's better at this Argentine-Italian place: the much-touted pasta, which deserves every one of the accolades heaped on it (try the gnocchi), or the atmosphere, which captures the dignified sexiness of Buenos Aires. Actually, it's no contest: you're the winner, as long as you eat here.

Fifi's Place   SEAFOOD $$
(Map p52; ☑305-865-5665; www.fifisseafood.com; 6934 Collins Ave; mains $13-30; ⊙noon-midnight) Latin seafood is the name of the game here – Fifi's does delicious seafood paella, a dish that mixes the supporting cast of *The Little Mermaid* with Spanish rice, and an equally good seafood *parrillada*, which draws on the same ingredients and grills them with garlic butter. Awesome.

Shuckers   AMERICAN $
(Map p52; ☑305-866-1570; www.shuckersbarand grill.com; 1819 79th St Causeway; mains $8-19; ⊙11am-late) With excellent views overlooking the waters from the 79th St Causeway, Shuckers has to be one of the best-positioned restaurants around. This is as much a bar as it is a grill, and as such the food is pub grub: burgers, fried fish and the like. We come here for one reason: the chicken wings. They're basted in several mouthwatering sauces, deep-fried and then grilled again, which results in what we can only describe as small pieces of heaven on a bone. We could sit here and devour a flock

of poultry if our willpower was low. Kitchen closes around 9pm.

El Rey del Chivito   URUGUAYAN $
(Map p52; ☑305-864-5566; www.elreydelchivito .com; 6987 Collins Ave; mains under $15; ⊙11am-midnight) Heart, meet the 'King of Chivitos' and his signature dish: a sandwich of steak, ham, cheese, fried eggs and mayonnaise (there may have been lettuce, peppers and tomatoes too, but the other ingredients just laughed at them). Now run, heart, run away! That's just the basic, by the way, and it comes with fries. We've never heard of Uruguayan restaurants in the US, and now we know why: anyone who could have spread the word died of a coronary long ago. El Rey also serves Uruguayan pizza; try it topped with *faina,* long strips of bread mixed with cheese and peppers.

La Perrada de Edgar   HOT DOGS $
(Map p52; 6976 Collins Ave; hot dogs from $5; ⊙10am-2am) Back in the day, Colombia's most (in)famous export to Miami was cocaine. But seriously, what's powder got on La Perrada and its kookily delicious hot dogs that were devised by some Dr Evil of the frankfurter world? Don't believe us? Try an *especial,* topped with plums, pineapple and whipped cream. How about shrimp and potato sticks? Apparently these are normal hot-dog toppings in Colombia. The homemade lemonade also goes down a treat.

DOWNTOWN MIAMI
Emily's Restaurante   LATIN AMERICAN $
(Map p56; ☑305-375-0013; 204 NE 1st St; mains $4-8; ⊙7am-4:30pm) A few bucks gets you two eggs, toast and coffee here; $5 gets you one of the best buffet deals in town. There are daily specials of Colombian, Cuban and Spanish cuisine: chicken soup, oxtail and *lengua en salsa* (marinated tongue).

La Moon   COLOMBIAN $
(Map p56; www.lamoonrestaurantmiami.com; 144 SW 8th St; meals $6-15) Nothing – and we're not necessarily saying this in a good way – soaks up the beer like a Colombian hot dog topped with eggs and potato sticks. Or fried pork belly and pudding. These delicacies are the preferred food and drink of Miami's 24-hour party people, and the best place for this wicked fare is here, within stumbling distance of bars like Tobacco Road. To really fit in, order a *refajo:* Colombian beer (Aguila) with Colombian soda (preferably the red one).

KEEP ON TRUCKIN'

The food-truck craze has rumbled into Miami with a vengeance. If you're not familiar with the trend, mobile kitchens drive around a city, perching on select spots where they serve ready-to-go, restaurant-quality fare for cheap – like fast food, except it's fast but not crap. Food trucks tend to have favored target destinations, but there are ways to track them down, with Twitter being the most popular. There are now more than 25 food trucks in Miami, and many congregate at **Tobacco Road** (626 S Miami Ave) on Sunday from 1pm to 5pm. Here's some of our favorite purveyors of mobile cuisine; we've included Twitter handles so you can follow their locations online:

» **Purple People Eatery** (@purpleppleatery; www.purpleppleatery.com; mains $4-8) Battered mahimahi, herb-crusted mac 'n' cheese and gourmet bison burgers.

» **Cheese Me** (@cheesememobile; www.cheeseme.com; mains $4-12) Gourmet grilled cheese, shoestring fries, braised short ribs and artisanal breads.

» **Miso Hungry** (@misohungryFT; www.misohungrymobile.com; mains $3-8) Asian-fusion options from curry to a pork burger with cilantro mayo, to vegan tofu with soy sauce.

» **Slow Food Truck** (@SlowFoodTruck; www.slowfoodtruck.com; mains $4-8) Seasonal, local food – a changing menu ensures variety and straight deliciousness.

Soya e Pomodoro   ITALIAN $

(Map p56; ☎305-381-9511; www.soyaepomodoro miami.com; 120 NE 1st St; mains $9-16; ⊙11:30am-4pm Mon-Fri, 7-11:30pm Thu-Sat) S&P is a nickname that sounds suspiciously corporate, but Soya e Pomodoro is anything but. Instead, this feels like a bohemian retreat for Italian artists and filmmakers, who can dine on bowls of fresh, mouth-watering pasta under vintage posters, glittery accoutrements and rainbow paintings and wall-hangings. Think what would happen if hippies were dropped into the set of *Casablanca*. As per this vibe, readings, jazz shows and other arts events take place here on select evenings.

Fresco California   MEDITERRANEAN $

(Map p56; ☎305-858-0608; 1744 SW 3rd Ave; mains $9-15; ⊙11:30am-3:30pm Mon-Fri, 5-10:30pm Mon-Thu, to 11pm Fri, 11am-11pm Sat) Fresco serves all kinds of West Coast takes on the Mediterranean palate. Relax in the candlelit backyard dining room, which feels like an Italian porch in summer when the weather is right (ie almost always). Pear and walnut salad and portobello sandwiches are lovely, while the pumpkin-stuffed ravioli is heaven on a platter. The prices are fairly low, but you'll inevitably be tempted to get wine, have multiple courses and turn a meal here into a long night out.

Azul   FUSION $$$

(Map p56; ☎305-913-8358; Mandarin Oriental Miami, 500 Brickell Key Dr; mains $30-72; ⊙7-11pm Mon-Sat) Falling-water windows, clean metallic spaces and curving copper facades complement one of the nicest views of the city. The Scandi-tastic decor works in harmony with a menu that marries the Mediterranean to Asia; try the oysters wrapped in beef and *hamachi* carpaccio.

La Cocotte   CARIBBEAN $

(Map p56; ☎305-377-6515; www.lacocottemiami .com; 150 W Flagler St, Suite 175; mains under $10; ⊙7:30am-3pm Mon-Fri) French Caribbean fare? Yes please! This innovative spot was sorely needed to spice up the otherwise slightly bland lunchtime fare usually found Downtown. The plantains Creole, served with scotch-bonnet slaw (hot!) and pulled pork or shrimp, or hearty brown stew chicken with carrots, onion and rosemary, are all as rich and tasty as they sound. Expect to leave lunch with a slightly expanded paunch.

Garcia's   SEAFOOD $

(Map p56; ☎305-375-0765; 398 NW River Dr; mains $8-18; ⊙11am-9:30pm) Crowds of Cuban office workers lunch at Garcia's, which feels more like you're in a smugglers' seafood shack than the financial district. Expect occasionally spotty service (a bad thing), freshly caught-and-cooked fish (a good thing) and pleasantly seedy views of the Miami River.

Mini Healthy Deli   DELI $

(Map p56; ☎305-523-2244; Station Mall, 48 E Flagler St; mains $6-10; ⊙11am-3pm; ☑) This excellent cafe, tucked into a half-vacant minimall, is where chef Carlos Bedoya works solo and churns out remarkably fresh and delicious specials such as grilled tilapia, fresh salad, and rice and beans. There are only two little tables, but it's worth waiting – or standing while you eat.

Granny Feelgoods HEALTH FOOD $

(Map p56; ☎305-377-9600; 25 W Flagler St; mains $9-15; ☺7am-4pm Mon-Fri; ✍) If you need karmic balance (or just tasty vegetarian fare), try this neighborhood health-food staple. Located next to the courthouse, Granny's must have the highest lawyer-to-bean-sprouts ratio in the USA. Try simple, vegetarian dishes such as tofu sandwiches and spinach lasagna. Carnivores are catered for too – there's a turkey burger.

WYNWOOD, DESIGN DISTRICT & LITTLE HAITI

TOP CHOICE Señora Martinez AMERICAN $$$

(Map p62; ☎305-424-9079; www.sramartinez .com; 3252 NE 1st Ave; mains $13-30; ☺noon-3pm Tue-Fri, 6-11pm Tue-Thu, to midnight Fri & Sat, to 10pm Sun; ✍) At the time of our research, Señora Martinez was the most exciting top-end restaurant in Miami, pushing the boundaries of experimentation and plain good food. The menu is eclectic, with no one overriding regional influence, besides perhaps Miami, entrepôt that it is. Squid-ink risotto comes with chimichurri sauce; roasted bone marrow is scooped out next to pickled onions; duck sausage swims in port wine. The cocktail menu is as exciting as the food; with bartenders mixing up stuff like espresso tequila, fernet and honey, or rum, allspice, cider and maple syrup. Eat up, drink up, revel in your own decadent excess and hit the town.

✍ Sustain AMERICAN $$$

(Map p62; ☎305-424-9079; www.sustainmiami .com; 3252 NE 1st Ave; mains $13-30; ☺11:30am-3pm, 5-10:30pm; ✍) Sustain is one of the leading – and more affordable – purveyors of locally sourced, organically grown, raised and caught food in the Miami area. The lovely dining room blends smooth white walls with warm wood paneling and rounded metallic edges. The food is fantastic; try the bright, meltingly textured fish sandwich or fired chicken swimming in creamy kale and barbecued beans. The menu changes with the season. Vegetarians and vegans are always catered to, although carnivores will find plenty to enjoy as well.

Michael's Genuine Food & Drink AMERICAN $$$

(Map p62; ☎305-573-5550; www.michaelsgenu ine.com; Atlas Plaza, 130 NE 40th St; mains $16-36; ☺11:30am-3pm Mon-Fri, 5:30-11pm Mon-Thu, to midnight Fri & Sat, 11am-2:30pm & 5:30-10pm Sun; ✍) The 'genuine' in Michael Schwartz' restaurant name refers to its use of locally sourced ingredients and healthy dose of innovation, moderated by its respect for the classics. Hence, the pork shoulder in parsley sauce and cheese grits that taste as though your grandma has just became a cordon-bleu chef. The chocolate-and-red interior feels cheerful and welcoming rather than snobbish and intimidating, and that goes for the attentive waitstaff as well.

Cheese Course CHEESE $

(Map p62; ☎786-220-6681; www.thecheesecourse .com; 3451 NE 1st Ave; mains under $16; ☺10:30am-9pm Sun-Wed, to 10pm Thu, 10:30am-11pm Fri & Sat; ✍) We love the idea at this place – pick out a few cheeses with the help of the staff and have them assemble a platter for you with fresh bread, candied walnuts, cornichons or whatever other accoutrement you so desire. There are also nice sandwiches, spreads and preserves, but for our money you can't beat a perfect lunch here of fermented dairy goodness.

Mandolin GREEK $$

(Map p62; ☎305-576-6066; www.mandolinmiami .com; 4312 NE 2nd Ave; mains $12-26; ☺noon-11pm Mon-Sat; ✍) Mandolin doesn't just provide good Greek food – although that is present in the form of fresh fish grilled in lemon and olive oil, tomato and Turkish chorizo sandwiches and light meze like smoked eggplant and creamy yogurt. What Mandolin also provides is excellent Greek atmosphere. It's all Aegean whites and blues, colors that come to life under the strong, melting Miami sun, especially if you sit in the back courtyard, shaded by the same trees that stretch over the surrounding Buena Vista neighborhood.

Lemoni Café CAFE $

(Map p62; ☎305-571-5080; www.mylemonicafe .com; 4600 NE 2nd Ave; mains under $10; ☺11am-10:30pm; ✍) Lemoni is as bright as its name suggests, a cute, cozy hole in the wall that serves up superlative sandwiches, wraps and salads. The salami sandwich with greens and olive oil is a simple revelation, and we'd probably rob a bank to get another slice of its Key lime pie. Located in the pretty Buena

NORTH BISCAYNE BOULEVARD

As North Biscayne Blvd continues to gentrify, better and better restaurants are opening up. Here are some winners from this foodie find:

Michy's (☎305-759-2001; 6927 Biscayne Blvd; meals $28-43; ☉6-10:30pm, 5:30-11pm Fri & Sat, Tue-Fri, 5:30-10pm Sun; ☑) Blue-and-white pop decor. Organic, locally sourced ingredients. A stylish, fantastical bar where Alice could drink before painting Wonderland red. Welcome to Michelle 'Michy' Bernstein's culinary lovechild – one of the brightest stars in Miami's culinary constellation. The emphasis is on good food and fun. The 'half plates' concept lets you halve an order and mix up delicious gastronomic fare, such as foie gras on corn cakes, chicken pot pie with wild mushrooms, white almond gazpacho, and blue-cheese croquettes.

Red Light Little River (☎305-757-7773; 7700 Biscayne Blvd; mains $14-28; ☉Tue-Thu 6-11pm, to midnight Fri & Sat) New Orleans comfort food gets mixed up with Florida ingredients in this laid-back, excellent-value eatery perched above its namesake, Little River. The result is cuisine both clean and rich; sour oranges with sea scallops and hearty lentils; spicy shrimp-grilled-cheese sandwiches; and skirt steak in decadent rosemary and gorgonzola demiglace.

Karma Car Wash (☎305-759-1392; www.karmacarwash.com; 7010 Biscayne Blvd; sandwiches & tapas $4.50-8; ☉8am-8pm) This ecofriendly car wash also serves soy chai lattes, organic tapas and good microbrews. The idea could have been be precocious in execution, but it ends up being fun – more fun than your average wash 'n' wait, anyway. Of course, hybrid drivers get a 25% discount, and the bar becomes a lounge at 8pm, with DJs spinning as you wonder, 'Should I have gotten the wax finish?'

Honey Tree (Map p62; ☎305-756-1696; 5138 Biscayne Blvd; mains under $10; ☉8am-8pm Mon-Thu, to 7pm Fri, 9am-6pm Sat; ☑) The Honey Tree is a health-food store that happens to serve excellent juices, smoothies and what many consider to be Miami's best vegan lunch. What's on offer varies day by day, but rest assured it will be cheap (it's priced by weight) and delicious. Lunch is usually served from noon to 2pm, but keep in mind that food often runs out due to high demand.

Jimmy's East Side Diner (☎305-754-3692; 7201 Biscayne Blvd; mains $5-13; ☉6:30am-4pm) Come to Jimmy's, a classic greasy spoon (that happens to be very gay-friendly; note the rainbow flag out front), for big cheap breakfasts of omelets, French toast or pancakes, and turkey clubs and burgers later in the day.

Vista neighborhood, this is a perfect place to grab a sidewalk alfresco lunch or dinner.

Enriqueta's　　　　　　　　　　LATIN **$**
(Map p62; ☎305-573-4681; 186 NE 29th St; mains $5-8; ☉6:30am-3:45pm Mon-Fri, to 2pm Sat) Back in the day, Puerto Ricans, not installation artists, ruled Wynwood. Have a taste of those times in this perpetually packed roadhouse, where the Latin-diner ambience is as strong as the steaming shots of *cortadito* (Cuban-style coffee) served at the counter. Balance the local gallery fluff with a steak-and-potato-stick sandwich.

Lost & Found Saloon　　　　　MEXICAN **$**
(Map p62; ☎305-576-1008; www.thelostandfound saloon-miami.com; 185 NW 36th St; mains $10-17; ☉11am-3am; ☑) The service is as friendly as the omelets and burritos are awesome (which is to say, very) at this little Wynwood spot, the sort of saloon where microbrews

are on tap and the wine list reads like a year abroad. Come the evening, this turns into a fun hipster kind of bar.

Garden of Eatin'　　　　　　　VEGAN **$**
(Map p62; ☎305-754-8050; 136 NW 62nd St; mains under $10; ☉11am-9pm Mon-Sat; ☑) The Garden of Eatin' is run by a Rastafarian Haitian that serves up *i-tal* (sort of like Rastafarian kosher – invariably vegetarian and in this case, vegan-friendly) food for customers. The menu changes a lot, and can include anything from soy fish to tofu and greens to brown rice in pea sauce. The Garden is a one-man show and located in a fairly tough part of Little Haiti, so you may want to call ahead to see if it's open. Cash only. A drum circle is held here on Monday evenings.

Lester's　　　　　　　　　　　CAFE **$**
(Map p62; ☎305-456-1784; www.lestersmiami .com; 2519 NE 2nd Ave; mains under $5; ☉9am-

10pm Tue-Thurs, 9am-midnight Fri & Sat) Lester's is the first of what will doubtless be the model for many future cafes in Wynwood: studiolike wide interior, pop art (for some reason focused on mustaches), graphic-design bookshelves and of course, wi-fi, coffees and snacks.

KEY BISCAYNE

Boater's Grill
SEAFOOD $$

(Map p64; ☑305-361-0080; 1200 S Crandon Blvd; mains $14-34; ⊙9am-9pm) Located in Crandon Park, this waterfront restaurant (actually there's water below and all around) feels like a Chesapeake Bay sea house from up north, except the menu is packed with South Florida maritime goodness: stone crabs, ma-himahi and lobster paella.

Rusty Pelican
SEAFOOD $$

(☑305-361-3818; 3201 Rickenbacker Causeway; mains $18-30; ⊙9am-sundown) More than the fare itself, it's the panoramic skyline views – among the best in Miami – that draw the faithful and romantic to this airy, tropical restaurant. But if you do come for a sunset drink, the fresh air could certainly seduce you into staying for some of the surf 'n' turf menu, which is good enough considering the setting and lack of options.

Oasis
CUBAN $

(Map p64; 19 Harbor Dr; mains $5-12; ⊙8am-8pm) This excellent Cuban cafe has a customer base that ranges from the working poor to city players, and the socioeconomic barriers come tumbling down fast as folks sip high-octane Cuban coffee. Between the super-strong coffee and *masas de puerco* – marinated pork chunks, which go great with hot sauce – we're in hole-in-the-wall heaven.

LITTLE HAVANA

Hy Vong Vietnamese Restaurant
VIETNAMESE $

(☑305-446-3674; www.hyvong.com; 3458 SW 8th; mains $7-22; ⊙6-11pm Wed-Sun, closed mid-late Aug) In a neighborhood full of exiles from a communist regime, it makes sense to find a Vietnamese restaurant. And it's telling that despite all the great Latin food around, Lit-tle Havanans still wait hours for a seat here. Why? Because this great Vietnamese food (with little touches of Florida, like Florida-style mango marinade) combines quality produce with Southeast Asian spice and a penchant for rich flavors inherited from the French colonial past. Just be prepared to wait a long time for your culinary reward. Check the website to learn about Hy Vong's cooking classes. Hy Vong is on 8th St, locat-ed about 2 miles west of the heart of Calle Ocho.

Islas Canarias
CUBAN $

(☑305-649-0440; 285 NW 27th Ave; mains $8-19; ⊙7am-11pm) Islas may not look like much, sitting in a strip mall, but it serves some of the best Cuban in Miami. The *ropa vieja* (shredded beef) is delicious and there are nice Spanish touches on the menu (the own-er's father is from the Canary Islands, hence the restaurant's name). Don't pass up the signature homemade chips, especially the ones cut from plantains.

El Cristo
CUBAN $

(Map p66; ☑305-643-9992; 1543 SW 8th St; mains $6-18; ⊙7am-11pm) A popular hangout among locals, the down-to-earth El Cristo has op-tions from all over the Spanish-speaking world. Lots of people say it's as good as Calle Ocho gets. The menu has daily specials, but the standout is fish – try it fried for a local version of fish & chips, or take away some excellent fish empanadas and *croquetas* (deep-fried in breadcrumbs). The outdoor area is an excellent perch for enjoying 8th St eye candy.

Versailles
CUBAN $

(☑305-444-0240; 3555 SW 8th St; mains $5-20; ⊙8am-2am) Versailles (ver-*sigh*-yay) is an in-stitution, and a lot of younger Cubans will tell you it's an overrated institution. We dis-agree – the food may not be the best Cuban in Miami, but it's certainly quite good (the ground beef in a gratin sauce is particu-larly good). And besides, older Cubans and Miami's Latin political elite still love com-ing here, so you've got a real chance to rub elbows with a who's who of Miami's most prominent Latin citizens. It's located 2 miles west of central Calle Ocho.

Yambo
LATIN AMERICAN $

(off Map p66; 1643 SW 1st St; mains under $10; ⊙24 hr) If you're a bit drunk in the mid-dle of the night and can find a cab or a friend willing to drive all the way out to Little Havana, direct them to Yambo. We've never actually been here during the day, although the restaurant is surely a pretty place for lunch or breakfast. At night Yambo does a roaring stock in trade selling trays and take-away boxes about to burst with juicy slices of carne asada, piles of rice and beans and sweet fried plantains. If you're going to soak up beer, this is a great sponge.

Los Pinareños Frutería   FRUIT STAND $
(Map p66; 1334 SW 8th St; snacks & drinks $2-4; ☺7am-7pm, to 2pm Sun) Nothing says refreshment on a sweat-stained Miami afternoon like a long, cool glass of fruit smoothie at this popular juice and veggie stand – try the sugarcane juice for something particularly sweet and bracing. The produce is pretty fresh and flavorful too.

El Rey de Las Fritas   BURGERS $
(Map p66; www.reydelasfritas.com; 1821 SW 8th St; snacks $2-3; ☺8am-10:30pm Mon-Sat) If you've never had a *frita* (Cuban-style burger) make your peace with McDonald's and come down to El Rey with the lawyers, developers, construction workers and every other slice of Miami's Latin life. These *fritas* are big, juicy and served under a mountain of shoestring fries. Plus, the *batidos* (Latin American milkshakes) definitely brings the boys to the yard.

COCONUT GROVE

Xixon   SPANISH $$
(☑305-854-9350; 1801 SW 22nd St; tapas $8-15; ☺11am-10pm Mon-Thu, to 11pm Fri & Sat, closed Sun) It takes a lot to stand out in Miami's crowded tapas-spot stakes. Having a Basque-country butcher-and-baker-turned-hip interior is a good start. Bread that has a crackling crust and a soft center, delicate explosions of *bacalao* (cod) fritters and the best eels cooked in garlic we've ever eaten secures Xixon's status as a top tapas contender. The *bocadillo* (sandwiches), with their blood-red Serrano ham and salty Manchego cheese, are great picnic fare. This place is a few miles north of the central Coconut Grove area.

Lulu   AMERICAN $$
(Map p69; ☑305-447-5858; 3105 Commodore Plaza; mains $9-25; ☺11:30am-1am Mon & Tue, to 2am Wed, to 3am Thu & Fri, 9am-3am Sat, 9am-midnight Sun; ☑) Lulu is the Grove's exemplar of using local, organic ingredients to provide gourmet versions of comfort food in a nice outdoor setting. Well, there is an interior dining space, and it is lovely, but the outdoor seating, shaded by the spreading boughs of Coconut Grove's many trees, is where we prefer to be. The truffle mac 'n' cheese is rich and immensely satisfying, while the Lulu burger is to die for.

Green Street Cafe   AMERICAN $$
(Map p69; ☑305-567-0662; 3468 Main Hwy; mains $10-23; ☺7:30am-1am) Sidewalk spots don't get more popular (and many say more delicious) than Green Street, where the Grove's young and gorgeous congregate at sunset. There's an excellent mix of lamburgers with goat cheese, salmon salads, occasional art shows and general indie defiance of Grove gentrification, which makes for an idiosyncratic dining experience.

Jaguar   LATIN $$
(Map p69; ☑305-444-0216; www.jaguarspot.com; 3067 Grand Ave; mains $17-32; ☺11:30am-11pm Mon-Thu, to 11:30 Fri & Sat, 11am-11pm Sun) The menu spans the Latin world, but really, everyone's here for the ceviche 'spoon bar.' The idea: pick from six styles of ceviche (raw, marinated seafood), ranging from swordfish with cilantro to corvina in lime juice, and pull a culinary version of DIY. It's novel and fun, and the $2 ceviche varieties are pretty damn delicious. Other mains include different kinds of grilled meats and fish – endearing in their simplicity, but lacking the tasty complexity of the ceviche.

George's in the Grove   FRENCH $$
(Map p69; ☑305-444-7878; 3145 Commodore Plaza; mains $13-29; ☺10am-11pm, Mon-Fri, from 8am Sat & Sun) George's has a manically over-the-top menu that throws in everything from French to Italian to Latin plus the kitchen sink. This all comes packaged with manic, over-the-top decor that looks like a cozy attic just exploded all over Coconut Grove. Mains are rich in the best rural French culinary tradition; standbys include steak frites, duck confit and grilled branzino.

Last Carrot   VEGETARIAN $
(Map p69; ☑305-445-0805; 3133 Grand Ave; mains $6; ☺10am-6:30pm Mon-Fri, to 4pm Sat, closed Sun; ☑) Folks of all walks, corporate suits included, come here for fresh juice, delicious wraps (veggie options are great but the tuna melt is divine) and old-Grove neighborliness. The Carrot's endurance next to massive CocoWalk is testament to the quality of its good-for-your-body food served in a good-for-your-soul setting.

CORAL GABLES

TOP CHOICE El Carajo   SPANISH $$
(☑305-856-2424; www.elcarajointernationaltapas andwines.com; 2465 SW 17th Ave; tapas $3.50-15; ☺11:30am-10pm Mon-Thu, to midnight Fri & Sat,

1-8pm Sun) Pass the Penzoil please. We know it is cool to tuck restaurants into unassuming spots, but the Citgo station on SW 17th Ave? Really? Really. Walk past the motor oil into a Granadan wine cellar and try not to act too fazed. And now the food, which is absolutely incredible: chorizo in cider blends burn, smoke and juice; frittatas are comfortably filling; and *sardinas* and *boquerones*... wow. These sardines and anchovies cooked with a bit of salt and olive oil are dizzyingly delicious. It is tempting to keep El Carajo a secret, but not singing its praises would be lying and we're not going to lie: if there's one restaurant you shouldn't miss in Miami, it's this one.

La Palme d'Or
FRENCH $$$

(Map p72; ☑305-913-3201; www.biltmorehotel.com/dining/palme.php; Biltmore Hotel, 1200 Anastasia Ave; fixed menus $39-89; ☺6:30-10:30pm Tue-Thu, to 11pm Fri & Sat) One of the most acclaimed French restaurants in the USA, Phillipe Ruiz' Palme is the culinary match for the Jazz Age opulence that ensconces it. With its white-gloved, old-world class and US attention to service, unmuddled by pretensions of hipness, the Palme captures, in one elegant stroke, all the exclusivity a dozen South Beach restaurants could never grasp. The menu shifts seasonally but remains consistently magnificent at one of Miami's best splurges.

Matsuri
JAPANESE $

(Map p72; ☑305-663-1615; 5759 Bird Rd; mains $7-20; ☺11:30am-2:30pm Tue-Fri, 5:30-10:30pm Tue-Sat) Note the customers here: Matsuri, tucked into a nondescript shopping center, is consistently packed with Japanese people. They don't want scene; they want a taste of home, although many of the diners are actually South American Japanese who order *unagi* (eels) in Spanish. Spicy *toro* (fatty tuna) and scallions, grilled mackerel with natural salt, and an ocean of raw fish are all *oishi* (delicious). The excellent $8 bento lunch makes the rest of the day somewhat disappointing in comparison.

Seasons 52
FUSION $$

(Map p72; ☑305-442-8552; 321 Miracle Mile; mains $14-32; ☺11:30am-11pm, to midnight Fri & Sat, to 10pm Sun) We love the concept and the execution at Seasons 52. The concept? A menu that partially rotates on a weekly basis depending on what is seasonally available (now the title makes sense). The execution?

Warm flatbreads overlaid with sharp melted cheese and steak; tiger shrimp tossed in a light pasta and chili that manages elegance and heartiness all at once.

Pascal's on Ponce
FRENCH $$$

(Map p72; ☑305-444-2024; www.pascalmiami.com; 2611 Ponce de León Blvd; mains $34-40; ☺11:30am-2:30pm Mon-Fri, 6-10pm Mon-Thu, to 11pm Fri & Sat) They're fighting the good fight here: sea scallops with beef short rib, crème brûlée and other French fine-dining classics set the elegant stage at this neighborhood hangout, a favorite night out among Coral Gables foodies who appreciate time-tested standards. The menu and the atmosphere rarely changes, and frankly we think this a good thing: if it ain't broke...

Caffe Abbracci
ITALIAN $$

(Map p72; ☑305-441-0700; www.caffeabbracci.com; 318 Aragon Ave; mains $17-37; ☺11:30am-3:30pm Mon-Fri, 6pm-midnight daily) Perfect moments in Coral Gables come easy. Here's a simple formula: you, a loved one, a muggy Miami evening, some delicious pasta and a glass of red at a sidewalk table at Abbracci – one of the finest Italian restaurants in the Gables.

GREATER MIAMI

Lots of Lox
DELI $

(www.originallotsoflox.com; 14995 S Dixie Hwy; mains $4-13; ☺8am-2:30pm) In a city with no shortage of delis, especially in mid-Miami Beach, who would have thought some of the best chopped liver on rye could be found in this unassuming place all the way down in Palmetto Bay? It is bustling, friendly and the excellent lunch meats sneer at their cousins over on Arthur Godfrey Rd, secure in their dominance of Greater Miami's deli ranks.

Graziano's
STEAKHOUSE $$

(☑305-225-0008; www.parrilla.com; 9227 SW 40th St; mains $14-34; ☺11am-11pm) People love to argue over who does the best South American steak in Miami, but among the Argentinian population the general consensus seems to be this very traditional *parilla* (grill), located on a strip of gas stations on Bird Rd. Everything is plucked out of Buenos Aires: the quebracho wood on the grill, the Argentinian customers and, most of all, the racks of *lomo* (steak), sweetbreads and blood sausage, gristly bits beloved by *portenos* (Buenos Aires natives), which are tough to find in more Yankee-friendly establishments.

SOUTH BEACH SIPPIN'

Starbucks has a pretty iron grip on the Miami coffee scene (we don't count stand-up Cuban coffee counters, as you can't sit there and read a book or work on your laptop, although if you speak Spanish, they're a good place for hearing local gossip). That said, there are some options besides Starbucks in Miami Beach.

» **A La Folie** (Map p44; www.alafoliecafe.com; 516 Española Way; mains $5-15; ⊙11am-8pm; ☑) A *tres* French cafe where the waiters have great accents. Why yes, we would like 'zee moka.'

» **Segafredo L'Originale** (Map p44; 1040 Lincoln Rd; mains $5-15; ⊙10:30am-1am; ☑) Immensely popular with Europeans and South Americans, this chic cafe always seems packed with gorgeous people. Credited with being the first Lincoln Rd business to open its trade to the outside street.

» **Nespresso** (Map p44; 1111 Lincoln Rd; mains $5-15; ⊙10:30am-11pm; ☑) This futuristic cafe, all done up in geometric swirls and shapes, has excellent (if overpriced) coffee.

🍷 Drinking

Too many people assume Miami's nightlife is all about being superattractive, super-rich and supersnooty. Disavow yourself of this notion, which only describes a small slice of the scene in South Beach. Miami has an intense variety of bars to pick from that range from grotty dives to beautiful – but still laid-back – lounges and nightclubs. Not to say you can't spot celebrities if you want to...

Dedicated gay nightlife in Miami consists largely of some South Beach clubs (and club nights) and a string of bars in the area around North Biscayne Blvd.

SOUTH BEACH

TOP CHOICE Abraxas BAR
(Map p48; 407 Meridian Ave) Abraxas is open, uncrowded, located in a classical deco building, serves fantastic beer from around the USA and the world, and has clientele and staff who are the friendly sort, the types who will quickly make friends with a stranger and then keep said stranger entertained and inebriated until closing time. It's tucked away in a residential area; take your traveling friends here and they'll wonder how you ever found it.

TOP CHOICE Room BAR
(Map p48; www.theotheroom.com; 100 Collins Ave) The Room's a gem: a crowded, dimly lit boutique beer bar where you can guzzle the best (brew) Miami has to offer and gawk at the best (hotties) South Beach has to show off. It's hip as hell, but the attitude is as low-key as the sexy mood lighting. Just beware, it gets crowded and it can be tough to find seats as the night goes on.

Abbey Brewery BAR
(Map p44; www.abbeybrewinginc.com; 1115 16th St) The only brew-pub in South Beach is on the untouristed end of South Beach (near Alton Rd). It's friendly and packed with folks listening to the Grateful Dead and slinging back some excellent homebrew: give Father Theo's stout or the Immaculate IPA a shot.

Jazid LOUNGE
(Map p44; www.jazid.net; 1342 Washington Ave) While the downstairs caters to folks seeking a mellow, candlelit spot to hear live jazz, soul and funk bands, the upstairs lounge has DJs spinning soul, funk and hip-hop to a cool, multiculti crowd. By being cool and not trying to be, this place has remained popular while places all around it have come and gone.

Zeke's BAR
(Map p44; 625 Lincoln Rd) Zeke's is a great beer bar and one of the few nightspots on Lincoln Rd where it feels like the focus is more on having fun than looking prettier than anyone else. The beer selection is pretty awesome – they have Beer Lao, from Laos! That's a find in the USA, as are the dozens of other brews.

Ted's Hideaway SPORTS BAR
(Map p48; 124 2nd St) Somewhere in the Florida panhandle is a bumpin', fabulous gay club, which clearly switched places with Ted's, a no-nonsense, pool table and sports-showin' 'lounge' smack in the middle of SoFi's elegance.

B Bar BAR
(Map p44; Betsy Hotel, 1440 Ocean Ave) This smallish basement bar, tucked under the Betsy Hotel, has two salient features. One

is a crowd of the beautiful, in-the-know SoBe-tastic types you expect at South Beach nightspots. The other is an odd, low-hanging reflective ceiling, built out of a sort of wobbly material that sinks in like soft Jell-o and ripples like a stone in a pond when you touch it. It's a pretty cool thing to witness, especially when all sorts of drunk, beautiful people try to (literally) raise the roof.

Lost Weekend
BAR
(Map p44; 218 Española Way) The Weekend is a grimy, sweaty, slovenly dive, filled with pool tables, cheap domestics and – hell yeah – Golden Tee arcade games and Big Buck Hunter. God bless it. Popular with local waiters, kitchen staff and bartenders.

Sagamore Bar
BAR
(Map p44; www.sagamorehotel.com; 1671 Collins Ave) Should you need a more refined vibe than the madness at the Delano (p88), walk into this cool white lobby, sit across from the rotating art projects and have a drink.

Mac's Club Deuce Bar
BAR
(Map p44; 222 14th St) The oldest bar in Miami Beach (established in 1926), the Deuce is a real neighborhood bar and hype-free zone. It's just straight-up seediness, which depending on your outlook can be quite refreshing. Plan to see everyone from transgendered ladies to construction workers – some hooking up, some talking rough, all having a good time.

Chesterfield Hotel Bar
BAR
(Map p48; Chesterfield Hotel, 855 Collins Ave) Perch on some prime Collins people-watching real estate and get crunk on the hip-hop and zebra-stripe theme they've got going. You'd think this would be a start-the-night-out sort of place, but the setting's so fly, folks end up stationary, sipping on mad martinis until they stumble into their rooms.

Dewey's Tavern
BAR
(Map p48; 852 Alton Rd) Dewey's is an art-deco dive (really; the exterior is a little gem of the genre) and it's as unpretentious as the best sordid watering holes out. Come here to get wasted and menace the crowds seeking serenity on quiet Alton Rd (just kidding – behave yourself!).

Bond Street Lounge
LOUNGE
(Map p44; www.townhousehotel.com/bond.asp; Townhouse Hotel, 150 20th St) The crowd in this white-and-red candy-cane-striped hotel bar like their litchitinis (lychee martinis) over sushi. Throw yourself over a white couch or cylindrical white ottoman, order up, sip and stare at the crowd.

NORTHERN MIAMI BEACH

Circa 39 Bar
LOUNGE
(Map p52; 3900 Collins Ave) Tucked off to the back of Circa 39's moody front lobby, the designer dream bar has a warm, welcoming feel to it. Definitely stop in for a cosmopolitan if you're up this way, before sauntering across the street and checking out the nighttime ocean.

Cabana Beach Club
BAR
(Map p52; 4525 Collins Ave) The back-porch bar at the Eden Roc is a surprisingly laid-back place for a drink. That's not to say the folks here aren't a beautiful bunch – they are – but the vibe is more 'chill out and enjoy the ocean view' (or the view into the pool via underwater porthole windows) than 'act like you're at a five-star resort'.

Boteco
BAR
(www.botecomiami.com; 916 NE 79th St) If you're missing São Paolo, come to Boteco on Friday evening to see the biggest Brazilian expat reunion in Miami. *Cariocas* (Rio natives) and their countrymen flock here to listen to samba and bossa nova, and chat each other up over the best caipirinhas in town.

Lou's Beer Garden
PUB
(Map p52; www.lousbeergarden.com; 7337 Harding Ave) We're frankly surprised it took so long for a beer garden to open in Miami. The weather's perfect, right? Nonetheless, this is the first beer garden to open in the Magic City in anyone's memory. Gather around long tables under tropical trees, order a cheese plate or a Kobe beef burger and down pints of Belgian craft ales. What could be better?

On the Rocks
SPORTS BAR
(Map p52; ☎305-531-0000; 217 71st St) Deep in mid-Miami Beach, this may be the only Cuban-Sports-Seedy-Dive-Bar we've visited in the USA.

DOWNTOWN MIAMI

Bar Black
LOUNGE
(Map p56; 28 NW 14th St) Bar Black is one of Miami's prime hipster hot spots – the sort of place that attracts artsy types with thick-framed glasses who mingle amid rotating art installations. This is still Miami, so folks are beautiful and there's a lovely backyard

court area to boot. But there's no cover and drinks are pretty cheap.

Tobacco Road
BAR

(Map p56; www.tobacco-road.com; 626 S Miami Ave) Miami's oldest bar has been on the scene since the 1920s. These days it's a little touristy, but it has stayed in business for a reason: old wood, blue lights, cigarette smoke and sassy bartenders greet you like a buddy. Cold beers are on tap and decent live acts crank out the blues, jazz and rock. The staff proudly reminds you its liquor license was the first one issued in a city that loves its mojitos. Tobacco Road has been here since the 1920s when it was a Prohibition-era speakeasy; today it remains a great place to order a drink or listen to live music. Film buffs may recognize it as the place where Kurt Russell has a drink in *The Mean Season* (1985).

D.R.B.
BAR

(Map p56; www.drbmiami.com; 255 NE 14th St) The acronym stands for Democratic Republic of Beer, and that's what's on offer here: a good variety of microbrews and hard-to-score imports, served in a small, understated bar area or outside on comfy couches within view of the Adrienne Arsht Center.

Kyma
LOUNGE

(Map p56; Epic Hotel, 270 Biscayne Blvd Way) Circle the round bar in the Epic Hotel, then wander past the Euro crowd onto a terrace that juts out over the slow-moving Miami river. Wander back in under 30ft ceilings for a drink, jam out to the soft pumping house music, and revel in this posh take on *Miami Vice.*

Level 25
BAR

(Map p56; Conrad Miami, 1395 Brickell Ave) When Neo buys Morpheus a drink, they probably meet at this Conrad Miami spot (guess which floor), where it's all long white lines, low black couches, pin-striped gorgeousity and God's-eye views over Biscayne Bay.

M Bar
BAR

(Map p56; Mandarin Oriental Miami, 500 Brickell Key Dr) The high-class lobby bar here may be tiny, but its martini menu – more than 250 strong – isn't. The views aren't bad either.

WYNWOOD, DESIGN DISTRICT & LITTLE HAITI

Electric Pickle
BAR

(Map p62; www.electricpicklemiami.com; 2826 N Miami Ave) Miami can work its magic on anyone, even Wynwood's angst-ridden artists and hipsters (Wypsters). Like Cinderella touched by a fairy godmother (or a very good DJ), they become glamorous club kids in this two-story hepcat hot spot. The Pickle is as sexy and gorgeous as Miami gets, but with its modish library and (semi)literati clientele, it's also intelligent enough to hold a conversation...though you should expect it to be a sloppy, fun drunk by midnight.

Churchill's
PUB

(Map p62; www.churchillspub.com; 5501 NE 2nd Ave, Little Haiti) Churchill's is a Brit-owned, East End–style pub in the midst of what could be Port-au-Prince. There's a lot of live music here, mainly punk, indie and more punk – expect a small cover charge if a show is on when you visit. Not insipid modern punk either: think the Ramones meets the Sex Pistols. While everyone's getting their ya-yas off, Haitians are waiting outside to park your car or sidle in and enjoy the gig and a beer with you. Brits, this is the place to watch your sports.

Magnum Lounge
GAY & LESBIAN

(709 NE 79th St) This gay piano lounge is... wait a second. Let's go over those three words again: "Gay piano lounge." Do we need to tell you more? Oh, fine: Magnum is located on the edge of gentrification, so it feels cool to 'discover' this spot. The interior is all dark shadows and deep reds but not to the point you're blind, and the clientele is a nice mix: gays, lesbians, straights on dates or just looking for something different – and by the way, the drinks are stiff, the prices are reasonable and the piano music is quite good.

LITTLE HAVANA

Casa Panza Bar
TAVERNA

(Map p66; 1620 SW 8th St) It doesn't get cornier than this 'authentic' Spanish taverna where the live shows, flamenco dancers, Spanish guitarists and audience participation reach new heights of sangria-soaked fun. Drop your cynicism, enter and enjoy.

COCONUT GROVE

Everything here closes at 3am.

Taurus
BAR

(Map p69; 3540 Main Hwy) The oldest bar in Coconut Grove is a cool mix of wood-paneling, smoky leather chairs, about 100 beers to choose from and a convivial vibe – as neighborhood bars go in Miami, this is one of the best.

ART WALKS: THE NEW CLUBBING?

It's hipsters gone wild! Or to put it another way: it's free wine! And artsy types, and galleries open till late, and the eye candy of a club, and the drunken momentum of a pub crawl and – best of all – no red ropes. The free Wynwood & Design District Art Walk is one of the best nightlife experiences in Miami. And we're not (just) being cheapskates. The experience of strolling from gallery to gallery ('That piece is *gorgeous*. Pour me another'), perusing the paintings ('No, I don't think there's a bathroom behind the performance artist') and delving into the nuances of aesthetic styles ('The wine's run out? Let's bounce') is as genuinely innovative as...well, the best contemporary art. Just be careful, as a lot of galleries in Wynwood are separated by short drives (the Design District is more walkable). Art Walks take place on the second Saturday of each month, from 7pm to 10pm (some galleries stretch to 11pm); when it's all over, lots of folks repair to Electric Pickle (p106) or Bardot (p107). Visit www.artcircuits.com for information on participating galleries.

Tavern in the Grove   BAR
(Map p69; 3416 Main Hwy) To say this sweatbox is popular with University of Miami students is like saying it rains sometimes in England. More of a neighborhood dive on weekdays.

Barracuda   BAR
(Map p69; 3035 Fuller St) The other place in the Grove to get overloaded on backwards baseball caps and coeds in miniskirts.

CORAL GABLES

Seven Seas   BAR
(Map p72; 2200 SW 57th Ave) Seven Seas is a genuine Miami neighborhood dive, decorated on the inside like a nautical theme park and filled with University of Miami students, Cuban workers, gays, straights, lesbians and folks from around the way. The best times to come are on Tuesday, Thursday and Saturday for the best karaoke in Miami – there's plenty of Spanish-language music, which adds some Latin spice.

The Bar   BAR
(Map p72; 172 Giralda Ave) All in a name, right? Probably the best watering hole in the Gables, The Bar is just what the title says (which is unusual in this neighborhood of extravagant embellishment). If you're in the 'hood on Friday, come here for happy hour (5pm to 8pm), when the young Gables professionals take their ties off and let loose long into the night.

Titanic   BAR
(☑305-668-1742; www.titanicbrewery.com; 5813 Ponce de León Blvd) By day, it's an All-American-type bar and grill, but at night Titanic turns into a popular University of Miami watering hole. Thursday tends to

be a big night. Located by the University entrance near Dixie Hwy and Red Rd (SW 57th Ave).

☆ Entertainment

Miami's artistic merits are obvious, even from a distance. Could there be a better creative base? There's Southern homegrown talent, migratory snowbirds bringing the funding and attention of northeastern galleries, and immigrants from across the Americas. These disparate cultures communicate their values via the language of expression. Creole, Spanish and English, after all, are poor languages compared to dance, music and theater.

Gay and lesbian nightlife used to be the province of South Beach, but today the scene is pretty integrated into straight Miami. Some clubs are still found in South Beach, while more casual gay bars are in Midcity, North Biscayne Blvd and Northern Miami Beach.

Clubs

Expect a cover charge at all of the following unless otherwise noted. In South Beach, covers range from $20 to $25 (sometimes higher!); elsewhere in the city you'll be paying around $5 to $10.

Bardot   CLUB
(Map p62; ☑305-576-5570; 3456 N Miami Ave) If you can't stand lines and crowds, we recommend visiting Bardot, in Wynwood, on a weekday. This could be said of any club in Miami, but you really should see the interior of Bardot before you leave the city. It's all sexy French vintage posters and furniture seemingly plucked from a private club

that serves millionaires by day, and becomes a scene of decadent excess by night. There are a lot of gorgeous Miamians here and we stress: the crowd is local, so while it's a glam scene, it's a much more friendly, laid-back one than the ridiculous posturing you might see in South Beach (not that there's no posturing going on). The entrance looks to be on N Miami Ave, but it's actually in a parking lot behind the building (indicated on our map).

Vagabond　　　　　　　　　　　　CLUB
(Map p56; ☑305-379-0508; www.thevagabondmiami.com; 30 NE 14th St) If the South Beach Clubs are Manhattan and Hollywood, then the Vagabond scene is Brooklyn or Silver Lake, which is a travel writer's way of saying: if you tire of the lame Top 40, plastic and mediocre big-name clubs in Miami Beach, come to the Vagabond, a cool club in a rough part of Overtown. The folks are still fine, but they're funkier, definitely more local and the music is more experimental. The animal-print furniture and flying, loopy lines and curves are made to be gawked at, which is possible as no one keeps the Vagabond too dimly lit. Friday night, hosted by indie record shop Sweat, is a blast.

La Covacha　　　　　　　　　LIVE MUSIC
(☑305-594-3717; www.lacovacha.com; 10730 NW 25th St, Doral) Drive out about halfway to the Everglades (just kidding, but only just) and you'll find Covacha, the most hidden, most hip Latin scene in Miami. Actually, it's not hidden; all the young Latinos know about Covacha and love it well, and we do too. It's an excellent spot to see new bands, up-coming DJs (almost all local), an enormous crowd and few tourists. Covacha is out in Doral, a good 14 miles west of Downtown Miami.

The Stage　　　　　　　　　LIVE MUSIC
(Map p62; ☑305-576-9577; www.thestagemiami.com; 170 NE 38th St) The Stage is many things: edgy art gallery, live music venue, arts and crafts bazaar, occasional bar, and sometimes all of these things at once. Check the website to see what shows are playing and try to catch a party here – you may see a more bohemian, creative side of Miami than you initially expected (on our last visit a one-man folk-bluegrass-punk band played for a crowd dressed in rockabilly chic). On Sunday afternoon The Stage hosts family-friendly all-ages shows starting at 2pm.

Skybar　　　　　　　　　　　　CLUB
(Map p44; ☑305-695-3900; Shore Club, 1901 Collins Ave) Skybar is one of those SoBe spots that is so impossibly full of beautiful people you wonder if you've walked into a dream – and it's not just the clientele who are gorgeous. The setting: the Moroccan garden of delights that is the courtyard of the Shore Club hotel. Chill alfresco in a sultan's pleasure garden under enormous, wrought-iron lanterns, gaze at the patricians lounging around the pool, or try (and fail, if you're an unlisted travel writer) to get into the all-crimson, all-A-list Red Room.

White Room　　　　　　　　　　　CLUB
(Map p56; ☑305-995-5050; www.whiteroomshows.com; 1306 N Miami Ave) Sitting as it does in edgy Overtown, it already feels like you're in on some secret when you find the White Room. Then the beautiful artists, hipsters and scenesters flock in, drinking, dancing and chatting as the requisite weird movies play on open-air projectors, near Lawrence of Arabia tents curving around an exposed-industrial main-stage. What we're saying is: hot hipsters get drunk and dance with other hot hipsters. You go, White Room.

Twist　　　　　　　　　　　　　GAY
(Map p48; ☑305-538-9478; www.twistsobe.com; 1057 Washington Ave) Never a cover, always a groove, and right across from the police station, this two-story gay club has some serious staying power and a little bit of something for everyone: six different bars; go-go dancers; drag shows; lounging areas and a small dance floor.

Nikki Beach Miami　　　　　　CLUB
(Map p48; ☑305-538-1111; www.nikkibeach.com; 1 Ocean Dr) Get your groove on outdoors, wandering from immaculate gossamer beach cabana to cabana at Nikki's, which feels like an incredibly upscale full-moon party. On Sunday (Sunday?!), starting around 4pm, it's the hottest party in town, as folks clamor to get in and re-live whatever it was they did the night before.

Florida Room at the Delano　　CLUB
(Map p44; ☑305-672-2000; 1685 Collins Ave) Framed posters of Snoop Dogg looking ghetto fabulous line the entrance to The Florida Room, which should give you an idea of the atmosphere here. This is as exclusive as clubs get – plus, there's a popular dancehall-samba piano lounge for local scenesters who eschew the tourist trap megaclubs further

If you're going out in Miami, ask yourself: what do I want? Do I want to dance? Hear good tunes? Score? See celebrities? If you answered yes to the first two questions, the downtown Miami and Wynwood scene might be more to your liking. If you answered yes to the last two questions, you may want to stay in South Beach.

Also, ask yourself another question: What do I bring? If it's good looks, money or promoter connections, the world is your oyster. If you have none of the above you can still party, but be prepared for some ego-crushing. Best overheard conversation in the course of this research:

Guy A: [Looking at model] 'How do you approach a girl like that?'

Guy B: 'In a Mercedes.'

Here's how it breaks down: the South Beach club scene plays on the appeal of celebrity. More famous customers equal more regular customers. Eventually, a strange equilibrium works out where enough regular customers make people assume famous people are there, even if they're not. But those regular customers can't appear too regular, so a little social engineering is committed by club owners and the titans of the cultural scene (bouncers) in the form of the red rope. How do you get by it?

» Be polite Don't be skittish, but don't act like you're J Lo either. And whatever you do, don't yell at the doorman – or touch him or yank on his clothing – to try to get his attention.

» Get guest-listed Ask the concierge at your hotel to help you out, or simply call the club and leave your name; it's often that simple.

» Remain confidently aloof Don't stare at the doorman. Look elsewhere – but look hot doing it.

» Be aggressive. Failing that, be rich If there's a clamoring crowd, standing at the back of it and hoping it'll part is about as effective as being meek when you need a seat on the New York subway. Push your way through to the front. Or order bottle service (an overpriced bottle of spirits), which usually guarantees you a pass to the front.

» Come correct For women, showing a sophisticated amount of skin is effective, although 'sophisticated' depends on the wearer. We've seen chic women in barely-there tops look less trashy than folks sporting a standard miniskirt ensemble. Men, don't wear T-shirts and jeans, unless you're one of those guys who can and still look put together. In which case, we're jealous, dude. Also, this is Miami – be a little more daring than a button-up shirt and slacks if you want to stand out.

» Get there early Do you want to be cool or do you want to get in? From 10:30pm to 11pm is a golden time for bouncer leniency, but you can't club-hop with this strategy.

» If you're a man, bring a woman A man alone is not worth much (unless you're at a gay club, natch); up your value by having a beautiful woman – or two or three – on your arm.

Though our listings represent the hottest parties as of press time, we urge you to do some follow-up research when you arrive: talk to friends and your concierge, and pick up a copy of the local arts weekly, *Miami New Times*, or a free monthly such as *Miami Living Magazine* or the pint-sized *Ego Miami Magazine*.

---

down the beach. Show up before 11pm or be on the list (or be Lenny Kravitz – who helped design this place) to get in.

Louis   CLUB
(Map p44; ☎305-531-4600; www.louismiami.com; 2325 Collins Ave) The resident club at the Gansevoort South is dark, crowded, expensive and loud, the music is meh and a 17% gratuity is automatically added to your bill, so the bartenders have little incentive to be nice to you. But Louis, whose interior resembles Marie Antoinette's boudoir after it collided with a Sex Pistols party, is located in the aforementioned Gansevoort, and as such this is the sort of place where you may well rub shoulders with a celebrity. It's Miami Beach; you came here to drink with models

and superstars, right? Well, here's a place to do just that.

Cameo
CLUB

(Map p44; ☎305-532-2667; www.cameomiami .com; 1445 Washington Ave) This enormous, touristy club, where Gwen Stefani tracks get smooshed into Oakenfold, is where the sexy times are to be had – if by sexy time you mean thumping music, a packed crowd and sweat to slip on. Sunday's gay night (the specific party name frequently changes) is one of the best in town.

Hoy Como Ayer
LIVE MUSIC

(Map p66; ☎305-541-2631; 2212 SW 8th St; cover $8-25) This Cuban hot spot – with authentic music, unstylish wood paneling and a small dance floor – is enhanced by cigar smoke and Havana transplants. Stop in nightly for *son* (a salsalike dance that originated in Oriente, Cuba), *boleros* (a Spanish dance in triple meter) and modern Cuban beats.

Mansion
CLUB

(Map p44; ☎305-532-1525; www.mansionmiami .com; 1235 Washington Ave) Every night the lines stretch around the block as plebs beg, cajole and strut in a vain attempt to get past that damned red rope. Inside? Well, they don't call it 'Mansion' for nothing. Expect megaclub grandiosity, plenty of attitude, waiting in line for hours and the chance to see young celebs do something tabloid-worthy.

Mynt
CLUB

(Map p44; ☎305-532-0727; www.myntlounge.com; 1921 Collins Ave) Join the partying stars – Justin Timberlake, Vin Diesel, Britney Spears etc – by bottle servicing yourself into the VIP section. Otherwise, make friends with the red rope until you can order a drink and then try not to spill it, which is tough in the sweaty scrum of models, Moët and mojitos.

Score
GAY

(Map p44; ☎305-535-1111; www.scorebar.net; 727 Lincoln Rd) Muscle boys with mustaches, glistening six-packs gyrating on stage, and a crowd of men who've decided shirts really aren't their thing: do we need to spell out the orientation of Score's customer base? It's still the best dedicated gay bar on the beach, and the addition of the more mature Crème Lounge upstairs will undoubtedly raise the cachet of this perennial favorite.

Space
CLUB

(Map p56; ☎305-375-0001; www.clubspace.com; 34 NE 11th St) This multilevel warehouse is Miami's main megaclub. With 30,000 sq ft to fill, dancers have room to strut, and an around-the-clock liquor license redefines the concept of after-hours. DJs usually pump each floor with a different sound – hip-hop, Latin, heavy trance – while the infamous rooftop lounge is the place to be for sunrise.

Performing Arts

Adrienne Arsht Center for the Performing Arts
THEATER

(Map p56; ☎305-949-6722, 786-468-2000; www .arshtcenter.org; 1300 Biscayne Blvd) This magnificent venue manages to both humble and enthrall visitors. Today the Arsht is where the biggest cultural acts in Miami come to perform; a show here is a must-see on any Miami trip. Get off the Metromover at Omni stop.

Colony Theatre
THEATER

(Map p44; ☎305-674-1040; www.colonytheatremi amibeach.com; 1040 Lincoln Rd, South Beach) The Colony is an absolute art-deco gem, with a classic marquee and Inca-style crenellations, which looks like the sort of place where gangsters would go to watch *Hamlet*. Built in 1935, this used to be the main cinema house in upper South Beach before it fell into disrepair in the mid-20th century. It was renovated and revived in 1976 and now boasts 465-seats and great acoustics. This treasure now serves as a major venue for performing arts – from comedy and occasional musicals to theatrical dramas, off-Broadway productions and ballet – as well as hosting movie screenings and small film festivals.

Gusman Center for the Performing Arts
THEATER

(Map p56; ☎305-374-2444; www.gusmancenter .org; 174 E Flagler St) This elegantly renovated 1920s movie palace services a huge variety of performing arts including film festivals, symphonies, ballets and touring shows. The acoustics are excellent.

Fillmore Miami Beach/Jackie Gleason Theater
THEATER

(Map p44; ☎305-673-7300; www.fillmoremb.com /index; 1700 Washington Ave, South Beach) Built in 1951, South Beach's premier showcase for touring Broadway shows, orchestras and other big musical productions has 2700 seats and excellent acoustics. Jackie Gleason chose to make the theater his home for the long-running 1960s TV show, but now you'll find an eclectic lineup of shows – Elvis Costello or

Albita one night, the Dutch Philharmonic or an over-the-top musical the next.

Light Box Theatre/Miami

Light Box Project THEATER
(Map p62; ☑305-576-4350; www.miamilightpro ject.com; 3000 Biscayne Blvd) The Miami Light Project is a nonprofit cultural foundation that represents innovative shows from theater troupes and performance artists from around the world. Shows are performed across the city, but the project is housed at Light Box Theatre.

THEATER

See www.southfloridatheatre.com for a comprehensive directory of playhouses in greater South Florida.

Actors Playhouse THEATER
(Map p72; ☑305-444-9293; www.actorsplayhouse .org; Miracle Theater, 280 Miracle Mile, Coral Gables; tickets $20-50) Housed within the 1948 deco Miracle Theater, this three-theater venue stages musicals and comedies, children's theater on its kids stage and more avant-garde productions in its small experimental black-box space. Recent productions have included *Footloose* and *The Wizard of Oz* for the little ones.

Gablestage THEATER
(Map p72; ☑305-446-1116; www.gablestage.org; 1200 Anastasia Ave, Coral Gables; tickets $15-40) Founded as the Florida Shakespeare Theatre in 1979 and now housed on the property of the Biltmore Hotel, this company still performs an occasional Shakespeare play, but mostly presents contemporary and classical pieces; recent productions have included *Frozen, Bug* and *The Retreat from Moscow.*

Jerry Herman Ring Theatre THEATER
(☑305-284-3355; www.miami.edu/ring; University of Miami, 1321 Miller Dr; tickets $8-15) This University of Miami troupe stages musicals, dramas and comedies, with recent productions including *Falsettos* and *Baby.* Alumni actors include Sylvester Stallone, Steven Bauer, Saundra Santiago and Ray Liotta.

Miami Improv COMEDY
(Map p69; ☑305-441-8200; www.miamiimprov .com; 3390 Mary St, Coconut Grove; tickets $10-70) Part of a national chain, this 3rd-floor club has the usual club-circuit suspects plus monthly Miami Comics, open-mic shows and Urban Nights, which feature stars from

MIAMI'S SMALL CINEMAS

Miami has a glut of art-house cinemas showing first-run, independent and foreign films. Here are some of our favorites:

» **Bill Cosford Cinema** (www.cosford cinema.com; Memorial Classroom Bldg, University of Miami, University Dr) On the University of Miami campus, this renovated art house was launched in memory of the *Miami Herald* film critic.

» **Coral Gables Art Cinema** (www .gablescinema.com; 260 Aragon Ave, Coral Gables) Indie and foreign films in a 144-seat cinema.

» **Tower Theater** (Map p66; www.mdc .edu/culture/tower; 1508 SW 8th St) In a gem of a deco building, managed by Miami Dade College.

» **O Cinema** (Map p62; www.o-cinema .org; 90 NW 29th St) Indie screenings in Wynwood.

Comedy Central's Showtime, HBO's Def Comedy Jam and BET's Comic View.

DANCE

Miami City Ballet DANCE
(Map p44; ☑305-929-7000; www.miamicityballet .org; 2200 Liberty Ave, South Beach) Formed in 1985, this troupe is guided by artistic director Edward Villella, who studied under the great George Balanchine at the NYC Ballet. So it's no surprise Balanchine's works dominate the repertoire, with shows held at a lovely three-story headquarters designed by famed local architectural firm Arquitectonica. The facade allows passers-by to watch the dancers rehearsing through big picture windows, which makes you feel like you're in a scene from *Fame,* except the weather is better and people don't spontaneously break into song.

Ifé-Ilé Afro-Cuban Dance DANCE
(☑305-476-0832; www.ife-ile.org) Ifé-Ilé is a nonprofit organization that promotes cultural understanding through dance and performs in a range of styles – traditional Afro-Cuban, mambo, rumba, conga, chancleta, son, salsa and ritual pieces. Call for further information.

Miami Hispanic Ballet   DANCE
([phone]305-549-7711;   www.miamihispanicballet.org;
900 SW 1st St) Directed by Cuban-trained Pe-
dro Pablo Peña, this troupe presents mainly
classical ballets based out of the lovely Manuel Artime Theater, the 'largest small venue'
in the city. It's located on SW 1st St between
Downtown and Little Havana.

CLASSICAL

Miami Chamber Symphony   ORCHESTRA
([phone]305-858-3500, 305-284-6477; Gusman Concert
Hall & University of Miami, 1314 Miller Dr; tickets $15-
30; ⊙performances Nov-May) Its yearly series
features world-renowned soloists at shows
held at the University of Miami's Gusman
Concert Hall (not to be confused with the
Downtown Gusman Center for the Performing Arts).

New World Symphony   ORCHESTRA
(NWS; [phone]305-673-3330; www.nws.edu; 500 17th
St) Housed in the New World Center (p43) –
a funky explosion of cubist lines and geometric curves, fresh white against the blue
Miami sky – the acclaimed New World Symphony holds performances from October
to May (tickets $20 to $70). The deservedly
heralded NWS serves as a three- to four-year
preparatory program for very talented mu-
sicians who have already graduated from
prestigious music schools.

Sports

Miami Heat   BASKETBALL
([phone]786-777-1000; www.nba.com/heat; tickets $22-
375; ⊙season Nov-Apr) At the time of research,
the Heat were (forgive us) one of the hottest
teams in the NBA. The team plays at American Airlines Arena (p55).

Miami Dolphins   FOOTBALL
([phone]305-943-8000; www.miamidolphins.com; Sun
Life Stadium, 2269 Dan Marino Blvd, Miami Gardens;
tickets $35-8500; ⊙season Aug-Dec) 'Dol-fans'
are respectably crazy about their team, even
if a Super Bowl showing has evaded them
since 1985. Games are wildly popular and
the Dolphins are painfully successful, in that
they always raise fans' hopes but never quite
fulfill them. Sun Life Stadium is in Miami
Gardens, 15 miles north of Downtown.

University of Miami Hurricanes   FOOTBALL
([phone]800-462-2637; www.hurricanesports.com; tickets $22-60; ⊙season Aug-Dec) The Hurricanes
were once undisputed titans of university
football, but experienced a slow decline in
2004. They've recovered a bit as of research,

and attending a game surrounded by UM's
pack of fanatics is lots of fun.

University of Miami Hurricanes BASKETBALL
([phone]800-462-2637;   www.hurricanesports.com;
tickets $20; ⊙season Nov-Apr) Catch the be-
loved college Hurricanes shooting hoops at
the BankUnited Center at the University of
Miami.

🛍 Shopping

There are two main shopping strips in South
Beach – Lincoln Road Mall, a pedestrian
road lined with a great mix of indie shops
and chain stores; and the southern end of
Collins Ave, below 9th St. Here you'll find
mostly high-end chains like A/X, Ralph Lauren and Barney's Co-op. Shooting way north
of here, you'll find two extremely popular
shopping malls: the **Aventura Mall** (www
.shopaventuramall.com; 19501 Biscayne Blvd, Aventura), a mainstream collection including JC
Penney and Bloomingdale's, and the chichi
Bal Harbour Shops (www.balharbourshops
.com; 9700 Collins Ave, Bal Harbor), a classy scene
boasting Prada, Gucci, Chanel and Saks
Fifth Avenue outposts. Bal Harbour is located about 3 miles north of North Miami
Beach; Aventura is 9 miles north of North
Miami Beach.

Move over to the mainland and there are
a few options, the hippest being the Design
District where you'll find a glut of art and
homewares plus clothing and accessories
hawkers. You'll have an easier time at the
touristy,   chain-store-drenched   **Bayside
Marketplace** (Map p56; www.baysidemarketpla
ce.com; 401 Biscayne Blvd), on the shores of
downtown Miami. Find more outdoor malls
in Coconut Grove, at the ever-popular **CocoWalk** (Map p69; 3015 Grand Ave) and **Streets
of Mayfair** (Map p69; www.mayfairinthegrove
.net; 2911 Grand Ave); Coral Gables meanwhile,
has the **Village of Merrick Park** (www.vil
lageofmerrickpark.com; 358 San Lorenzo Ave), located a mile south of Coral Gables' Miracle
Mile, near the intersection of S Le Jeune Rd
and Dixie Hwy, anchored by the classy department stores Neiman Marcus and Nord-
strom.

Art, Furniture & Home Design

Miami Mid Century   ANTIQUES
(Map p62; [phone]305-572-0558; 3404 N Miami Ave;
⊙10am-7pm) Miami Mid Century has a
playful approach to antiques and retro
homewares – big sunglasses, old stacks of
magazines, cool geometric lamps – sorely

lacking in the more snooty shops of the Design District.

Española Way Art Center
ART
(Map p44; ☑305-673-0946; 405 Española Way) There are three levels of studios here, plus excellent original work and prints for sale, all by local artists. Hours vary by studio.

Clothing & Accessories

Consign of the Times
VINTAGE
(Map p44; ☑305-535-0811; www.consignofthe times.com; 1635 Jefferson Ave; ⏰11am-9pm) Cute vintage boutique that carries labels as lovely as Gucci (patent-leather shoes!), Von Furstenberg (leather slingbacks!) and Versace (silver bustier!).

C Madeleine's
VINTAGE
(☑305-945-7770; 13702 Biscayne Blvd; ⏰11am-6pm Mon-Sat, noon-5pm Sun) The undisputed queen of vintage Miami, C Madeleine's is more than your standard used-clothes write-off. This is a serious temple to classical style, selling Yves Saint Laurent couture and classic Chanel suits. Come here for the sort of timeless looks that are as beautiful now as when they first appeared on the rack. Located on North Biscayne Blvd about 7.5 miles north of the Design District.

Hip.e
CLOTHING
(Map p72; ☑305-445-3693; 359 Miracle Mile; ⏰11am-7pm Mon-Sat) A bit more hip than hippie, the clothes and jewelry here manage to mix up indie and hip-hop aesthetics in an admirably wearable way. Think Lucite bangles just slightly embellished by bling and you've got an idea of the vibe.

Alchemist
CLOTHING
(Map p44; ☑305-531-4653; www.shopalchemist .com; 438 Lincoln Rd; ⏰10am-9pm) This high-end boutique eschews bling and snootiness for friendly attitude, minimalism and simply beautiful clothes – standout labels include Zara and Proenza Schouler. Has another location on the 5th floor of the 1111 Lincoln Rd garage

Pepe Y Berta
CLOTHING
(Map p66; ☑305-266-1007, 305-857-3771; 1421 SW 8th St; ⏰10am-6:30pm, 9am-7pm Sat) The most gorgeous collection of *guayaberas* in Miami can be found in this family-run shop, where the friendly owner will hand measure you and tailor a shirt to your tastes.

Boy Meets Girl
CHILDREN
(Map p72; ☑305-445-9668; 355 Miracle Mile; ⏰10am-7pm Mon-Fri, 11am-6pm Sat) Fantastically upscale and frankly expensive

clothing for wee ones – if the kids are getting past puberty, look elsewhere, but otherwise they'll be fashionable far before they realize it.

Olian
MATERNITY
(Map p72; ☑305-446-2306; 356 Miracle Mile; ⏰10am-7pm Mon-Fri) Flagship of the Olian empire and Miami's premier maternity boutique, this is where expecting mommies can outfit themselves to look as glam as any South Beach model.

Hiho Batik
CLOTHING
(Map p52; ☑305-892-7733; www.hihobatik.com; 2174 NE 123rd St; ⏰11am-6pm Mon-Sat) Hiho is a neat little shop where you can design your own batik (wax-and-dyed artwork; here they usually put it on T-shirts) with a friendly staff of artsy types. Located about 7 miles north of the Design District.

U Rock Couture
CLOTHING
(Map p44; ☑305-538-7625; 928 Ocean Dr; ⏰10am-1am, to 2am Sat) U Rock is the quintessential Miami Beach clothing store. Loud, flashy and in your face, it resembles a mangled clash of rhinestones, tight clothes, revealing dresses, deep tans, euro accents and the cast of *Jersey Shore*. Somehow, this is all strangely appealing... rather like Lincoln Rd itself.

Gifts

Books and Books
BOOKS
(Map p72; ☑305-442-4408; 265 Aragon Ave St; ⏰10am-11pm, to midnight Fri & Sat) The best indie bookstore in South Florida is a massive emporium of all things literary. Hosts frequent readings and is generally just a fantastic place to hang out. Has other outposts on Lincoln Rd (☑305-532-3222; 927 Lincoln Rd) and the Bal Harbour shops.

Metta Boutique
GIFTS
(Map p69; ☑305-648-0250; 3435 Main Hwy; ⏰9am-5pm) A cute store that exemplifies the evolution of the Grove from hippie hangout to massive market, in that it sells consumer goodies – clothes, journals, accessories, gifts and tchotchkes – that are decidedly green/organic/sustainable/fair trade.

Celestial Treasures
GIFTS
(Map p69; ☑305-461-2341; 3444 Main Hwy; ⏰noon-8pm, to 10pm Fri & Sat) Your one-stop shop for spiritual and metaphysical needs, this shop has accoutrement, books, cards and components for those interested in Zen, Kabbalah, Wicca, Yoga, Buddhism

and Hinduism. Also has staff psychics on hand.

Bookstore in the Grove   BOOKS
(Map p69; ☑305-483-2855; 3399 Virginia St; ☺7am-10pm, from 8am Sat & Sun) Coconut Grove's independent bookstore is a good spot for all kinds of lit, and has a great cafe (try the empanadas) to boot.

Taschen   BOOKS
(Map p44; ☑305-538-6185; 1111 Lincoln Rd; ☺11am-9pm Mon-Thu, to 10pm Fri & Sat, noon-9pm Sun) Ridiculously cool, well-stocked collection of art, photography, design and coffee-table books to make your hip home look that much smarter.

Ricky's NYC   GIFTS
(Map p44; ☑305-674-8511; 536 Lincoln Rd; ☺10am-midnight, to 1am Sat) This South Beach standby boasts hundreds of tacky gifts (boxing-nun puppets), pop art para-phernalia and, well, 'adult' accoutrements of sex toys, games, costumes and other unmentionables.

El Crédito Cigars   TOBACCONIST
(Map p66; ☑305-858-4162; 1106 SW 8th St; ☺8am-6pm Mon-Fri, to 4pm Sat) In one of the most popular cigar stores in Miami, and one of the oldest in Florida, you'll be treated as a venerated member of the stogie-chomping club.

Little-Havana-To-Go   SOUVENIRS
(Map p66; ☑305-857-9720; www.littlehavanatogo .com; 1442 SW 8th St) This is Little Havana's official souvenir store, and has some pretty cool items, from Cuban-pride T-shirts to posters, flags, paintings, photo books, cigar-box purses and authentic clothing.

M&N Variedades   BOTANICA
(Map p66; ☑305-649-3040; 1753 SW 8th St; ☺9am-8pm) This *Santeria botanica* offers spell components, magic candles, *cosultas espirituales* (spiritual consultation) and computer repair.

Eyes on Lincoln   EYEWEAR
(Map p44; ☑305-532-0070; 708 Lincoln Rd; ☺10am-8pm) The most sexy, impressive col-lection of glasses, sunglasses and optical accoutrement we've seen in South Florida.

Genius Jones   TOYS
(Map p62; ☑866-436-4875; 49 NE 39th St; ☺noon-8pm Tue-Sun, to 10pm Fri & Sat) High-end toys, dolls and gear for babies and toddlers and their parents. Fatboy 'bean-bag' chairs, Primo Viaggio car seats and Bugaboo strollers – geek out, parents.

Music

Sweat Records   MUSIC
(Map p62; ☑786-693-9309; 5505 NE 2nd Ave; ☺noon-10pm Tue-Sat, to 5pm Sun) Sweat's al-most a stereotypical indie record store – there's funky art and graffiti on the walls, it has big purple couches, it sells weird Japanese toys and there are skinny guys with thick glasses arguing over LPs and EPs you've never heard of, and of course, there's coffee and vegan snacks.

ⓘ Information

Dangers & Annoyances
There are a few areas considered by locals to be dangerous: Liberty City, in northwest Miami; Overtown, from 14th St to 20th St; Little Haiti and stretches of the Miami riverfront. In these and other reputedly 'bad' areas you should avoid walking around alone late at night, use common sense and travel in groups. If in doubt, it's best to take a taxi and to know your address.

Deserted areas below 5th St in South Beach are more dangerous at night, but your main concerns are aggressive drunks or the occa-sional strung-out druggie, rather than muggers. In downtown Miami, use caution near the Grey-hound station and around causeways, bridges and overpasses where homeless people and some refugees have set up shanty towns.

Natural dangers include the strong sun (use a high-SPF sunscreen), mosquitoes (use a spray-on repellent) and hurricanes (between June and November). There's a **hurricane hotline** (☑305-229-4483), which will give you informa-tion about approaching storms, storm tracks, warnings and estimated time to touchdown – all the things you will need to make a decision about if and when to leave.

Emergency
Ambulance (☑911)
Beach Patrol (☑305-673-7714)
Hurricane Hotline (☑305-468-5400)
Poison Information Center (☑305-585-5250)
Rape Hotline (☑305-585-7273)
Suicide Intervention (☑305-358-4357)

Internet Access
Most hotels and hostels (and increasingly, even camping grounds) offer wi-fi access. Free wi-fi is also available in libraries, Starbucks and McDonald's.

Media
Beach Channel (www.thebeachchannel.tv) Local 24-hour TV station on channel 19, like a quirky infomercial about goings-on in Miami Beach.

Diario Las Americas (www.diariolasamericas .com) Spanish-language daily.

El Nuevo Herald (www.elnuevoherald.com) Spanish-language daily of the *Herald*.

Miami Herald (www.miamiherald.com) Major daily covering local, national and international news.

Miami New Times (www.miaminewtimes.com) Free alternative weekly paper.

Miami Sun Post (www.miamisunpost.com) In-depth news and lifestyle coverage.

Sun-Sentinel (www.sun-sentinel.com) Daily covering South Florida.

WLRN (www.wlrn.org) Local National Public Radio affiliate, at 91.3FM on the dial.

Medical Services

Beach Dental Center (☑305-532-3300; 1680 Michigan Ave, South Beach) For dental needs.

Coral Gables Hospital (☑305-445-8461; 3100 Douglas Rd, Coral Gables) A community-based facility with many bilingual doctors.

Eckerd Drugs (☑305-538-1571; 1421 Alton Rd, South Beach; ☺24hr) One of many 24-hour Eckerd pharmacies.

Miami Beach Community Health Center (☑305-538-8835; 710 Alton Rd, South Beach) Walk-in clinic with long lines.

Mount Sinai Medical Center (☑305-674-2121; 4300 Alton Rd, Miami Beach) The area's best emergency room. Beware that you must eventually pay, and fees are high.

Visitor's Medical Line (☑305-674-2222; ☺24hr) For physician referrals.

Money

Bank of America has branch offices all over Miami and Miami Beach. To get currency exchanged you can go to **Amex** (☑305-358-7350; www.amex.com; 100 N Biscayne Blvd, downtown Miami; ☺9am-5pm Mon-Fri).

Post

The following branches have hours extended until evening thanks to self-serve machines in the lobbies:

Post office Mid-Beach (Map p52; 445 W 40th St; ☺8am-5pm Mon-Fri, 8:30am-2pm Sat); South Beach (Map p44; 1300 Washington Ave; ☺8am-5pm Mon-Fri, 8:30am-2pm Sat)

Tourist Information

Art Deco Welcome Center (Map p48; ☑305-672-2014; www.mdpl.org; 1001 Ocean Dr, South Beach; ☺10am-7:30pm Mon-Sat, to 6pm Sun) Run by the Miami Design Preservation League (MDPL); has tons of art-deco district information and organizes excellent walking tours.

Black Archives History & Research Center of South Florida (☑305-636-2390; www .theblackarchives.org; 5400 NW 22nd Ave,

ste 101, Liberty City) Information about black culture.

Coconut Grove Chamber of Commerce (Map p69; ☑305-444-7270; www.coconutgrove chamber.com; 2820 McFarlane Rd, Coconut Grove; ☺9am-5pm Mon-Fri)

Coral Gables Chamber of Commerce (Map p72; ☑305-446-1657; www.coralgablescham ber.org; 224 Catalonia Ave, Coral Gables; ☺9am-5pm Mon-Fri)

Downtown Miami Welcome Center (Map p56; ☑786-472-5930; www.downtownmiami.com; 900 S Miami Ave; ☺9am-5pm Mon-Fri) Provides maps, brochures and tour information for the downtown area.

Greater Miami Convention & Visitors Bureau (Map p56; ☑305-539-3000, 800-933-8448; www.miamiandbeaches.com; 701 Brickell Ave; ☺8:30am-5pm Mon-Fri) Located in an oddly intimidating high-rise building.

Miami Beach Chamber of Commerce (Map p44; ☑305-672-1300; www.miamibeachguest .com; 1920 Meridian Ave, South Beach; ☺9am-5pm Mon-Fri)

Websites

Art Circuits (www.artcircuits.com) The best insider info on art events; includes excellent neighborhood-by-neighborhood gallery maps.

Mango & Lime (www.mangoandlime.net) The best local food blog is always ahead of the curve on eating events in the Magic City.

Meatless Miami (www.meatlessmiami.com) Vegetarians in need of an eating guide, look no further.

Miami Beach 411 (www.miamibeach411.com) A great guide for Miami Beach visitors, covering just about all concerns.

Miami Nights (www.miaminights.com) Get a good, opinionated lowdown on Miami's ever-shifting after-dark scene.

Beached Miami (www.beachedmiami.com) The best independent arts website in Miami.

Miami Favs (www.miamifavs.tumblr.com) A great list of the best of Miami.

❶ Getting There & Away

Air

Miami is served by all major carriers via two main airports: Miami International Airport (MIA) and the Fort Lauderdale-Hollywood International Airport (FLL), half an hour north of MIA. **MIA** (Map p40; ☑305-876-7000; www.miami -airport.com) is the third-busiest airport in the country. Just 6 miles west of downtown Miami, the airport is open 24 hours and is laid out in a horseshoe design. There are left-luggage facilities on two concourses at MIA, between B and C, and on G; prices vary according to bag size.

The **Fort Lauderdale-Hollywood Internation-al Airport** (☑954-359-6100, 866-435-9355; www.broward.org/airport; 320 Terminal Dr), about 15 miles north of Miami just off I-95, often serves as a lower-cost alternative to MIA, especially because it's serviced by popular, cut-rate flyers including Southwest Airlines and JetBlue.

Boat

Though it's doubtful you'll be catching a steamer to make a trans-Atlantic journey, it is quite possible that you'll arrive in Miami via a cruise ship, as the **Port of Miami** (☑305-347-4800; www .miamidade.gov/portofmiami), which received nearly four million passengers in 2003, is known as the 'cruise capital of the world.' Arriving in the port will put you on the edge of downtown Miami; taxis and public buses to other local points are available from nearby Biscayne Blvd. See p167 for details on the Key West Express ferry to Key West from Miami.

Bus

Greyhound (☑800-231-2222; www.grey hound.com) is the major carrier in and out of town. There are four major terminals: **Airport terminal** (☑305-871-1810; 4111 NW 27th St); **Main Downtown terminal** (Map p56; ☑305-374-6160; 1012 NW 1st Ave); **Northern Miami terminal** (Map p52; ☑305-945-0801; 16560 NE 6th Ave); and the **Southern Miami terminal** (☑305-296-9072; Cutler Ridge Mall, 20505 S Dixie Hwy). There are several buses daily that head both up the East Coast and across the panhandle through the Gulf Coast.

Train

The main Miami terminal of **Amtrak** (☑305-835-1222, 800-872-7245; www.amtrak.com; 8303 NW 37th Ave) connects the city with the rest of continental USA and Canada. Travel time between New York and Miami is a severe 27 to 30 hours and costs $99 to $246 one-way. The Miami Amtrak station has a left-luggage station, which costs $2 per bag.

❶ Getting Around

To/From the Airport

MIAMI INTERNATIONAL AIRPORT It's a cinch to get from the airport to just about anywhere in Miami, especially Mid-Beach. If you're driving, follow Rte 112 from the airport, then head east on the Julia Tuttle Causeway or the I-195 to get to South Beach. Other options include the free shuttles offered by most hotels or a taxi ($38 flat rate from the airport to South Beach). Alternatively, catch the Airport Owl night-only public bus, or the SuperShuttle (☑305-871-8210; www.supershuttle.com) shared-van service, which will cost about $26 to South Beach. Be sure to reserve a seat the day before.

FORT LAUDERDALE HOLLYWOOD INTERNATIONAL AIRPORT Put the money you save on flights toward getting to Miami once you land; either rent a car at one of the many Fort Lauderdale agencies (see p233), or take the free shuttle from terminals 1 and 3 to the airport's **Tri-Rail station** (☑800-874-7245; www.tri-rail.com; one-way $2-5.50); you can ride this commuter train into Miami. The schedule is infrequent, though, so you may want to opt for the **GOShuttle** (☑954-561-8888; http:// floridalimo.hudsonltd.net), which will cost about $40 to South Beach.

Bicycle

A bike-share program on Miami Beach makes cycling around the beaches, at least, a cinch.

The Miami area may be as flat as a pancake, but it's also plagued by traffic backups and speedy thoroughfares, so judge the bikeability of your desired route carefully.

The city of Miami Beach offers the **DecoBike** (☑305-532-9494; www.decobike.com; 1-/3-day access $14/30) bike-share program. Bike stations are located in dozens of spots around Miami Beach (there's a map on the website, plus a link to an iPhone app that tells you where the nearest station is).

Places that rent bicycles:

BikeAndRoll (☑305-604-0001; www.bikeand roll.com; 401 Biscayne Blvd; ⏰10am-6pm; per hr/day from $5/15) Also does bike tours.

Mangrove Cycles (☑305-361-5555; 260 Crandon Blvd, Key Biscayne; ⏰10am-6pm Tue-Sun; per 2hr/day/week from $20/25/75)

Highgear Cycling (☑305-444-2175; www .highgearcycling.com; 3423 Main Hwy, Coconut Grove; ⏰10am-7pm Mon-Fri, to 6pm Sat, noon-5pm Sun; per hr/day from $12/35)

Bus

The local bus system is called **Metrobus** (☑305-891-3131; www.miamidade.gov/transit /routes.asp; tickets $2). An easy-to-read route map is available online. You may spend more time waiting for a bus than you will riding on one.

In South Beach, an excellent option is the **South Beach Local Circulator** (☑305-891-3131; $0.25), a looping shuttle bus with disabled-rider access that operates along Washington between South Pointe Dr and 17th St and loops back around on Alton Rd on the west side of the beach. Rides come along every 10 to 15 minutes.

Car & Motorcycle

If you drive around Miami there are a few things to keep in mind. Miami Beach is linked to the mainland by four causeways built over Biscayne Bay. They are, from south to north: the MacArthur (the extension of US Hwy 41 and Hwy A1A);

Venetian ($1.50 toll); Julia Tuttle and John F Kennedy.

The most important north–south highway is I-95, which ends at US Hwy 1 south of downtown Miami. US Hwy 1, which runs from Key West all the way north to Maine, hugs the coastline. It's called Dixie Hwy south of downtown Miami and Biscayne Blvd north of downtown Miami. The Palmetto Expressway (Hwy 826) makes a rough loop around the city and spurs off below SW 40th St to the Don Shula Expressway (Hwy 874, a toll road). Florida's Turnpike Extension makes the most western outer loop around the city. Hwy A1A becomes Collins Ave in Miami Beach.

Miami has an annoying convention of giving major roads multiple names. So for example, Bird Rd is both SW 40th St and Hwy 976. Hwy 826 is the Palmetto Expressway. US 1 is the Dixie Hwy – except in Downtown, when it becomes Biscayne Blvd. Hwy 836 is the Dolphin Expressway, while in Miami Beach 5th St becomes A1A. Calle Ocho is SW 8th St, as well as the Tamiami Trail, and US 41 (phew), and Hwy 959 is Red Rd, except when it's SW 57th St. Somehow, this isn't as confusing as it reads on paper – most signage indicates every name a route may have, but it can be frustrating to first-time Miami drivers.

Besides the causeways to Miami Beach, the major east–west roads are SW 8th St; Hwy 112 (also called Airport Expressway); and Hwy 836 (also called Dolphin Expressway), which slices through downtown Miami and connects with I-395 and the MacArthur Causeway, and which runs west to the Palmetto Expressway and Florida's Turnpike Extension.

Miami drivers are...how can we put this delicately?...aggressive, tailgating jerks who'd cut off their grandmother if they could figure out how to properly change lanes. We are, of course, kidding. Not all Miami drivers fit the above description, but there are enough of these maniacs about to make driving here a nightmare.

PARKING Parking is pretty straightforward. Regulations are well signposted and meters are plentiful (except perhaps on holiday-weekend evenings in South Beach). Downtown, near the **Bayside Marketplace**, parking is cheap but a bit confusing: you must find a place in the head-on parking lots (backing into the parking space not allowed), buy a ticket from a central machine, and display it in your windshield.

On South Beach there's metered street parking along most streets (except Lincoln Rd and residential areas). Meters are enforced from 9am to as late as 3am in some parts of South Beach. Most allow you to pay for up to three hours, although some have increased that range to 12 hours. Most Miami Beach meter machines include a credit-card option; parking rates vary, but it rarely costs more than $1.50 per hour.

There are many **municipal parking garages**, which are usually the easiest and cheapest option – look for giant blue 'P' signs. You'll find several located along Collins Ave and Washington Ave. If you park illegally or if the meter runs out, parking fines are about $30, but a tow could cost much more.

Taxi

Central Cabs (☑305-532-5555)
Dispatch Service (☑305-525-2455)
Flamingo Taxis (☑305-759-8100)
Metro (☑305-888-8888)
Sunshine (☑305-445-3333)
Yellow (☑305-400-0000)

Train

Around Miami the **Metromover** (www.miami dade.gov/transit), which is equal parts bus, monorail and train, is helpful for getting around downtown Miami. It offers visitors a great perspective on the city and a free orientation tour of the area.

Metrorail (www.miamidade.gov/transit) is a 21-mile-long heavy-rail system that has one elevated line running from Hialeah through downtown Miami and south to Kendall/Dadeland. Trains run every five to 15 minutes from 6am to midnight. The fare is $2, or $1 with a Metromover transfer.

The regional **Tri-Rail** (☑800-874-7245; www .tri-rail.com) double-decker commuter trains run the 71 miles between Dade, Broward and Palm Beach counties. Fares are calculated on a zone basis; the shortest distance traveled costs $4.40 round-trip, the most you'll ever pay is for the ride between MIA and West Palm Beach ($11.55 round-trip). No tickets are sold on the train, so allow time to make your purchase before boarding. All trains and stations are accessible to riders with disabilities. For a list of stations, log on to the Tri-Rail website.

The Everglades

Includes »

Best Places to Eat

» Robert is Here (p129)

» Joannie's Blue Crab Café (p126)

» JT's Island Grill & Gallery (p127)

» Rosita's (p130)

» Oyster House (p127)

Best Places to Stay

» Everglades International Hostel (p129)

» Everglades City Motel (p127)

» Ivey House Bed & Breakfast (p127)

» Wilderness Camping (p132)

» Rod & Gun Club Lodge (p127)

Why Go?

The Everglades truly make South Florida unique, even more so than Miami. Called the 'River of Grass' by its initial Native American inhabitants, this is not just a wetland, or a swamp, or a lake, or a river or a prairie, or a grassland – it is all of the above, twisted together into a series of soft horizons, long vistas, sunsets that stretch across your entire field of vision and the creeping grin of a large population of dinosaur-era reptiles.

When you watch anhinga flexing their wings before breaking into a corkscrew dive, or the slow, Jurassic flap of a great blue heron gliding over its domain, or the sun kissing miles of unbroken saw grass as it sets behind humps of skeletal cypress domes, you'll have an idea of what we're speaking of. In a nation where natural beauty is measured by its capacity for drama, the Everglades subtly, contentedly flows on.

When to Go

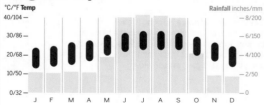

Everglades City

Dec–Mar Dry season: top wildlife viewing along watercourses, but some kayaking will be difficult.

Apr–Jun Although the weather gets pretty hot, there's a good mix of water and wildlife.

Jul–Nov Lots of heat, lots of bugs and (except October and November) chances of hurricanes.

EVERGLADES NATIONAL PARK

Tamiami Trail

Although the grassy waters – the Everglades ecosystem – extend outside Everglades National Park (the third-largest in continental USA), you really need to enter the park to experience it. There are three main entrances and three main areas of the park: one along the southeast edge near Homestead and Florida City (Ernest Coe section); at the central-north side on the Tamiami Trail (Shark Valley section); and a third at the northwest shore (Gulf Coast section), past Everglades City. The Shark Valley and Gulf Coast sections of the park come one after the other in geographic succession, but the Ernest Coe area is entirely separate. At all of these entrances you'll pay $10 for a vehicle pass, or $5 if you're a cyclist, both of which are good for entrance for seven consecutive days into any entrance in the park.

These entrances allow for two good road trips from Miami. The first choice is heading west along the Tamiami Trail, past the Miccosukee reservation and Shark Valley, all the way to Everglades City, the Gulf Coast and the crystal waters of the 10,000 Islands.

The other option is to enter at Ernest Coe and take Hwy 9336 to Flamingo through the most 'Glades-y' landscape in the park, with unbroken vistas of wet prairie, big sky and long silences.

❶ Getting There & Away

The largest subtropical wilderness in the continental USA is easily accessible from Miami. The Glades, which comprise the 80 southernmost miles of Florida, are bound by the Atlantic Ocean to the east and the Gulf of Mexico to the west. The Tamiami Trail (US Hwy 41) goes east–west, parallel to the more northern (and less interesting) Alligator Alley (I-75).

❶ Getting Around

You need a car to properly enter the Everglades and once you're in, wearing a good pair of walking boots is essential to penetrate the interior. Having a canoe or kayak helps as well; these can be rented from outfits inside and outside of the park, or else you can seek out guided canoe and kayak tours. Bicycles are well suited to the flat roads of Everglades National Park, particularly in the area between Ernest Coe and Flamingo Point, but they're useless off the highway. In addition, the road shoulders in the park tend to be dangerously small.

Calle Ocho, in Miami's Little Havana (p67) happens to be the eastern end of the Tamiami Trail/US 41, which cuts through the Everglades to the Gulf of Mexico. So go west, young traveler, along US 41, a few dozen miles and several different worlds away from the city where the heat is on. This trip leads you onto the northern edges of the park, past long landscapes of flooded forest, gambling halls, swamp-buggy tours, roadside food shacks and other Old Florida accoutrements.

Past Hialeah, Miami fades like a trail of diminishing Starbucks until...*whoosh*...it's all huddled forest, open fields and a big canal off to the side (evidence of US 41's diversion of the Glades' all-important sheet flow). The surest sign the city is gone and the Glades have begun is the Confederate flag decals on **Pit BBQ** (p126). The empty road runs past the **Miccosukee Resort & Convention Center** (✆305-925-2555, 877-242-6464; www.miccosukee.com; 500 SW 177th Ave; r Dec-Mar/Apr-Nov $150/120; ✿⚓). It's essentially a casino-hotel complex full of slot machines and folks chunking coins into them – not really an ecological wonderland. Rooms have attractive geometric Native American designs worked into the furniture, but again, there's no need to stay here unless you're gambling.

As you head west you'll see fields and fields of pine forest and billboards advertising swamp tours. Airboats tours are an old-school way of seeing the Everglades (and there is something to be said for getting a tour from a raging Skynyrd fan with killer tatts and better camo), but there are other ways of exploring the park as well.

SHARK VALLEY
◎ Sights & Activities

Shark Valley   PARK

(✆305-221-8776; www.nps.gov/ever/planyourvisit/svdirections; car/cyclist $10/5; ◷8:30am-6pm) Shark Valley sounds like it should be the headquarters for the villain in a James Bond movie, but it is in fact a slice of National Park Service grounds heavy with informative signs and knowledgeable rangers. Shark Valley is located in the cypress-and-hardwood-and-riverine section of the Everglades, a more traditionally jungly section of the park than the grassy fields and forest domes surrounding the Ernest Coe visitor center. A 15-mile/24km paved trail takes you past

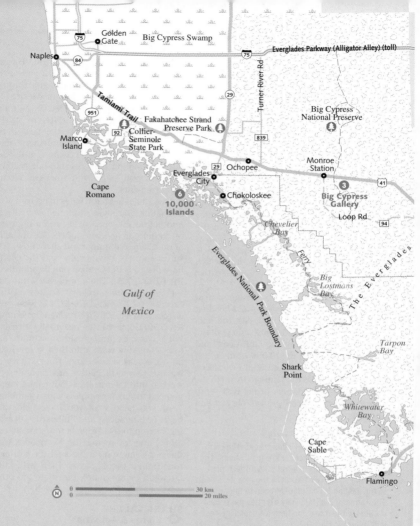

Everglades Highlights

1 Watching the sun set over the ingress road to **Pa-hay-okee Overlook** (p130) from the roof of your car

2 Canoeing or kayaking into **Hell's Bay Paddling Trail**

(p130), a tangled morass of red creeks, slow blackwater and the heavy vegetative curtain of a preserved marsh

3 Checking out some of the best photography of the

surrounding swamps, forests, beaches and sea at **Big Cypress Gallery** (p124)

4 Helping support the animal rescue operations

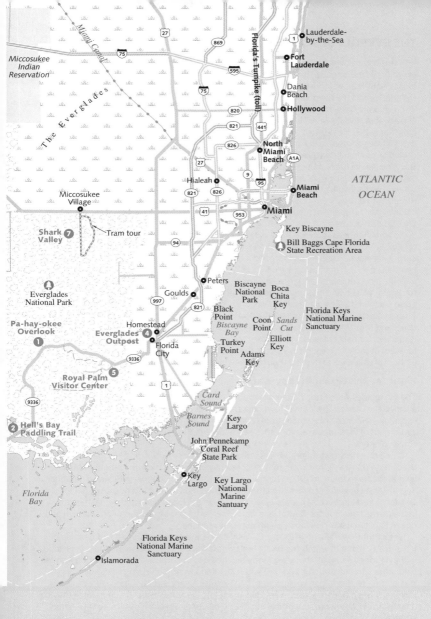

Miami Canal

Miccosukee
Indian
Reservation

The Everglades

27

869

75

75

595

1

Lauderdale-
by-the-Sea

Fort
Lauderdale

820

821

441

Dania
Beach

Hollywood

826

North
Miami
Beach

A1A

ATLANTIC
OCEAN

Miccosukee
Village

27

821

826

Hialeah

9

95

Miami
Beach

41

953

Miami

Shark
Valley

7

Tram tour

94

Key Biscayne

Bill Baggs Cape Florida
State Recreation Area

Peters

Goulds

997

821

Biscayne
National
Park

Boca
Chita
Key

Everglades
National Park

Pa-hay-okee
Overlook

1

Homestead

Everglades
Outpost

4

Florida
City

9336

Black
Point

Biscayne
Bay

Turkey
Point

Coon
Point

Adams
Key

Sands
Cut

Elliott
Key

Florida Keys
National Marine
Sanctuary

Royal Palm
Visitor Center

5

9336

Hell's Bay
Paddling Trail

2

1

Card
Sound

Barnes
Sound

Key
Largo

John Pennekamp
Coral Reef
State Park

Florida
Bay

Key
Largo

Key Largo
National
Marine
Sanctuary

Florida Keys
National Marine
Sanctuary

Islamorada

underway at the **Everglades
Outpost** (p129)

5 Spotting alligators at
night at the **Royal Palm
Visitor Center** (p130)

6 Riding your bicycle or the
excellent public tram at **Shark
Valley** (p119)

7 Canoeing or kayaking
through the scattered islands
of **10,000 Islands** (p128).

THE EVERGLADES: AN OVERVIEW

It's tempting to think of the Everglades as a swamp, but 'prairie' may be a more apt description. The Glades, at the end of the day, are grasslands that happen to be flooded for most of the year: visit during the dry season (winter) and you'd be forgiven for thinking the Everglades was the Everfields.

So where's the water coming from? Look north on a map of Florida, all the way to Lake Okeechobee and the small lakes and rivers that band together around Kissimmee. Florida dips into the Gulf of Mexico at its below-sea-level tip, which happens to be the lowest part of the state geographically and topographically. Run-off water from central Florida flows down the peninsula via streams and rivers, over and through the Glades, and into Florida Bay. The glacial pace of the flood means this seemingly stillest of landscapes is actually in constant motion. Small wonder the Calusa Indians called the area Pa-hay-okee (grassy water). Beloved conservationist Marjory Stoneman Douglas (1890–1998) called it the River of Grass; in her famous book of the same title, she revealed that Gerard de Brahm, a colonial cartographer, named the region the River Glades, which became Ever Glades on later English maps.

So what happens when nutrient-rich water creeps over a limestone shelf? The ecological equivalent of a sweaty orgy. Beginning at the cellular level, organic material blooms in surprising ways, clumping and forming into algal beds, nutrient blooms and the ubiquitous periphyton, which are basically clusters of algae, bacteria and detritus (ie stuff). Periphyton ain't pretty: in the water they resemble puke streaks and the dried version looks like hippo turds. But you should kiss them when you see them (well, maybe not), because in the great chain of the Everglades, this slop forms the base of a very tall organic totem pole. The smallest tilt in elevation alters the flow of water and hence the content of this nutrient soup, and thus the landscape itself: all those patches of cypress and hardwood hammock (not a bed for backpackers; in this case, hammock is a fancy Floridian way of saying a forest of broadleaf trees, mainly tropical or subtropical) are areas where a few inches of altitude create a world of difference between biosystems.

Fight for the Green Grassy Waters

The Everglades were utter wilderness for thousands of years. Even Native Americans avoided the Glades; the 'native' Seminole and Miccosukee actually settled here as exiles escaping war and displacement from other parts of the country. But following European settlement of Florida, some pioneers saw the potential for economic development of the Grassy Waters.

Cattle ranchers and sugar growers, attracted by mucky waters and Florida's subtropical climate (paradise for sugarcane), successfully pressured the government to make land available to them. In 1905, Florida governor Napoleon Bonaparte Broward personally dug the first shovelful of a diversion that connected the Caloosahatchee River to Lake Okeechobee. Hundreds of canals were cut through the Everglades to the coastline to 'reclaim' the land, and the flow of lake water was restricted by a series of dikes. Farmland began to claim areas previously uninhabited by humans.

Unfortunately, the whole 'River of Grass' needs the river to survive. And besides being a pretty place to watch the birds, the Everglades acts as a hurricane barrier and kidney. Kidney? Yup: all those wetlands leeched out pollutants from the Florida Aquifer (the state's freshwater supply). But when farmland wasn't diverting the sheet flow, it was adding fertilizer-rich wastewater to it. Result? A very sweaty (and well-attended) biological orgy. Bacteria, and eventually plant life, bloomed at a ridiculous rate (they call it fertilizer for a reason), upsetting the fragile balance of resources vital to the Glades' survival.

Enter Marjory Stoneman Douglas, stage left. Ms Douglas gets the credit for almost single-handedly pushing the now age-old Florida issue of Everglades conservation; for more on this titan of the US environmental movement, see the boxed text, p126.

Despite the tireless efforts of Douglas and other environmentalists, today the Florida Aquifer is in serious danger of being contaminated and drying up. In 2011, the water level in Okeechobee was almost 2.7 inches below normal level. The number of wading birds nesting has declined by 90% to 95% since the 1930s. Currently, there are 67 threatened and endangered plant and animal species in the park.

The diversion of water away from the Glades and run-off pollution are the main culprits behind the region's environmental degradation. This delicate ecosystem is the neighbor of one of the fastest-growing urban areas in the US. The current water-drainage system in South Florida was built to handle the needs of two million people; the local population topped six million in 2010. And while Miami can't grow north or south into Fort Lauderdale or Homestead, it can move west, directly into the Everglades. At this stage, scientists estimate the wetlands have been reduced by 50% to 75% of their original size.

Humans are not the only enemy of the Everglades. Nature has done its share of damage as well. During 2055's Hurricane Wilma, for example, six storm-water treatment areas (artificial wetlands that cleanse excess nutrients out of the water cycle) were lashed and heavily damaged by powerful winds. Without these natural filtration systems, the Glades are far more susceptible to nutrient blooms and external pollution. In 2011, wildfires caused by drought incinerated huge patches of land near the Tamiami Trail.

Restoration of the Everglades

Efforts to save the Everglades began in the late 1920s, but were sidelined by the Great Depression. In 1926 and 1928, two major hurricanes caused Lake Okeechobee to overflow; the resulting floods killed hundreds. The Army Corps of Engineers did a really good job of damming the lake. A bit too good: the Glades were essentially cut off from their source, the Kissimmee watershed.

In the meantime, conservationists began donating land for protection, starting with 1 sq mile of land donated by a garden club. The Everglades was declared a national park in 1947, the same year Marjory Stoneman Douglas' *The Everglades: River of Grass* was published.

By draining the wetlands through the damming of the lake, the Army Corps made huge swaths of inland Florida inhabitable. But the environmental problems created by shifting water's natural flow, plus the area's ever-increasing population, now threaten to make the whole region uninhabitable. The canal system sends, on average, over 1 billion gallons of water into the ocean every day. At the same time, untreated runoff flows unfiltered into natural water supplies. Clean water is disappearing from the water cycle while South Florida's population gets bigger by the day.

Enter the **Comprehensive Everglades Restoration Project** (CERP; www.everglades plan.org). CERP is designed to address the root of all Everglades issues: water – where to get it, how to divert it and ways to keep it clean. The plan is to unblock the Kissimmee, restoring remaining Everglades lands to predevelopment conditions, while maintaining flood protection, providing freshwater for South Florida's populace and protecting earmarked regions against urban sprawl. It sounds great, but political battles have significantly slowed the implementation of CERP. The cost of the project has bloomed from around $7.8 billion to $15 billion, and rather than sharing a 50-50 split, as of research Florida has footed 79% of the CERP bill. In the meantime, Florida funding has fallen from $200 million during the Jeb Bush years to $17 million under Rick Scott.

Bringing back the Everglades is one of the biggest, most ambitious environmental restoration projects in US history, one that combines the needs of farmers, fishers, urban residents, local governments and conservationists. The success or failure of the program will be a bellwether for the future of the US environmental movement.

THE EVERGLADES EVERGLADES NATIONAL PARK

Airboats are flat-bottomed skiffs that use powerful fans to propel themselves through the water. Their environmental impact has not been determined, but one thing is clear: airboats can't be doing much good, which is why they're not allowed in the park. Swamp buggies are enormous balloon-tired vehicles that can go through wetlands, creating ruts and damaging wildlife.

Airboat and swamp-buggy rides are offered all along US Hwy 41 (Tamiami Trail). Think twice before going on a 'nature' tour. Loud whirring fanboats and marsh jeeps really don't do the quiet serenity of the Glades justice. That said, many tourists in the Everglades are there (obviously) because of their interest in the environment, and they demand environmentally knowledgeable tours. The airboat guys are pretty good at providing these – their livelihood is also caught up in preservation of the Glades, and they know the back country well. We recommend going with the guys at **Cooperstown** (☑305-226-6048; www.cooperstownairboats.com; 22700 SW 8th St; adult/child $22/11; ⛟), one of the first airboat operators you encounter heading west on 41. Just expect a more touristy experience than the National Park grounds.

small creeks, tropical forest and 'borrow pits' (manmade holes that are now basking spots for gators, turtles and birdlife). The pancake-flat trail is perfect for bicycles, which can be rented at the entrance for $7.50 per hour. Bring water with you.

Tram Tour
(☑305-221-8455; www.sharkvalleytramtours.com; adult/child under 12yr/senior $18.25/11.50/17.25; ⏰departures 9:30am, 11am, 1pm, 3pm May-Dec, 9am-4pm every hour on the hour Jan-Apr) If you don't feel like exerting yourself, the most popular and painless way to immerse yourself in the Everglades is via the two-hour tram trip that runs along Shark Valley's entire 15-mile trail. If you only have time for one Everglades activity, this should be it, as guides are informative and witty, and you'll likely see gators sunning themselves on the road. Halfway along the trail is the 50ft-high **Shark Valley Observation Tower**, an ugly concrete tower that offers dramatically beautiful views of the park.

Trails
At the park entrance, the easy **Bobcat Boardwalk** makes a loop through a thick copse of tropical hardwoods before emptying you out right back into the Shark Valley parking lot. A little ways past is the **Otter Cave Trail**, which heads over a limestone shelf that has been Swiss-cheesed into a porous sponge by rainwater. Animals now live in the eroded holes (although it's not likely you'll spot any) and Native Americans used to live on top of the shelf.

Miccosukee Village　　　PARK
(www.miccosukee.com; village/airboat ride $8/10; ⏰9am-5pm) Just across the road from Shark Valley, this 'village' is an informative, entertaining open-air museum that showcases the culture of the Miccosukee via guided tours of traditional homes, a crafts gift store, dance and music performances, an airboat ride into a hammock-cum-village of raised 'chickee' (wooden platforms built above the waterline) huts and (natch) gator wrestling. There's a somewhat desultory on-site restaurant if you get hungry. The on-site art gallery and the handmade crafts make a good souvenir.

BIG CYPRESS & OCHOPEE
The better part of the Tamiami Trail is fronted on either side by long cypress trees overhung with moss and endless vistas of soft prairie, flooded in the wet season into a boggy River of Grass.

◉ **Sights & Activities**

Big Cypress Gallery　　　GALLERY
(☑941-695-2428; www.clydebutcher.com; Tamiami Trail; ⏰10am-5pm Wed-Mon) The highlight of many Everglades trips, this gallery showcases the work of Clyde Butcher, an American photographer who follows in the great tradition of Ansel Adams. His large-format black-and-white images elevate the swamps to a higher level. Butcher has found a quiet spirituality in the brackish waters and you might, too, with the help of his eyes. Every Labor Day (first weekend in September), the gallery holds a gala event, which includes a fun $20 swamp walk onto his 30-acre property; the party attracts swamp-stompers from across

the state. At the time of writing, the gallery was setting up two homes located in the cypress woods as guesthouses – the properties look pretty nice, can sleep from four to six people and will cost around $200 per night.

Big Cypress National Preserve   PARK
(☎239-695-4758; 33000 Tamiami Trail E; ⊙8:30am-4:30pm) The 1139-sq-mile Big Cypress Preserve (named for the size of the park, not its trees) is the result of a compromise between environmentalists, cattle ranchers and oil-and-gas explorers. The area is integral to the Everglades' ecosystem: rains that flood the Preserve's prairies and wetlands slowly filter down through the Glades. About 45% of the cypress swamp (actually a group of mangrove islands, hardwood hammocks, slash pine, prairies and marshes) is protected. Great bald cypress trees are nearly gone, thanks to pre-Preserve lumbering, but dwarf pond cypress trees (more impressive than the name suggests) fill the area with their own understated beauty. The **Oasis Visitor Center** (☎941-695-1201; ⊙8am-4:30pm Mon-Fri;🖰), about 20 miles west of Shark Valley, has great exhibits for the kids and an outdoor, water-filled ditch popular with alligators.

Florida National Scenic Trail
(www.nps.gov/bicy/planyourvisit/florida-trail.htm) There are some 31 miles of the Florida National Scenic Trail within Big Cypress National Preserve. From the southern terminus, which can be accessed via Loop Rd, the trail runs 8.3 miles north to US 41. The way is flat, but it's hard going: you'll almost certainly be wading through water, and you'll have to pick your way through a series of solution holes (small sinkholes) and thick hardwood hammocks. There is often no shelter from the sun, and the bugs are... *plentiful.* There are three primitive campsites with water wells along the trail; pick up a map at the visitor center. Most campsites are free, and you needn't register. **Monument Lake** (May-Dec 14 free, Dec 15-Apr $16) has water and toilets.

Ochopee   VILLAGE
(GPS 25.901529, -81.306023) Drive to the hamlet of Ochopee (population about four)...no... wait...turn around, you missed it! Then pull over and break out the cameras: Ochopee's claim to fame is the country's smallest **post office**. It's housed in a former toolshed and set against big park skies; a friendly postal worker patiently poses for snapshots.

Skunk Ape Research Headquarters   PARK
(☎239-695-2275; www.skunkape.info; 40904 Tamiami Trail E; ⊙7am-7pm, 'zoo' closes around 4pm) Sometimes we think Florida needs to change its state motto to 'Florida; You Can't Make This Stuff Up.' To whit: the Skunk Ape Research Center, topped by a giant panther statue, dedicated to tracking down Southeastern USA's version of Bigfoot, the eponymous Skunk Ape (a large gorilla-man who supposedly stinks to high heaven). We never saw a Skunk Ape here, but you can see a corny gift shop and, in the back, a reptile and bird zoo run by a true Florida eccentric, the sort of guy who wraps albino pythons around his neck for fun. Donate a few bucks at the entrance.

Everglades Adventure Tours   TOURS
(EAT; ☎800-504-6554; www.evergladesadventuretours.com; tours from $69) We already like the guys at EAT for being based out of the same headquarters as the Skunk Ape people; we like them even more for offering some of the best private tours of the Everglades

---

DETOUR: LOOP ROAD

Loop Rd, off Tamiami Trail (Hwy 41), offers some unique sites. One: the homes of the **Miccosukee**, some of which have been considerably expanded by gambling revenue. You'll see some traditional chickee-style huts and some trailers with massive add-on wings that are bigger than the original trailer – all seem to have shiny new pickup trucks parked out front. Two: great pull-offs for viewing flooded forests, where egrets that look like pterodactyls perch in the trees. Three: houses with large Confederate flags and 'Stay off my property' signs; these homes are as much a part of the landscape as the swamp. And four: the short, pleasantly jungly **Tree Snail Hammock Nature Trail**. Be warned the Loop is a rough, unpaved road; you'll need a 4WD vehicle (there has been talk of repaving the road, so it may have improved by the time you read this). True to its name, the road loops right back onto the Tamiami; expect a good long jaunt on the Loop to add two hours to your trip.

we've found. Swamp hikes, 'safaris,' airboats and, best of all, being poled around in a canoe or skiff by some genuinely funny guys with genuine local knowledge of the Grassy Waters; it's an absolute treat. The Eat guys have set up a campsite at Skunk Ape HQ; it costs $30 to camp here, and there's wi-fi throughout the camp.

✕ Eating

Joannie's Blue Crab Café　　　AMERICAN $
(joaniesbluecrabcafe.com; Tamiami Trail; mains $9-17; ⊙9am-5pm) This quintessential shack, east of Ochopee, with open rafters, shellacked picnic tables and alligator kitsch, serves delicious food of the 'fried everything' variety on paper plates. There's live music most days.

Pit BBQ　　　AMERICAN $
(16400 SW 8th St, btwn Miami & Shark Valley; mains $4-9; ⊙11am-11:30pm) The barbecue is decent and served on picnic tables with a side of country music and Confederate-flag accoutrement. It is as cheesy as a dairy, so if you can't arm yourself with irony, drive on.

EVERGLADES CITY

The end of the track is an old Florida fishing village of raised houses, turquoise water and scattershot emerald-green mangrove islands. Hwy 29 runs south through town into the peaceful residential island of Chokoloskee, past a great psychedelic mural of a gator on a shed. 'City' is an ambitious name for Everglades City, but this is a friendly fishing town where you can easily lose yourself for a day or three.

◉ Sights & Activities

Gulf Coast Visitor Center　　　PARK
(☑239-695-3311; Hwy 29, Everglades City, 815 Oyster Bar Ln; ⊙9am-4:30pm May-Oct, from 8am Nov-Apr; tours from $25, boat rentals per hr from $13) This is the northwest-most ranger station for Everglades National Park, and provides access to the 10,000 Islands area. Boat tours depart from the downstairs marina into the mangrove flats and green islands – if you're lucky you may see dolphins springing up beside your craft. This tangled off-shore archipelago was a major smuggling point for drugs into the mainland USA

GLADES GUARDIAN

In a state known for iconoclasts, no one can hold a candle to Marjory Stoneman Douglas. Not just for her quirks, but for her drive. A persistent, unbreakable force, she fueled one of the longest conservation battles in US history.

Born in 1890, Douglas moved to Florida after her failed first marriage. She worked for the *Miami Herald* and eventually as a freelance writer, producing short stories that are notable for both the quality of the writing and their progressive themes: *Plumes* (1930) and *Wings* (1931), published in the *Saturday Evening Post,* addressed the issue of Glades bird-poaching when the business was still immensely popular (the feathers were used to decorate ladies' hats).

In the 1940s, Douglas was asked to write about the Miami River for the Rivers of America Series and promptly chucked the idea in favor of capturing the Everglades in her classic, *The Everglades: River of Grass*. Like all of Douglas' work the book is remarkable for both its exhaustive research and lyrical, rich language.

River of Grass immediately sold out of its first print-run, and public perception of the Everglades shifted from 'nasty swamp' to 'national treasure.' Douglas went on to be an advocate for environmental causes ('It is a woman's business to be interested in the environment. It's an extended form of housekeeping.'), women's rights and racial equality, fighting, for example, for basic infrastructure in Miami's Overtown.

Today she is remembered as Florida's favorite environmentalist. Always immaculately turned out in gloves, dress, pearls and floppy straw hat, she would bring down engineers, developers, politicians and her most hated opponents, sugar farmers ('They should go at any time, now, as far as I'm concerned. Pick up and go. Any minute. We won't miss them a bit.') by force of her oratory alone. She kept up the fight, speaking and lecturing without fail, until she died in 1998 at the age of 108.

Today it seems every environmental institution in Florida is named for Douglas, but were she around, we doubt she'd care for those honors. She'd be too busy planting herself in the CERP office, making sure everything was moving along on schedule, and playing the disappointed older woman if it weren't.

during the late 1970s and early '80s; bales of marijuana were nicknamed 'square grouper' by local fishermen. It's great fun to go kayaking and canoeing around here; boats can be rented from the marina, but make sure to take a map with you (they're available for free in the visitor center).

Museum of the Everglades
MUSEUM
(NACT; www.evergladesmuseum.org; 105 W Broadway; ⊙9am-5pm Tue-Fri, to 4pm Sat) This small museum, located in an old library, has some placards and information on the settlement of the Everglades – the focus is far more concerned with the human history of the area than the natural environment. It's a decidedly community museum, with the feel of an attic full of everyone's interesting stuff and heirlooms, but charming for all that as well.

If you're up for a tour, try Everglades Adventure Tours (p125) or the guys at **North American Canoe Tours** (NACT; ☑941-695-3299/4666; www.evergladesadventures.com; Ivey House Bed & Breakfast, 107 Camellia St; ⊙Nov–mid-Apr) rent out camping equipment and canoes for full/half-days ($35/$25) and touring kayaks ($45 to $65). You get 20% off most of these services and rentals if you're staying at the Ivey House Bed & Breakfast (below), which runs the tours. Tours shuttle you to places like Chokoloskee Island, Collier Seminole State Park, Rabbit Key or Tiger Key for afternoon or overnight excursions (from $99).

🛏 Sleeping

All lodging is family-friendly, and comes with air-conditioning and parking.

TOP CHOICE Everglades City Motel
MOTEL $$
(☑239-695-4244, 877-567-0679; www.evergladescitymotel.com; 310 Collier Ave; r from $80; ❄🕸📶🐾) With large renovated rooms that have flat-screen TVs, arctic air-conditioning and a fantastically friendly staff that will hook you up with whatever tours your heart desires, this is an exceptionally good-value lodge for those looking to spend some time near the 10,000 Islands.

Ivey House Bed & Breakfast
B&B $$
(☑239-695-3299, 877-567-0679; www.iveyhouse.com; 107 Camellia St; lodge $74-120, inn $99-209; ❄🕸📶🐾) This family-run tropical inn serves good breakfasts in its small Ghost Orchid Grill. Plus it operates some of the best nature trips around (North American Canoe Tours).

Ivey offers an entire range of package vacations (www.iveyhouse.com/package-vacation .htm), from day trips to six-day excursions including lodging, tours and some meals; trips run from $300 to $2290.

Rod & Gun Club Lodge
B&B $$
(☑239-695-2101; www.evergladesrodandgun.com; 200 Riverside Dr; r July–mid-Oct $95, mid-Oct-Jun $110-140; P❄🐾) Built in the 1920s as a hunting lodge by Barron Collier (who needed a place to chill after watching workers dig his Tamiami Trail), this masculine place, fronted by a lovely porch, has a restaurant that serves anything that moves in them thar waters.

Parkway Motel & Marina
MOTEL $
(☑239-695-3261; 1180 Chokoloskee Dr; www .parkwaymotelandmarina.com; r $99-120; P❄🐾) An extremely friendly owner (and an even friendlier dog) runs this veritable testament to the old-school Floridian lodge: cute small rooms and one cozy apartment in a one-story motel building.

🍴 Eating

JT's Island Grill & Gallery
AMERICAN $
(238 Mamie St, Chokoloskee; mains $5-16; ⊙11am-3pm late Oct-May) Just a mile or so past the edge of town, this awesome cafe-cum-art-gallery sits in a restored 1890 general store. It's outfitted with bright retro furniture and piles of kitschy books, pottery, clothing and maps (all for sale). But the best part is the food (lunch only) – fresh crab cakes, salads, fish platters and veggie wraps, made with locally grown organic vegetables.

Oyster House
SEAFOOD $
(on Chokoloskee Causeway; mains $8-22; ⊙10am-11pm) Besides serving the Everglades staples of excellent fried seafood and burgers, Oyster House has a friendly bar with a screened-in porch where you can drink, slap mosquitoes and have a chat with friendly local boozehounds.

Seafood Depot
SEAFOOD $
(102 Collier Ave; mains $14-33; ⊙10:30am-9pm) Don't totally sublimate your desire for fried food, because the gator tail and frog's legs here offer an excellent way to honor the inhabitants of the Everglades: douse them in Tabasco and devour them.

ℹ Information
Everglades Area Chamber of Commerce
(☑239-695-3941; cnr US Hwy 41 & Hwy 29; ⊙9am-4pm)

CANOE CAMPING ON 10,000 ISLANDS

One of the best ways to experience the serenity of the Everglades – somehow desolate yet lush, tropical and foreboding – is by paddling the network of waterways that skirt the northwest portion of the park. The **10,000 Islands** consist of many (but not really 10,000) tiny islands and a mangrove swamp that hugs the southwestern-most border of Florida. The **Wilderness Waterway**, a 99-mile path between Everglades City and Flamingo, is the longest canoe trail in the area, but there are shorter trails near Flamingo.

Most islands are fringed by narrow beaches with sugar-white sand, but note that the water is brackish, and very shallow most of the time. It's not Tahiti, but it's fascinating. You can camp on your own island for up to a week.

Getting around the 10,000 Islands is pretty straightforward if you religiously adhere to National Oceanic & Atmospheric Administration (NOAA) tide and nautical charts. Going against the tides is the fastest way to make a miserable trip. The Gulf Coast Visitor Center (p126) sells nautical charts and gives out free tidal charts. You can also purchase charts prior to your visit – call ☑305-247-1216 and ask for chart numbers 11430, 11432 and 11433.

EVERGLADES CITY TO NAPLES

Fakahatchee Strand Preserve PARK
(www.floridastateparks.org/fakahatcheestrand/; Coastline Dr, Copeland; admission free; ⊘8am-sunset) The Fakahatchee Strand, besides having a fantastic name, also houses a 20-mile by 5-mile estuarine wetland that could have emerged directly out of the *Jurassic Park* franchise. A 2000ft boardwalk traverses this wet and wild wonderland, where panthers still stalk their prey amid the black waters. While it's unlikely you'll spot any, there's a great chance you'll see a large variety of bird life and reptiles ranging in size from tiny skinks to grinning alligators.

Homestead to Flamingo Point

Head south of Miami to drive into the heart of the park and the best horizons of the Everglades. Plus, there are plenty of side paths and canoe creeks to detour onto. You'll see some of the most quietly exhilarating scenery the park has to offer on this route, and have better access to an interior network of trails for those wanting to push off the beaten track into the buggy, muggy solar plexus of the wetlands.

HOMESTEAD & FLORIDA CITY

Homestead is not the prettiest town in the USA. After getting battered into rubble by Hurricane Andrew in 1992 and becoming part of the expanding subdivisions of South Miami, it's been poorly planned around fast-food stops, car dealerships and gas stations. A lot of Mexicans have moved here seeking farm work (or moved here providing services for farm laborers), and as a result, if you speak Spanish, it's impossible not to notice the shift in accent as Cuban Spanish gives way to Mexican. Radio stations also shift from Cuban reggaeton and hip-hop to brass-style mariachi music.

You could pass a mildly entertaining afternoon walking around Homestead's almost quaint **Main Street** (www.homestead mainstreet.org) which essentially comprises a couple of blocks of Krome Ave extending north and south of **Old Town Hall** (41 N Krome Ave). It's a good effort at injecting some character into 'downtown' Homestead.

With that said, let us give Homestead huge props: it houses two of the great attractions of the Florida roadside, one of its best hostels and an incredible farmers' market. Yup: four 'top picks' in one town.

◉ Sights

Coral Castle CASTLE
(www.coralcastle.com; 28655 S Dixie Hwy; adult/ child 7-18yr $12/7; ⊘8am-6pm, to 8pm Sat & Sun) 'You will be seeing unusual accomplishment,' reads the inscription on the rough-hewn quarried wall. That's an understatement. There is no greater temple to all that is weird and wacky about South Florida than the legend: a Latvian gets snubbed at the altar. Comes to the US. Moves to Florida. Hand carves, unseen, in the dead of night, a monument to unrequited love: a rock compound that includes a 'throne room,' a sun dial, a stone stockade (his intended's 'timeout area') and a revolving boulder gate that engineers around the world, to this day, cannot

explain. Oh, and there are audio stations situated around the place that explain the site in a replicated Latvian accent, so it feels like you're getting a narrated tour by Borat.

TOP CHOICE **Everglades Outpost** WILDLIFE SANCTUARY (www.evergladesoutpost.org; 35601 SW 192nd Ave; recommended donation $20; ⊙10am-4pm Sat & Sun, by appointment Mon-Fri) If the Coral Castle is amusing, the Everglades Outpost is moving and heart-warming. An effort cobbled together by a dedicated family and friends, all animal-lovers to the core, the outpost houses, feeds and cares for wild animals that have been seized from illegal traders, abused, neglected or donated by people who could not care for them. Residents of the outpost include gibbons, a lemur, wolves, cobras, alligators and a pair of majestic tigers (one of whom was bought by an exotic dancer who thought she could incorporate it into her act). Your money goes into helping the outpost's mission; we can think of few better causes in the area. During the week, just call ahead to visit.

🛏 Sleeping

There are plenty of chains like Best Western, the Days Inn and similar hotels and motels all along Rt 1 Krome Ave.

TOP CHOICE **Everglades International Hostel** HOSTEL $ (☑305-248-1122, 800-372-3874; www.evergladeshostel.com; 20 SW 2nd Ave, Florida City; camping $18, dm $28, d $61-75; ℗✳🛜🏊) Located in a cluttered, comfy 1930s boarding house, this friendly hostel has good-value dorms, private rooms and 'semi-privates' (you have an enclosed room within the dorms and share a bathroom with dorm residents). But what

they've done with their back yard – wow. It's a serious garden of earthly delights. There's: a tree house; a natural rock-cut pool with a waterfall; a Bedouin pavilion that doubles as a dancehall; a gazebo; an open-air tented 'bed room'; an oven built to resemble a tail-molting tadpole. It all needs to be seen to be believed, and best of all you can sleep anywhere in the back for $18. Sleep in a tree house! We think that's an amazing deal. We should add the crowd is made up of all those funky international traveler types that made you fall in love with backpacking in the first place, and the hostel conducts some of the best tours into the Everglades around.

Redland Hotel HOTEL $$ (☑305-246-1904; www.redlandhotel.com; 5 S Flagler Ave, Homestead; r $83-150; ℗🛜) This historic inn has clean, individualized rooms with a distinct doily vibe. The building served as the town's first hotel, mercantile store, post office, library and boarding house (for real!) and is now favored by folks who want more of a personal touch than you can get from the chains.

🍴 Eating

TOP CHOICE **Robert Is Here** MARKET $ (www.robertishere.com; 19200 SW 344th St, Homestead; ⊙8am-7pm Nov-Aug) More than a farmer's stand, Robert's is an institution. This is Old Florida at its kitschy best, in love with the Glades and the agriculture that surrounds it. There's a petting zoo for the kids, live music at night, plenty of homemade preserves and sauces, and while everyone goes crazy for the milkshakes – as they should – do not leave without having the fresh orange juice. It's the best in the world. What's up with the funny name? Well, back in the day

---

AH-TAH-THI-KI MUSEUM

If you want to learn about Florida's Native Americans, come to this **Seminole museum** (☑877-902-1113; www.ahtahthiki.com; Big Cypress Seminole Indian Reservation, Clewiston; adult/child/senior $9/6/6; ⊙9am-5pm), 17 miles north of I-75. All of the excellent educational exhibits on Seminole life, history and the tribe today were founded on gaming proceeds, which provide most of the tribe's multimillion-dollar operating budget.

The museum is actually located within a cypress dome cut through with an interpretive boardwalk, so from the start it strikes a balance between environmentalism and education. The permanent exhibit has several dioramas with life-sized figures depicting various scenes out of traditional Seminole life, while temporary exhibits have a but more academic polish (past ones have included lengthy forays into the economic structure of the Everglades). There's an old-school 'living village' and recreated ceremonial grounds as well. Overall, the Ah-tah-thi-ki is making an effort to not be a cheesy Native American theme park, and the Seminole tribe is to be commended for its effort in this regard.

129

THE EVERGLADES HOMESTEAD TO FLAMINGO POINT

the namesake of the pavilion was selling his daddy's cucumbers on this very spot, but no traffic was slowing down for the produce. So a sign was constructed that announced, in big red letters, that Robert was, in fact, here. He has been ever since, too.

Rosita's
MEXICAN $

(☑305-246-3114; 199 W Palm Dr, Florida City; mains under $10; ☺8:30am-9pm) There's a working-class Mexican crowd here, testament to the sheer awesomeness of the tacos and burritos. Everyone is friendly, and best of all, they'll give you a takeaway plate if you're staying at the next-door Everglades International Hostel.

Farmers Market Restaurant
AMERICAN $

(☑305-242-0008; 300 N Krome Ave, Florida City; lunch mains $8-13, dinner mains $12-16; ☺5:30am-9pm) This restaurant's as fresh and hardy as the produce in the next-door farmers' market and its rural-worker clientele. It's a bit barebones on the inside, but the food will fill you up, and nicely too.

🛍 Shopping

ArtSouth
GALLERY

(☑305-247-9406; www.artsouthhomestead.org; 240 N Krome Ave, Homestead; ☺10am-6pm Tue-Fri) This colony of artists' studios is a good place to see local talent and pick up Glades-inspired artwork. It's also a nice sight in and of itself. Outdoor exhibits make the compound feel like a dreamy sculpture garden (or at least a decent free museum), and provide a good aesthetic anchor to the north side of Homestead's main-street project.

ℹ️ Information

Chamber of Commerce (☑305-247-2332; www.chamberinaction.com; 455 N Flagler Ave, Homestead; ☺9am-noon & 1-5pm Mon-Fri)

ERNEST COE & ROYAL PALM TO FLAMINGO

Drive past Florida City, through miles of paper-flat farmland and past an enormous, razor-wired jail (it seems like an escapee heads for the swamp at least once a year) and turn left when you see the signs for Robert Is Here (p129) – or stop in so the kids can pet a donkey at Robert's petting zoo.

👁 Sights & Activities

Ernest Coe Visitor Center
PARK

(☑305-242-7700; www.nps.gov/ever; 40001 State Rd 9336; ☺8am-5pm) As you go past Homestead and Florida City, the farmland loses its uniformity and the flat land becomes more

tangled, wild and studded with pine and cypress. After a few more miles you'll enter Everglades National Park at this friendly visitor center. Have a look at the excellent exhibits, including a diorama of 'typical' Floridians (the fisherman looks like he should join ZZ Top).

Royal Palm Visitor Center
PARK

(☑305-242-7700; State Rd 9336; ☺8am-4:15pm) Four miles past Ernest Coe Visitor Center, Royal Palm offers the easiest access to the Glades in these parts. Two trails, the **Anhinga** and **Gumbo Limbo** (the latter named for the gumbo-limbo tree, also known as the 'tourist tree' because its bark peels like a sunburned Brit), take all of an hour to walk and put you face to face with a panoply of Everglades wildlife. Gators sun on the shoreline, anhinga spear their prey and wading birds stalk haughtily through the reeds. Come at night for a ranger walk on the boardwalk and shine a flashlight into the water to see one of the coolest sights of your life: the glittering eyes of dozens of alligators prowling the waterways.

Kayaking & Canoeing
BOATING

The real joy here in this part of the park is canoeing into the bracken heart of the swamp. There are plenty of push-off points, all with names that sound like they were read off Frodo's map to Mordor, including **Hell's Bay**, the **Nightmare**, **Snake Bight** and **Graveyard Creek**. Our favorite is Hell's Bay. 'Hell to get into and hell to get out of,' was how this sheltered launch was described by old Gladesmen, but damn if it isn't heaven inside: a capillary network of mangrove creeks, saw-grass islands and shifting mudflats, where the brambles form a green tunnel and all you can smell is sea salt and the dark organic breath of the swamp. Three chickee sites are spaced along the trail.

Hiking Trails
HIKING

State Rd 9336 cuts through the soft heart of the park, past long fields of marsh prairie, white, skeletal forests of bald cypress and dark clumps of mahogany hammock. There are plenty of trails to detour down; all of the following are half a mile (800m) long. **Mahogany Hammock** leads into an 'island' of hardwood forest floating on the waterlogged prairie, while the **Pinelands** takes you through a copse of rare spindly swamp pine and palmetto forest. Further on, **Pa-hay-okee Overlook** is a raised platform that

Gators

Alligators are common in the park, although not so much in the 10,000 Islands, as they tend to avoid saltwater. If you do see an alligator, it probably won't bother you unless you do something overtly threatening or angle your boat between it and its young. If you hear an alligator making a loud hissing sound, get the hell out of Dodge. That's a call to other alligators when a young gator is in danger. Finally, never feed an alligator – it's stupid and illegal.

Crocs

Crocodiles are less common in the park, as they prefer coastal and saltwater habitats. They are more aggressive than alligators, however, so the same rules apply. With perhaps only a few hundred remaining in the USA, they are also an endangered species.

Panthers

The Florida panther is critically endangered, and although it is the state's official animal its survival in the wild is by no means assured. There are an estimated 100 panthers left in the wild, and although that number has increased from around 20 to 30 since the 1980s, it's not cause for big celebration either. As usual, humans have been the culprit behind this predator's demise. Widespread habitat reduction (ie the arrival of big subdivisions) is the major cause of concern. In the past, poor data on panther populations and the approval of developments that have been harmful to the species' survival have occurred; environmental groups contend the shoddy information was linked to financial conflicts of interest. Breeding units, which consist of one male and two to five females, require about 200 sq miles of ground to cover, and that often puts panthers in the way of one of Florida's most dangerous beasts: drivers. Sixteen panthers were killed by cars in 2010.

If you're lucky enough to see one (and you gotta be pretty damn lucky), Florida panthers are rather magnificent brown hunting cats (they are, in fact, cougars). They are extremely elusive and only inhabit 5% of their historic range. Many are relatively concentrated in **Big Cypress National Preserve** (p125).

Weather

Thunderstorms and lightning are more common in summer than in winter. But in summer the insects are so bad you won't want to be outside anyway. In emergency weather, rangers will search for registered campers, but under ordinary conditions they won't unless they receive information that someone's missing. If camping, have a friend or family member ready to contact rangers if you do not report back by a certain day.

Insects

You can't overestimate the problem of mosquito and no-see-ums (tiny biting flies) in the Everglades; they are, by far, the park's worst feature. While in most national parks there are warning signs showing the forest-fire risk, here the charts show the mosquito level (call ☎305-242-7700 for a report). In summer and fall, the sign almost always says 'extremely high.' You'll be set upon the second you open your car door. The only protections are 100% DEET or, even better, a pricey net suit.

Snakes in a Glade!

There are four types of poisonous snake in the Everglades: diamondback rattlesnake *(Crotalus adamanteus);* pigmy rattlesnake *(Sistrurus miliarius);* cottonmouth or water moccasin *(Agkistrodon piscivorus conanti),* which swims along the surface of water; and the coral snake *(Micrurus fulvius).* Wear long thick socks and lace-up boots – and keep the hell away from them. Oh, and now there are Burmese pythons prowling the water too. Pet owners who couldn't handle the pythons (this happens with depressing frequency) have dumped the animals into the swamp, where they've adapted like...well, a tropical snake to a subtropical forest. The python is an invasive species that is badly mucking up the natural order of things.

WILDERNESS CAMPING

Three types of backcountry campsites are available: beach sites, on coastal shell beaches and in the 10,000 Islands; ground sites, which are basically mounds of dirt built up above the mangroves; and 'chickees,' wooden platforms built above the waterline where you can pitch a free-standing (no spikes) tent. Chickees, which have toilets, are the most civilized – there's a serenity found in sleeping on what feels like a raft levitating above the water. Ground sites tend to be the most bug-infested.

Warning: if you're just paddling around and see an island that looks pleasant for camping but isn't a designated campsite, beware – you may end up submerged when the tides change.

From November to April, camping permits cost $10, plus $2 per person per night; from May to October sites are free, but you must still self-register at Flamingo and Gulf Coast Visitor Centers or call ☑239-695-2945.

Some backcountry tips:

» Store food in a hand-sized, raccoon-proof container (available at gear stores).

» Bury your waste at least 10in below ground, but keep in mind some ground sites have hard turf.

» Use a backcountry stove to cook. Ground fires are only permitted at beach sites, and you can only burn dead or drowned wood.

peeks over one of the prettiest bends in the River of Grass. The **West Lake Trail** runs through the largest protected mangrove forest in the Northern Hemisphere. Further down you can take a good two-hour, 1.8-mile (2.9km) hike to **Christian Point**. This dramatic walk takes you through several Glades environments: under tropical forest, past columns of white cypress and over a series of mudflats (particularly attractive on grey, cloudy days), and ends with a dramatic view of the windswept shores of Florida Bay.

Flamingo Visitor Center   PARK
(☑239-695-2945; State Rd 9336; ⊙8am-4:15pm)
The most isolated portion of the park is a squat **marina** (☑239-696-3101, 239-695-2591) where you can go on a backcountry boat tour or rent boats, but facilities were shut down for renovations during our visit. In the past, boat tours ran for around $20/10 for adult/child, while canoes (one hour/half-day/full day $8/22/32) and sea kayaks (half-/full day $35/45) were available for rental. You're largely left to explore the channels and islands of Florida Bay on your own. Be careful in coastal areas here during rough weather, as storm surges can turn an attractive spread of beach into a watery stretch of danger fairly quickly.

🛏 Sleeping

National Park Service
Campsites   CAMPGROUND $
(NPS;   ☑800-365-2267;   www.nps.gov/ever/plan
yourvisit/camping; sites May-Oct free, Nov-Apr $16)

There are campgrounds run by the NPS located throughout the park. Sites are primitive and do not have hookups. Depending on the time of year, cold-water showers are either bracing or a welcome relief. The NPS information office at Royal Palm can provide a map of all campsites, as does the park website.

Long Pine Key Campground   CAMPGROUND $
(☑305-242-7873; May-Oct free, Nov-Apr $16)
This is a good bet for car campers, just west of Royal Palm Visitor Center.

Flamingo Campground   CAMPGROUND $
(☑877-444-6777; May-Oct free, Nov-Apr $30)
There are 41 car camping sites at the Flamingo Visitor Center that have electrical hookups.

BISCAYNE NATIONAL PARK

Just to the east of the Everglades is Biscayne National Park, or the 5% of it that isn't underwater. Let us explain: a portion of the world's third-largest reef sits here off the coast of Florida, along with mangrove forests and the northernmost Florida Keys. Fortunately this unique 300-sq-mile park is easy to explore independently with a canoe, or via a glass-bottom boat tour.

A bit unfairly shadowed by the Everglades, Biscayne is unique as national parks go, requiring both a little extra planning and a lot more reward for your effort. The offshore keys, accessible only by boat, offer pristine opportunities for camping. Generally, summer and fall are the best times to visit the park; you'll want to snorkel when the water is calm. This is some of the best reef-viewing and snorkeling you'll find in the US, outside Hawaii and nearby Key Largo.

◉ Sights

Biscayne National Park   PARK
(☑305-230-7275, 305-230-1100; www.nps.gov /bisc, www.biscayneunderwater.com; 9700 SW 328th St) The park itself offers canoe rentals, transportation to the offshore keys, snorkeling and scuba-diving trips, and glass-bottom boat viewing of the exceptional reefs. All tours require a minimum of six people, so call to make reservations. Three-hour glass-bottom boat trips ($45) depart at 10am and are very popular; if you're lucky you may spot some dolphins or manatees. Canoe

rentals cost $12 per hour and kayaks $16; they're rented from 9am to 3pm. Three-hour snorkeling trips ($45) depart at 1:15pm daily; you'll have about 1½ hours in the water. Scuba trips depart at 8:30am Friday to Sunday ($99). You can also arrange a private charter boat tour around the park for $300.

Offshore Keys   ISLANDS
Long **Elliott Key** has picnicking, camping and hiking among mangrove forests; tiny **Adams Key** has only picnicking; and equally tiny **Boca Chita Key** has an ornamental lighthouse, picnicking and camping. These little islands were settled under the Homestead Act of 1862, which gave land freely to anyone willing to take five years at turning a scratch of the tropics into a working pineapple and Key-lime farm. No-see-ums are invasive, and their bites are devastating. Make sure your tent is devoid of minuscule entry points.

MANATEES' BIGGEST THREAT

Manatees are shy, utterly peaceful mammals that are, for all intents, the poster children of Floridian environmentalism. They look like obese seals with vaguely elephantine noses. Back in the day, sailors apparently mistook them for mermaids and sirens, which suggests these guys had been at sea for entirely too long.

Jokes aside, the manatee is a major environmental concern for Florida. Pollution is a problem for these gentle giants, but their biggest killers are boaters, and of those, the worst offenders are pleasure boaters.

Manatees seek warm, shallow water and feed on vegetation. South Florida is surrounded by just such an environment, but it also has one of the highest concentrations of pleasure boats in the world. Despite pleas from environmental groups, wildlife advocates and the local, state and federal governments, which have declared many areas 'Manatee Zones,' some pleasure boaters routinely exceed speed limits and ignore simple practices (see p211) that would help protect the species.

After grabbing a bite, manatees come up for air and often float just beneath the surface, chewing and hanging around. When speedboats zoom through the area, manatees are hit by the hulls and either knocked away or pushed under the boat, whose propeller then gashes the mammal as the boat passes overhead. Few manatees get through life without propeller scars, which leave slices in their bodies similar to the diagonal slices on a loaf of French bread.

There are several organizations throughout the state that rescue and rehabilitate injured manatees, but they're fighting what would appear to be a losing battle. Some of these organizations include **Save the Manatee** (www.savethemanatee.org) and the Miami Seaquarium (p65). Divers, animal experts and veterinarians of Seaquarium's Marine Mammal Rescue Team patrol South Florida waters, responding to reports of stranded manatees, dolphins and whales. While the Seaquarium's program has been successful, pleasure boaters still threaten the manatees' survival. In 2010, the Florida Fish & Wildlife Commission reported that 83 manatees were killed by watercraft.

In February of 2011, a man was charged with killing a nursing manatee mother while speeding his boat through a slow-water area. He was put on probation for a year and had his boat seized by authorities. The ruling was welcomed by conservationists, but decisions like this are few and far between – the speeder was caught in the act of killing the manatee, but most such incidents are not reported.

Maritime Heritage Trail DIVE SITE

One of the only trails of its kind in the USA, the Maritime Heritage Trail was still technically under development at the time of research, but already taking 'hikers'. If you've ever wanted to explore a sunken ship, this may well be the best opportunity in the country. Six are located within the park grounds; the trail experience involves taking visitors out, by boat, to the site of the wrecks where they can swim and explore among derelict vessels and clouds of fish – there are even waterproof information site cards placed among the ships. Five of the vessels are suited for scuba divers, but one, the *Mandalay,* a lovely two-masted schooner that sank in 1966, can be accessed by snorkelers.

🏃 Activities

Boating and **fishing** are naturally very popular and often go hand in hand, but to do either you'll need to get some paperwork in order. Boaters will want to get tide charts from the park (or from www.nps.gov/bisc /planyourvisit/tide-predictions.htm). And make sure you comply with local slow-speed zones, designed to protect the endangered manatee (see p133).

The slow zones currently extend 1000ft out from the mainland, from Black Point south to Turkey Point, and include the marinas at Black Point and Homestead Bayfront Parks. Another slow zone extends from Sands Cut to Coon Point; maps of all of the above can be obtained from rangers, and are needed for navigation purposes in any case.

Although Biscayne is a national park, it is governed by state law when it comes to fishing, so if you want to cast a line, you'll need a state license. These come in varieties many and sundry, all of which can be looked up at http://myfwc.com/fishing, which also provides a list of places where licenses can be obtained. At the time of writing, nonresident seven-day salt- and freshwater fishing permits cost $50 each.

For information on boat tours and rental, contact **Biscayne Underwater** (www.biscayneunderwater.com), which can help arrange logistics.

The water around Convoy Point is regarded as prime **windsurfing** territory. Windsurfers may want to contact outfits in Miami (p79)

🛏 Sleeping

Primitive camping on Elliott and Boca Chita Keys costs $15 per tent, per night; you pay on a trust system with exact change on the harbor (rangers cruise the Keys to check your receipt). Bring all supplies, including water, and carry everything out. There's no water on Boca Chita, only saltwater toilets, and since it has a deeper port, it tends to attract bigger (and louder) boats (and boaters). Bring your own water to the island. There is potable water on the island, but it always pays to be prepared. It costs $20 to moor your boat overnight at Elliott or Boca Chita harbors, but that fee covers the use of one campsite for up to six people and two tents.

ℹ Information

Dante Fascell Visitor Center (☎305-230-7275; www.nps.gov/bisc; 9700 SW 328th St; ⊙8:30am-5pm) Located at Convoy Point, this center shows a great introductory film for an overview of the park and has maps, information and excellent ranger activities. The grounds around the center are a popular picnic grounds on weekends and holidays, especially for families from Homestead. Also showcases local artwork.

ℹ Getting There & Away

To get here, you'll need to drive about 9 miles east of Homestead (the way is pretty well signposted) on SW 328th St (North Canal Dr) into a long series of green-and-gold flat fields and marsh.

Florida Keys & Key West

Includes »

Best Places to Eat

» Café Solé (p163)

» Keys Fisheries (p148)

» Seven Fish (p163)

» Midway Cafe (p144)

» Key Largo Conch House (p141)

Best Places to Stay

» Deer Run Bed & Breakfast (p151)

» Curry Mansion Inn (p162)

» Mermaid & Alligator (p162)

» Casa Morada (p144)

» Bahia Honda State Park Campground (p151)

Why Go?

The Keys are a place separate from mainland USA. They march to the beat of their own drum, or Alabama country band, or Jimmy Buffett single, or Bahamanian steel calypso set...whatever. The point is, this is a place where those who reject everyday life in the Lower 48 escape to. What do they find? About 113 mangrove-and-sandbar islands where the white sun melts over tight fists of deep green mangroves, long, gloriously soft mudflats and tidal bars, water as teal as Arizona turquoise and a bunch of people often like themselves: freaks, geeks and lovable weirdoes all.

Key West is still defined by its motto, which we love – One Human Family – an ideal that equals a tolerant, accepting ethos where anything goes and life is always a party (or at least a hungover day after). The color scheme: watercolor pastels cooled by breezes on a sunset-kissed Bahamian porch. Welcome to the End of the USA.

Have a drink.

When to Go
Key West

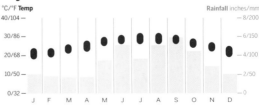

Dec–Mar It's dry, the sun is out, weather is grand and lodging is at its most expensive.

Apr–Jun Sea breezes help to keep the summer heat down, and hotel rates drop precipitously.

Jul–Nov There's some rain (and maybe even some hurricanes), but plenty of festivals happening too.

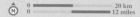

Gulf of
Mexico

Everglades National Park Boundary

Shark
Point

INSET

Hospital
Key
Middle
Key
East
Key
Loggerhead
Key
Bush Key
Garden Key
Long Key

⑩ **Dry Tortugas
National Park**

Marquesas
Keys

Note: Same scale as main map

See Inset

Great White
Heron
National
Wildlife
Refuge

Florida Keys
National Marine
Sanctuary

Great White
Heron
National
Wildlife
Refuge

Little
Torch
Key

Big Torch
Key

Big Pine
Key

Little Pine
Key

Seven Mile
Bridge

Marquesas
Keys

Snipe
Keys

Cudjoe
Key

② ②

No
Name
Key

Bahia
Honda
Key

Pigeon
Key

Boca Chica
Key

Sugarloaf
Key

Summerland
Key

Big
Pine

Bahia
Honda
State Park

Key West

⑦⑥③①

Key West
Key West
International
Airport

Ramrod
Key

Looe Key
National Marine
Sanctuary

Lower Keys

Florida Keys & Key West Highlights

① Getting friendly with the locals as you down drinks at the oldest bar in Key West, the **Green Parrot** (p164).

② Spotting Key deer while you wander on Big Pine and No Name Keys at the **National Key Deer Refuge** (p150)

③ Watching the sun set over the ocean as you sit and take in the raucous show at **Mallory Square** (p153).

④ Diving around the rainbow reefs of **John Pennekamp Coral Reef State Park** (p139).

⑤ Paddling out to eerie, lonely, beautiful **Indian Key State Historic Site** (p143)

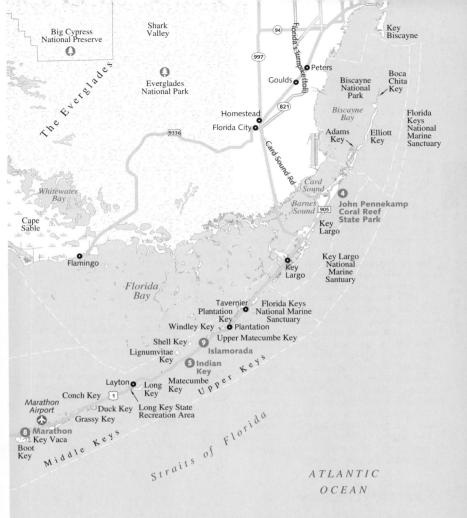

The Everglades

Big Cypress
National Preserve

Shark
Valley

Key
Biscayne

94

997

Florida's Turnpike (toll)

Peters

Goulds

Biscayne
National
Park

Boca
Chita
Key

821

Biscayne
Bay

Florida
Keys
National
Marine
Sanctuary

Homestead

Florida City

Adams
Key

Elliott
Key

9336

Card Sound Rd

Card
Sound

Whitewater
Bay

Barnes
Sound

905

4 John Pennekamp
Coral Reef
State Park

Cape
Sable

Key
Largo

Flamingo

Key
Largo

Key Largo
National
Marine
Santuary

Florida
Bay

Tavernier

Florida Keys
National Marine
Sanctuary

Plantation
Key

Windley Key

Plantation

Shell Key

9

Upper Matecumbe Key

Lignumvitae
Key

Islamorada

5 Indian
Key

Layton

Long
Key

Matecumbe
Key

Upper Keys

Conch Key

1

Marathon
Airport

Duck Key

Long Key State
Recreation Area

Grassy Key

8 Marathon

Key Vaca

Boot
Key

Middle Keys

Straits of Florida

ATLANTIC
OCEAN

6 Donning a purple and
green crocodile costume and
partying in the streets at Key
West's **Fantasy Fest** (p161)

7 Scratching Papa's six-toed
cats behind their ears at the

lovely **Hemingway House**
(p157)

8 Strolling through the palm
hammock and pineland scrub
at eco-educational **Crane
Point Museum** (p147)

9 Feeding the giant tarpon
swimming in circles at
Robbie's Marina (p142)

10 Making an island-hopping
daytrip and detour to **Dry
Tortugas National Park** (p160)

History

Calusa and Tequesta Indians plied these waters for thousands of years, but that era came to a depressingly predictable end with the arrival of the Spanish, the area's first European settlers. Upon finding Native American burial sites, Spanish explorers named Key West Cayo Hueso (pronounced kah-ya way-so, meaning Bone Island), a title since anglicized into its current incarnation. From 1760 to 1763, as the Spaniards transferred control of Florida to Great Britain, all of the islands' indigenous peoples were transferred to Cuba, where they either died in exile or integrated into the local ethnic mélange.

Key West itself was purchased by John Simonton in 1821, and developed as a naval base in 1822. For a long while, the area's cycle of boom and bust was tied to the military, salt manufacturing, lime production (from coral), shipwrecks (see p161) and sponges, which were harvested, dried and turned into their namesake bath product.

In the late 1800s, the area became the focus of mass immigration as Cubans fled Spanish rule and looked to form a revolutionary army. Along with them came cigar manufacturers, who turned Key West into the USA's cigar-manufacturing center. That would end when workers' demands convinced several large manufacturers, notably Vicente Martínez Ybor and Ignacio Haya, to relocate to Tampa in southwest Florida. Immigrants from the Caribbean settled in the Keys in this period, and as a result, today's local African Americans tend to be descended from Bahamian immigrants rather than Southern slaves – something of a rarity in the US.

During the Spanish-American War (1898), Key West was an important staging point for US troops, and the military presence lasted through to WWI. In the late 1910s, with Prohibition on the horizon, Key West became a bootlegging center, as people stocked up on booze. The Keys began to boom around 1938 when Henry Flagler constructed his Overseas Hwy, replacing the by-then defunct Overseas Railroad.

Key West has always been a place where people buck trends. A large society of artists and craftspeople congregated here at the end of the Great Depression because of cheap real estate, and that community continues to grow (despite today's pricey real estate). While gay men have long been welcomed, the gay community really picked up in earnest in the 1970s; today it's one of the most renowned and best organized gay communities in the country.

Climate

Though it's warm and tropical in the Keys, it never gets higher than about 97°F; the peak in summer is usually about 89°F, with the temperature staying a few degrees cooler than Miami because the Keys are surrounded by ocean (and refreshing ocean breezes). The coldest it gets is usually in the 50s (when some people dress like a blizzard has descended), and water temperature stays in the 80s most of the time. The thunderstorm season begins by late May, and then everyone buckles down for the feared hurricanes – if they arrive, expect them in late summer and early fall.

KEYS FOR CHILDREN

Check out some of the following options to entertain the kids:

» **Florida Keys Eco-Discovery Center** (p157) Get an understanding of the region's environment.

» **Glass-bottom boat tours at John Pennekamp Coral Reef State Park** (p139) Your own window to the underwater world.

» **Key West Butterfly & Nature Conservatory** (p158) Pretty flying things.

» **Turtle Hospital** (p147) Save (or watch) the turtles.

» **Conch Tour Train** (p161) Kitschy, corny, enjoyable tour.

» **Ghost tours** (p161) Only slightly spooky; younger kids may find this one a bit scary.

» **Key-deer spotting** (p150) Kids go crazy for cute mini-deer.

» **Key West Cemetery** (p157) Get Gothic with these often humorus tombs.

» **Robbie's Marina** (p142) All sorts of activities, including the ever-popular tarpon (giant fish) feeding frenzy.

ⓘ Information

The Monroe County Tourist Development Council's **Florida Keys & Key West Visitor's Bureau** (☎800-352-5397; www.fla-keys.com) runs an excellent website, which is packed with information on everything the Keys has to offer.

Check www.keysnews.com for good daily online news and information about the islands.

ⓘ Getting There & Away

Getting here can be half the fun – or, if you're unlucky, a whopping dose of frustration. Imagine a tropical-island hop, from one bar-studded mangrove islet to the next, via one of the most unique roads in the world: the Overseas Hwy (US Hwy 1). On a good day, driving down the Overseas with the windows down, the wind in your face and the twin sisters of Florida Bay and the Atlantic stretching on either side, is the US road trip in tropical perfection. On a bad day, you end up sitting in gridlock behind some fat guy who is riding a midlife-crisis Harley.

Greyhound (☎800-229-9424) buses serve all Keys destinations along US Hwy 1 and depart from downtown Miami and Key West; you can pick up a bus along the way by standing on the Overseas Hwy and flagging one down. If you fly into Fort Lauderdale or Miami, the **Keys Shuttle** (☎888-765-9997) provides door-to-door service to most of the Keys ($70/80/90 to the Upper and Middle Keys/Lower Keys/Key West). Reserve at least a day in advance.

See also p167.

UPPER KEYS

No, really, you're in the islands!

It is a bit hard to tell when you first arrive, as the huge, rooty blanket of mangrove forest that forms the South Florida coastline spreads like a woody morass into Key Largo. In fact, the mangroves become Key Largo, which is more famous for its underwater than aboveground views. Keep heading south and the scenery becomes more archipelagically pleasant as the mangroves give way to wider stretches of road and ocean, until – bam – you're in Islamorada and the water is everywhere. If you want to avoid traffic on US 1, you can try the less trafficked FL 997 and Card Sound Rd to FL 905 (toll $1), which passes Alabama Jack's (p142).

Key Largo & Tavernier

We ain't gonna lie: Key Largo (both the name of the town and the island it's on) is slightly underwhelming at a glance. 'Under' is the key word, as its main sights are under the water, rather than above. As you drive onto the islands, Key Largo resembles a long line of low-lying hammock and strip development. But that's Key Largo from the highway. Head down a side road and duck into this warm little bar, or that converted Keys plantation house, and the island idiosyncrasies become more pronounced.

The 33-mile long Largo, which starts at MM 106, is the longest island in the Keys, and those 33 miles have attracted a lot of marine life, all accessible from the biggest concentration of dive sites in the islands. The town of Tavernier (MM 93) is just south of the town of Key Largo.

⊙ Sights & Activities

John Pennekamp Coral Reef State Park   PARK
(www.pennekamppark.com, www.floridastateparks.org/pennekamp; MM 102.5 oceanside; car/motorcycle/cyclist or pedestrian $8/4/2; ☺8am-sunset; 🅿) John Pennekamp has the singular distinction of being the first underwater park in the USA. There's 170 acres of dry parkland here and over 48,000 acres (ie 75 sq miles) of wet: the vast majority of the protected area is the ocean. Before you get out in that water, make sure to dig around some pleasant beaches and stroll over the nature trails. The **Mangrove Trail** is a good boardwalk introduction to this oft-maligned, ecologically awesome arboreal species (the trees, often submerged in water, breathe via long roots that act as snorkels – neat). Stick around for nightly campfire programs and ranger discussions.

The visitor center is well run and informative and has a small, cute **aquarium** (☺8am-5pm) that gives a glimpse of what's under them thar waters. To really get beneath the surface of this park (pun intended), you should take a 2½-hour **glass-bottom boat tour** (☎305-451-6300; adult/child $24/17; ☺tours 9:15am, 12:15pm & 3pm). You won't be ferried around in some rinky-dink fishing boat; you're brought out in a safe, modern 38ft catamaran from which you'll ooh and aah at filigreed flaps of soft coral, technicolor schools of fish, dangerous-looking barracudas and massive, yet ballerina-graceful sea turtles. Besides the swirl of natural coral life, interested divers can catch a glimpse of the *Christ of the Abyss*, an 8.5ft, 4000lb bronze sculpture of Jesus – a copy of a similar sculpture off the coast of Genoa, Italy, in the Mediterranean Sea.

DIVER DOWN

If you go diving in the Keys, Florida state law requires you to raise a 'Diver Down' flag whenever you are underwater. If you don't have one, they can be bought at any Keys dive shop.

If you want to go even deeper, try straight-up **snorkeling trips** (☑305-451-6300; adult/child $29.95/24.95) or **diving excursions** (☑305-451-6322, 877-727-5348; dive excursions with/without own gear $60/90). DIYers may want to take out a canoe ($12 per hour) or kayak (single/double per hour $12/$17) to journey through a 3-mile network of trails. Call ☑305-451-6300 for boat-rental information.

To learn more about the reef in this area, go to www.southeastfloridareefs.net.

Florida Keys Wild Bird Rehabilitation Center WILDLIFE SANCTUARY
(www.fkwbc.org; 93600 Overseas Hwy, MM 93.6; suggested donation $5; ☉sunrise-sunset) This sanctuary is the first of many animal hospitals you'll come across built by critter-loving Samaritans throughout the Keys. You'll find an alfresco bird hospital that cares for birds that have swallowed fish hooks, had wings clipped in accidents, been shot by BB pellets etc. A pretty trail leads back to a nice vista of Florida Bay and a wading bird pond. Just be warned, it does smell like bird doo back here.

Harry Harris Park PARK
(MM 93.5; ☉sunrise-sunset; ⊕) This small park is a good place to take the kids – there's a small playground, picnic table and other such accoutrements, and (rare for the Keys) a good patch of white sand fronting a warm lagoon that's excellent for swimming. There are good boat ramps here as well.

Jacob's Aquatics Center PARK
(☑305-453-7946; 320 Laguana Ave, MM 99.6; ☉11am-6pm Mon-Fri, 10am-7pm Sat & Sun; adult/child/student $8/5/6 Mon-Fri, $10/6/8 Sat & Sun; ⊕) Jacob's is a complex of all kinds of aquatic fun. There's an eight-lane pool for lap and open swimming, a therapy pool with handicapped access, courses on water aerobics and a small waterpark for the kids with waterslides, a playground and of course, kiddie-sized pools.

Caribbean Club Bar FILM LOCATION
(MM 104 bayside; ☉7am-4am) Here's one for the movie fans, particularly Bogie buffs: the Caribbean Club Bar is, in fact, the only place in Key Largo where *Key Largo,* starring Humphrey Bogart and Lauren Bacall, was filmed (the rest of the island was a Hollywood soundstage). If that's not enough, the original *African Queen,* of the same-titled movie, is docked in a channel at the Holiday Inn at MM 100 – just walk around the back and there she is.

Crocodile Lake National Wildlife Refuge WILDLIFE SANCTUARY
(www.fws.gov/nationalkeydeer/crocodilelake; FL 905) If you approach Key Largo from FL 905, you'll be driving through one of the last wild sanctuaries for the threatened American crocodile, indigo snake and Key Largo woodrat – the latter is an enterprising fellow who likes to build 4ft by 6ft homes out of forest debris. Unfortunately, this really is a refuge; the wildlife areas are closed to the public, and your chances of seeing the species we've mentioned from the road are negligible.

🛏 Sleeping

Key Largo House Boatel HOTEL $$
(☑305-766-0871; www.keylargohouseboatel.com; Shoreland Dr, MM 103.5 oceanside; houseboat small/medium/large from $75/100/150) If you can't afford to sleep underwater at Jules' Undersea Lodge, why not sleep on it here? There are five houseboats available, and they're a steal. The largest one is incredibly spacious and fairly well decorated for the Keys, with minimal sea-themed decor and enough room to sleep six people comfortably. The boats are right on the docks (and across from a bar), so no possibility of being isolated from land (or booze). Call ahead for directions, as the 'boatel' is a little off the beaten track.

Largo Lodge HOTEL $$
(☑305-451-0424, 800-468-4378; www.largolodge.com; MM 102 bayside; winter apt/cottages $150/195, summer apt $95-115, cottages $125-155; ℗) The manager of the property couldn't be friendlier, and his six hidden cottages, tucked into a glimmery secret tropical garden with a private swimming cove, couldn't be cozier. And, as a side note, there couldn't be more squirrels having the run of the joint. The interior of the rooms get lots of soothing green light thanks to that strong Keys sunshine slashing in over the copses of trees in the back.

KEY LIME PIE

Many places claim to serve the original Key lime pie, but no one knows who discovered the tart treat. Types of crust vary, and whether or not the pie should be topped with meringue is debated. However, the color of Key lime pie is not open to question. Beware of places serving green Key lime pie: Key limes are yellow, not green. Restaurants that add green food coloring say that tourists expect it to be green. Steer clear.

Kona Kai Resort & Gallery HOTEL $$$
(☑305-852-7200, 800-365-7829; www.konakairesort.com; MM 97.8 bayside; r $199-369, ste $249-975; Ⓟ🛜🏊) This intimate hideaway features 11 airy rooms and suites (with full kitchens). They're all bright and comfortable, with good natural light and linoleum floors, but some feel a little too old-fashioned. Kona Kai also happens to house one of the better galleries in this corner of the Keys and extensive botanical gardens; guided tours are offered Tuesday and Thursday at 9:30am and 4:30pm, and on Saturdays at 9:30am, for $15. There's plenty to do otherwise – from tennis, kayaking and paddleboating to lounging in one of the hammocks that dot the palm-strewn, white-sand beach.

Hilton Key Largo Resort HOTEL $$
(☑888-871-3437; www.keylargoresort.com; MM 102 bayside; summer apt $95-115, cottage $170-230, ste from $315; Ⓟ🛜🏊🐾) For an enormous outpost of a largely impersonal hotel chain, the Hilton Key Largo has a lot of friendliness and character. Folks just seem to get all laid back when lounging in clean, designer rooms outfitted in blues, greens and (why not?) blue-green. Throw in some beiges and you've got a supremely soothing sleeping experience. The grounds are enormous and include an artificial waterfall-fed pool and frontage to a rather large stretch of private white-sand beach.

Jules' Undersea Lodge HOTEL $$$
(☑305-451-2353; www.jul.com; 51 Shoreland Dr, MM 103.2 oceanside; per person $400-500) For a while, it seemed like some fancy hotel in Dubai was going to supplant tiny, kitschy Jules as the world's only underwater hotel. But then there was a financial crisis, the Dubai hotel tanked and bam! Key Largo: 1; Dubai: 0. Jules' Undersea Lodge, the world's only underwater hotel is still the only place you and your significant other can join the 'five-fathom club' (we're not elaborating). Once a research station, this module has been converted into a delightfully cheesy Keys motel, but wetter. In addition to two private guest rooms (there's just the *teensiest* nautical theme – everywhere), there are common rooms, a fully stocked kitchen-dining room, and a wet room with hot showers and gear storage. Telephones and an intercom connect guests with the surface. Guests must be at least 10 years old and you gotta dive to get here – plus, there's no smoking or alcohol. If you just want to visit, sign up for a three-hour mini-adventure ($125), which also gives access to breathing hookahs (120ft-long air hoses for tankless diving). There's a good variety of PADI certification courses here (an open-water course runs $595).

John Pennekamp Coral Reef State Park CAMP GROUND $
(☑800-326-3521, ☑305-451-1202; www.pennekamppark.com; MM 102.5 oceanside; per night $31.49, hire of pavilion $32.25-53.75; Ⓟ) You don't even have to leave Pennekamp at closing time if you opt for tent or recreational vehicle (RV) camping, but be sure to make a reservation, as the sites fill up fast.

Stone Ledge Paradise Inn HOTEL $
(☑305-852-8114; www.stoneledgeparadiseinn.com; 95320 Overseas Hwy; r winter $88-118, summer $78-98, villas winter $250-300, summer $185-250; Ⓟ) This is a pink palace (well, squat bunch of motel blocks) of old-school US seaside kitsch. The wooden fish hung on every door are only the tip of the nautical-tack iceberg, but the real joy is the sweeping view over Florida Bay at the back of the property. Rooms are pretty simple on the inside.

🍴 Eating

TOP CHOICE Key Largo Conch House FUSION $$
(☑305-453-4844; MM 100.2 oceanside; lunch $8-14, dinner $13-25; ⊙7am-9:30pm Sun-Thu, to 10pm Fri & Sat; 🛜) A wi-fi hotspot, coffeehouse and innovative kitchen that likes to sex up local classics (conch in a lime and white-wine sauce, or in a vinegar sauce with capers), set in a restored old-school Keys mansion wrapped in a *Gone With the* Wind veranda? Yes please, and more of it. It's hard not to love the way the period architecture blends in seamlessly with the local tropical fauna. A justifiably popular spot with tourists and locals. The fish tacos are intensely good.

DETOUR: FLORIDA KEYS OVERSEAS HERITAGE TRAIL

One of the best ways to see the Keys is by bicycle. The flat elevation and ocean breezes are perfect for cycling, and the **Florida Keys Overseas Heritage Trail** (FKOHT; www.dep.state.fl .us/gwt/state/keystrail) will connect all the islands from Key Largo to Key West. At the time of writing about 70 miles of the trail were paved, but there have been significant delays to its completion.

If you are keen to ride, it's currently possible to bike through the Keys by shoulder riding (it takes three days at a good clip). There are particularly pleasant rides around Islamorada, and if you're uncomfortable riding on the shoulder, you can contact the FKOHT through its website for recommended bike excursions.

Mrs Mac's Kitchen   AMERICAN **$**
(MM 99.4 bayside; breakfast & lunch $7-11, dinner $9-18; ☺7am-9:30pm Mon-Sat) When Applebee's stuffs its wall full of license plates, it's tacky. When Mrs Mac's does it, it's homey. Probably because the service is warm and personable, and the breakfasts are delicious. Plus, the food packs in the locals, tourists, their dogs and pretty much everyone else on the island (plus, admittedly, a fair few calories, but that's why it tastes good).

Fish House   SEAFOOD **$$**
(☑305-451-4665; 1024021 Overseas Hwy; mains $12-28; ☺11:30am-10pm) The Fish House delivers on the promise of its title – very good fish, bought whole from local fishermen and prepared fried, broiled, jerked, blackened or char-grilled. This sort of cooking lets you taste the fish, which is as it should be. Because the Fish House only uses fresh fish, the menu changes daily based on what is available. We prefer the original Fish House over the more sushi-centered next door Fish House Encore.

DJ's Diner   AMERICAN **$**
(99411 Overseas Hwy; mains $6-14; ☺7am-9pm, to 3pm Sat & Sun) You're greeted by a mural of Humphrey Bogart, James Dean *and* Marilyn Monroe – that's a lot of Americana. It's all served with a heapin' helpin' of diner faves, vinyl-boothed ambience, and South Florida staples like *churrasco* (skirt steak) and conch.

🍷 Drinking & Entertainment

Alabama Jack's   BAR
(58000 Crad Sound Rd; ☺11am-7pm) Welcome to your first taste of the Keys: zonked-out fishermen, exiles from the mainland, and Harley heads getting drunk on a mangrove bay. This is the line where Miami-esque South Florida gives way to the country-fried American South. Wildlife-lovers: you may spot the rare mulleted version of *Jacksonvillia Redneckus*! But seriously, everyone raves about the conch fritters, and the fact they have to close because of nightly onslaughts of mosquitoes means this place is as authentically Florida as they come. Country bands take the stage on weekends from 2pm to 5pm.

Tavernier Towne Cinemas   CINEMA
(☑305-853-7003; MM 92) This multiplex, showing new releases, is a perfect rainy-day option.

ℹ Information

Key Largo Chamber of Commerce (☑305-451-1414, 800-822-1088; www.keylargo.org; MM 106 bayside; ☺9am-6pm) Helpful office; has area-wide information.

Key Largo post office (☑305-451-3155; MM 100 bayside)

Mariner Hospital (☑305-434-3000; www .baptisthealth.net; Tavernier, MM 91.5 bayside)

ℹ Getting There & Away

The Greyhound bus stops at MM 99.6 oceanside.

Islamorada

Islamorada (eye-luh-murr-*ah*-da) is also known as 'The Village of Islands.' Doesn't that sound pretty? Well, it really is. This little string of pearls (well, keys) – Plantation, Upper and Lower Matecumbe, Shell and Lignumvitae (lignum-*vite*-ee) – shimmers as one of the prettiest stretches of the islands. This is where the scrubby mangrove is replaced by unbroken horizons of ocean and sky, one perfect shade of blue mirroring the other. Islamorada stretches across some 20 miles, from MM 90 to MM 74.

◎ Sights & Activities

Robbie's Marina   MARINA
TOP CHOICE
(☑800-979-3370, 305-664-9814; www.robbies .com; MM 77.5 bayside; tours from $35; ☺8am-6pm; ⊕) Robbie's really may be the happiest dock on Earth. More than a boat launch, Robbie's is a local flea market, tacky tour-

ist shop (all the shells you ever wanted), sea pen for tarpons (very big-ass fish) and jump-off for excellent fishing expeditions, all wrapped into one driftwood-laced compound. There's a glut of boat-rental and tour options here. The party boat (half-day/night/full-day trips $35/40/60) is just that: a chance to drink, fish and basically achieve Keys Zen. Or, for real Zen (ie the tranquil kind as opposed to drunken kind), take an ecotour ($35) on an electrically propelled silent boat deep into the mangroves, hammocks and lagoons. Snorkeling trips are a good deal; for adult/child $35/20 you get a few hours on a very smooth-riding Happy Cat vessel and a chance to bob amid some of the USA's only coral reefs. If you don't want to get on the water, at least feed the freakishly large tarpons from the dock ($2.79 per bucket, $1 to watch).

Indian Key State Historic Site ISLAND
(http://floridastateparks.org/indiankey; ☉8am-sunset) You may have encountered spooky abandoned houses, mansions, even towns in your travels – but how about a derelict island? In 1831, renegade wrecker (shipwreck salvager) Jacob Housman turned this quiet island into a thriving city, complete with a warehouse, docks, streets, hotel and about 40 to 50 permanent residents. By 1836, Indian Key was the first seat of Dade County, but four years later the inhabitants of the island were killed or scattered by a Native American attack during the Second Seminole War. There's not much left at the historic site – just foundation, some cisterns, Housman's grave and jungly tangle. There are trails that follow the old layout of the city streets, and there is an observation tower, or you can walk among ruins and paddle around spotting rays and dolphins in utter isolation in a canoe or kayak – which, by the way, is the only way out here. Robbie's used to bring boats this way, and still does boat rental (single/double/glass-bottom kayak/canoe per hour $20/27.50/30/30). You can also see the island from the water on an ecotour with Robbie's ($35).

Lignumvitae Key State Botanical Site ISLAND
(☏305-664-2540; http://floridastateparks.org/lignumvitaekey; ☉9am-5pm Thu-Mon) This key, only accessible by boat, encompasses a 280-acre island of virgin tropical forest and is home to roughly a zillion jillion mosquitoes. The official attraction is the 1919 **Matheson**

House, with its windmill and cistern; the real draw is a nice sense of shipwrecked isolation. Strangler figs, mastic, gumbo-limbo, poisonwood and lignum vitae trees form a dark canopy that feels more South Pacific than South Florida. Guided walking tours (1¼ hours) are given at 10am and 2pm Friday to Sunday. You'll have to get here via Robbie's Marina (p142); boats depart for the 15-minute trip (adult/child $20/12) about 30 minutes prior to each tour and reservations are recommended.

Florida Keys History of Diving Museum MUSEUM
(☏305-664-9737; www.divingmuseum.org; MM 83; adult/child $12/6; ☉10am-5pm, to 7pm Wed) You can't miss the diving museum – it's the building with the enormous mural of swimming manatees on the side – and we mean that in every sense of the phrase. In other words, don't miss this museum, a collection of diving paraphernalia from around the world, including diving 'suits' and technology from the 19th century. This is the sort of charmingly eccentric museum that really reflects how many quirks live in the Keys. The hall of dozens of variations of the diving helmet from around the world, from Denmark to Japan, is particularly impressive. Folks in the museum can also provide information on diving in a vintage Mark V diving suit (the ones with the bulbous onion-heads connected to surface pumps), or you can call ☏305-394-1706 for more information.

Anne's Beach BEACH
(MM 73) Anne's is one of the best beaches in these parts. The small ribbon of sand opens upon a sky-bright stretch of tidal flats and a green tunnel of hammock and wetland. Nearby mudflats are a joy to get stuck in, and will be much loved by the kids.

Windley Key Fossil Reef Geological State Park PARK
(☏305-664-2540; www.floridastateparks.org/windleykey; MM 85.5; per person $2.50) To get his railroad built across the islands, Henry Flagler had to quarry out some sizable chunks of the Keys. The best evidence of those efforts can be found at this former quarry-cum-state-park. Besides having a mouthful of a name, Windley has leftover quarry machinery scattered along an 8ft former-quarry wall. The wall offers a cool (and rare) public peek into the stratum of coral that forms the substrate of the Keys. Ranger tours are offered at 10am and 2pm Friday to Sunday for $3.

Rain Barrel
ARTS CENTER

(☎305-852-8935; 86700 Overseas Hwy; ☺9am-5pm) We want to tell you the Rain Barrel, Islamorada's local artists' village, strikes a balance between the beautiful and the tacky. But you're more likely to find souvenir-y tourist tat here than a truly striking work of art. That said, strolling around the seven studios and galleries that make up the Rain Barrel is a nice way to pass about an hour of your time, and who knows, you may find the piece of your dreams, or at least a handpainted sign that says 'It's always 5 o'clock somewhere.'

🛏 Sleeping

Casa Morada
HOTEL $$$

(☎305-664-0044, 888-881-3030; www.casamorada .com; 136 Madeira Rd, off MM 82.2; ste winter $299-659, summer $239-459; [P][🛜][🏊]) Contemporary chic comes to Islamorada, but it's not gentrifying away the village vibe. Rather, the Casa adds a welcome dab of sophistication to Conch chill: a Keystone standing circle, freshwater pool, manmade lagoon, plus a *Wallpaper* magazine-worthy bar that overlooks Florida Bay; all make this boutique hotel worth a reservation. It's a bit of South Beach style over the usual Keys-style Jimmy Buffett blah. The slick back bar is one of our favorite places to catch a drink and a sunset in the Keys.

La Siesta Resort & Marina
RESORT $$$

(☎305-664-2132; www.lasiestaresort.com; MM 80.5 oceanside; ste $190-340; [P][🏊]) This pretty option consists of renovated suites and apartments that let in generous amounts of light and are decorated to feel modern and classy, but still refreshingly un-hip and family-friendly. Service is amiable, the pool is busy and the ocean views are lovely.

Ragged Edge Resort
RESORT $$

(☎305-852-5389; www.ragged-edge.com; 243 Treasure Harbor Rd; apt $69-259; [P][🏊]) This low-key and popular efficiency and apartment complex, far from the maddening traffic jams, has 10 quiet units and friendly hosts. The larger studios have screened-in porches, and the entire vibe is happily comatose. There's no beach, but you can swim off the dock and at the pool.

Conch On Inn
MOTEL $

(☎305-852-9309; conchoninn.com; MM 89.5, 103 Caloosa St; apt $59-129; [P]) A simple motel popular with yearly snowbirds, Conch On Inn has basic rooms that are reliable, clean and comfortable.

✖ Eating

Midway Cafe
CAFE $

(☎305-664-2622; 80499 Overseas Hwy; mains under $5; ☺7am-3pm Thu-Tue, to 2pm Sun) The lovely folks who run this cafe – stuffed with every variety of heart-warming art the coffee shop trope can muster – roast their own beans, make baked goods that we would swim across the Gulf for, and are friendly as hell. You're almost in the Middle Keys: celebrate making it this far with a cup of joe.

Pierre's
FRENCH $$$

(☎305-664-3225; www.pierres-restaurant.com; MM 81.6 bayside; mains $28-42; ☺5-10pm Sun-Thu, to 11pm Fri & Sat) Why hello two-story waterfront plantation – what are you serving? A tempura-ed spiny lobster tail…good, decadent start. Hogfish meunière? Well, that's rich enough to knock out a rhino. A filet mignon with black truffle mash potatoes? Splurge, traveler, on possibly the best food between Miami and Key West.

Morada Bay
AMERICAN $$

(☎305-664-0604; MM 81.6 bayside; lunch $10-15, dinner $21-29; ☺11:30am-11pm Sun-Thu, to midnight Fri & Sat) If you can ignore the service from staff who can get overwhelmed by customers and the awful bands that occasionally 'headline' the lunch rush, this is a lovely, laid-back Caribbean experience, complete with imported powder-white sandy beach, nighttime torches, tapas and fresh seafood.

Spanish Gardens Cafe
SPANISH $

(☎305-664-3999; MM 80.9 oceanside; mains $9.50-19; ☺11am-9pm Tue-Sun) A great option for those sick of fried everything, this pink, Barcelona-esque cafe serves sandwiches and salads dripping with manchego cheese, chorizo, *piquillo* peppers and other Iberian foodstuffs that get foodies going.

Bob's Bunz
CAFE $

(www.bobsbunz.com; MM 81.6 bayside; mains $6-12; ☺6am-2pm) The service at this cute cafe is energetic and friendly in an only-in-America kinda way, and the food is fine, filling and cheap. Key lime pie is a classic Keys dish and Key-lime anything at this bakery is highly regarded, so buy that souvenir pie here.

🍷 Drinking

Hog Heaven
BAR

(☎305-664-9669; MM 85 oceanside) We're tempted to place this joint in the eating section, as the seafood nachos are so good. But it deserves pride of place in Drinking thanks to huge crowds that trip all the way down from Fort Lauderdale for back-porch, alfresco imbibing.

Morada Bay   BAR
(☎305-664-0604; MM 81.6 bayside) In addition to its excellent food (p144), the Bay holds monthly full-moon parties that attract the entire party-people population of the Keys. The whole shebang typically starts around 9pm and goes until whenever the last person passes out; check www.moradabay -restaurant.com for dates.

❶ Information
Islamorada Chamber of Commerce (☎305-664-4503, 800-322-5397; www.islamorada chamber.com; MM 83.2 bayside; ☺9am-5pm Mon-Fri, 10am-3pm Sat & Sun) Located in an old caboose.
Post office (☎305-664-4738; MM 82.9 oceanside)

❶ Getting There & Away
The Greyhound bus stops at the Burger King at MM 82.5 oceanside.

Long Key
The 965-acre **Long Key State Recreation Area** (☎305-664-4815; www.floridastateparks .org/longkey; MM 67.5 oceanside; per car/motorcycle/cyclist $5/4/2) takes up much of Long Key. It's about 30 minutes south of Islamorada, and comprises a tropical clump of gumbo-limbo, crabwood and poisonwood trees; a picnic area fronting a long, lovely sweep of teal water; and lots of wading birds in the mangroves. Two short nature trails head through distinct plant communities. The park also has a 1.5-mile canoe trail through a saltwater tidal lagoon and rents out canoes (per hour/day $5/10) and ocean-going kayaks (per two/four hours $17.20/32.25).

If you want to stay here, make reservations this minute: it's tough to get one of the 60 sites at the **campground** (☎305-326-3521, 888-433-0287; www.reserveamerica.com; MM 67.5 oceanside; sites $38.50; ℗). They're all waterfront, making this the cheapest (and probably most unspoiled) ocean view – short of squatting on a resort – you're likely to find in Florida.

As you truck down the Keys, the bodies of water get wider until you reach the big boy: Seven Mile Bridge, one of the world's longest causeways and a natural divider between the Middle and Lower Keys. In this stretch of islands you'll cross specks like Conch Key and Duck Key, green, quiet Grassy Key, and finally Key Vaca (MM 54 to MM 47), where Marathon, the second-largest town and most Key-sy community in the islands, is located.

Grassy Key

At first blush Grassy Key seems pretty sedate. Well spotted; Grassy is very much an island of few attractions and lots of RV lots and trailer parks. These little villages were once the heart of the Keys, where retirees, escapists, fishermen and the wait staff who served them lived, drank and dreamed (of a drink). Some of these communities remain, but development is relentless, and so, it seems, is the migration of the old Conch trailer towns.

◉ Sights & Activities
Dolphin Research Center   WILDLIFE RESERVE
(☎305-289-1121; www.dolphins.org; MM 59 bayside; adult/child under 4yr/child 4-12yr/senior $20/ free/15/17.50, swim program $180-650; ☺9am-4pm) By far the most popular activity on this island is swimming with the descendants of Flipper. Of all the dolphin swimming spots in the Keys, we prefer this one; the dolphins are free to leave the grounds and a lot of marine-biology research goes on behind the (still pretty commercial) tourist activities, such as getting a dolphin to paint your T-shirt or playing 'trainer for a day' ($650).

Curry Hammock State Park   PARK
(☎305-289-2690; http://floridastateparks.org /curryhammock; MM 56.2 bayside; per car/motorcycle/cyclist $5/4/2; ☺8am-sunset) This park is small but sweet and the rangers are just lovely. Like most parks in the Keys, it's a good spot for preserved tropical hardwood and mangrove habitat – a 1.5-mile hike takes you through both environments. Local waters are blissfully free of power boats, which is a blessing down here. Rent a kayak (single/double for two hours $17.20/21.50) or, when the wind is up, join the crowds of windsurfers and kiteboarders. You can also

SHOULD YOU SWIM WITH DOLPHINS?

There are four swim-with-the-dolphin (SWTD) centers in the Keys, and many more arguments for and against the practice.

For

» While SWTD sites are commercial, they are also research entities devoted to learning more about their charges.

» The dolphins raised on-site are legally obtained and have not been not captured from the wild.

» The dolphins are used to humans and pose a negligible danger to swimmers, especially when overseen by expert trainers.

» Dolphin swim programs increase our knowledge of dolphins and promote conservation.

» At places such as the **Dolphin Research Center** (p145), the dolphins can actually swim out of their pens into the open water, but choose not to.

Against

» Dolphins are social creatures that require interaction, which is impossible to provide in captivity.

» SWTD tourism encourages the capture of wild dolphins in other parts of the world.

» Dolphin behavior is never 100% predictable. Dolphins can seriously injure a human, even while playing.

» SWTD centers encourage customers to think of dolphins as anthropomorphized 'friends,' rather than wild animals.

» Dolphins never appreciate captivity. Those that voluntarily remain in SWTD sites do so to remain close to food.

SWTD Centers

If you decide to swim or see dolphins in the Keys, you can contact one of the following:
  Theater of the Sea (☑305-664-2431; www.theaterofthesea.com; Islamorada, MM 84.5 bayside; swim programs $175; ⊙9:30am-4pm) has been here since 1946. Structured dolphin swims and sea-lion programs ($135) include 30 minutes of instruction and a 30-minute supervised swim. You can also swim with stingrays ($55).
  Dolphins Plus (☑305-451-1993, 866-860-7946; www.dolphinsplus.com, off MM 99.5 bayside; swim programs $135-220), a Key Largo center, specializes in recreational and educational unstructured swims. They expect you know a good deal before embarking upon the swim, even though a classroom session is included.
  There is also dolphin swimming at Grassy Key's **Dolphin Research Center** (p145) and **Hawk's Cay Resort** (p146).

camp at the park for $36 per night – sites have toilets and electric hookups.

🛏 Sleeping & Eating

Hawk's Cay Resort   RESORT $$$
(☑888-395-5539; 305-743-7000; www.hawkscay.com; 61 Hawk's Cay Blvd, Duck Key, off MM 61 oceanside; r & ste winter $350-1600, summer $150-500; [P][🛜][🏊][🐾]) Now, if after one dolphin swim center and fish ranch you're thinking, Man, I *still* want to play with some sealife..., don't worry: Hawk's Cay Resort is there for you. The Cay is an enormous luxury compound that could well have its own zip code, and besides a series of silky-plush rooms and nicely appointed townhouses, it has more activities than you can shake a... flipper at. Which is to say, the Cay has its own dolphin pool where you can swim with the dolphins – plus a sailing school, snorkeling, tennis and boat rentals.

Rainbow Bend   HOTEL $$$
(☑800-929-1505; www.rainbowbend.com; MM 58 oceanside; r $150-270; [P][🏊]) You'll be experiencing intensely charming Keys-kitsch in

these big pink cabanas, where the apartments and suites are bright, the tiki huts are shady, the bedsheets are ghastly, the beach swing is...um, swing-y and the ocean is (splash)...right there. Half-day use of the Bend's Boston whalers (motorboats), kayaks and canoes is complimentary.

Wreck Galley & Grill AMERICAN **$$**
(☎ 305-743-8282; MM 59 bayside; mains $10-25; ⏱ 11am-10pm) The Wreck is a Keys classic, where fisherman types knock back brew and feast on wings – but it's definitely a local haunt, where island politicos like to tongue wag about the issues (fishing). The food is excellent; it grills one of the best burgers in the Keys, and the aforementioned wings go down a treat with a tall beer.

Marathon

Marathon sits right on the halfway point between Key Largo and Key West, and is a good place to stop on a road trip across the islands. It's perhaps the most 'developed' key outside Key West (that's really pushing the definition of the word 'developed') in the sense that it has large shopping centers and a population of a few thousand. Then again it's still a place where exiles from the mainland fish, booze it up and have a good time, so while Marathon is more family-friendly than Key West, it's hardly G-rated.

⦿ Sights & Activities

Crane Point Museum PARK
(www.cranepoint.net; MM 50.5 bayside; adult/child over 5yr/senior $12.50/8.50/11; ⏱ 9am-5pm Mon-Sat, noon-5pm Sun; 🚼) This is one of the nicest spots on the island to stop and smell the roses. And the pinelands. And the palm hammock – a sort of palm jungle (imagine walking under giant, organic Japanese fans) that only grows between MM 47 and MM 60. There's also Adderly House, a preserved example of a Bahamian immigrant cabin (which must have *baked* in summer) and 63 acres of green goodness to stomp through. This is a great spot for the kids, who'll love the pirate exhibits in an on-site museum and yet another bird hospital.

Turtle Hospital WILDLIFE SANCTUARY
(☎ 305-743-2552; www.theturtlehospital.org; 2396 Overseas Hwy; adult/child $15/7.50; ⏱ 9am-6pm 🚼) Be they victims of disease, boat propeller strikes, flipper entanglements with fishing lines – whatever, really – any injured

sea turtle in the Keys will hopefully end up in this motel-cum-sanctuary. We know we shouldn't anthropomorphize animals, but these turtles just seem so sweet, so it's sad but heartening to see the injured and sick ones well looked after. The whole setup is a labor of love by Richard Moretti, who's quite the Keys character himself. Tours are educational and fun, and offered at 10am, 1pm and 4pm. It's recommended you call ahead before visiting, as hospital staff may be away 'on call' at any moment.

Pigeon Key ISLAND
(☎ 305-289-0025, 305-743-5999; www.pigeon key.net; MM 47; adult/child $12/9; ⏱ tours 10am, 11:30am, 1pm & 2:30pm) For years, tiny Pigeon Key, located 2 miles west of Marathon (basically below the Old Seven Mile Bridge) housed the rail workers and maintenance men who built the infrastructure that connected the Keys. Today you can tour the historic structures of this National Historic District or just relax on the beach and get in some snorkeling. Ferries leave from Knight's Key (to the left of the Seven Mile Bridge if you're traveling south) to Pigeon; the last one returns at 4pm. The **Old Seven Mile Bridge**, meanwhile, is closed to traffic and now serves as 'the World's Longest Fishing Bridge'; park at the northeastern foot of the bridge and have a wander.

Marathon Community Park & Marina MARINA
(12222 Overseas Hwy) Has athletic fields and a skate park for disaffected adolescents. The marina, better known as **Boot Key Harbor** (☎ 305-289-8877; www.bootkeyharbor.com; VHF 16), is one of the best maintained working waterfronts in the Keys, and an excellent spot to book charter-fishing and diving trips. Come during Christmas to see a 'boat parade' of boats decked out with Christmas lights.

Sombrero Beach BEACH
(Sombrero Beach Rd, off MM 50 oceanside) One of the few white-sand, mangrove-free beaches in the Keys. It's a good spot to lay out or swim, and it's free.

Marathon Kayak KAYAKING
(☎ 305-395-0355; www.marathonkayak.com; 6363 Overseas Hwy) Does guided mangrove ecotours, sunset tours and boat rentals starting from around $45.

Sombrero Reef Explorers (☎ 305-743-0536; www.marathoncharters.com; 19 Sombrero Rd, off MM 50 oceanside) and **Tilden's Scuba Center**

It's easy to think of the Keys, environmentally speaking, as a little boring. The landscape isn't particularly dramatic (with the exception of those sweet sweeps of ocean visible from the Overseas Hwy); it tends toward low brush and...well, more low brush.

Hey, don't judge a book by its cover. The Keys have one of the most unique, sensitive environments in the US. The difference between ecosystems here is measured in inches, but once you learn to recognize the contrast between a hammock and a wetland, you'll see the islands in a whole new tropical light. Some of the best introductions to the natural Keys can be found at **Crane Point Museum** (p147) and the **Florida Keys Eco-Discovery Center** (p157).

But here, we want to focus on the mangroves, the coolest, if not most visually arresting habitat in the islands. They rise from the shallow shelf that surrounds the Keys (which also provides that lovely shade of Florida teal), looking like masses of spidery fingers constantly stroking the waters. Each mangrove traps the sediment that has accrued into the land your tiki barstool is perched on. That's right, no mangroves = no Jimmy Buffett.

The three different types of mangrove trees are all little miracles of adaptation. Red mangroves, which directly front the water, have aerial roots, called propagules, which allow them to 'breathe' even as they grow into the ocean. Black mangroves, which grow further inland, survive via 'snorkel' roots called pneumatophores. Resembling spongy sticks, these roots grow out from the muddy ground, gasping in fresh air. White mangroves grow furthest inland and actually sweat out the salt they absorb through air and water to keep healthy.

The other tree worth a prop here isn't a mangrove, but the lignum vitae, which is restricted to the Keys in the US, is just as cool. Its sap has long been used to treat syphilis, hence the tree's Latin name, which translates to 'tree of life.'

(☎305-743-7255; www.tildensscubacenter.com; 4650 Overseas Hwy) both offer snorkeling and diving expeditions through nearby sections of the coral reef.

🛏 Sleeping

Seascape   B&B $$
(☎305-743-6212; 1275 76th St, between MM 51 & 52; r from $125; P❀≋☷) The classy, understated luxury in this B&B manifests in the nine rooms, which all have a different feel, from old-fashioned cottage to sleek boutique. Seascape also has a waterfront pool, kayaks for guests to use and a lovely lobby-lounge where you'll find breakfast, and afternoon wine and snack (all included).

Tranquility Bay   RESORT $$$
(☎888-755-7486; www.tranquilitybay.com; MM 48.5 bayside; r $280-650; P❀≋☷) If you're serious about going upscale, you should be going here. Tranquility Bay is a massive condotel resort with plush townhouses, high-thread-count sheets and all-in-white chic. The rooms really do have a dollhouse effect going on – between shades of eggwhite and sea blue they resemble nothing so much as pieces of delicate china. The grounds are enormous and activity-filled; they really don't want you to leave.

Siesta Motel   MOTEL $
(☎305-743-5671; www.siestamotel.net; MM 51 oceanside; r $75-105; P❀☷) Head here for one of the cheapest, cleanest flops in the Keys, located in a friendly cluster of cute Marathon homes – and it's got great service, to boot.

Seadell Motel   MOTEL $$
(☎305-743-5161; 5000 Overseas Hwy; r $79-180; P@) The Seadell is a Keys classic: low-slung huts containing linoleum-floored rooms that sport tropical bedspreads. The rooms are more or less self-sufficient small apartments, and can comfortably accommodate small families.

🍴 Eating

Keys Fisheries   SEAFOOD $
(3502 Gulf View Ave; mains $7-16; ⊙11am-9pm) The lobster reuben is the stuff of legend here. Sweet, chunky, creamy, so good it's making us leave unsightly drool all over our keyboard. But you can't go wrong with any of the excellent seafood here, all served with

sass (to order you have to identify your favorite car, color, etc; a question that depends on the mood of the guy behind the counter). Expect pleasant levels of seagull harassment as you dine on a working waterfront.

Hurricane
AMERICAN **$$**

(☎305-743-2200; MM 49.5 bayside; mains $12-19; ☺11am-midnight) Besides being our favorite bar in Marathon, the Hurricane also serves an excellent menu of creative South Florida–inspired goodness. Snapper stuffed with crabmeat comes after an appetizer of conch sliders (miniburgers) jerked in Caribbean seasoning. Save room for the chicken wings, an amazing blend of hot, sweet and plain delicious. The $5 lunch specials are a hell of a deal.

Wooden Spoon
AMERICAN **$**

(MM 51 oceanside; mains $3-9; ☺7am-3pm) It's the best breakfast around, served by sweet Southern women who know their way around a diner. The biscuits are fluffy, but they drown so well in that thick, delicious sausage gravy, and the grits are the most buttery soft starch you'll ever have the pleasure of seeing beside your eggs.

Villa Blanca
CUBAN **$**

(2211 Overseas Hwy; mains $7-12; ☺7am-8pm Mon-Sat) Villa Blanco's roast pork is a superlative example of the genre (of Cuban pork – a method cuisine with many practitioners in South Florida). It's pillowy soft, luscious, citrus tangy – yet comforting. It's also freakishly huge, as you will be if you eat in this friendly, barebones cafeteria too often.

Dion's
FRIED CHICKEN **$**

(MM 51 bayside; fried-chicken dinner $4-6; ☺24hr) Hold on – it's a gas station. Well, gas stations treated you right in Miami, didn't they (see El Carajo, p102)? Dion's serves our favorite fried chicken in South Florida: crisp but juicy, plump and rich, with gooey, melty mac and cheese and sweet fried-but-just-firm-enough plantains on the side...Oh man, we'll be right back.

🍸 Drinking & Entertainment

TOP
CHOICE **Hurricane**
BAR

(☎305-743-2200; MM 49.5 bayside) The staff is sassy, sarcastic and warm. The drinks will kick your ass out the door and have you back begging for more. The ambience: locals, tourists, mad fishermen, rednecks and the odd journalist saddling up for endless

Jägerbombs before dancing the night away to any number of consistently good live acts. It's the best bar before Key West, and it deserves a visit from you.

Island Fish Company
BAR

(☎305-743-4191; MM 54 bayside) The Island's got friendly staff pouring strong cocktails on a sea-breeze-kissed tiki island overlooking Florida Bay. Chat with your friendly Czech or Georgian bartender, tip well, and they'll top up your drinks without you realizing it. The laid-back by-the-water atmosphere is quintessentially Keys.

Brass Monkey
BAR

(☎305-743-4028; Marathon, MM 52) When Colonel Kurtz whispered, 'The horror, the horror,' in *Apocalypse Now* he was probably thinking about the night he got trashed in this scuzziest of dives, the preferred watering hole for off-the-clock bar and wait staff in Marathon.

Marathon Cinema
& Community Theater
CINEMA

(☎305-743-0408; www.marathontheater.org; 5101 Overseas Hwy) A good, old-school, single-stage theater that shows movies and plays in big reclining seats (with even bigger cup-holders).

ℹ Information

Fisherman's Hospital (☎305-743-5533; www.fishermanshospital.com; 3301 Overseas Hwy) Has a major emergency room.

Marathon Visitors Center Chamber of Commerce (☎305-743-5417, 800-262-7284; www.floridakeysmarathon.com; MM 53.5 bayside; ☺9am-5pm) Sells Greyhound tickets.

ℹ Getting There & Away

You can fly into the **Marathon Airport** (☎305-289-6060; MM 50.5 bayside) or go Greyhound, which stops at the airport.

LOWER KEYS

The Lower Keys are fierce bastions of Conch Keys native culture. Some local families have been Keys castaways for generations, and there are bits of Big Pine that feel more Florida Panhandle than Overseas Hwy. It's an odd contrast, the islands get at their most isolated, rural and quintessentially 'Keez-y' before opening onto (relatively) cosmopolitan, heterogeneous (yet strongly homosexual) Key West.

DON'T MISS

KEY DEER

While we can't guarantee you'll spot one, if you head down the side roads of Big Pine Key, there's a pretty good chance you'll spot the Key deer, roughly the size of a large dog. Once mainland dwellers, the Key deer were stranded on the islands during the formation of the Keys. Successive generations grew smaller and had single births, as opposed to large litters, to deal with the reduced food resources in the Keys. While you won't see thundering herds of dwarfish deer, the little cuteballs are pretty easy to spot if you're persistent and patient. In fact, they're so common you need to pay careful attention to the reduced speed limits. Note: speed limits drop further at night, because cars are still the biggest killer of Key deer.

To visit the official Key deer refuge (although the deer can be spotted almost anywhere on Big Pine) take Key Deer Blvd (it's a right at the lights off the Overseas Hwy at the southern end of Big Pine) north for 3.5 miles from MM 30.5.

Big Pine, Bahia Honda & Looe Key

Big Pine is home to endless stretches of quiet roads, Key West employees who found a way around astronomical real-estate rates, and packs of wandering Key deer. Bahia Honda has got everyone's favorite sandy beach, while the coral-reef system of Looe offers amazing reef-diving opportunities.

⊙ Sights & Activities

Bahia Honda State Park   PARK
(✆305-872-3210; www.bahiahondapark.com; MM 36.8; per car/motorcycle/cyclist $5/4/2; ◷8am-sunset; ⊕) This park, with its long, white-sand (and seaweed-strewn) beach, named Sandspur Beach by locals, is the big attraction in these parts. As Keys beaches go, this one is probably the best natural stretch of sand in the island chain, but we wouldn't vote it best beach in the continental USA (although Condé Nast did...in 1992). As a tourist, the more novel experience is walking a stretch of the **old Bahia Honda Rail Bridge**, which offers nice views of the surrounding islands. Or check out the nature trails (ooh, butterflies!) and science center, where helpful park employees help you identify stone crabs, fireworms, horseshoe crabs and comb jellies.

The **park concession** (✆305-872-3210; MM 36.8 oceanside) offers daily 1½-hour snorkeling trips at 9:30am and 1:30pm (adult/child $30/25). Reservations are a good idea in high season.

Looe Key National Marine Sanctuary   MARINE PARK
(✆305-292-0311; floridakeys.noaa.gov) Looe (pronounced 'loo') Key, located five nauti-cal miles off Big Pine, isn't a key at all but a reef, part of the Florida Keys National Marine Sanctuary. This is an area of some 2800 square nautical miles of 'land' managed by the National Oceanic & Atmospheric Administration. The reef here can only be visited through a specially arranged charter-boat trip, best arranged through any Keys diving outfit, the most natural one being **Looe Key Dive Center** (✆305-872-2215; www.diveflakeys.com; snorkel/dive $44/84). The marine sanctuary is named for an English frigate that sank here in 1744, and the Looe Key reef contains the 210ft *Adolphus Busch,* used in the 1957 film *Fire Down Below* and then sunk (110ft deep) in these waters in 1998.

National Key Deer Refuge Headquarters   WILDLIFE RESERVE
(✆305-872-2239; www.fws.gov/nationalkeydeer; Big Pine Shopping Center, MM 30.5 bayside; ◷8am-5pm Mon-Fri; ⊕) What would make Bambi cuter? Mini Bambi. Introducing: the Key deer, an endangered subspecies of white-tailed deer that prance about primarily on Big Pine and No Name Keys. The folks here are an incredibly helpful source of information on the deer and all things Keys. The refuge sprawls over several islands, but the sections open to the public are on Big Pine and No Name. The headquarters also administers the Great White Heron National Wildlife Refuge, 200,000 acres of open water and mangrove islands north of the main Keys that is only accessible by boat; there is no tourism infrastructure in place to get out here, but you can inquire about nautical charts and the heron themselves at the office.

Blue Hole   POND

(off MM 30.5; ☉24hr) This little pond (and former quarry) is now the largest freshwater body in the Keys. That's not saying much, but the hole is a pretty little dollop of blue (well, algal green) surrounded by a small path and information signs. The water is home to turtles, fish, wading birds and two alligators, including a hefty sucker named 'Bacardi.' Apparently people have taken to (illegally) feeding the wildlife here; please don't follow in their footsteps. A quarter mile further along the same road is **Watson's Nature Trail** (less than 1 mile long) and **Watson's Hammock**, a small Keys forest habitat.

No Name Key   ISLAND

Perhaps the best named (or lack thereof) island in the Keys gets few visitors, as it's basically a residential island. It's one of the most reliable spots for Key deer watching. From Overseas Hwy, go on to Watson Blvd, turn right, then left onto Wilder Blvd. Cross Bogie Bridge and you'll be on No Name.

Veterans Memorial Park & Beach   PARK

(MM 39 oceanside; ☉sunrise-sunset; ⊞) This small park has covered picnic tables and good access to the mudflat and mangrove habitat that makes up most of the Keys' coastline. The views onto the ocean are pristine.

Big Pine Flea Market   MARKET

(MM 30.5 oceanside; ☉8am-sunset Sat & Sun) This market, which attracts folks from across the Keys, rivals local churches for weekly attendance. You know how we keep harping on about how weird Keys residents are? Well, imagine rummaging through their closets and seeing their deepest, darkest secrets – on sale for 50¢?!

Strike Zone Charters   SNORKELING, DIVING

(☎305-872-9863, 800-654-9560; www.strikezonecharter.com; MM 29.5 bayside) Runs snorkeling ($35) and diving trips ($45) aboard glass-bottom boats, in which you can explore the thousands of varieties of colorful tropical fish, coral and sea life in the Looe Key sanctuary.

🛏 Sleeping

TOP
CHOICE **Deer Run Bed & Breakfast**   B&B $$$
(☎305-872-2015; www.deerrunfloridabb.com; 1997 Long Beach Dr, Big Pine Key, off MM 33 oceanside; r $235-355; Ⓟ☀) This state-certified green lodge and vegetarian B&B is isolated on a

lonely, lovely stretch of Long Beach Dr. It's a garden of quirky delights, complemented by assorted love-the-earth paraphernalia, street signs and four simple but cozily scrumptious rooms with names such as Eden, Heaven and Utopia. The helpful owners will get you out on a boat or into the heated pool for some chillaxation, while they whip up organic, vegetarian meals. We should add: the vibe is decidedly not self-righteous vegetarian. You could take home a steak-and-bacon sandwich and the staff wouldn't mind.

TOP
CHOICE **Bahia Honda State Park
Campground**   CAMP GROUND $
(☎305-872-2353; www.reserveamerica.com; MM 37, Bahia Honda Key; sites $36, cabins $160; Ⓟ) Bahia Honda has the best camping in the Keys. There's nothing quite like waking up to the sky as your ceiling and the ocean as your shower (Ow! Damned sand flies. OK, it's not paradise...). The park has six cabins, each sleeping six people, and 200 sites a short distance from the beach. Reserve well in advance.

Barnacle Bed & Breakfast   B&B $$

(☎305-872-3298; www.thebarnacle.net; 1557 Long Beach Dr, Big Pine Key; r $145-195; Ⓟ☀) Another great Keys B&B, the Barnacle welcomes you into its atrium with the promise of fresh ocean breezes. Wander around the pool and Jacuzzi, past the swinging hammocks, into highly individualized rooms that nonetheless all share a lovingly crazy design sense: tropical knickknacks and big windows that let in lots of Keys sunlight are standard. Meals should be enjoyed on the excellent deck, which overlooks a gorgeous clean sweep of the sea.

Big Pine Key Fishing Lodge   HOTEL $

(☎305-872-2351; MM 33 oceanside, Big Pine Key; sites with/without electricity $40/35, motel apt $80-120; Ⓟ☀⊞) This tidy canalside spot has a loyal clientele of snowbirds who wouldn't call anywhere else their Keys home. Key deer wander the clean grounds, staff is friendly and there are plenty of activities for the kids. The lodge, geared toward fishing and diving types, does boat rental.

Parmer's Place Guesthouse   HOTEL $$

(☎305-872-2157; www.parmersresort.com; 565 Barry Ave, Little Torch Key, off MM 28.5 bayside; r winter $134-294, summer $99-209; 🛜☀) Appearing deceptively small from the outside, this 5-acre property takes up a nice chunk of Little Torch Key and fills it with inviting rooms that overlook local cuts and channels. The rooms are spacious, although you'd be mad not to step outside them and enjoy a view of the islands from your balcony.

Little Palm Island Resort & Spa   RESORT $$$
(☑305-872-2524, 800-343-8567; www.littlepalmis land.com; ste $1091-2072; @☎) How do you get here? By boat or by plane, accompanied by a big wad of money. If you can afford to get here you can afford to spoil yourself, and this exclusive island, with its Zen gardens, blue lagoons and general Persian-empire air of decadent luxury, is very good at spoiling you.

✕ Eating

No Name Pub   PIZZA $
(☑305-872-9115; N Watson Blvd, Big Pine Key, off MM 30.5 bayside; mains $7-18; ☺11am-11pm) The No Name's one of those off-the-track places that everyone seems to know about. It feels isolated, it looks isolated, yet somehow, the tourists are all here – and this doesn't detract in the slightest from the kooky ambience, friendly service, excellent locally brewed beer and primo pizzas served up at this colorful semidive. Note, the name of this place implies that it is located on No Name Key, but it is on Big Pine Key, just over the causeway.

Coco's Kitchen   DINER $
(Big Pine Key Shopping Center, MM 30.5 bayside; mains & sandwiches $10.50; ☺7am-2pm & 4-7pm Tue-Sat) Enter through the oddly mirrored storefront into this tiny luncheonette, where local fishers join shoppers from the Winn Dixie next door for diner fare and local gossip. Serves a good mix of American standards and Cuban diner fare such as *picadillo* (ground beef cooked in Cuban spices).

Good Food Conspiracy   VEGETARIAN $
(Big Pine Key, MM 30 oceanside; mains under $10; ☺9:30am-7pm Mon-Sat, 11am-5pm Sun; ☑) This place serves pork-fat and baby-seal tacos. Just kidding! Rejoice, health-food nuts, all the greens, sprouts, herbs and tofu you've been dreaming about during that long, fried-food-studded drive down the Overseas are for sale in this friendly little macrobiotic organic shop. There is a good smoothie and fresh-juice bar on site. Note the big pink shrimp out front – Keezy kitsch as its best.

ⓘ Information

Lower Keys Chamber of Commerce (☑305-872-2411; www.lowerkeyschamber.com; MM 31

oceanside; ☺9am-5pm Mon-Fri, 9am-3pm Sat) Stocked with brochures and tourist information.

Sugarloaf & Boca Chica Keys

This is the final stretch before the holy grail of Key West. There's not much going on – just a few good eats and a thoroughly batty roadside attraction.

This lowest section of the Keys goes from about MM 20 to the start of Key West.

◎ Sights

Perky's Bat Tower   TOWER
(Sugarloaf Key, MM17) It resembles an Aztec-inspired fire lookout, but this wooden tower is actually one real-estate developer's vision gone utterly awry. In the 1920s Richter C Perky had the bright idea to transform this area into a vacation resort. There was just one problem: mosquitoes. His solution? Build a 35ft tower and move in a colony of bats (he'd heard they eat mosquitoes). He imported the flying mammals, but they promptly took off, leaving the tower empty. Perky never built in this area again.

Sheriff's Animal Farm   ZOO
(☑305-293-7300; 5501 College Rd, Stock Island; ☺1-3pm every other Sun or by appt; ☑) Just before you hit Key West, you may be tempted to stop into this farm, located near the Monroe County Sheriff's Office and Detention Center (seriously). This shelter for Monroe County animals that have been abandoned or given up is a lovely place to take the kids (call ahead to visit and farmer Jeanne Selander will be happy to show you around). There are tortoises, South American cavvies (a kind of rodent), birds, llamas, an albino python – it's a zoo, folks, and a fun one at that.

▭ Sleeping

Sugarloaf Key Resort KOA   CAMP GROUND $
(☑305-745-3549, 800-562-7731; www.koa.com /campgrounds/sugarloaf-key; 251 County Rd, off MM 20 oceanside; sites tent/RV from $55/72; P☎☎) This highly developed KOA (Kampground of America) has about 200 tent sites and 200 RV sites, with amenities including beachfront volleyball, swimming pool, minigolf and sunset cruises.

Sugarloaf Lodge   HOTEL $$
(☑800-553-6097; www.sugarloaflodge.net; Sugarloaf Key, MM 17; r $115-165; P☎) The 55 motel-

Conchs (pronounced 'conk' as in 'bonk', not 'contsh' as in 'bunch') are people who were born and raised in the Keys. It's a rare title to achieve. Even transplants can only rise to the rank of 'freshwater Conch.' You will hear reference to, and see the flag of, the Conch Republic everywhere in the islands, which brings us to an interesting tale.

In 1982 US border patrol and customs agents erected a roadblock at Key Largo to catch drug smugglers and illegal aliens. As traffic jams and anger mounted, many tourists disappeared. They decided they'd rather take the Shark Valley Tram in the Everglades, thank you very much. To voice their outrage, a bunch of fiery Conchs decided to secede from the USA. After forming the Conch Republic, they made three declarations (in this order): secede from the USA; declare war on the USA and surrender; and request $1 million in foreign aid. The roadblock was eventually lifted, and every February, Conchs celebrate the anniversary of those heady days with nonstop parties, and the slogan 'We Seceded Where Others Failed.'

Today the whole Conch Republic thing is largely a marketing gimmick, but that doesn't detract from its official motto: 'One Human Family.' This emphasis on tolerance and mutual respect has kept the Keys' head and heart in the right place, accepting gays, straights, and peoples of all colors and religions.

FLORIDA KEYS & KEY WEST   KEY WEST

like rooms are nothing special, though every single one has a killer bay view. There is also an on-site restaurant, a tiki bar, a marina and an airstrip, from which you can charter a seaplane tour or go skydiving.

✖ Eating

Sugarloaf Food Company   AMERICAN $
(MM 24 bayside; breakfast $2.25-4.25, lunch $5-9; ⊙6:30am-3pm Tue-Sat) A cozy, airy alternative to fried dullness, the Food Company specializes in excellent sandwiches and salads, plus some cute handcrafted postcards. An almost impossibly cute artsy retreat-cum-restaurant.

Mangrove Mama's   CARIBBEAN $$
(MM 20 oceanside; lunch $10-15, dinner $19-29; ⊙11:30am-3:30pm & 5:30-10pm) This groovy roadside eatery serves Caribbean-inspired seafood – coconut shrimp, spicy conch stew, lobster – best enjoyed on the backyard patio and accompanied by a little live reggae.

Baby's Coffee   CAFE $
(☏800-523-2326; MM 15 oceanside; ⊙7am-6pm Mon-Fri, 7am-5pm Sat & Sun) This very cool coffeehouse has an on-site bean-roasting plant and sells bags of the aromatic stuff along with excellent hot and cold java brews – many locals consider this to be some of the best coffee in the islands. Other essentials are sold, from yummy baked goods to Dr Brommer's liquid soap.

KEY WEST

The Keys, like any frontier, have always attracted two 'E's': edges and eccentrics. And when it came to the far frontier, the very edge, the last outpost of America – out here, only the most eccentric would dare venture. And thus, Key West, is the most beautifully strange (or is it strangely beautiful?) island in the US. This place is seriously screwy, in a (mostly) good way. There's no middle separating the high and low brow, that's for sure. On one side of the road, literary festivals, Caribbean villas, tropical noir and expensive art galleries. On the other, an S&M fetishist parade, frat boys vomiting on their sorority girlfriends and 'I Love to Fart' T-shirts (seriously).

Where the other Keys are a bit more country-fried, Key West, a historical haven for homosexuals and artists, remains a little more left of center. The locals revel in their funky nonconformity here, probably because weirdness is still integral to the Key West brand. But past these idiosyncrasies is simply a beautiful tropical island, where the moonflowers bloom at night and the classical Caribbean homes are so sad and romantic it's impossible not to sigh when you see them.

◉ Sights

TOP CHOICE **Mallory Square**   SQUARE
(⊙sunset; ⭗) Take all those energies, subcultures and oddities of Keys life – the hippies, the rednecks, the foreigners and, of course, the tourists – and focus them into one

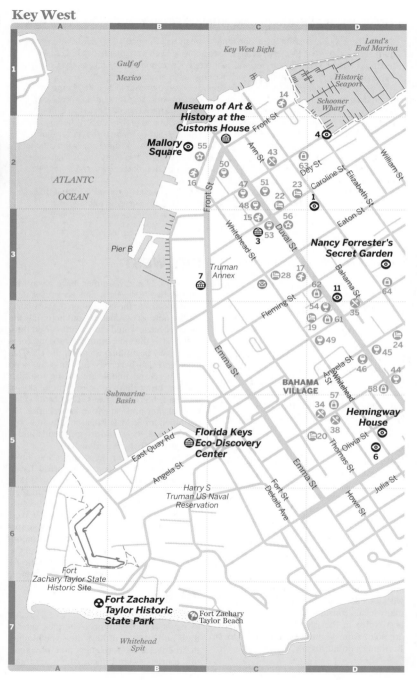

Key West

Key West Bight

Land's
End Marina

Gulf of
Mexico

Historic
Seaport

Schooner
Wharf

14

**Museum of Art &
History at the
Customs House**

Front St

4

**Mallory
Square** 55

50

43

63

Dey St

Ann St

ATLANTC
OCEAN

16

47 51

48 22 23 1

15 56

3 53

Whitehead St

Duval St

Caroline St

Eaton St

Elizabeth St

William St

**Nancy Forrester's
Secret Garden**

Pier B

7

Truman
Annex

17

28

Bahama St

62

11

64

Fleming St

54 61

19

Emma St

49

45 24

46 44

58

Angela St

Whitehead St

**BAHAMA
VILLAGE**

57

34

**Hemingway
House**

35

Submarine
Basin

**Florida Keys
Eco-Discovery
Center**

East Quay Rd

38

20

Olivia St

Thomas St

6

Angela St

Harry S
Truman US Naval
Reservation

Fort St

Emma St

Dekalb Ave

Howe St

Julia St

Fort
Zachary Taylor State
Historic Site

**Fort Zachary
Taylor Historic
State Park**

Fort Zachary
Taylor Beach

Whitehead
Spit

Key West

◎ Top Sights

Florida Keys Eco-Discovery
Center...B5
Fort Zachary Taylor Historic
State Park..A7
Hemingway House D5
Key West Cemetery...............................F3
Mallory Square.......................................B2
Museum of Art & History at the
Customs House C2
Nancy Forrester's Secret
Garden..D3

◎ Sights

1 Casa Antigua..D2
2 Gay & Lesbian Trolley Tour of
Key West F6
3 Heritage House C3
4 Jolly II Rover...D2
5 Key West Butterfly & Nature
Conservatory E6
6 Key West Lighthouse D5
7 Little White House B3
8 Mathieson's 4th of July.......................G4
9 Office of the Secretary General
of the Conch Republic.......................E4
Pelican Poop Gift Shoppe..............(see 1)
San Carlos Institute.....................(see 62)
10 Southernmost Point.............................E6
11 Strand Building.....................................D3
12 Studios of Key West F2
13 Subtropic Dive Center.........................H3

◎ Activities, Courses & Tours

14 Conch Tour Train..................................C1
15 Ghosts & Legends of Key West C3
Historic Key West Walking Tour
office...(see 16)
16 Old Town Trolley Tours........................B2
17 Original Ghost Tours C3

⬛ Sleeping

18 Avalon Bed & Breakfast.......................E6
19 Big Ruby's Guesthouse........................D4
20 Caribbean House...................................D5
21 Chelsea House.......................................F4
22 Curry Mansion Inn C2
23 Cypress House C2
24 Gardens Hotel D4
25 Key Lime Inn F4

26 Key West Youth Hostel &
Seashell Motel G6
27 La Mer & Dewey Hotel F6
28 L'habitation...C3
29 Merlin Inn E4
30 Mermaid & Alligator F4
31 Pearl's Rainbow F6
32 Santa Maria F6
33 Truman Hotel E5

◉ Eating

34 Blue Heaven...D5
35 Café...D4
36 Café Solé...F3
37 Camille's F5
38 Conch Town Café..................................D5
39 El Siboney G5
40 Mo's Restaurant G4
41 Nine One Five..E5
42 Seven Fish...E4
43 Thai Cuisine C2

◉ Drinking

44 801 Bourbon Bar D4
45 Aqua..D4
46 Bourbon St Pub.....................................D4
47 Captain Tony's Saloon.........................C2
48 Garden of Eden Bar..............................C2
49 Green Parrot D4
50 Hog's Breath...C2
51 Irish Kevin's C2
52 La Te Da E5
Pearl's Rainbow...........................(see 31)
53 Porch...C3
54 Virgilio's D4

◉ Entertainment

55 Key West Players B2
56 Red Barn Theatre..................................C3
Tropic Cinema ....(see 28)

◉ Shopping

57 Bésame Mucho D5
58 Dogs on Duval..D4
59 Frangipani Gallery E5
60 Haitian Art Co F2
61 Leather Master D4
62 Montage D3
63 Peppers of Key West.............................C2
64 Project Lighthouse................................D3

torchlit, family-friendly (but playfully edgy), sunset-enriched street party. The child of all these raucous forces is Mallory Sq, one of the greatest shows on Earth. It all begins as the sun starts to set, a sign for the madness that it's OK to break out. Watch a dog walk a tightrope, a man swallow fire, British acrobats tumble and sass each other. Have a beer. And a conch fritter. And wait for the sun to dip behind the ocean and for the carnival to really get going.

Duval Street   STREET

Key West locals have a love-hate relationship with the most famous road in Key West (if not the Keys). Duval, Old Town Key West's main drag, is a miracle mile of booze, tacky everything and awful behavior (and not awful in an awfully good way either). It's more like awful in a loud, belligerently drunk, omigodthatshirtsays 'Put some lipstick on my dipstick' *really*? kinda way). But it's fun. The 'Duval Crawl' is one of the best pub crawls in the country. The mix of live music drink-o-ramas, T-shirt kitsch, local theaters, art studios and boutiques is more charming than jarring. And the experience is quintessentially Key West ('Keezy'). Have some perspective, have a laugh, and appreciate Duval for her pimples-and-all, to see why this street continues to be the island's tipsy heart.

Hemingway House   HISTORIC SITE

(www.hemingwayhome.com; 907 Whitehead St; adult/child 6-12yr $12.50/6; ☺9am-5pm) Key West's biggest darling, Ernest Hemingway, lived in this gorgeous Spanish colonial house from 1931 to 1940. Papa moved here in his early 30s with wife No 2, a *Vogue* fashion editor and (former) friend of wife No 1. *The Short Happy Life of Francis Macomber* and *The Green Hills of Africa* were produced here, but Hemingway didn't just work; like all writers he wasted a lot of time, specifically by installing Key West's first saltwater swimming pool. The construction project set him back so badly he pressed his 'last penny' into the cement on the pool's deck. It's still there today, along with the evil descendants of his famous six-toed cat, who basically rule the house and grounds. The author's old studio is preserved as he left it – when he ran off in 1940 with wife No 3.

FREE Florida Keys
Eco-Discovery Center   MUSEUM

(eco-discovery.com/ecokw.html; 35 East Quay Rd, Truman Annex; ☺9am-4pm Tue-Sat; P♿) So, you've been making your way down the Keys, visiting all these lovely state parks and nature reserves, thinking, Gosh, could there be a place that ties all the knowledge of this unique ecological phenomenon into one fun, well-put-together educational exhibit? OK, maybe those weren't your exact thoughts, but this is exactly what you get at this excellent center. This place does a marvelous job of filling in all the wild details of the natural Keys. The kids love it, and by the way, it's free *and* has free parking, an abnormality around here.

Fort Zachary Taylor
Historic State Park   PARK

(☎305-292-6713; www.floridastateparks.org/fort taylor; Truman Annex; per car/motorcycle/pedestrian & cyclist $6/4/2; ☺8am-sunset) 'America's Southernmost State Park,' this park is oft-neglected by authorities and visitors, which is a shame as it's a nice place to while away a quiet afternoon. The actual fort walls are still standing, and within the compound those most-blessed of nerds – historical re-enactors – put on costumes and act out scenes from Civil War and pirate days (we have yet to see a Civil War soldiers vs pirates fight here. But we can hope). Butterflies flit over the grounds, and the beach here is the best one Key West has to offer – it's got white sand to lounge on, deep enough water to swim in and tropical fish under the waves. Beach divers who head about 20ft from shore may spot some decent fish life.

Key West Cemetery   CEMETERY

(Margaret & Angela St; ☺sunrise-sunset; ♿) A darkly alluring Gothic labyrinth beckons (rather incongruously) at the center of this pastel town. Built in 1847, the cemetery crowns Solares Hill, the highest point on the island (with an elevation of all of 16ft). Some of the oldest families in the Keys rest in peace – and close proximity – here. With body space at a premium, the mausoleums stand practically shoulder to shoulder. Island quirkiness penetrates the gloom: seashells and green macramé adorn headstones with inscriptions like, 'I told you I was sick.' Get chaperoned by a guide from the Historic Florida Keys Foundation (☎305-292-6718), with guided tours for $10 per person at 9:30am on Tuesday and Thursday; departs from the main gate at Margaret and Angela Sts.

Key West Butterfly & Nature Conservatory
WILDLIFE SANCTUARY

(☑305-296-2988; www.keywestbutterfly.com; 1316 Duval St; adult/child/seniors & military $12/8.50/9; ☺9am-5pm; ✪) This vast domed conservatory lets you stroll through a magic garden of flowering plants, colorful birds and up to 1800 fluttering butterflies, all live imports from around the globe.

Nancy Forrester's Secret Garden
GARDEN

(www.nfsgarden.com; 1 Free School Lane; admission $10; ☺10am-5pm) Nancy, a local artist and fixture of the Keys community, invites you to bring lunch (but no cell phones!) into her oasis of lush palms, orchids, and chatty caged parrots and macaws. Although the place is called a secret garden, Nancy considers it to be a piece of art in and of itself – the last acre of undeveloped (although tended and cared for by human hands) natural space within the heart of Key West. The garden-artwork becomes a bridge between the natural world and the Key West that surrounds it. However you choose to interpret it, most agree this is a serene, near-magical place.

Museum of Art & History at the Customs House
MUSEUM

(www.kwahs.com/customhouse; 281 Front St; adult/child/senior $7/5/6; ☺9:30am-4:30pm) There is art at the end of the road, and you'll find the best at this museum, which is worth a look-see if only for its gorgeous home – the grand Customs House, long abandoned until its impressive renovation in the '90s. Actually, this place is worth a look-see for any number of reasons, including a permanent display of massive portraits and some of the best showcases of international (particularly Caribbean) art in the region. The raw, almost cartoonish paintings of Key West done on wood by Mario Sanchez are a particular draw.

Fort East Martello Museum & Gardens
MUSEUM

(www.kwahs.com/martello.htm; 3501 S Roosevelt Blvd; adult/child/senior $7/5/6; ☺9:30am-4:30pm) This old fortress was built to resemble old Italian Martello-style coastal watchtowers (hence the name), a design that quickly became obsolete with the advent of the explosive shell. Now the fort serves a new purpose: preserving the old. That is to say, the historical memorabilia, artifacts, the folk art of Mario Sanchez and 'junk' sculptor Stanley Papio, who worked with scrap metal and (cue ominous music)...Robert

the Doll. Perhaps the most haunted thing in Key West, Robert is a genuinely creepy looking child's doll from the 19th century who reportedly causes much misfortune to those who question his powers. Honest, he looks like something out of a Stephen King novel; see www.robertthedoll.org for more information.

Studios of Key West
GALLERY

(TSKW; ☑305-296-0458; www.tskw.org; 600 White St; ☺10am-6pm) This nonprofit showcases about a dozen artists' studios in a gallery space located in the old Armory building, which includes a lovely sculpture garden. Besides its public visual-arts displays, TSKW hosts readings by local authors like Robert Stone, literary and visual workshops, concerts, lectures and community discussion groups. Essentially, it has become the accessible heart of this city's enormous arts movement, and offers a good point-of-entry for visitors who want to engage in Key West's creative scene but don't have a clue where to start. You may want to call ahead before you visit in case exhibits are being installed.

Little White House
HISTORIC BUILDING

(☑305-294-9911; www.trumanlittlewhitehouse.com; 111 Front St; adult/child 5-12yr/senior $16/5/13.50; ☺9am-4:30pm) While we were first tempted here by the prospect of a Lego-sized execution of the presidential digs, this is in fact the spot where ex-president Harry S Truman used to vacation when he wasn't molding post-WWII geopolitics. It is as lushly luxurious as you'd expect and open only for guided tours, although you are welcome to walk around the surrounding botanical gardens (☺7am-6pm) for free. Plenty of Truman's possessions are scattered about, but the real draw is the guides, who are intensely intelligent, quirky and helpful.

Heritage House
HISTORIC BUILDING

(☑305-296-3573; www.heritagehousemuseum.org; 410 Caroline St; admission $5; ☺10am-4pm Mon-Sat) Of all the many historic Key West homes open to visitors, this Caribbean-Colonial house is among the most wonderful to walk through. That's because it's rarely crowded, has passionate guides, and contains original furnishings and antiques, from a piano from the court of Marie Antoinette to a set of dining chairs from the 1600s. All have been collected and preserved by seven generations of a local family. The Robert Frost Cottage, where the poet stayed for 16 winters, is out back, along with another wonderful garden.

Numerous lectures, readings, writers' workshops and weddings are held here.

San Carlos Institute
HISTORIC BUILDING

(www.institutosancarlos.org; 516 Duval St) Founded in 1871 by Cuban exiles, the San Carlos is a gorgeous building constructed in classical Spanish mission style. The current structure dates from 1924 and received an extensive overhaul in 1992. The interior is spackled with Cuban tile work, Italian marble and statues of Cuban luminaries, including Jose Marti, who spoke here and dubbed the building 'La Casa Cuba.' Today the building serves as a library, art gallery, lecture hall, theater and general multipurpose building; it is only open during events, but these occur pretty often.

Bahama Village
NEIGHBORHOOD

Bahama Village was the old Bahamian district of the island, and in days past it had a colorful Caribbean feel about it – which is resurrected a bit during the **Goombay Festival** (p161). But today the village is pretty gentrified; many areas have been swallowed into a sort of pseudo-Duval periphery zone, but some retain their old Caribbean charm. At the **Office of the Secretary General of the Conch Republic** (☑305-296-0213; 613 Simonton St) you can see all manner of Conch Republic tat – flags, souvenirs and such.

Casa Antigua
HISTORIC BUILDING

(314 Simonton St; ◷10am-6pm) This was technically Hemingway's first house in Key West and the spot where he wrote *A Farewell to Arms,* but it isn't all that notable, except for a lush garden in the back and one of the kitschiest 'guided tours' in the US. Here's how it breaks down: go to the **Pelican Poop Gift Shoppe** (www.pelicanpoop.com; 314 Simonton St), which now occupies the Casa, pay the $2 garden entrance fee and let the kitsch begin! Go into the peaceful green area out the back, then a recorded tape plays at the volume God uses whenever he says anything that begins with 'Let there be...' At this ear-splitting volume, a man with a voice that can only be described as Big Gay Al raised in Dixie lays down the history of the Casa for you. It's gloriously hilarious.

Strand Building
HISTORIC BUILDING

(527 Duval St) The historic Strand Theater was one of the Key West's great old-time movie houses, and was used to stand in as a movie house in the 1993 film *Matinee.* Today it's a Walgreens pharmacy, but the exterior is as romantic as ever.

Key West Lighthouse
LIGHTHOUSE

(www.kwahs.com; 938 Whitehead St; adult/student over 7yr/senior $10/5/9; ◷9:30am-4:30pm) You can climb up 88 steps to the top of this lighthouse, built in 1846, for a decent view. But honestly, it's just as enjoyable to gaze up at the tower from the leafy street below.

Southernmost Point
LANDMARK

(cnr South & Whitehead Sts) The most photographed spot on the island, this red-and-black buoy isn't even the southernmost point in the USA (that's in the off-limits naval base around the corner). The most overrated attraction in Key West.

🏃 Activities

Beach Going
BEACH

Key West is *not* about beach going. In fact, for true sun 'n' surf, locals go to Bahia Honda (p150) whenever possible. Still, the three city beaches on the southern side of the island are lovely and narrow, with calm and clear water. **South Beach** is at the end of Simonton St. **Higgs Beach**, at the end of Reynolds St and Casa Marina Ct, has barbecue grills, picnic tables, and a big crowd of gay sunbathers and Key West's Eastern European seasonal workforce. **Smathers Beach**, further east off S Roosevelt Blvd, is more popular with jetskiers, parasailers, teens and college students. The best local beach, though, is at Fort Zachary Taylor (p157); it's worth the admission to enjoy the white sand and relative calm.

Boating

Check www.charterboatkeywest.com for a directory of the many fishing and cruising charters offered in Key West.

⌐TOP⌐ Jolly II Rover
CHOICE
BOAT TOUR

(☑305-304-2235; www.schoonerjollyrover.com; cnr Greene & Elizabeth Sts, Schooner Wharf; cruises $39) This outfit has a gorgeous tanbark (reddish-brown) 80ft schooner that embarks on daily sunset cruises under sail. It looks like a pirate ship and has the cannons to back the image up.

Reelax Charters
KAYAKING

(☑305-304-1392, 305-744-0263; www.keyskayaking.com; MM 17 Sugarloaf Key Marina; kayak trips $200) Get your paddle on and slip silently into the surrounding mangroves and mudflats of the Lower Keys with Andrea Paulson. Based on Sugarloaf Key.

DETOUR: DRY TORTUGAS NATIONAL PARK

After all those keys, connected by all that convenient road, the nicest islands in the archipelago require a little extra effort. Ponce de León named them Las Tortugas (The Turtles) for the sea turtles that roamed here. A lack of freshwater led sailors to add a 'dry.' Today the Dry Tortugas are a national park under the control of the **National Park Service** (☎305-242-7700; www.nps.gov/drto; admission $5) and are accessible by boat or plane.

Originally the Tortugas were the US's naval perch into the Gulf of Mexico. But by the Civil War, **Fort Jefferson**, the main structure on the islands, had become a prison for Union deserters and at least four people, among them Dr Samuel Mudd, who had been arrested for complicity in the assassination of Abraham Lincoln. Hence, a new nickname: Devil's Island. The name was prophetic; in 1867 a yellow-fever outbreak killed 38 people, and after an 1873 hurricane the fort was abandoned. It reopened in 1886 as a quarantine station for smallpox and cholera victims, was declared a national monument in 1935 by President Franklin D Roosevelt, and was upped to national-park status in 1992 by George Bush Sr.

The park is open for day trips and overnight camping, which provides a rare phenomenon: a quiet Florida beach. Garden Key has 13 campsites ($3 per person, per night), which are given out on a first-come, first-served basis. Reserve early by calling the National Park office. There are toilets, but no freshwater showers or drinking water; bring everything you'll need. The sparkling waters offer excellent snorkeling and diving opportunities. A **visitor center** is located within fascinating Fort Jefferson.

If you're hungry, watch for Cuban-American fishing boats trolling the waters. They'll happily trade for lobster, crab and shrimp; you'll have the most leverage trading beverages. Just paddle up and bargain for your supper. In March and April, there is stupendous bird-watching, including aerial fighting. Star-gazing is mind-blowing any time of the year.

Getting There

If you have your own boat, the Dry Tortugas are covered under National Ocean Survey chart No 11438. Otherwise, the **Yankee Freedom II** (☎305-294-7009, 800-634-0939; www.yankeefreedom.com; Historic Seaport) operates a fast ferry between Garden Key and the Historic Seaport (at the northern end of Margaret St). Round-trip fares cost $165/120 per adult/child. Reservations are recommended. Continental breakfast, a picnic lunch, snorkeling gear and a 45-minute tour of the fort are all included.

Key West Seaplanes (☎305-294-0709; www.seaplanesofkeywest.com) can take up to 10 passengers (flight time 40 minutes each way). A four-hour trip costs $250/free/160/190 per adult/child under two years/child two to six years/child under 12 years; an eight-hour trip costs $515/free/320/365. Again, reserve at least a week in advance.

The $5 park admission fees are included in the above prices.

Diving & Snorkeling

The diving is better in Key Largo and Biscayne National park, but there is some decent wreck diving near Key West.

The website of the **Keys Association of Dive Operators** (http://divekeys.com; 3128 N Roosevelt Blvd) is a clearing house for information on diving opportunities in the islands; it also works on enhancing local sustainable underwater activities by creating artificial reefs and encouraging safe boating and diving practices.

Subtropic Dive Center   DIVING
(☎305-296-9914, 800-853-3483; www.subtropic.com; 1605 N Roosevelt Blvd) Reliable operator

with a good reputation. Does open-water certification for $499, and offers numerous other levels of PADI certification.

Dive Key West   DIVING
(☎305-296-3823, 800-426-0707; www.divekeywest.com; 3128 N Roosevelt Blvd) Largest dive facility on the island. Wreck-diving trips cost $144 with all equipment and air provided.

Tours

Worth noting is *Sharon Wells' Walking & Biking Guide to Historic Key West,* a booklet of self-guided walks available free at inns and businesses around town, written by a local. See www.seekeywest.com.

Old Town Trolley Tours
TROLLEY

(☑305-296-6688; www.trolleytours.com/key-west; adult/child under 13yr/senior $29/free/26; ⊗tours 9am-4:30pm; 🚻) These tours are a great introduction to the city. The 90-minute, hop-on, hop-off narrated tram tour starts at Mallory Sq and makes a large, lazy loop around the whole city, with nine stops along the way. Trolleys depart every 15 to 30 minutes from 9am to 4:30pm daily. The narration is hokey, but you'll get a good overview of Key West, its history, and gossipy dirt about local issues and people in the news.

Conch Tour Train
TRAIN

(☑305-294-5161; www.conchtourtrain.com; adult/ child under 13yr/senior $29/free/26; ⊗tours 9am-4:30pm; 🚻) Run by the same company as trolley tours, though this one seats you in breezier linked train cars with no on/ off option. Offers discounted admission to sights like the Hemingway House.

Historic Key West Walking Tour
WALKING

(☑800-844-7601; 1 Whitehead St; www.trusted tours.com; adult/child $18/9) A walking tour that takes in some of the major architecture and historical sights of the island. Takes about two hours. You need to book in advance.

Ghosts & Legends of Key West
GHOST

(☑305-294-1713; www.keywestghosts.com; Porter House Mansion, 429 Caroline St; adult/child $18/10; ⊗tours 7pm & 9pm) Promises to take you 'off the beaten track' to places 'only a Conch could show you,' including the old city morgue and a small cemetery.

Original Ghost Tours
GHOST

(☑305-294-9255; www.hauntedtours.com; 423 Fleming St; adult/child $15/10; ⊗tours 8pm & 9pm) Stories about souls who inhabit locations that include about half the bars and hotels on the island.

⚘ Festivals & Events

Contact the **Key West Art & Historical Society** (☑305-295-6616; www.kwahs.com) to get the skinny on upcoming studio shows, literary readings, film festivals and the like.

Annual Key West Literary Seminar LITERARY
(http://keywestliteraryseminar.org/lit) Now in its 23rd year, draws top writers from around the country each January (although it costs hundreds of dollars to attend).

Robert Frost Poetry Festival LITERARY
(www.robertfrostpoetryfestival.com) Held in April.

Hemingway Days LITERARY
Held in late July, brings parties, a 5km run and an Ernest look-alike contest.

WomenFest LESBIAN & TRANSEXUAL
(www.womenfest.com) Nothing says dignified sexiness like this festival, held in early September, which attracts thousands of lesbians who just want to party.

Fantasy Fest CULTURAL
You gotta see this festival held throughout the week leading up to Halloween in late October. It's when all the inns get competitive about decorating their properties, and everyone gets decked out in the most outrageous costumes they can cobble together (or decked down in daring body paint).

Goombay Festival CULTURAL
(www.goombay-keywest.org) Held during the same out-of-control week as Fantasy Fest, this is a Bahamian celebration of food, crafts and culture.

Parrot Heads in Paradise Convention MUSIC
(www.phip.com/motm.asp) This festival in November is for, you guessed it, Jimmy Buffett fans (rabid ones only, natch).

🛏 Sleeping

There's a glut of boutique hotels, cozy B&Bs and four-star resorts here at the end of the USA, so sleepers won't want for accommodations. Although we've labeled some options as more central than others, the fact is that any hotel in Old Town will put you within walking distance of all the action. Though all people, gay and straight, are welcome just about anywhere, there are some exclusively gay inns, noted here.

All of the following properties have air-con. Lodgings have higher rates during the high season (mid-December to April). In addition, many properties add a 'shoulder' (midseason) that runs from May to June; rates may fall somewhere between low (July to November) and high during midseason. Many hotels (especially smaller properties) enforce two-night minimum stays. Expect rates to be extremely high during events such as New Year's and Fantasy Fest, when some places enforce up to seven-night minimum stays.

Curry Mansion Inn
HOTEL $$$

(☎800-253-3466, 305-294-5349; http://curry mansion.com; 511 Caroline St; r low season $195-285, high season $240-365; P☀︎♠︎🐾) In a city full of stately 19th-century homes, the Curry Mansion is especially handsome. All the elements of an aristocratic American home come together here, from plantation-era Southern colonnades to a New England–style widow's walk and, of course, bright Floridian rooms with canopied beds. Enjoy bougainvillea and breezes on the veranda.

Mermaid & Alligator
GUESTHOUSE $$

(☎305-294-1894, 800-773-1894; www.kwmermaid .com; 729 Truman Ave; r low season $148-198, high season $218-298; P☀︎@♠︎🐾) It takes a real gem to stand out amid the jewelry store of Keys hotels, but this place, located in a 1904 mansion, more than pulls off the job. Each of the nine rooms is individually designed with a great mix of modern comfort, Keys Colonial ambience and playful laughs. The treetop suite, with its exposed beams and alcoved bed and bathroom, is our pick of this idiosyncratic litter.

La Mer & Dewey Hotel
BOUTIQUE HOTEL $$$

(☎305-296-6577; www.southernmostresorts.com /lamer; 504 South St; r $200-350; ☀︎♠︎) Nineteen rooms are spread across two historic homes, one Victorian, the other fashioned like an old-school Keys cottage. Inside, the rooms come equipped with a lovely mix of European twee antiques and sleek modern amenities. Your porch basically looks out onto the Atlantic Ocean, whose breezes make for nice natural air-conditioning (not that you can't crank up the A/C in your room).

Santa Maria
BOUTIQUE HOTEL $$$

(☎305-600-5165; www.santamariasuites.com; 1401 Simonton St; r $300-450; P☀︎♠︎🐾) The Santa Maria looks like it took a wrong turn on South Beach, Miami, and ended up in Key West. First, it's an incredible deco edifice. The exterior should rightly be studied by architecture students looking to identify the best of deco design. Second, the interior rooms are an airy, luxurious dream, each one calling to mind the leisure lounge of a businessman from the 1950s. Finally, this place boasts in its central courtyard one of the finest hotel pools in Key West. Go ahead – splurge and let yourself go.

Gardens Hotel
HOTEL $$$

(☎305-294-2661, 800-526-2664; www.gardensho tel.com; 526 Angela St; r & ste low season $165-420, high season $325-645; P☀︎@🐾) Would we be stating the obvious if we mentioned this place has really nice gardens? In fact, the 17 rooms are located in the Peggy Mills Botanical Gardens, which is a longish way of saying 'tropical paradise.' Inside, Caribbean accents mesh with the fine design to create a sense of green-and-white-and-wood space that never stops massaging your eyes.

L'habitation
GUESTHOUSE $$

(☎800-697-1766, 305-293-9203 www.lhabitation .com; 408 Eaton St; r $109-179; ☀︎♠︎) A beautiful classical Keys cottage with cute rooms kitted out in light tropical shades, with lamps that look like contemporary art pieces and skittles-bright quilts. The friendly bilingual owner welcomes guests in English or French. The front porch, shaded by palms, is a perfect place to post and engage in Keys people-watching.

Cypress House
HOTEL $$$

(☎800-525-2488, 305-294-6969; www.cypress housekw.com; 601 Caroline St; r $165-305; P☀︎♠︎🐾) This plantationlike getaway has wrap-around porches, leafy grounds, a secluded swimming pool and spacious, individually designed bedrooms with four-poster beds. It's lazy, lovely luxury in the heart of Old Town, and one of the most extensively renovated and converted mansions we've seen anywhere. We'd recommend rooms in the Main House and Simonton House over the blander guest studios. Parking costs $10 per day.

Truman Hotel
HOTEL $$$

(☎866-487-8626; www.trumanhotel.com; 611 Truman Ave; r low season $195-285, high season $240-365; P☀︎♠︎🐾) Close to the main downtown drag, these playful rooms have huge flatscreen TVs, kitchenettes, zebra-print throw rugs and midcentury modern furniture. The bouncy fluff-erific beds will serve you well after the inevitable Duval Crawl (which is only steps from your door). Make sure to grab a drink by the lovely courtyard pool at the bar, seemingly carved from a single stone.

Big Ruby's Guesthouse
HOTEL $$

(☎305-296-2323, 800-477-7829; www.bigrubys .com; 409 Applerouth Lane; r $193-305; P☀︎♠︎🐾) This gay-only place looks like a refined Conch mansion on the outside, but once you get to your room, you'll see it's all contemporary, white and sleeker than a designer's decadent dreams. The clothing-optional lagoon pool is capped by a treetop walkway, elegant decking and tropical palms; plus there are fine linens and lots of privacy.

Caribbean House
GUESTHOUSE $

(☎305-296-0999; www.caribbeanhousekw.com; 226 Petronia St; r incl breakfast from $85; P ❋ @) This is a cute, canary-yellow Caribbean cottage in the heart of Bahama Village. The 10 small, brightly colored guest rooms aren't too fancy, but it's a happy, cozy bargain.

Avalon Bed & Breakfast
B&B $$

(☎305-294-8233; www.avalonbnb.com; 1317 Duval St; r low season $89-189, high season $169-289; ❋ ⑦ ❋) A cute, restored Victorian house on the quiet end of Duval blends attentive service with stately old ceiling fans, tropical lounge-room rugs, and black-and-white photos of olde-timey Key West. Music the cat likes to greet guests at reception.

Pearl's Rainbow
B&B $$

(☎305-292-1450, 800-749-6696; www.pearlsrainbow.com; 525 United St; r incl breakfast $99-200; ❋ ⑦ ❋) Pearl's is one of the best low-key lesbian resorts in the country, an intimate garden of tropical relaxation and enticing rooms scattered across a few cottages. A clothing-optional backyard pool bar is the perfect spot for alfresco happy hour, or to enjoy your brekkie.

Chelsea House
HOTEL $$

(☎305-296-2211; www.historickeywestinns.com/the-inns/chelsea-house; 707 Truman Ave; r low season $120-180, high season $200-250; P ❋ @ ⑦ ❋) This perfect pair of Victorian mansions beckons with large vaulted rooms and big comfy beds, with the whole shebang done out in floral, but not dated, chic. The old-school villa ambience clashes – in a nice way – with the happy vibe of the guests and the folks at reception.

Merlin Inn
GUESTHOUSE $$

(☎305-296-3336, 800-642-4753; 811 Simonton St; low season $89-225, high season $135-300; P ❋ @ ❋) Set in a secluded garden with a pool and elevated walkways, everything here is made from bamboo, rattan and wood. Throw in the rooms' high ceilings and exposed rafters, and this hotel oozes Colonial-tropical atmosphere.

Key Lime Inn
HOTEL $$

(☎800-559-4430; www.historickeywestinns.com; 725 Truman Ave; r $99-229; P ❋ ⑦ ❋) These cozy cottages are all scattered around a tropical hardwood backdrop. Inside, the blissfully cool rooms are greener than a jade mine, with wicker furniture and tiny flat-screens on hand to keep you from ever leaving.

Key West Youth Hostel & Seashell Motel
HOSTEL $

(☎305-296-5719; www.keywesthostel.com; 718 South St; dm from $44, motel r from $75; P ❋) This isn't our favorite hostel, but it's about the only youth-oriented budget choice on the island. That said, both dorms and motel rooms are overpriced.

✗ Eating

For such a small island, Key West has a superlative range of places to eat, from delicious neighborhood joints in the wall to top-end purveyors of haute cuisine that could easily compete with the best restaurants in Miami.

Café Solé
TOP CHOICE
FRENCH $$$

(☎305-294-0230; www.cafesole.com; 1029 Southard St; lunch $5-11, dinner $25-32; ⊗5:30-10pm) Conch carpaccio with capers? Yellowtail fillet and foie gras? Oh yes. This locally and critically acclaimed venue is known for its cozy back-porch ambience and innovative menus, cobbled together by a chef trained in southern French techniques who works with island ingredients. The memory of the anchovies on crostini makes us smile as we type. It's simple – fish on toast! – but it's the sort of simple yet delicious that makes you feel like Mom's whipped up something special for Sunday dinner.

Seven Fish
SEAFOOD $$

(☎305-296-2777; www.7fish.com; 632 Olivia St; mains $17-20; ⊗6-10pm Wed-Mon) This simple yet elegant tucked-away storefront is the perfect place for a romantic feast of home-made gnocchi or sublime banana chicken. All that said, the way to go here is to order the fresh fish of the day. The dining room might be the Zen-est interior in the islands. In point of fact, the entire experience here is one of minimalism (except for the flavors, which are abundant in the extreme).

Nine One Five
FUSION $$$

(☎305-296-0669; www.915duval.com; 915 Duval St; mains $18-34; ⊗6pm-midnight; ✍) Classy Nine One Five certainly stands out from the nearby Duval detritus of alcoholic aggression and tribal band tattoos. Ignore all that and enter this immaculate, modern and elegant space, which serves a creative, New

American-dips-into-Asia menu. It's all quite rich – imagine a butternut squash and almond risotto, or local lobster accompanied by duck confit potatoes.

Mo's Restaurant
CARIBBEAN $

(http://salsalocakeywest.com; 1116 White St; mains $11-16; 11am-10pm Mon-Sat) The words 'Caribbean,' 'home' and 'cooking', when used in conjunction, are generally always enough to win over. But it's not just the genre of cuisine that wins us over at Mo's – it's the execution. The dishes are mainly Haitian, and they're delicious – the spicy pickles will enflame your mouth, which can get cooled down with a rich vegetable 'mush' over rice, or try the incredible signature snapper.

Camille's
FUSION $$

(1202 Simonton St; breakfast $3-13, lunch $4-13, dinner $14-25; 8am-10pm;) This healthy and tasty neighborhood joint is the kind of place where players on the Key West High School softball team are served by friends from their science class, and the hostess is the pitcher's mom – when Conchs head out for a casual meal, they often come here. For 20 years the homey facade of Camille's has concealed a sharp kitchen that makes a mean chicken-salad sandwich, stone crab claws with Dijon mayo and a macadamia-crusted yellowtail we shudder (with pleasure) to recall.

Blue Heaven
AMERICAN $$

(305-296-8666; http://blueheavenkw.homestead.com; 729 Thomas St; dinner mains $19-38; 8am-10:30pm Mon-Sat, from 9am Sun) Proof that location is *nearly* everything, this is one of the quirkiest venues on an island of oddities. Customers and a local chicken flock dine in the spacious courtyard where Hemingway once officiated boxing matches; restrooms are in the adjacent former brothel. This place gets packed with customers who wolf down Southern-fried takes on Keys cuisine – the barbecued shrimp, drunk in a spicy sauce, are gorgeous.

Conch Town Café
SEAFOOD $

(801 Thomas St; mains $5-18; 11:30am-7:30pm) Too many people ignore this walk-up/carry-out, with its plastic patio furniture and scruffy island vibe. It's a shame, as it serves conch – good for more than listening to the ocean – deliciously 'cracked' (deep-fried) with a lip-puckeringly sour-lime marinade. You'll be tempted to wash it down with

the homemade smoothies, but be warned: they're more milky than refreshing.

Café
VEGETARIAN $

(509 Southard St; mains $7-17; 11am-10pm Mon-Sat;) The Café is the only place in Key West that exclusively caters to herbivores (OK, they have one fish dish). By day, it's a cute, sunny, earthy-crunchy luncheonette; by night, with flickering votive candles and a classy main dish (grilled, blackened tofu and polenta cakes), it's a sultry-but-healthy dining destination.

Thai Cuisine
THAI $$

(513 Greene St; lunch $10-12, dinner $15-24; 11:30-10pm) There's surprisingly good Thai to be had here near the top of Duval. It's not Bangkok, but the weather's just as nice and there are no *tuk-tuk* drivers or ladyboys interrupting your meal. There's sushi on the premises as well, although we don't think it's much compared to the curry and noodles.

Mathieson's 4th of July
AMERICAN $

(1110 White St; ice cream $3.50-6, mains $7-12; 11am-10pm Tue-Thu, to 11pm Fri & Sat, to 9pm Sun) The poodle skirts, ponytails and even the occasional pair of roller skates lay the '50s Americana diner vibe on as thick as they douse the excellent ice cream in toppings like gorgeous hot melted chocolate. The menu of burgers and such is really good, but we come to Mathieson's mainly for the ice cream, which is perfect relief from the heat of a Key West day.

El Siboney
CUBAN $

(Catherine St; mains $9.50-16; 11am-9:30pm) This is a rough-and-ready Cuban joint where the portions are big and there's no screwing around with either high-end embellishment or bells and whistles. It's rice, it's beans, it's shredded beef and roasted pork, it's cooked with a craftman's pride, and it's good.

Drinking

Basically, Key West is a floating bar. 'No, no, it's a nuanced, multilayered island with a proud nautical and multicultural histo...' *bz-zzt*! Floating bar. Make your memories (or lack thereof) at one of the following. Bars close at 3am; for gay venues, see p165.

TOP CHOICE Green Parrot
BAR

(601 Whitehead St) The oldest bar on an island of bars, this rogues' cantina opened in the late 19th century and hasn't closed yet. The

owner tells you the parachute on the ceiling is 'weighed down with termite turds,' while a blues band howls through clouds of smoke. Defunct business signs and local artwork litter the walls and, yes, that's the city attorney showing off her new tattoo at the pool table. Men: check out the Hieronymus Bosch–like painting *Proverbidioms* in the restroom, surely the most entertaining urinal talkpiece on the island.

Porch   BAR

(429 Caroline St) If you're getting tired of the frat-boy bars on the Duval St strip, head to the Porch. It's a friendly little artisan beer bar that's more laid back (but hardly civilized) than your average Keys watering hole. The knowledgeable bartenders will trade jokes with you and point you in the right direction for some truly excellent brew. Then sit on the porch of the Porch and watch the Keys stumble on by.

Garden of Eden Bar   BAR

(224 Duval St) Go to the top of this building and discover Key West's own clothing-optional drinking patio. Lest you get too excited, cameras aren't allowed, most people come clothed, and those who do elect to flaunt their birthday suits are often...erm...older.

Captain Tony's Saloon   BAR

(428 Greene St) Propagandists would have you believe the nearby megabar complex of Sloppy Joe's was Hemingway's original bar, but the physical place where the old man drank was right here, the original Sloppy Joe's location (before it was moved onto Duval St and into frat-boy hell). Hemingway's third wife (a journalist sent to profile Papa) seduced him in this very bar, wallpapered with business cards from around the world (including this travel writer's).

Irish Kevin's   BAR

(211 Duval St) One of the most popular megabars on Duval, Kevin's has a pretty good entertainment formula pinned down: nightly live acts that are a cross between a folk singer, radio shock jock and pep-rally cheerleader. The crowd consistently goes ape-poo for acoustic covers of '80s favorites. Basically, this is a good place to see 50 women from New Jersey do tequila shots, scream 'Livin' on a Prayer' at the top of their lungs and then inexplicably sob into their Michelob. It's more fun than it sounds.

Hog's Breath   BAR

(400 Front St) A good place to start the infamous Duval Pub Crawl, the Hog's Breath is a rockin' outdoor bar with good live bands and better cold Coronas.

FLORIDA KEYS & KEY WEST KEY WEST

GAY & LESBIAN KEY WEST

Key West's position at the edge of the USA has always attracted artists and eccentrics, and with them a refreshing dose of tolerance. The island had one of the earliest 'out' communities in the USA, and though less true than in the past, visiting Key West is a rite of passage for many LGBT (lesbian, gay, bisexual and transgender) Americans. In turn, this community has had a major impact on the local culture. Just as there is a straight trolley tour, you can hop aboard the **Gay & Lesbian Trolley Tour of Key West** (☑305-294-4603; tour $25), departing from the corner of South St and Simonton St at 11am on Saturday. The tour provides commentary on local gay lore and businesses (you'll also see the sites of the infamous Monster club). It's organized by the Key West Business Guild, which represents many gay-owned businesses; the guild is housed at the **Gay & Lesbian Community Center** (☑305-292-3223; www.glcckeywest.org; 513 Truman Ave), where you can access free internet on one of the few computers, plus pick up loads of information about local gay life. For details on gay parties and events, log onto www.gaykeywestfl.com.

Gay nightlife, in many cases, blends into mainstream nightlife, with everybody kind of going everywhere these days. But the backbone of the gay bar scene can be found in a pair of cruisey watering holes that sit across the street from one another, **Bourbon St Pub** (724 Duval St) and **801 Bourbon Bar** (801 Duval St), and can be summed up in five words: drag-queen-led karaoke night. For a peppier scene that includes dancing and occasional drag shows, men and women should head to **Aqua** (☑305-294-0555; 711 Duval St), while women will enjoy the backyard pool bar at the women's inn **Pearl's Rainbow** (☑305-292-1450; 525 United St).

☆ Entertainment

La Te Da CABARET
(www.lateda.com; 1125 Duval St) While the out-side bar is where locals gather for mellow chats over beer, you can catch high-quality drag acts – big names come here from around the country – upstairs at the fabulous Crystal Room on weekends. More low-key cabaret acts grace the downstairs lounge.

Virgilio's JAZZ
(524 Duval St) This bar-stage is as un-Keys as they come, and frankly, thank God for a little variety. This town needs a dark, candlelit martini lounge where you can chill to jazz and get down with some salsa, and Virgilio's handsomely provides. Enter on Applerouth Lane.

Red Barn Theatre THEATER
(☑305-296-9911; www.redbarntheatre.org; 319 Duval St) An occasionally edgy and always fun, cozy little local playhouse.

Tropic Cinema CINEMA
(☑877-761-3456; www.tropiccinema.org; 416 Eaton St) Great art-house movie theater with deco frontage.

Key West Players THEATER
(☑305-294-5015; www.waterfrontplayhouse.com; Waterfront Playhouse, Mallory Sq) Catch high-quality musicals and dramas from the oldest-running theater troupe in Florida. The season runs November through April.

Key West Symphony Orchestra OPERA
(☑305-292-1774; www.keywestsymphony.com; Tennessee Williams Theatre, 5901 Collage Rd) This critically acclaimed orchestra performs classics from Debussy, Beethoven and Mendelssohn from December through April.

🛍 Shopping

Bright and breezy art galleries, excellent cigars, leather fetish gear and offensive T-shirts – Key West, what don't you sell?

Montage SOUVENIRS
(512 Duval St; ⊙9am-10pm) Had a great meal or wild night at some bar or restaurant in the Keys? Well, this store probably sells the sign of the place (along with lots of Conch Republic tat), which makes for a nice souvenir.

Peppers of Key West FOOD
(602 Greene St; ⊙10am-8pm Mon-Sat) For a downright shopping party, you should bring your favorite six-pack with you into this store and settle in at the tasting bar, where the entertaining owners use double entendres to hawk seriously mouth-burning hot sauces, like their own Right Wing Sauce (use Liberally).

Project Lighthouse ARTS & CRAFTS
(418 Eaton St) Lighthouse is a community organization that runs programs for street kids (Key West is a popular runaway destination); it partly supports itself by selling arts and crafts made by its charges.

Bésame Mucho GIFTS
(315 Petronia St; ⊙10am-6pm, to 4pm Sun) This place is well stocked with high-end beauty products, eclectic jewelry, clothing and housewares.

Dogs on Duval PETS
(800 Duval St; ⊙10am-9pm) Pet accoutrement, like university sports jerseys for dogs, is on the rack behind – puppies! Heart-wrenchingly cute puppies.

Leather Master LEATHER
(415 Applerouth Lane; ⊙11am-10pm, to 11pm Fri & Sat, noon-5pm Sun) Besides the gladiator outfits, studded jockstraps and S&M masks, they do very nice bags and shoes here. Which is what you came for, right?

Frangipani Gallery ARTS & CRAFTS
(1102 Duval St; ⊙10am-6pm) One of the best galleries of local artists' work.

Haitian Art Co ARTS & CRAFTS
(600 Frances St; ⊙9am-5pm Mon-Fri) Haitian arts and crafts.

❶ Information

Media

Keeping up with local goings-on is easy, as this well-read town has nearly 10 newspapers (though some are entertainment-only rags). Also among the following are Key West's most accessible medical services.

Bank of America (☑305-296-1204; 510 Southard St, Key West)

Citizen (www.keysnews.com) A well-written, oft-amusing daily.

Key West Chamber of Commerce (☑305-294-2587; www.keywestchamber.org; 510 Greene St; ⊙8:30am-6:30pm Mon-Sat, to 6pm Sun) An excellent source of information.

Lower Keys Medical Center (☑305-294-5531, 800-233-3119; www.lkmc.com; 5900 College Rd, Stock Island, MM 5) Has a 24-hour emergency room.

National Public Radio (NPR) Tune into 91.3FM.

Post office (400 Whitehead St; ☺8:30am-9pm Mon-Fri, 9:30am-noon Sat)

Solares Hill (www.solareshill.com) Weekly, slightly activist take on community interests.

South Med (☎305-295-3838; www.southmed .us; 3138 Northside Dr) Dr Scott Hall caters especially to the gay community, but serves all visitors.

❶ Getting There & Around

Key West International Airport (EYW) is off S Roosevelt Blvd on the east side of the island. You can fly into Key West from some major US cities such as Miami or New York. Flights from Los Angeles and San Francisco usually have to stop in Tampa, Orlando or Miami first. **American Airlines** (☎800-433-7300) and **US Airways** (☎800-428-4322) have several flights a day. **Cape Air** (☎305-352-0714, 800-352-0714; www.flycapeair.com) flies between Key West and Fort Myers. From the Key West airport, a quick and easy taxi ride into Old Town will cost about $15.

Greyhound (☎305-296-9072; www.grey hound.com; 3535 S Roosevelt Blvd) has two buses daily between Key West and downtown Miami. Buses leave Miami for the 4¼-hour journey at 12:35pm and 6:50pm and Key West at 8:55am and 5:45pm going the other way (from US$40 each way).

You can boat from Miami to the Keys on the **Key West Express** (☎888-539-2628; www .seakeywestexpress.com; adult/child round-trip $146/81, one-way $86/58), which departs from Fort Myers and does a 3½-hour cruise to Key West. Returning boats depart the seaport at 6pm. You'll want to show up 1½ hours before your boat departs. During winter and fall the Express also leaves from Marco Island (adult/child round-trip $125/81, one-way $86/58).

Once you're in Key West, the best way to get around is by bicycle (rentals from the Duval St area, hotels and hostels are about $10 a day). Other options include the **City Transit System** (☎305-292-8160; tickets 75¢), with color-coded buses running about every 15 minutes; mopeds, which generally rent for $35 for four hours ($50 for a six-hour day); or the ridiculous electric tourist cars, or 'Conch cruisers,' which travel at 35mph and cost about $50/200 per hour/day.

Understand Miami & the Keys

›

population per sq miles

USA   FLORIDA   MIAMI

♰ ≈ 90 people

Miami & the Keys Today

Pride in Place

South Florida has always been a region apart from the rest of the USA. While small communities here can trace their roots to colonial America (and in the case of Everglades Native Americans, further back), by and large this is an old land with a young people drawn from all over Latin America, the Caribbean and the rest of the USA.

As a result, in the past many locals pined for feeling, well, local. South Beach, the epicenter of local tourism, had the cachet of a consumer playground, where the hot spots were populated not by locals, but jet-setters who flew in, partied and flew out.

Yet this perception, both external and internal, is changing. Jordan Melnick, who writes the excellent Beached Miami (www.beachedmiami .com) arts blog, told us over coffee, 'People who grew up in Miami used to think there was nothing in Miami, and the cool places to go were all filled with people from out of town. Now we're discovering there's a lot more Miami for people from Miami.'

Melnick was speaking of the growth of Wynwood, Overtown's nightlife, North Biscayne Boulevard's renaissance, and creative infrastructure like the New World Center, and we'd add: yes, these places are fantastic for locals, but they're open to visitors too. Miami has always tied growth to 'lifestyle': to bars, restaurants and shopping, rather than industry and manufacturing. That lifestyle is now appealing to locals by drawing on local creative talent, be it in the kitchen, club, concert hall or studio space. At the same time, because locals here are often from everywhere, there's a cosmopolitanism that couples with this homegrown spirit forming an intensely local, fiercely proud sense of place.

Miami is a truly bilingual (and sometimes trilingual) city. In order of popularity, the languages spoken here are Spanish, English and Haitian Creole. The last has its roots in French, and many (but not all Haitians) can speak that language. But Spanish is king here, and while most Miamians can speak English, even a few phrases of Spanish goes a long ways here.

Wilderness Way

» When hiking, stay on the trail, pick up your trash.

» Never pick wildflowers, especially orchids.

» Never chase or feed wild dolphins or manatees; admire but don't touch.

» Never feed alligators; they bite.

» On beaches, never approach nesting sea turtles or hatchling runs. Adhere to nighttime lights-out policies when posted (usually May to October).

» When snorkeling or diving, never touch coral reefs.

Media

Miami Herald (www.miami herald.com)

Miami New Times (www.miami newtimes.com)

Key West Citizen (http://keys news.com)

South Dade News Leader (www .southdadenewsleader.com)

belief systems
(% of population)

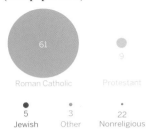

61
Roman Catholic

9
Protestant

5
Jewish

3
Other

22
Nonreligious

if Miami were 100 people

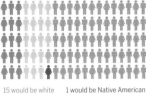

15 would be white (non-Hispanic)
18 would be black
1 would be Asian

1 would be Native American
65 would be Hispanic

Boom & Bust

Miami-Dade county, Florida's largest, may be reveling in a newfound regional pride on an aesthetic and cultural level, but in the arena of the environment and economics, things aren't as cheery.

Florida Governor Rick Scott, at the time of this writing, wanted to cut funding for restoration of the Everglades by 66%. An Everglades Foundation poll found that 55% of Floridian voters opposed Scott's decision, which could have a dire impact on more than alligators: the fate of the entire water supply of South Florida is tied to the health of the Glades.

The national real-estate-market collapse, which began in 2007, hit Florida like a brick, and Miami like several sacks of bricks. By 2011, local home prices hit their lowest since 2002, but few people were buying property; in Miami-Dade there was a 12% housing-vacancy rate. Along with tourism, construction and real estate are major pillars of the local economy, and the housing crisis kicked these particular pillars away with savage force. Thanks to this faltering economy, Miami-Dade had the second-worst unemployment rate – 13.7% – in Florida during our research.

With Florida facing major budget shortfalls, the resolution to the above issues will be down to forces economic and political. On the plus side, Miami and the Keys have done a good job of promoting expanded tourism in South Florida. If this baseline can pump enough money into the local economy, the surrounding environment and livelihood of South Florida's citizens has a chance of weathering the financial storm.

The *Miami Herald*'s Spanish-language version, *El Nuevo Herald* (www.elnuevoherald.com), is more than a translation; it's different news aimed at Miami's Cuban and Latin citizens, and treats events in Cuba and Latin America with the same urgency English-language media give to Washington.

Film

Key Largo (1948) Bogart, Bacall.
Scarface (1983) Al Pacino.
The Birdcage (1996) Robin Williams, Nathan Lane as gay lovers.
There's Something about Mary (1998) On love, Miami, hair gel.
Adaptation (2002) Surreal adaption of *The Orchid Thief*.

Books

Swamplandia! (Karen Russell) Surreal saga of a family of Everglades alligator wrestlers.
Cold Case Squad (Edna Buchanan) Miami noir.
Continental Drift (Russell Banks) New Hampshire worker flees for shallow promises in Florida. Beautiful, haunting prose.
The Everglades: River of Grass (Marjory Stoneman Douglas, 1947) Rich tribute to the Glades.
Hoot (Carl Hiaasen) Carl Hiaasen on kids, Coconut Grove, conservation, spotted owls.

History

South Florida has been built on boom and bust, by dreamers who took advantage of nice weather and opportunists who took advantage of natural disasters – nothing clears out old real estate like a hurricane, after all. Every chapter of the region's saga is closed by a hurricane, building boom or riot. It took 400 years for Miami to turn into a city since Spanish explorer Ponce de León missed the long-sought-after fountain of youth. But when this town decided to go large, it played catch-up with a vengeance.

South Florida is a region that has historically treated slow growth with contempt, and this attitude has paid off huge financial dividends (and economic catastrophes), but the local environment pays the price of success, wreaking a mighty toll on the Everglades and the Keys.

This chapter primarily focuses on Miami, which has long been the bellwether for culture, politics and growth in South Florida; for more information on the history of Key West, see p138. For background on the Everglades, see the boxed text, p123.

Spain, Britain & Spain Again

The Spanish settled Florida in 1565, several decades before Pilgrims landed on Plymouth Rock and English aristocrats starved in Jamestown, Virginia. The territory changed hands from Spain (until 1763) to Britain (1763–83) and back to Spain again (1783–1821). And then came American Independence. The Spanish had to deal with a big, land-hungry new nation lying just to the north.

Relations chilled when escaped American slaves made for Spanish Florida, where slavery was illegal and freed slaves were employed as standing militia members. White American Southerners saw armed black militia and started sweating the notion of slave revolts in their back plantation yard. By 1821, the USA had purchased Florida from Spain, but the presence of Native Americans and escaped slaves meant the price of the land was to be paid for in blood.

Historic Homes

» Merrick House

» Vizcaya

» Biltmore Hotel

» Heritage House, Key West

» Hemingway House, Key West

TIMELINE

10,000 BC	500 BC	AD 500
After crossing the Bering Strait from Siberia some 50,000 years earlier, humans arrive in Florida, hunting mastodon and saber-toothed tigers, at the end of the last Ice Age.	Pottery from this period is attributed to the Glades Culture, which stretches from the Keys to present-day Martin county, north of Miami. The Glades Culture does not survive European contact.	The Caloosahatchee Culture develops and thrives in the area that now includes the western Everglades and 10,000 Islands. This complex society lasts till 1750.

The Unconquered People

In the late 18th century, elements of the Creek nation in Georgia and other tribes from the north migrated into Florida. These tribes intermingled and intermarried, and in the late 1700s were joined by runaway black slaves. Black newcomers were generally welcomed into Native American society and were occasionally kept as slaves, although this slavery was more akin to indentured servitude (slaves, for example, had their own homes that they inhabited with their families).

At some point, these fugitive, mixed peoples occupying Florida's interior were dubbed 'Seminoles,' a corruption of the Spanish word *cimarrones,* meaning 'free people' or 'wild ones'. Defying European rule and ethnic category, they were soon considered too free for the newly independent United States, which coincidentally was growing hungrier for land.

When the majority of the Creek were forced west across the Mississippi River in 1817, Americans figured everything east of that body of water was now theirs for the settling. But the Seminoles had no intention of leaving their homes.

Bad blood and sporadic violence between Americans and Seminoles eventually gave the US the excuse it needed to make a bid for Florida, which it finally bought from Spain in 1821. Before and after that the US military embarked on several campaigns against the Seminoles and their allies, who took to the swamps, fought three guerilla wars, and scored a respectable amount of victories against an enemy several times their size. In fact, the Second Seminole War (1835–42) was the longest in American history between the American Revolution and the Vietnam War.

Indeed, operationally the Seminole wars were a 19th-century version of Vietnam, a never-ending parade of long, pointless patrols into impenetrable swamps, always searching for an ever-invisible enemy. By 1830 Congress came up with the shocking Removal Act, a law that told Native Americans to pack up their things and move across the country to Oklahoma. Some went, enticed by bribe money, but Seminole Chief

Native American Resources

» Ah-Tah-Thi-Ki Museum (www .ahtahthiki.com)

» Tequesta Indians (www .floridiannature .com/tequesta)

» Heritage of the Ancient Ones (www.ancient native.org)

» Miccosukee Tribe (www .miccosukee .com/tribe)

TEQUESTA INDIANS

In 1998, 24 holes, inscribed in bedrock and arranged in the shape of a perfect circle, were found in downtown Miami. The 'Miami Circle,' as it was dubbed, is thought to be the foundations of a permanent structure and, at some 2000 years old, it's the oldest contender for that title on the US East Coast.

Archaeologists think the Circle was built by Miami's earliest known inhabitants, the Tequesta (Tekesta) Indians, who are otherwise a mystery. The tribe was mostly wiped out by Spanish first contact, which brought violence and disease, and survivors likely melted into the local Miccosukee and Seminole nations.

1513	1702	1763	1776
Ponce de León discovers Florida, landing south of Cape Canaveral, believing it an island. Since it's around Easter, he names it La Florida, 'The Flowery Land' or 'Feast of Flowers.'	In their ongoing struggle with Spain and France over New World colonies, the British burn St Augustine to the ground; two years later they destroy 13 Spanish missions in Florida.	The mixed Spanish-Native American community in Key West is resettled in Havana after the island is seized by the British. For years, the island has little real authority.	The American Revolution begins, but Florida's two colonies don't rebel. They remain loyal to the British crown, and soon English Tories flood south into Florida to escape the fighting.

Osceola and his band (never exceeding more than 100 warriors) refused to sign the treaty and fled into the Everglades. After keeping thousands of soldiers jumping at the barest hint of his presence for years, Osceola was finally captured under a false flag of truce in 1837. Yet resistance continued, and while the Seminoles gave up on fighting, the government also gave up on moving them west.

By 1842 the warring had ended, but no peace treaty was ever signed, which is why the Seminoles to this day call themselves 'the unconquered people'. Those Seminoles who remained in Florida are now organized under a tribal government and run the Ah-Tah-Thi-Ki Museum (p129) and, um, the Hard Rock Café. Not one Hard Rock Café: the entire Hard Rock chain, bought for $965 million in 2007 with money made from gambling revenue. The Seminoles were the first Native American tribe to cash in on gambling, starting with a bingo hall in 1979 that has since expanded to a multi-billion-dollar empire. That's not bad for a Seminole population of a little over 3000.

Freezes, Flagler & Tuttle Too

For decades, Florida was farming country: sugar, citrus and drained swamps. Julia Tuttle arrived from Cleveland, Ohio in this largely agricultural empire in 1875 with a tubercular husband, and after his death she moved to South Florida to take over the land she had inherited as a widow. Proving her worth as a true Floridian, over the next 20 years she proceeded to buy up property like crazy.

In the meantime, Henry Morrison Flagler, a business partner of John D Rockefeller, realized Florida's tourism potential and had been busy developing the northern Florida coast in St Augustine and Palm Beach. He also built the Florida East Coast Railroad, which extended down as far as Palm Beach. Tuttle saw a business opportunity and contacted Fla-

---

FIVE WHO SHAPED SOUTH FLORIDA

» **Henry Morrison Flagler** The developer whose Florida East Coast Railroad brought scores of visitors to sunny paradise.

» **Julia Tuttle** The woman behind Flagler, who (supposedly) lured the skeptical developer to Miami with a handful of orange blossoms.

» **Fidel Castro** He may be reviled by local Cubans, but then again, said Cubans wouldn't be here if it wasn't for the bushy-bearded Caribbean communist.

» **Morris Lapidus** The Fontainebleau, Eden Roc, Lincoln Rd Mall...is there anything this MiMo (Miami Modern) god didn't design?

» **Pardon C Greene** One of the founding fathers of Key West; also a member of the city council and (briefly) mayor of the town.

Late 1700s	1818	1822	1835
Elements of the Creek Nation, supplemented by black runaway slaves and their descendants, begin settling South Florida, displacing local Calusa and Mayaimi Indians.	Andrew Jackson invades Western Florida after violence between settlers and a coalition of Native Americans and blacks. The First Seminole War essentially ends when the USA buys Florida from Spain.	Commodore Matthew C Perry lands on Key West and plants the American flag, claiming the entire Keys island chain for the USA.	In attacks coordinated by Seminole leader Osceola, Seminoles destroy five sugar plantations on Christmas Day and soon after kill 100 US soldiers marching near Tampa, launching the Second Seminole War.

gler with a proposition: if he would extend his railroad to Miami, Tuttle would split her property with him. Miami? Way down at the end of nowhere? Flagler wasn't interested.

Then, in 1895, a record freeze enveloped most of Florida (but not Miami), wiping out citrus crops and sending vacationers scurrying. Legend has it that Tuttle – who is said to have been rather quick both on the uptake and with an 'I told you so' – went into her garden at Fort Dallas on the Miami River, snipped off some orange blossoms and sent them to Flagler, who hightailed it down to Miami to see for himself.

Flagler was hooked. He and Tuttle came to terms, and all those Floridians whose livelihoods had been wiped out by the freeze followed Flagler south. Passenger-train services to Miami began on April 22, 1896, the year the city of Miami became incorporated. Incidentally, this was the same year John S Collins began selling lots out of a 5-mile strip between the Atlantic and Biscayne Bay, or what is now 14th to 67th Sts on Miami Beach (ie most of the city).

Of Miami's 502 original inhabitants, 100 of them were black, conscripted for hard labor and regulated to the northwest neighborhood of Colored Town.

The First Big Booms

The promise of money and the expansion of Flagler's railway fueled waves of settlement. Population growth peaked during WWI, when the US military established an aviation training facility in Miami. Many of the thousands who came to work and train figured, 'Hey, the weather's nice,' and Miami's population shot from 1681 people in 1900 to almost 30,000 by 1920. The new Floridians wrote home and got relatives in on the act, and after the war came the first full-fledged Miami boom (1923–25), when Coconut Grove and Allapattah were annexed into what was dubbed, for the first time, Greater Miami.

Even then, Miami was built for good times. People wanted to drink and gamble, because although it was illegal, liquor flowed freely here throughout the entire Prohibition period.

Depression, Deco & Another World War

Miami's growth was astronomical, and so was her eventual fall: the Great Miami Hurricane of 1926, which left about 220 people dead and some 25,000 to 50,000 homeless; and the Great Depression. But it's in Miami's nature to weather every disaster with an even better resurgence, and in the interwar period Miami's phoenix rose in two stages. First, Franklin Roosevelt's New Deal brought the Civilian Conservation Corps, jobs and a spurt of rise-from-the-ashes building projects.

In the early 1930s, a group of mostly Jewish developers began erecting small, stylish hotels along Collins Ave and Ocean Dr, jump-starting

The main (downtown) branch of the Miami-Dade Public Library has an extensive Florida collection that constitutes one of the best repositories of state history anywhere. The collection includes some 17,000 photos by photojournalist Gleason Romer, who snapped South Florida as a photojournalist and amateur shooter from 1925 to the 1950s.

1845	1861	1905	1912
Florida is admitted to the Union as the 27th state. Since it is a slave state, its admission is balanced by that of Iowa, a free state.	Voting 62 to 7, Florida secedes from the US, raising its fifth flag, the stars-and-bars of the Confederacy. Florida's farms and cattle provide vital Confederate supplies during the ensuing Civil War.	The first of many attempts to drain the Everglades begins. In coming decades, thousands of acres are destroyed as water is diverted from its natural flow from Lake Okeechobee.	'Flagler's Folly,' Henry Flagler's 128-mile overseas railroad connecting the Florida Keys, reaches Key West. It's hailed as the 'Eighth Wonder of the World,' but is destroyed by a 1935 hurricane.

BLACK-MARKET FLORIDA

In 1919, when the US passed the 18th Amendment – making liquor illegal and inaugurating Prohibition – bootleggers discovered something that previous generations of black slaves and Seminoles knew well: Florida is a good place to hide.

Interestingly, Florida rumrunning was conducted mostly by local 'mom-and-pop' operations, not the mob, despite the occasional vacationing mobster like Al Capone. In this way, Prohibition did its turn to stimulate certain sectors of the Florida economy. When times were good, as in the 1920s, all that (illicit) money got launder-...um...pumped into real estate, making the good times unbelievably great for those criminals doing the laundering. When hard times fell in the 1930s, out-of-work farmers could still make bathtub gin and pay the bills. Because of this often-explicit understanding, Miami bars served drinks with impunity throughout the 1920s, and local police simply kept walking.

In the 1960s and '70s, the story was repeated with marijuana. Some down-on-their-luck commercial fisherfolk made a mint smuggling plastic-wrapped bails of pot. In tiny Everglades City, dozens of fisherfolk were indicted by the FBI for catching 'square grouper' – slang for marijuana.

In the 1980s, cocaine became the illegal drug of choice. But this time the smugglers were Colombian cartels, and they did business with a gun, not a handshake. Bloody shoot-outs on Miami streets shocked Floridians, but it didn't slow the estimated $10 billion drug business.

a miniboom that resulted in the creation and development of Miami Beach's famous art-deco district. This led to a brief rise in anti-Semitism, as the Beach became segregated and 'Gentiles Only' signs began popping up. The election of a Jewish governor of Florida in 1933 led to improvement, as did airplane travel, which brought plenty of Jewish visitors and settlers from the north.

Cuba Comes Over

During the 1950s progress seemed inexorable; in 1954 Leroy Collins became the first Southern governor to publicly declare racial segregation 'morally wrong,' while an entire 'Space Coast' was created around Cape Canaveral (between Daytona and Miami on the east coast) to support the development of the National Aeronautics & Space Administration (NASA).

Then, in 1959, Fidel Castro marched onto the 20th-century stage and forever changed the destiny of Cuba and Miami.

As communists swept into Havana, huge portions of the upper and middle classes of Cuba fled north and established a fiercely anti-Castro Cuban community, now 50 years old and, in some ways, as angry as ever about the dictator to the south. At the time, counter-revolutionary politics were

1925
Coral Gables, one of the first planned communities in the USA, is officially founded. The 'City Beautiful' was designed by real-estate developer George Edgar Merrick.

JON DAVISON / LONELY PLANET IMAGES ©

1926
The Great Miami Hurricane devastates South Florida, killing 220 people, leaving 25,000 to 50,000 homeless and causing some $100 million in damages. The Great Depression slows recovery.

1928
Ernest Hemingway pens *A Farewell to Arms* in Key West, supposedly while awaiting the delivery of a car. His wife's uncle gifts the Hemingways a local house in 1931.

» Coral Gables (p71)

discussed, and a group of exiles formed the 2506th Brigade, sanctioned by the US government, which provided weapons and Central Intelligence Agency (CIA) training for the purpose of launching a US attack on Cuba.

The resulting badly executed attack is remembered today as the Bay of Pigs fiasco. The first wave of counter-revolutionaries, left on the beach without reinforcements or supplies, were all captured or killed. All prisoners were released by Cuba about three months later.

In the meantime, Castro attracted Soviet missiles to his country, but couldn't keep his people. In 1965 alone some 100,000 Cubans hopped the 'freedom flight' from Havana to Miami.

Racial Tensions

Riots and skirmishes broke out between Cubans and blacks and blacks and whites in Miami. In 1968 a riot broke out after it was discovered that two white police officers had arrested a 17-year-old black male, stripped him naked and hung him by his ankles from a bridge.

In 1970 the 'rotten meat' riot began when black locals picketed a white-owned shop they had accused of selling spoiled meat. After three days of picketing, white officers attempted to disperse the crowds and fired on them with tear gas. During the 1970s, there were 13 other race-related violent confrontations.

Racial tensions exploded on May 17, 1980, when four white police officers, being tried on charges that they beat a black suspect to death while he was in custody, were acquitted by an all-white jury. When the verdict was announced, race riots broke out all over Miami and lasted for three days.

The Mariel Boatlift

In the late 1970s, Fidel suddenly declared that anyone who wanted to leave Cuba had open access to the docks at Mariel Harbor. Before the ink was dry on the proclamation, the largest flotilla ever launched for non-military purposes set sail (or paddled) from Cuba in practically anything that would float the 90 miles between Cuba and the USA.

The Mariel Boatlift, as the largest of these would be called, brought 125,000 Cubans to Florida, including an estimated 25,000 prisoners and mental patients. Mariel shattered the stereotype of the wealthy Batista-exiled Cuban. The resulting strain on the economy, logistics and infrastructure of South Florida added to still-simmering racial tensions; by 1990, it was estimated that 90% of Miami's Caucasian populace was Hispanic.

The tension carried over from Hispanic-Anglo divisions to rifts between older Cubans and the new *Marielitos*. The middle- to upper-class white Cubans of the 1960s were reintroduced to that nation in the form of thousands of Afro-Cubans and *santeros*, or worshippers of Santeria, Cuba's version of *vodou* (voodoo).

Best Florida Histories

» *The New History of Florida*, Michael Gannon

» *The Everglades: River of Grass*, Marjory Stoneman Douglas

» *Dreamers, Schemers & Scalawags*, Stuart McIver

» *The Enduring Seminoles*, Patsy West

» *Miami Babylon*, Gerald Posner

1920s–30s	1933–40	1941–45	1942
A small spit of land located across Biscayne Bay, known as Miami Beach, becomes dotted with hotels and resorts, presaging its emergence as a tourism hot spot.	New Deal public-works projects employ 40,000 Floridians and help save Florida from the Depression. The most notable construction project is the Overseas Highway through the Keys.	US enters WWII. Two million men and women receive basic training in South Florida. At one point, the army commandeers 85% of Miami Beach hotels to house personnel.	From January to August, German U-boats sink over two dozen tankers and ships off Florida's coast. By war's end, Florida holds nearly 3000 German POWs in 15 labor camps.

Miami Not So Nice

In the 1980s Miami became the major East Coast entry port for drug dealers and their product and earned the nickname 'Mi-Yay-Mi', 'yay' being slang for cocaine. As if to keep up with the corruption, many savings and loans (S&Ls) opened in newly built Miami headquarters. While *Newsweek* magazine called Miami 'America's Casablanca', locals dubbed it the 'City with the S&L Skyline.'

A plethora of businesses – legitimate concerns as well as drug-financed fronts – and buildings sprang up all over Miami. Downtown was completely remodeled. But it was reborn in the grip of drug smugglers: shoot-outs were common, as were gangland slayings by cocaine cowboys. At one stage, up to three people per week were being killed in cocaine-related clashes.

The police, Coast Guard, Drug Enforcement Agency (DEA), Border Patrol and Federal Bureau of Investigation (FBI) were trying to keep track of it all. Roadblocks were set up along the Overseas Hwy to Key West (prompting the quirky and headstrong residents down there to call for a secession, which eventually sent the cops on their way).

Miami Vice was single-handedly responsible for Miami Beach rising to international fabulousness in the mid-1980s, its slick soundtrack and music-video-style montages glamorizing the rich South Florida lifestyle. Before long, people were coming down to check it out for themselves – especially photographer Bruce Weber, who began using South Beach as a grittily fashionable backdrop for modeling shoots in the early 1980s.

Celebrities were wintering in Miami, international photographers were shooting here, and the Art Deco Historic District, having been granted federal protection, was going through renovation and renaissance. Gay men, always on the cutting edge of trends, discovered South Beach's gritty glamour. The city was becoming a showpiece of fashion and trendiness.

BUG SPRAY

After WWII, the advent of effective bug spray and affordable air-conditioning did more for Florida tourism than anything else. With these two technological advancements, Florida's subtropical climate was finally safe for delicate Yankee skin.

The 1990s & 2000s

A combination of Hurricane Andrew and a crime wave against tourists, particularly carjackings, equaled a drop in visitors, until tourist-oriented community policing and other visible programs reversed the curse. Miami went from being the US city with the most violent crime to one with average crime statistics for a city its size. From 1992 to 1998, tourist-related crimes decreased by a whopping 80%.

The Cuban-American population dominated headlines again during the Elián Gonzalez nightmare, an international custody fight that ended with federal agents storming the Little Havana house where the seven-year-old was staying to have him shipped back to Cuba while anti-Castro Cubans protested in Miami streets.

On the bright side, corruption was slightly cleaned out after the removal of Mayor Xavier Suarez in 1998, whose election was overturned

1947	1961	May 1980	1980
Everglades National Park is established, successfully culminating a 19-year effort, led by Ernest Coe and Marjory Stoneman Douglas, to protect the Everglades from the harm done by dredging and draining.	Brigade 2506, a 1300-strong volunteer army, invades Cuba's Bay of Pigs on April 16. President Kennedy withholds air support, leading to Brigade 2506's immediate defeat and capture by Fidel Castro.	In the McDuffie trial, white cops are acquitted of wrongdoing in the death of a black man, igniting racial tensions and Miami's Liberty City riots; 18 people are killed.	Cuba's Castro 'opens the floodgates'. The USA's ensuing Mariel Boatlift rescues 125,000 *Marielitos*, who face intense discrimination in Miami.

MIAMI HISTORY BOOKS

» **Miami** (1987), by Joan Didion. How Cuban politics shape US policy.

» **The Corpse Had a Familiar Face** (1987), by Edna Buchanan. Written by a former *Miami Herald* reporter, this is an addictive read on real-life Miami murders.

» **Black Miami in the Twentieth Century** (1997), by Marvin Dunn. This was the first book devoted to the issue of race in Miami.

» **This Land Is Our Land: Immigrants and Power in Miami** (2003), by Alex Stepick. Stepick and other authors break it down.

» **Miami, USA** (2000), by Helen Muir. A newly expanded 1950s title that's full of anecdotes.

following the discovery of many illegal votes. Manuel 'Manny' Diaz, who had been a lawyer for the Miami-based Gonzalez family, followed Suarez as mayor; his two terms were marked by relatively low levels of scandal and decent economic growth. Diaz pushed for cementing ties between Miami and the Latin American world – he was fond of saying, 'When Venezuela or Argentina sneezes, Miami catches a cold.'

During the 2000s Miami proper underwent more 'Manhattan-ization,' with more and more skyscrapers altering the city skyline. At the same time, Diaz began working to use arts districts and buildings – the former represented by Wynwood and Midtown, the latter by the Arsht Center for the Performing Arts – to revitalize blighted areas of town.

The Recent Past

Journalist Tomas Regalado was elected mayor of Miami in 2009 in the wake of a financial crisis and recession. At the time of this writing the issues dogging his term are economic; policemen and firefighters face stagnant salaries and higher costs of living, leading to some vicious riffs between city hall and city services.

Miami is still, by far, the largest Cuban city outside of Cuba, and most Cubans here still don't like the Castro regime. At the same time, there has been some relaxing of ultraorthodox anti-Castroism. The original Batista refugees of the 1950s are aging, to be replaced by a new generation of 'YUCAs' – young, urban Cuban-Americans. The YUCAs don't like Castro either. But they are not single-issue voters like their parents (that issue being isolating Cuba) – many vote Democrat – and in general, they are more interested in subverting Cuba via commerce and consumer goods rather than the CIA. That's an approach that was facilitated by Barack Obama, who in 2011 relaxed some elements of the US–Cuba travel ban and trade embargo.

Richard Heyman, who served two terms as mayor of Key West (1983–85 and 1987–89), was perhaps the first openly gay mayor of a sizable US town (and perhaps any US town, period). In 2010, a documentary on his life, *The Newcomer*, was released. Heyman died of AIDS-related pneumonia in 1994.

1992	1999	2000	2009
On August 24, Hurricane Andrew devastates Dade County, leaving 41 people dead, over 200,000 homeless, and causing about $15.5 billion in damage.	On Thanksgiving, five-year-old Elián Gonzalez is rescued at sea, his Cuban mother having died en route. Despite wild protests by Miami's Cuban exiles, the US returns the then seven-year-old Elián to his father in Cuba.	The Comprehensive Everglades Restoration Plan is put into action. The 30-year plan aims to restore natural water flow to the Everglades and replenish South Florida's water reservoirs	Tomas Regalado, a former journalist and centrist Republican, is elected the 33rd mayor of Miami by a 72% margin, inheriting a growing city with serious financial problems.

More South than South

There's an old saw about US geography that goes as such: drive down I-95, the main highway on the East Coast, into Virginia and you enter the American South. Keep driving roughly 800 miles until you get past Orlando and into South Florida and you reenter the Northeast.

How's that? Well, you leave the Carolinas, Georgia and North Florida, where families are only a generation or two removed from the farm and demographics are fairly homogenous, and enter a region defined by diversity, where most folks are either immigrants from another country or from another part of this country (and often enough, they're transplanted from New York or New England, making the Northeast analogy seem even tighter).

But we take issue with the South-Florida-as-sunny-northeast comparison. It reduces South Florida to aping another part of the country, while diminishing the considerable increasing diversity (and shrinking regional identity) of the old Confederacy. South Florida, in any case, is not just Manhattan with a tan. It's an intersection of Middle America, Latin America and the Caribbean, and a clash of the idiosyncratic types who decided miles of marshland, beach and a few mangrove-y islets were a place where the American Dream could be realized to subtropical perfection. In short, it's interesting here. South Florida possesses far more culture, creativity and intellectual energy then you might guess as you drive by acres of glass condos and strip malls.

You can count among Florida's snowbirds some of the USA's best writers, like Robert Frost, Isaac Bashevis Singer and Annie Dillard, and every January, the literati of the US hold court at the Annual Key West Literary Seminar.

Greater Multicultural Miami

Contemporary South Florida is certainly more than Miami, but if the local distinct regional identity has an anchor city, Miami is that town. With that said, while Miami's energy impacts the Keys and the Glades (particularly the former), these other areas are more demographically homogenous, and in the case of Key West, have their own unique histories of settlement.

Miami

With all we've said above, it'd still be silly not to recognize Miami as the center of South Florida's cultural gravity. Which begs the question: what makes Miami, well, Miami? Basically, it's the mix: that conspicuous jumble of Cubans, Haitians, Anglos and Jews. It possesses the best and worst of its parent cultures, immigrant and migrant narratives that are embraced and rejected and spliced and diced into entirely new paradigms (and sometimes all of these things occur at once). How else does a Cuban-American proudly show off a Matanzas accent on the one hand while shrugging off the pork and rum of her island ancestors in favor of vegetarianism and yoga? As they say here, only in Miami.

It can be difficult to meet someone from Miami who has more than two generations of connection to the place. At the negative end, this lack of connection can manifest as a detached sense of place and resentment towards other newcomers; Miami is not without tensions between her myriad communities. On the positive side are those Miamians concerned with building an identity for their town, the ones who patronize local sport and arts and extend a helping hand rather than a rude gesture towards newcomers from across America or the Gulf of Mexico. It almost goes without saying, but Miami's cultural capital, even among Asian and Anglo citizens, is largely derived from the Caribbean and Latin America. There's an energy here that is cheerful, loud and colorful. It infects the place, and it will get under your skin the longer you stay.

Florida's Division of Cultural Affairs (www.florida-arts.org) is a great resource for statewide arts organizations and agencies. Their Florida Artists Hall of Fame memorializes the Sunshine State's creative legacy.

The Everglades

Rural Florida can still evoke America's western frontier, and the Everglades, the wildest part of the state, are still very much a hinterland. The Old West trope is exacerbated by the fact there is still a settlement pattern here of colonizers and Native Americans; the Seminole and Miccosukee tribes constitute a major part of the 'Glades' population. Their neighbors in Homestead and Everglades City are largely descended from those who came here in the 19th century, after the West was won, when Florida became one of the last places where pioneers could simply plant stakes and make a life. These pioneers became Florida's 'Crackers,' the poor rural farmers, fisherfolk, cowhands and outlaws who traded life's comforts for independence on their terms. Many Crackers came from the old Southern states, and created a culture not too far removed, geographic or otherwise, from the Confederacy.

A bit of Southern-fried hospitality and Western independence is a feisty combination, but therein are the roots of many Glades citizens. Even the local Native Americans share these qualities, although they also retain elements of indigenous culture. Most Everglades citizens, like rural people in much of the USA, place a high value on self-reliance and perceived freedom from government.

Finally, we'd be remiss not to mention the large number of Mexicans who now call Homestead home, the majority attracted by jobs working on nearby farms.

The Keys

The Keys constitute a fascinating combination of Crackers (called 'Conchs' here), Caribbean islanders and just about every ethnicity attracted by living an island lifestyle that's still technically in the USA. As the Keys have been settled by non-Native Americans longer than Miami, there is a distinct local culture that's a little bit country in the Outer Keys, and elegantly eccentric in Key West. There's a great deal of pride in the Keys themselves and their independence from the mainland. And while many people, especially in the Outer Keys, have conservative attitudes on gun control and the environment (ie less regulation related to both), there's also a great deal of tolerance for alternative lifestyles. Maybe because just choosing to live out here is an alternative lifestyle decision in its self.

The Arts in South Florida

If we're going to speak of local culture, we have to speak of art, music and literature, which permeate South Florida's daily life. Because this region has a pretty face, a lot of people think it's stupid as a result. The stereotype isn't fair. Because what makes South Florida beautiful, from the bodies on the beach to the structure of the skyline, is diversity. The energies of the Western Hemisphere have been channeled into this Gateway to the

EXPERIENCING MULTICULTURAL MIAMI

To understand some of Miami's most prominent ethnic groups, we suggest the following:

Cuban Miami

Cuban Miami is stereotypically associated with Little Havana, but to be fair, so much of Miami is Cuban it's more accurate to refer to Cubans as the norm, the default ethnicity. With that said, the most important cultural symbols of Cuban Miami are concentrated in Little Havana, particularly near 8th Street/Calle Ocho. Other parts of town where you can get a strong sense of Cuban identity include Hialeah, where over 90% of the population speaks Spanish as a first language.

» Little Havana (p67)
» Viernes Culturales (p68)
» Versailles (p101)
» Cuba Ocho (p68)
» Máximo Gómez Park (p67)

Haitian Miami

Haitian Miamians speak Creole (also spelled 'Kreyol'), which is related to French. If you speak French, you may be able to converse with local Haitians, but we want to stress that Kreyol is its own language, with its own grammar and syntax, and French alone may not get you far. Little Haiti is by far one of the most colorful neighborhoods in the city, but it can be rough after dark, so try and visit during the day, unless a Big Night in Little Haiti (a monthly street party) is happening.

» Big Night in Little Haiti (p63)
» Tap Tap (p93)
» Libreri Mapou (p39)
» Botanicas (p39)
» Little Haiti Cultural Center (p63)

Jewish Miami

Jews were some of the first developers and residents of Miami Beach. They've maintained a strong presence here for decades, which helps explain why the Miami metro area has the nation's second-largest concentration of Jews. While many of these Jews are descended from northeast families, many are also the children of Latin American exiles. There is a significant Cuban, Puerto Rican, Brazilian and Colombian Jewish presence in Miami.

» Arthur Godfrey Rd/41st St (p54)
» Jewish Museum of Florida (p47)
» Temple Emanu El (p51)
» Lots of Lox (p103)
» Roasters' n Toasters (p97)

Argentine Miami

Argentines are mainly concentrated in Northern Miami Beach, although they are not restricted to any one part of the city. In South America, Argentines are often stereotyped as snooty compared to other South American nationalities. Many Spanish-speaking Miamians, especially ones from South America, like to riff on this cliché with Argentine friends, but the comments are almost always good-natured teasing and taken as such.

» Normandy Isle & Ocean Terrace (p54)

Americas, and a lot of that drive is rooted in creativity and a search for self-expression.

This artistic impulse tends to derive from the immigrant experience, which this region has in spades. There's the pain of exile. The conditions of a country where you can't be arrested for public expression. The

Spanish Miami

Spaniards have settled in Miami in large numbers. They tend to be, if not affluent, not desperate either – Spanish immigrants are not boat people. There is no one part of Spain that produces these new arrivals; in one part of Miami you'll find people from the Basque country who resent being called 'Spanish,' while in another you may break bread with Catalans in one restaurant, and Castillians in another. Many of the best high-end grocery stores, bakeries, cheese shops and meat shops in Miami seem to be, perhaps unsurprisingly, run by Spaniards.

» El Carajo (p102)

Japanese Miami

Miami does not have a particularly large Japanese community, but there are some Japanese here. Many are businessmen participating in the global economy and international commerce, but there is also a large amount of contemporary artists and designers who are attracted by Miami's growing cultural credibility. No one neighborhood in Miami can be said to be Japanese.

» Matsuri (p103)

Vietnamese Miami

Miami is not a major center for Vietnamese immigration, but those Vietnamese who are here (assuming they came from South Vietnam, which is generally the case) find lots of common ground with the Cuban community. At least as regards the older generation, both groups share a sense of exile, nurse grievances against communism, use the label 'communist' as a serious insult, and often, share a devout belief in Catholicism.

» Hy Vong Vietnamese Restaurant (p101)

Brazilian Miami

Miami's Brazilians are mainly found in Northern Miami Beach. Well, those Brazilians who live in Greater Miami proper. Many Brazilians in this city are fashionistas, models and their respective entourages; these Brazilians tend to base themselves in South Beach with the other jet-setters. In Northern Miami Beach you'll find Brazilian immigrants working, partying, eating and blending into the Miami milieu.

» Boteco (p105)

Colombian Miami

You'll find many Colombians with their South American brethren in Northern Miami Beach, but there are also plenty of Colombians in Coral Gables (where the Colombian consulate is) and poorer parts of downtown. Colombian politics are difficult to pigeonhole, as Colombian migrants have come to the USA fleeing from both left- and right-wing overthrows.

» La Moon (p97)

Nicaraguan Miami

Nicaraguans actually make up a large percentage of the population of 'Cuban' areas like Little Havana. Nicaraguans are easily recognizable, as they tend to look more indigenous and less European than most other Miamians. It is the Nicaraguans who are leading the way, currently, to more settlement from Central America.

» Yambo (p101)

flush of financial success and the frustration of being shut out of the sometimes callous American Dream. Miami's greatest quality, her inborn tolerance for eccentricity, is at the root of such public innovations as the Arab fantasyland architecture of Opa Locka, and the modernistic design of the Art Deco Historic District.

BRIGHT BRITTO

If the top public artist of a given city determines how said city sees itself, we must conclude Miami is a cartoon-y, cubist, chaotic place of bright-happy-shiny-joy-joy-iness.

That's the aesthetic legacy Romero Britto is leaving this town, anyways. The seemingly perpetually grinning Brazilian émigré, clad in jackets leftover from a 1980s MTV video, was the hot face of public art in the 2000s, having designed the mural of the **Miami Children's Museum** (p76), the 'Welcome' structure at Dadeland North Station, the central sculpture at the shops at Midtown and many others. You might need sunglasses to appreciate his work, which appeals to the islander in all of us: Saturday-morning cartoon brights, sharp geometric lines and woopy, loopy curls, inner-child character studies and, underlying everything, a scent of teal oceans on a sunny day.

Gloria Estefan loves the guy, and former governor Jeb Bush gave Tony Blair an original Britto when the ex-PM visited Miami in 2006. Of course, not everyone feels the Romero love; plenty of critics have dubbed Britto more commercial designer than pop artist (but, like, what is art man?). Rather than get mired in the debate, we suggest you go check out a Britto installation for yourself, or **Britto Central** (818 Lincoln Rd). The man's work is as ubiquitous as palm trees and, hey, if you've got a spare $20,000, you can buy an original before you go home.

In addition, there is always a sense of the possible coupled with the fantasy of excess here. Plenty of people dismiss Coral Gables and the Vizcaya as gauche and tacky, and through modern eyes they may appear as such. But they were revolutionary for their time. Concepts like a Mediterranean revival village that would serve as an aesthetic bulwark against sprawl, or an Italianate villa carved out of the seashore, were not likely to be accepted by conservative Northeastern Americans untouched by the risk-inducing Florida sun.

Putting Miami on the Arts Map

Miami's citizens and their memories, realities and visions have created a burgeoning art scene that truly began to be noticed with the 2002 introduction of Art Basel Miami Beach (p83), the US outpost of an annual erudite gathering that's based in Switzerland. By its second year, the event had created electricity throughout the national art world – and had succeeded in wooing 175 exhibitors, more than 30,000 visitors and plenty of celebs to take over the galleries, clubs and hotels of South Beach and the Design District. It has grown, in both size and strength, each year since, and its impact on the local art scene here cannot be overstated; today, Art Basel Miami is the biggest contemporary arts festival in the western hemisphere.

Public Art

This city's always been way ahead of the curve when it comes to public art. Miami and Miami Beach established the Art in Public Places program way back in 1973, when it voted to allocate 1.5% of city construction funds to the fostering of public art; since then more than 700 works – sculptures, mosaics, murals, light-based installations and more – have been created in public spots. Here's just a few examples.

Barbara Neijne's *Foreverglades,* in Concourse J of Miami International Airport, uses mosaic, art-installed text from *River of Grass* (by Marjory Stoneman Douglas) and waves representing the movement of water over grass to give new arrivals a sense of the flow of Florida's most unique ecosystem. A series of hand-prints representing Miami's many immigrant communities link into a single community in *Reaching for Miami Skies,* by Connie Lloveras, which greets Metromover commuters at Brickell Station. In Miami-Dade Library, the floating text of *Words Without Thought Never to Heaven Go* by Edward Ruscha challenges readers to engage in thought processes that are inspired by, but go beyond, the books that surround them. The team of Roberto Behar and Rosario Marquardt, hailing from Argentina, have been among the most prolific public artists in town, to the degree that their work is deliberately meant to warp conceptions of what is or isn't public space; they created the giant red *M* at the Metromover Riverwalk Station for the city's centennial back in 1996.

Literature

Writers need to be around good stories to keep their narrative wits sharp, and no place provides this like South Florida, where farmers clash with environmentalists who fight financiers, while immigrants arrive from a hundred different countries and, every summer, a hurricane hits. This proximity to real-life drama means, unsurprisingly, many of Miami's best authors cut their writing teeth in journalism. As a result, there's a breed of Miami prose that has the terse punch of the best newspaper writing. Beginning with former *Miami Herald* crime-beat reporters Edna Buchanan and Carl Hiaasen, and leading to new names like Jeff Lindsay, the Miami crime-writing scene is alive and well. On the other hand, local immigrant communities have lent this town's literature the poetry of exiled tongues, narratives that find a thread through the diaspora alleyways that underline Florida's identity. Look out for Carolina Garcia-Aguilera, Edward Danticat and Diana Abu-Jaber. And finally, the subtle beauty of South Florida has produced a certain breed of nature writer that is able to capture the nuances of the region's subdued scenery while explaining the complicated science that runs through it all – Marjory Stoneman Douglas and Ted Levin spring to mind.

Music

As in all things, it's the mad diversity of Miami that makes her music so appealing. The southbound path of American country and Southern rock, the northbound rhythms of the Caribbean and Latin America,

CARL HIAASEN: LOVING THE LUNACY

In Carl Hiaasen's Florida the politicians are corrupt, the rednecks are violent, the tourists are clueless, the women are fast and the ambience is smoky noir, brightened by a few buckets of loony pastel. Some would say the man knows his home state.

Hiaasen, who worked at the *Miami Herald* for decades and is now a Keys resident (he met his wife while reading in the Keys bar she managed), is both a writer gifted with crisp prose and a journalist blessed by a reporter's instinct for the offbeat. His success has rested in his ability to basically take the hyperbolic reality that is Florida and tell it to the world. Although his fiction is just that, in many ways it simply draws off the day-to-day eccentricities of the Sunshine State and novelizes them. So: *Tourist Season,* where Hiaasen turns his pen on ecozealots with a story about a terrorist group that tries to dissuade tourists from coming to Florida and further wrecking the state – namely, by feeding them to a crocodile named Pavlov. In complete thematic contrast comes *Hoot,* a heart-warming tale (odd for Hiaasen) catering to young adults about a 12-year-old boy's fight against a corporation that threatens to pave over a Coconut Grove colony of burrowing owls. *Stormy Weather* takes on the corruption, bureaucracy and disaster tourism that fills the vacuum of the devastation trail left by a hurricane.

Hiaasen's work tends to career between satire and thriller, and betrays both an unceasingly critical eye and deep affection for all of Florida's quirks. Which ironically makes Hiaasen – enemy of almost every special-interest group in the Sunshine State – the state's biggest promoter. He is a man who loves Florida for her warts, not her curves, and that, folks, is true romance.

MIAMI TRACKS (& WHERE TO PLAY THEM)

» 'Conga', by Gloria Estefan & the Miami Sound Machine – Ocean Dr
» 'Rakata', by Wisin y Yandel – Little Havana
» 'Moon Over Miami', by Joe Burke and Edgar Leslie – Julia Tuttle Causeway
» 'Miami', by Will Smith – I-95 past Downtown
» 'Miami', by U2 – Wynwood or North Miami Beach
» 'Save Hialeah Park', by Los Primeros – Hialeah
» 'Swamp Music', by Lynyrd Skynyrd – Tamiami Trail to Everglades City
» 'Jaspora', by Wyclef Jean – Little Haiti
» 'Your Love', by the Outfield – A1A

and the homegrown beats of Miami's African-American community get mixed into a musical crossroads of the Americas. Think about the sounds the above influences produce, and you'll hear a certain thread: bouncy, percussive, with a tune you can always dance to.

The above sounds, rooted in the New World, are fighting against interlopers from a far shore: Europeans and their waves of techno, house and electronica. In the narrative of Miami immigrants, we can't leave out the gay community and the Euro-expats, and the latter have brought a strong club-music scene, best evidenced by the annual Winter Music Conference each March, which brings thousands of DJs and producers to town for workshops and parties. Sometimes, the competing thumpa-thumpa of house and hip-hop get along, but usually the scenes stay distinct.

Miami's heart and soul is Latin, and that goes for her music as well. Producers and artists from across Latin America come here for high-quality studio facilities, the lure of global distribution and the Billboard Latin Music Conference & Awards, held here each April. The Magic City has been the cradle of stars such as Gloria Estefan, Ricky Martin and Albita, and a scan over the local airwaves always yields far more Spanish-language stations than English, playing a mix of salsa, *son* (itself an Afro-Cuban-Spanish mélange of musical styles), conga and reggaeton. A night out in La Covacha (p108) is a good intro to the scene.

Here's a quick crib sheet for your Miami nightclub explorations.

Salsa is the most commonly heard word used to reference Latin music and dance, which makes sense as it's actually a generic term developed in the mid-'60s and early '70s as a way to pull all Latin sounds under one umbrella name for gringos who couldn't recognize the subtle differences between beats. From the Spanish word for 'sauce,' salsa has its roots in Cuban culture and has a sound that's enhanced by textures of jazz. Music that lends itself to salsa dancing has four beats per bar of music.

One specific type of Cuban salsa is *son* – a sound popularized by the release of 1999's *Buena Vista Social Club*. It has roots in African and Spanish cultures and is quite melodic, usually incorporating instruments including the *tres* (a type of guitar with three sets of closely spaced strings), standard guitars and various hand drums.

Merengue originates from the Dominican Republic and can be characterized by a very fast beat, with just two beats to each bar. It's typically played on the tamboura, guiro (a ridged cylindrical percussion instrument made of metal or dried gourd) and accordion.

Hailing from the Andalusian region of Spain is the folk art of flamenco, which consists of hand clapping, finger snapping, vocals, guitar and the flamboyant dance. Miami's Argentines love to tango, a Buenos Aires invention that draws off European classical dance and the immigrant experience of South America's French, Italian, African and indigenous ethnic enclaves.

The popular reggae sound, originating in Jamaica and having strong Rastafarian roots, is a total movement most popularly associated with Bob Marley. It's characterized by rhythm chops on a backbeat and, at least in its beginnings, a political-activist message. There are various styles within reggae, including roots (Marley's sound), dancehall (ie Yosexygirlwannagetboomshackalacka), raga and dub.

But it's rare to just hear one of the above. Miami is a polyglot kind of town, and it loves to blend techno with *son,* give an electronic backbeat to salsa, and overlay everything with dub, hip-hop and *bomba* (African-influenced Puerto Rican dance music). This mixed marriage produces a lot of musical children, and the most recognizable modern sound derived from the above is reggaeton, a driving mash-up that plays like Spanish rap shoved through a sexy backbeat and thumpin' dancehall speakers. Pioneers of the genre include Daddy Yankee, Don Chezina, Tito El Bambino, Wisin Y Yandel, Calle 13 and producers such as Luny Tunes and Noriega. Although it largely originated in Puerto Rico, reggaeton is one of the few musical styles that can get Latinos from across the Americas – from Nicaraguans to Mexicans to Colombians – shaking it.

Miami's hip-hop has had a bit of a circular evolution, from early '90s Miami bass (dirrrty dance music, exemplified by 2 Live Crew) to more aggressive, street-style rap, which has blended and morphed into today's club-oriented tracks. These modern sounds draw off the crunk beats, Southern drawls and Atlanta overproduction of the Dirty South sound. The hit 2008 single 'Low' by Flo Rida encapsulates the genre, which sounds, in a lot of ways, like the club child of Miami bass and everything that has come since. Local hip-hop heroes work hard to keep Miami on the map and strongly rep neighborhoods such as Opa Locka, Liberty City and Overtown; artists to listen for include DJ Smallz, Pitbull, Rick Ross, Flo Rida and Uncle Luke.

There's been a small but strong indie-rock boom over the past decade, and it's mainly centered on Sweat Records (p114) and Churchill's (p106) in Little Haiti. The crop of homegrown bands is growing; events like Sweatstock (p21) are a good means of accessing the scene. Besides Churchill's, other good spots to see the cutting edge of Miami rock are Vagabond (p108) and Bardot (p107).

Film

Crime sells this city – at least cinematically. Sam Katzman chose Miami for B-movies about gang wars, and several (lowbrow) classics – as well as the *Jackie Gleason Show,* shot here for TV – in the 1960s. *Scarface,* Brian DePalma's over-the-top story of the excesses of capitalism, entered Miami into hip-hop's common lexicon; and *Miami Vice,* the 1980s TV series about a couple of pastel-clad vice-squad cops, put Miami on the international map. The images – of murders, rapes and drug-turf wars – were far from positive, and the powers-that-be in the city were not initially happy. But *Vice* was more about Ferraris, speedboats and booty than gang-banging, and as branding goes, it depicted Miami as more than a high-crime slum where everyone's grandparents retired. As William Cullom, a President of the Greater Miami Chamber of Commerce put it, '*[Miami Vice]* has built an awareness of Miami in young people who had never thought of visiting Miami.' A pretty mediocre Hollywood film version starring Colin Farrell and Jamie Foxx, released in 2006, capitalized on the '80s nostalgia market. There have been loads of comedies filmed here as well, but for our money, *The Birdcage* best captures the fabulosity and, yes, even community vibe, of South Beach. We're forgetting

MORE SOUTH THAN SOUTH THE ARTS IN SOUTH FLORIDA

FILM FESTIVALS

Two of the best film festivals in the US are the Miami International Film Festival (www .miamifilmfesti val.com) a showcase for Latin cinema (March), and the up-and-coming Florida Film Festival (www .floridafilmfesti val.com) in Orlando (April).

one other genre: porn. Well, what did you expect with all the silicone? There's a fair amount of homegrown adult industry going on here.

Today, Miami and Miami Beach governments love the idea of producers coming to town so much that in early 2005 they instituted the One Stop Permitting system, providing a streamlined, online way for makers of films, TV shows and commercials to apply for permits (at www .filmiami.org).

Fashion

With Miami now a hub of cool food, nightlife and arts, it makes sense that it would gain acclaim as an influencer in the world of fashion. And it has, with the annual Miami Fashion Week (p21) playing a large role in putting this region on the most stylish global maps.

The event is renowned globally, from Paris to Hong Kong – but it's by no means the only game in town. Miami has gained enormous cred among European designers (ironically ever since one of them, Gianni Versace, was killed here) and draws mavens from all over the Old World who find something inspiring in the combination of a Latin emphasis on appearance versus the American love of comfort and the dare-to-bare styles inspired by the sunny weather. Today Miami is the base city for Perry Ellis International, while GenArt, a national nonprofit dedicated to film, art and fashion, holds an annual Fresh Faces in Fashion showcase focusing on Miami's burgeoning designer scene.

So what defines the 'Miami look'? 'Go to a supermarket. Any supermarket. Nine out of 10 girls: wearing high heels. That's Miami,' says a local journalist. Yup, if you want to hang here, you gotta come correct. But it's a weird style – part laid-back yet totally glam.

On the one hand, you'll see a desperate desire for brand-name cred, of Louis Vuitton–endowed affirmation. But on the flip side is the understated (yes, Miami can do understatement) sense of cool that comes from all that heat, exemplified by a casual dressiness the best-looking Miamians accomplish without any apparent effort. Note, for example, the older Cuban man in his guayabera, an elegant but simple brocaded men's shirt; he's classy because he's looking good without seeming to try.

There is a distinctive South Beach style and there's no better place to buy it than at the source, but be warned: you must be bold, unabashed and bikini-waxed to pull off some of the more risqué outfits on display, which is to say, pretty much all of them. For information on shopping in Miami, see Shopping (p112).

MYSTERY NOVEL

Naked Came the Manatee (1998) is a collaborative mystery novel by a constellation of famous Florida writers: Carl Hiaasen, Dave Barry, Elmore Leonard, James Hall, Edna Buchanan, and more. It's like nibbling a delectable box of cyanide-laced chocolates.

Haute or Not

When South Florida sits at the table, it doesn't know what to order. Hell, it might not even know what language the menu is written in.

This region has a rich culinary identity, which is simply an extension of an already rich demographic identity. Florida offers as much culinary excellence and adventure as you'd like. The entire area – Miami most recognizably, but surrounding suburbs and the Keys as well – is one of the most immigrant-rich regions of America. Recipes are derived from countless ethnic backgrounds, and as a result the local culinary scene is somewhat paradoxical: on one hand a free-floating gastronomy for people unmoored from their homeland, detached from native tradition, and on the other an attempt to connect to the roots of homeland and traditions via the immediacy of taste.

And never forget that there is local bounty here – an agriculturally rich backyard of citrus, cattle and water filled with an incredible bounty of marine life. If there is no native South Florida cuisine, there are certainly indigenous ingredients. The trick, traveler, is finding food that connects this local bounty to clever students of South Florida's many culinary backgrounds.

Defining Local Dining

It's hard to isolate a 'native' South Florida cuisine (actual Native American dishes like chili and frybread found in Everglades-area restaurants are imported from the American Southwest). The first white settlers here came from all over America, and thus the American South and its foodways, which heavily influence Northern Florida, is one of many dozens of influences in Miami, although more keenly felt in the Everglades region and the Keys.

But in general, South Florida is a region defined not by any one, but a hemisphere's-worth of cultures: Southern, Creole, Cuban, Caribbean, and Central and South American, but also Jewish, Japanese, Vietnamese, Nigerian, Thai, Chinese, Spanish and more. The expression 'Jack of all trades, master of none' occasionally applies in these circumstances. Local restaurants that are dedicated to a particular style of cuisine are usually a better bet than places that jumble their influences. As an

FLORIBBEAN CUISINE

Okay, somebody worked hard to come up with 'Floribbean' – a term for Florida's tantalizing gourmet mélange of just-caught seafood, tropical fruits and eye-watering peppers, all dressed up with some combination of Nicaraguan, Salvadoran, Caribbean, Haitian, Cajun, Cuban and even Southern influences. Some call it 'Fusion,' 'Nuevo Latino,' 'New World,' 'Nouvelle Floridian' or 'Palm Tree Cuisine,' and it could refer to anything from a ceviche of lime, conch, sweet peppers and scotch bonnets to grilled grouper with mango, adobo and fried plantains.

example: when in Miami, you'll note dozens of 'Thai-Japanese' restaurants. These two cuisines are pretty far apart in terms of their flavor profiles, and inevitably, we've found this attempt at Asian fusion to be disappointing. Dedicated Japanese or Thai restaurants, on the other hand, are another matter entirely.

It must also be said: South Florida in general, and Miami in particular, is obsessively trendy. If barnacles are the 'it' recipe in Manhattan, you better believe barnacle sorbet will feature on at least a dozen South Beach menus within a week. This attitude is a double-edged sword, because while you're in no danger of missing culinary trends in Miami, there's a chance you'll eat at a place where the afore-mentioned barnacles are prepared carelessly and sold at sky high costs.

This cynical attitude most often manifests in South Beach. Tourists aren't as likely to hold a bad restaurant as accountable as locals, and the fact is, most of the folks going out in South Beach are tourists. With that said there are some fantastic restaurants in South Beach, places that are not just on top of culinary trends but redefining them, and similar restaurants downtown, in Wynwood and the Design District and even in Key West.

Few places can boast Florida's sublime fresh bounty from land and sea, and menus playfully nick influences. Gourmets can genuflect before celebrity chefs, while gourmands hunt Florida's bizarre delicacies, like boiled peanuts, frog's legs, snake, and gator. Strip malls can contain gastronomic gems, while five-star hotel restaurants can be total duds. Smell, taste, enjoy and indulge – our advice to you, and a fitting motto for Floridians and food.

For pricing and tipping information, see p222.

Bounty of the Sea

Florida has always fed itself from the sea, which lies within arm's reach from nearly every point. If it swims or crawls in the ocean, you can bet some enterprising local has shelled or scaled it, battered it, dropped it in a fryer and put it on a menu.

Grouper is far and away the most popular fish. Grouper sandwiches are to Florida what the cheesesteak is to Philadelphia or pizza to Manhattan – a defining, iconic dish, and the standard by which many places are measured. Hunting the perfect grilled or fried grouper sandwich is an obsessive Floridian quest, as is finding the creamiest bowl of chowder (Sustain, in Midtown Miami, does excellent versions of both; see p99).

Of course, a huge range of other fish are offered. Other popular species include snapper (with dozens of varieties), mahimahi and catfish.

Florida really shines when it comes to crustaceans: try pink shrimp and rock shrimp, and don't miss soft-shell blue crab – Florida is the only place with blue-crab hatcheries, making them available fresh year-round. Winter (October to April) is the season for Florida spiny lobster and stone crab (out of season, both will be frozen). Florida lobster is all tail, without the large claws of its Maine cousin, and stone crab is heavenly sweet, served steamed with butter or the ubiquitous mustard sauce.

Finally, the Keys popularized conch (a giant sea snail); now fished out, most conch is from the Bahamas. For information on sustainable seafood, check out www.montereybayaquarium.org/cr/seafoodwatch.aspx.

Cuban & Latin American Cuisine

Cuban food, once considered 'exotic,' is itself a mix of Caribbean, African and Latin American influences, and in Tampa and Miami, it's a staple of everyday life. Sidle up to a Cuban *loncheria* (snack bar) and order a *pan cubano:* a buttered, grilled baguette stuffed with ham, roast pork, cheese, mustard and pickles.

SOUTH FLORIDA'S BEST CUBAN

» Islas Canarias (p101)

» El Cristo (p101)

» Garcia's (p98)

» Versailles (p101)

» El Siboney (p164)

Integral to many Cuban dishes are *mojo* (a garlicky viniagrette, sprinkled on sandwiches), *adobo* (a meat marinade of garlic, salt, cumin, oregano and sour orange juice) and *sofrito* (a stew-starter mix of garlic, onion and chili peppers). Main-course meats are typically accompanied by rice and beans and fried plantains.

With its large number of Central and Latin American immigrants, the Miami area offers plenty of authentic ethnic eateries. Seek out Haitian *griots* (marinated fried pork), Jamaican jerk chicken, Brazilian barbecue, Central American *gallo pinto* (red beans and rice) and Nicaraguan *tres leches* ('three milks' cake).

In the morning, try a Cuban coffee, also known as *café cubano* or *cortadito*. This hot shot of liquid gold is essentially sweetened espresso, while *café con leche* is just *café au lait* with a different accent: equal parts coffee and hot milk.

Another Cuban treat is *guarapo,* or fresh-squeezed sugarcane juice. Cuban snack bars serve the greenish liquid straight or poured over crushed ice, and it's essential to an authentic mojito (rum, sugar, mint, lemon and club soda). It also sometimes finds its way into *batidos,* a milky, refreshing Latin American fruit smoothie.

Self-Catering

Epicure Market (1656 Alton Rd; dishes $7-15; ☺10am-8pm Mon-Fri, to 7pm Sat, to 6pm Sun), a gourmet food shop just off Lincoln Rd in South Beach, has a beautiful selection of international cheeses and wines, fresh produce, baked goods and prepared dishes. Many of the more than 25 Publix supermarkets throughout Miami are quite upscale, and the **Whole Foods Market** (1020 Alton Rd; ☺7am-11pm) is the biggest health-food store around, with an excellent produce department, pretty good deli and so-so salad bar; its biggest draw is for vegetarians (not so well catered for by markets in these parts) who are seeking a particular brand of soy milk or wheat-free pasta.

For the freshest picnic items around, hit one of several **farmers' markets** (☎305-531-0038), which are held in various areas on different days, roughly 9am to 4pm. The one on Lincoln Rd on Sundays is perhaps best known, but you'll find others on Española Way (Sunday), Normandy Village Fountain at 71st St (Saturday), the Aventura Mall (Saturday and Sunday), Downtown on Flagler St at Miami Ave (8am until 2pm Saturday), Coconut Grove on Grand Ave at Margaret St (Saturday) and Coral Gables City Hall (Saturday).

FARMERS' MARKETS

If you love farmers' markets, visit www.florida -agriculture.com and click on 'Info for Consumers' and 'Community Farmers' Markets' to find a statewide list.

Eating in Miami, Hood by Hood

Let's break down the Miami eating experience neighborhood by neighborhood:

South Beach

Restaurants open and close with the frequency of celebrity-spottings, which is to say, a lot – sometimes eating here feels like opening the pages of a British tabloid, although to be fair, usually you're surrounded by other tourists. There is no shortage of food variety, price options and presentation, but the trend is towards ostentatiousness. Even the stripped-back places are ostentatiously underdone, if you know what we mean. All those restaurants with loud hostesses fronting Ocean Dr get mixed traveler reviews, so be warned that the price of pedestrian-watching might be an expensive, mediocre meal.

North Miami Beach

There are three good clusters of eats here: Mid-Beach, particularly 41st St, with its Jewish delis, steakhouses and sushi bars; Normandy Isle, with its expat South Americans, Brazilians, Uruguayans and their penchant for coronary-inducing cuisine; and far North Beach, around Sunny Isles, home to some eclectic little gems. In general, this is an area that excels in the cheap to midrange ethnic eatery category.

Downtown

Downtown's eating options run, like Downtown itself, between extremes: from high-end corporate power lunches in glass and steel hotels in Brickell to down-home Latin hole-in-the-walls. The latter characterizes the center of Downtown, where you can easily find a filling, likely Latino meal for well under $10.

Wynwood, the Design District & Little Haiti

This area, collectively known as Midtown Miami, and nearby neighborhoods like Buena Vista and North Biscayne Boulevard, is where the best food in Miami is being served. It's as trendy as South Beach but far more reliant on local clientele. Eating out here is a joy, be it in a cute cafe, fine-dining restaurant or cowboy-hipster-burrito joint.

Little Havana

Cuban cuisine is only a small slice of Little Havana's pan-Latin palate; there are menus from all over *el Sud,* from Ecuador to El Salvador and Mexico to Mendoza, Argentina. And while locals say you have to go a bit further afield than Calle Ocho for the best *comida latino,* you'll rarely go wrong when you stroll into ethnic eateries in this part of town.

Key Biscayne

For an eensy island, Biscayne's got good options that'll keep you from trekking all the way over the causeway back into the city.

Coconut Grove

The Grove may look chain heavy, but it's actually a strong spot for healthy eats, while the pedestrian-friendly nature of the neighborhood makes for pleasant culinary strolling. At night the sidewalk cafes come alive, and the nearby University of Miami means both nightlife and eating out can be fun and affordable.

Coral Gables

The Gables is a goldmine for foodies, with an ample supply of international, eclectic and high-end dining options. Many restaurants are clustered on or near 'Restaurant Row,' on Giralda Ave between Ponce de León Blvd and Le Jeune Rd.

Southern Cooking

You are technically in the South down here, but much of South Florida is so south it's *sud* as opposed to Southern if you catch our drift. Basically, we're saying Miami is too international to be classified as the American South. And as such, Southern cooking basically skips Miami as a city. That said, in the Everglades and the Keys, the Southern influence is much more keenly felt.

Florida Cookbooks

» *Cross Creek Cookery* by Marjorie Kinnan Rawlings

» *New World Cuisine* by Allen Susser

» *Miami Spice: The New Florida Cuisine* by Steve Raichlen

» *The Florida Cookbook: From Gulf Coast Gumbo to Key Lime Pie,* by Jeanne Voltz and Caroline Stuart

» *Florida Bounty* by Eric and Sandra Jacobs

Southern makes up in fat and pure tastiness what it may lack in refinement. Standard Southern fare is a main meat – like fried chicken, catfish, barbecued ribs, chicken-fried steak or even chitlins (hog's intestines) – and three sides: perhaps some combination of hushpuppies, cheese grits, cornbread, coleslaw, mashed potatoes, black-eyed peas, collard greens or buttery corn. End with pecan pie, and that's living.

In the Keys, Southern-style cooking melds with Caribbean gastronomy. In truth, there's a lot of room for overlap, as black slaves developed many of the same recipes in the US and the Caribbean. Plus, Southern and Caribbean cooking are both unapologetically rich and heavy, and that latter description may apply to you too if you're not careful when you eat in the Keys.

A good (and mouth-watering) example of the phenomenon we're describing is the fried chicken at Dion's gas station (yes, gas station) in

SUNSHINE STATE FOOD FESTIVALS

Many of Florida's food festivals have the tumultuous air of county fairs, with carnival rides, music, parades, beauty pageants and any number of wacky, only-in-Florida happenings.

Food Fest! by Joan Steinbacher is the definitive guide; her companion website (www.foodfestguide.com) lists festivals for the coming three months.

» **Key West Food & Wine Festival** (www.keywestfoodandwinefestival.com) Key West; three-day weekend, late January. A weekend-long party and celebration of the finest in Key West gastronomy.

» **Everglades Seafood Festival** (www.evergladesseafoodfestival.com) Everglades City; three-day weekend, early February. Not just seafood, but gator, frog's legs and snakes, oh my!

» **South Beach Food & Wine Festival** (www.sobefest.org) Miami; four days, late February. This Food Network–sponsored party is one of the largest food festivals in the country.

» **Swamp Cabbage Festival** (www.swampcabbagefestival.org) La Belle; three-day weekend, late February. Armadillo races and crowning of the Miss Swamp Cabbage Queen.

» **Carnaval Miami** (www.carnaval-miami.org) Miami; fortnight, early March. Negotiate drag queens and in-line skaters to reach the Cuban Calle Ocho food booths.

» **Grant Seafood Festival** (www.grantseafoodfestival.com) Grant; two-day weekend, early March. This small Space Coast town throws one of Florida's biggest seafood parties.

» **Florida Strawberry Festival** (www.flstrawberryfestival.com) Plant City; 11 days, early March. Since 1930, over half a million folks come annually to pluck, eat and honor the mighty berry.

» **Island Fest** (www.islamoradachamber.com) Islamorada; early April. Essentially a county fair for all things Keys-y.

» **Taste of Key West** (www.fla-keys.com/keywest. www.keywestcity.com) Key West; mid-April. Dozens of local restaurants turn their kitchens into food carts along the Truman waterfront.

» **Isle of Eight Flags Shrimp Festival** (www.shrimpfestival.com) Amelia Island; three-day weekend, early May. Avast, you scurvy dog! Pirates invade for shrimp and a juried art show.

» **Palatka Blue Crab Festival** (www.bluecrabfestival.com) Palatka; four-day Memorial Day weekend (weekend before last Monday in May). Hosts the state championship for chowder and gumbo. Yes, it's that good.

» **Florida Seafood Festival** (www.floridaseafoodfestival.com) Apalachicola; two days, early November. Stand way, way back at their signature oyster shucking and eating contests.

» **Ribfest** (www.ribfest.org) St Petersburg; three days, mid-November. Three words: ribs, rock, Harleys.

Marathon (p149). This is seriously the best fried chicken in the Keys, similar in initial execution to standard American fried chicken, but spiced with some secret (but distinctly Caribbean) seasoning that has us drooling on our computer at the memory of it.

Cracker cooking is Florida's rough-and-tumble variation on Southern cuisine, but with more reptiles and amphibians. And you'll find a good deal of Cajun and Creole as well, which mix in spicy gumbos and bisques from Louisiana's neighboring swamps. Southern Floridian cooking is epitomized by writer Marjorie Kinnan Rawlings' famous cookbook *Cross Creek Cookery*.

Ice tea is ubiquitous in the Everglades and the Keys, but watch out for 'sweet tea,' which is an almost entirely different Southern drink – tea so sugary your eyes will cross.

South Florida Specialties

While South Florida has an international palate, some dishes have been here long enough to constitute something like a local cuisine.

Cuban Sandwich

South Florida Food Blogs
» Jan Norris (www.jannorris.com)

» Mango & Lime (http://mango andlime.net)

» Meatless Miami (www.meatless miami.com)

The traditional Cuban sandwich is a thing of some beauty, and a possible genuine native Florida dish; that Cubans invented the thing is agreed upon, but where they did so, here or Tampa or Havana, is a subject of debate. Anyways, here's the skinny: Cuban bread is buttered or oiled and hit with mustard. Layer on thin pickles, ham, roast pork or salami, and Swiss cheese. Press the thing in a *plancha* (a smooth panino grill) and ta-da: yumminess on warm bread.

Colombian Hot Dog

The Colombian *perro caliente* is a work of mad genius. Colombians have...a different take on hot dogs; toppings we've seen include quail eggs, plum sauce, potato chips, pineapple and 'pink sauce' (we didn't ask). These crazy creations may not be native to South Florida, but this is about the only place you'll find them in the US outside of a few neighborhoods in New York.

Alligator

Alligator tastes like a cross between fish and pork. The meat comes from the tail, and is usually served as deep-fried nuggets, which overwhelms the delicate flavor and can make it chewy. Try it grilled. Most alligator is legally harvested on farms and is often sold in grocery stores. It's also healthier than chicken, with as much protein but half the fat, fewer calories and less cholesterol.

Frog's Legs

Those who know say the 'best' legs come from the Everglades; definitely ask, since you want to avoid imported ones from India, which are smaller and disparaged as 'flavorless'.

Stone Crabs

The first recycled crustacean: only one claw is taken from a stone crab – the rest is tossed back in the sea (the claw regrows in 12 to 18 months, and crabs plucked again are called 'retreads'). The claws are so perishable that they're always cooked before selling. October through April is less a 'season' than a stone-crab frenzy. Joe Weiss of Miami Beach is credited with starting it all.

Key Lime Pie

Key limes are yellow, and that's the color of an authentic Key lime pie, which is a custard of Key lime juice, sweetened condensed milk and egg yolks in a cracker crust, then topped with meringue. Avoid any slice that's green or stands ramrod straight. The combination of extratart Key lime with oversweet milk nicely captures the personality of Key West Conchs.

Conch

Speaking of conchs, the shellfish Keys natives are named for (A 'conch' is a shellfish, while a capitalized 'Conch' is a Keys native) happen to be delicious, and are difficult to find outside of South Florida (in the US). Conch meat is pleasantly springy and usually prepared according to Caribbean recipes: most of the time it's either curried or 'cracked' (fried). Either way it is seriously tasty. Café Solé, in Key West (p163), is famous for its conch carpaccio, oft-imitated but yet to be improved upon.

Arepas

The greatness of a city can be measured by many yardsticks. The arts. Civic involvement. Infrastructure. What you eat when you're plowed at 3am. In Miami, the answer is often enough arepas, delicious South American corn cakes that can be stuffed with any manner of deliciousness; generally, you can't go wrong with cheese.

From Farm (& Grove) to Table

Florida has worked long and hard to become an agricultural powerhouse, and it's famous for its citrus. The state is the nation's largest producer of oranges, grapefruits, tangerines and limes, not to mention mangoes and sugarcane. Scads of bananas, strawberries, coconuts, avocados (once called 'alligator pears'), and the gamut of tropical fruits and vegetables are also grown in Florida. Homestead is a major agricultural region, with citrus groves and fields of crops extending all the way to the edge of the Everglades.

However, only relatively recently – with the advent of the USA's locavore, farm-to-table movement – has Florida started featuring vegetables in its cooking and promoting its freshness on the plate. Florida's regional highlights – its Southern and Latin American cuisines – do not usually emphasize greens or vegetarianism. But today, most restaurants with upscale or gourmet pretensions promote the local sources of their produce and offer appealing choices for vegetarians.

Inside Miami you'll find a delightful variety of vegetarian options, including a few vegan-friendly places. Funnily enough, folks here choose vegetarianism for reasons both ethical and vain; in the latter case, you'll find a lot of SUV-driving fitness nuts who don't give a fig for being green, but are obsessed with looking good. Outside Miami, dedicated vegetarian restaurants are few, and in many Keys and Everglades restaurants vegetarians can be forced to choose between iceberg-lettuce salads and pastas. We list some of our favorite vegetarian options below.

One indigenous local delicacy is heart of palm, or 'swamp cabbage,' which has a delicate, sweet crunch. The heart of the sabal palm, Florida's state tree, it was a mainstay for Florida pioneers. Try it if you can find it served fresh (don't bother if it's canned; it's not from Florida).

Edible Communities (www.edi blecommunities .com) is a regional magazine series (print and online) that celebrates and supports local, sustainable farming, culinary artisans and seasonal produce. It publishes editions for Orlando and South Florida.

HAUTE OR NOT FROM FARM (& GROVE) TO TABLE

VEGGING OUT: BEST VEGETARIAN IN SOUTH FLORIDA

» Sustain (p99)
» Honey Tree (p100)
» Michy's (p100)
» Last Carrot (p102)
» Granny Feelgoods (p99)

Libations

Be it a lime stuffed into a Corona on a dock in the Keys, or rum served in countless permutations, South Florida really likes a drink. Or 10. There's a phrase you'll hear in the Keys that describes the islands as 'Drinking towns with a fishing problem', which more or less nails it.

Miami loves its booze too, but as with food, the focus is often on whatever happens to be the trendy drink of the moment (this rule, admittedly, does not apply to Miami's many excellent dives and neighborhood joints). And as with food, this trend-consciousness has its good and bad sides. During our research, unique cocktails created by professional 'mixologists' were all the drinking rage. You could find some incredible concoctions out there too – Señora Martinez (on p99), we're looking in your direction. But we also had far too many poorly mixed drinks that cost a rich man's price tag served in the umpteenth variation of a 'hip' Miami Beach bar.

Funnily enough, Miami's obsession with mixology represents a bit of a cocktail renaissance down here. Cuban bartenders became celebrities in the 1920s for what they did with all that sugarcane and citrus: the two classics are the *Cuba libre* (rum, lime and cola) and the mojito, traditionally served with *chicharrónes* (deep-fried pork rinds).

The beer market in Miami has definitely improved over the past few years. A demand for quality brew means you can find a gallery of international beers at some bars; on the other hand, you can go from being very international to totally local and trying a brew pub. Miami is known for its celebrity nightlife scene, but one of the first famous drinkers here was down in Key West. Old Ernest Hemingway, it was said, favored piña coladas, lots of them. In the same neighborhood, Jimmy Buffett memorialized the margarita – so that now every sweaty beach bar along the peninsula claims to make the 'best'. Welcome, good friends, to Margaritaville.

ORANGE JUICE

Coinciding with modern refrigeration, frozen concentrated orange juice was invented in Florida in 1946: this popularized orange juice as a year-round drink and created a generation of 'orange millionaires'.

Bikes, Boats & Beaches

The American outdoors experience is often associated with quality of rugged: jagged mountains, crashing waterfalls, deep forests. It's beauty expressed by elevation, horizons defined by their intervening topography.

You know what South Florida doesn't have? Elevation or topography.

What it does have is a gentle, user-friendly prettiness, and water. And not just bodies of water (the ocean, the bays, the rivers, the marsh, the swamp) but water existing in countless permutations and evolutions thanks to its complicated relationship with the land: flooded prairies, blackwater cypress domes, mangrove coastlines, squidgy mudflats, 10,000 Islands and beach, beach, beach. And more beach.

Likely as not you came here for the beach. Good for you! There's a lot to do on that beach, and perhaps more pertinently, off it: fishing, swimming, boating, snorkeling, diving – and several different brands of boarding. Why not get under the water while you're at it? Herein you will find the largest coral reef system in North America.

South Florida can give the Netherlands a run for its money in the race to the bottom of the topographic map, and as such, should be traversed by the means of exploring below sea level: via bicycle, or boat or scuba gear (ie really below sea level). Enjoy the land, and the water too. They exist in tandem, and are almost always experienced as such.

Trails & Tents

Boardwalk paths run by still-water swamps, noodle-thin tracks lace into boonies studded with lakes and rivers, and mangrove walkways encircle white beaches. And the whole while, there's tents, cabins and pavilions for sleeping under the stars. Lace up your boots (or don some sandals; there's some very gentle trails here) and roll up your canvas.

Trails

One thing Florida hikers never have to worry about is elevation gain. But the weather more than makes up for it, especially in the dry season. From November through March rain, temperature, humidity and mosquitoes decrease to tolerable levels. In summer (June to September), make sure to hike first thing, before noon, to avoid the midday heat and afternoon thundershowers.

South Florida swamps tend to favor 1- to 2-mile boardwalk trails; these are excellent, and almost always wheelchair accessible. You'll also find lovely short trails in many state parks. The best trails in South Florida can be found in Everglades National Park and surrounds.

Miami

» Oleta River State Park (p54) A gentle series of nature trails stretches across this, Florida's largest urban park.

Great Hiking & Camping Guides

» *30 Eco-Trips in Florida* (2005), Holly Ambrose

» *A Hiker's Guide to the Sunshine State* (2005), Sandra Friend

» *The Best in Tent Camping: Florida* (2010), John Malloy

TREAD LIGHTLY, EXPLORE SAFELY

These days, it should go without saying that any wilderness, even a swamp, is a fragile place. Whether hiking, biking, paddling, or snorkeling, always practice 'Leave No Trace' ethics (see www.lnt.org for comprehensive advice). In short, this boils down to staying on the trail, cleaning up your own mess, and observing nature rather than plucking or feeding it. See also A Kinder, Gentler Wilderness Encounter, p211.

As you enjoy Florida's natural bounty, take care of yourself, too. In particular, carry lots of water, up to a gallon per person per day, and always be prepared for rain. Line backpacks with plastic bags, and carry rain gear and extra clothes for when (not if) you get soaked. Reid Tillery's *Surviving the Wilds of Florida* will help you do just that, while Tillery's website **Florida Adventuring** (www.floridaadventuring.com) covers backcountry essentials.

» Arch Creek Park (p54) This small park has family-friendly nature trails.

» Bill Baggs Cape Florida State Park (p66) Sandy trails lead past beaches and mangroves.

» Crandon Park (p65) Nature trails abound in this lovely coastal ecosystem.

» Fairchild Tropical Garden (p74) Not many hikes, per se, but the park is so large you'll get a good walk traversing its length and breadth.

The Everglades

» Florida National Scenic Trail (p125) One of America's 11 national scenic trails. Enters South Florida north from the swamps of Big Cypress National Preserve; you can feasibly trek from here to Lake Okeechobee. Just expect a few mosquitoes here and there, a description we'll lovingly admit is the understatement of this book.

» Royal Palm Visitor Center (p130) Classic wetlands boardwalk walkway

» Shark Valley (p124) Two small trails pierce the unique environment of the northern Glades.

» Fakahatchee Strand Preserve (p128) Follow a long boardwalk deep into the heart of a genuine blackwater swamp.

The Keys

» John Pennekamp Coral Reef State Park (p139) While this park is primarily known for its water activities, there are some small, friendly trails here for when you're done diving.

» Windley Key Fossil Reef Geological State Park (p143) Part of this Key has been carved out, which gives you a glimpse into the complex geology of the archipelago.

» Indian Key State Historic Site (p143) Rotting buildings and groves of shady trees add an almost eerie touch to trekking across this island.

» Lignumvitae Key State Botanical Site (p143) Genuine jungle has reclaimed this small, isolated island.

» Curry Hammock State Park (p145) Narrow trails finger through the local mangrove and beachside biomes.

» Crane Point Museum (p147) The interpretative trails attached to this museum are a great introductory lesson on the ecology of the Keys.

» Bahia Honda State Park (p150) Probably the best park in the Keys, filled with nature, beach and boardwalk trails.

» Dry Tortugas National Park (p160) A small series of walks stretches around this old naval fort.

Tents

When you're done hiking, take time to camp under Florida's starry skies. Camping opportunities abound. You'll be close to nature, and this is a good way of saving money on accommodations. If you want to hear the heartbeat of wild Florida, nothing beats sleeping in the Everglades in a *chickee* (wooden platform above the waterline, p132).

Miami

» Oleta River State Park (p54) There are 14 cabins here for your camping pleasure.
» Bill Baggs Cape Florida State Park (p66) Boat and chaperoned youth group camping only.

The Everglades & Around

» 10,000 Islands (p128) Pure backcountry camping calm when you're isolated on these specks of green goodness.
» Everglades International Hostel (p129) The backyard of this hostel is a surreal, lovely spot to pitch a tent.
» National Park Service Campsites (p132) Manages dozens of campsites within Everglades National Park
» Off-shore Islands in Biscayne National Park (p133) Boat camping and camping on lonely beaches.

The Keys

» John Pennekamp Coral Reef State Park (p139) Excellent camping, but make sure you reserve in advance.
» Curry Hammock State Park (p145) This 28-site campground includes hookups.
» Bahia Honda State Park (p150) The most popular campground in the Keys has cabins, 80 full-facility campsites and boat camping.
» Dry Tortugas National Park (p160) Self-service camping out here at the end of America.

For a complete listing of campgrounds operated by Miami-Dade County, see www.miamidade.gov/parks/facility-find_campground.asp. For information on backcountry camping in the Everglades, see p132.

Canoeing & Kayaking

To really experience South Florida's swamps and rivers, its estuaries and inlets, its lagoons and barrier islands, you need watercraft, preferably the kind you paddle. The intimate quiet of dipping among mangroves, startling alligators and ibis, stirs wonder in the soul. It's not only the Everglades that are great for paddling. Don't forget the coasts. There are some choice options for coastal kayaking and canoeing in Miami and around.

As with hiking, the winter 'dry' season is best for paddling. If it's summer, canoe near cool freshwater springs and swimming beaches, 'cause you'll be dreaming about them.

Miami

» Oleta River State Park (p54) You'll find both open water and mangrove tunnels here; the calm water sits next to the Haulover inlet.
» Bill Baggs Cape Florida State Park (p66) Has a new boat launch and a seawall that fronts No Name Harbor.
» Crandon Park (p65) This gorgeous beach faces waters that are lovely for off-shore paddling.

BIKES, BOATS & BEACHES CANOEING & KAYAKING

Wildlife-watching Resources

» Florida Fish & Wildlife Conservation Commission (http://myfwc.com)
» Audubon of Florida (www.audubonofflorida.org)
» Great Florida Birding Trail (http://floridabirdingtrail.com)
» Florida Wildlife Viewing (www.floridawildlifeviewing.com)

GUIDE BOOK

A great all-in-one paddling guide – with everything from the state's best water trails to nitty-gritty advice about weather, equipment and supplies – is *A Paddler's Guide to the Sunshine State* (2001) by Sandy Huff.

The Everglades

» Everglades National Park (p119) You'll tell your grandchildren about kayaking here. Hell's Bay paddling trail (p130) is heavenly.

» 10,000 Islands (p128) Just as amazing, and for the ultimate Florida paddling adventure, you can try and tackle the 99-mile-long Wilderness Waterway.

» Biscayne National Park (p133) A national park that's 95% water.

The Keys

» Anne's Beach (p143) Offshore paddling near clumps of mangrove forest.

» John Pennekamp Coral Reef State Park (p139) Boat over the continent's largest coral-reef formations.

» Curry Hammock State Park (p145) A quiet mangrove creek, plus offshore paddling – this is a no-combustion zone.

» Bahia Honda State Park (p150) One of the most popular spots for boating in the Florida Keys.

» Indian Key State Historic Sight (p143) The only way out here is via paddling.

» Lignumvitae Key State Botanical Sight (p143) Again, this lovely spot is only boat-accessible.

We'll particularly highlight the latter two options, as they give you the chance to actually boat between different islands in the Keys – a fairly magical experience, believe us.

Diving & Snorkeling

South Florida has, hands down, the best reef and wreck diving in the continental USA. The snorkeling is just as magical. At times, the clarity of the water is disconcerting, as if you were floating on air; every creature and school of fish all the way to the bottom feels just out of reach, so that, as William Bartram once wrote, 'the trout swims by the very nose of the alligator and laughs in his face'. North America's largest coral-reef system is at your fingertips and wreck diving in Florida is equally epic.

The Everglades

» Biscayne National Park (p132) Is developing a wreck-centric maritime *trail,* for goodness sake.

LIFE'S A BEACH

Best beach in South Florida? Well, it depends what you're after. If you want to sunbathe next to models and fashionistas, go to South Beach and hit the sand anywhere between 23rd St and 1st St. We're not saying it's a nonstop Madonna video out there, but in the area around Nikki Beach it can feel like one (p108). If you want family-friendly beaches, check our Travel With Children chapter (p30).

For a list based on 'science,' consult Dr Beach (www.drbeach.org).

Best Beaches (In Our Very Humble Opinion)

» Bahia Honda (p150)

» Bill Baggs Cape Florida State Park (p66)

» Sombrero Beach (p147)

» Haulover Beach Park (p54)

» The Beach at The South Beach Promenade (p51)

GET ON BOARD

South Florida is no surfing hot spot; if you want to ride waves in this state, it's generally best to head north to at least Jupiter Beach (see p80). But surfing isn't the only means of using a board to access the water. Kiteboarding and wakeboarding are growing in popularity, and are accessible to first-timers looking to try something new.

The equipment for wake- and kiteboarding is the same: the wakeboard is a smaller version of a surfboard. In either activity you're pulled along the water; by a boat with a wakeboard and, if it wasn't already blessedly obvious, by a kite while kiteboarding. Either evolution allows you to achieve some serious speed and work some magnificent tricks, although beginners aren't going to be flipping Triple Maddog Overhang Bazooka Busters off the bat (we made that up). The flat, shallow waters around Key Biscayne are wake- and kiteboard central. Check out the following:

» **Miami Kiteboarding** (☑305-345-9774; www.miamikiteboarding.com; Crandon Park, Key Biscayne, Key Biscayne) Offers a range of private lessons starting from $150 for one hour of one-on-one instruction. Couples get discounted rates.

» **Gator Bait Wakeboard School** (☑305-282-5706; www.gatorbaitwakeboard.com; 3301 Rickenbacker Causeway, Key Biscayne) Half-/one-hour lessons run $80/160.

» **Miami Wakeboard Cable Complex** (MWCC; ☑305-476-9253; www.miamiwake boardcablecomplex.com; Amelia Earhart Park, 401 E 65th St, Hialeah) Offers lessons in cableboarding, wherein the rider is pulled along by an overhead cable system. That means no boat, less pollution and less noise. Half-/one-hour lessons are $80/140.

Biscayne, by the way, is also a good place to take up windsurfing; see p79 for more information.

The Keys

» Dry Tortugas National Park (p160) Named for its abundant sea turtles; it's well worth the effort to reach them.

» John Pennekamp Coral Reef State Park (p139) A standout. Some of the best diving in the lower 48 states.

» Looe Key National Marine Sanctuary (p150) Good for small marine life.

» Bahia Honda State Park (p150) Also a good bet.

» Key West (p160) Diving usually takes in the reefs of Looe Key and numerous wreck sites in the vicinity of Key West.

» Marathon (p147) Has extensive diving infrastructure.

» Islamorada has the fantastic Florida Keys History of Diving Museum (p143), which is pretty awesome whether you dive or not.

Biking

Florida is generally too flat for mountain biking (there are exceptions), but there are plenty of off-road opportunities, along with hundreds of miles of paved trails for those who prefer to keep their ride clean. As with hiking, avoid biking in summer, unless you like getting hot and sweaty.

Cruiser bikes and city bikes are great here. If you're Dutch, a classic *oma* bicycle would be perfect for Miami Beach and Key West. In fact, folks from the Netherlands will find, topographically at least, the biking conditions here are close to that of their below-sea-level home; just throw in a *lot* more sunshine and a *lot* fewer bike lanes. Miami Beach operates a bike share program (p116) and bicycles are easy to rent in Key West (p167), so there's really no excuse not to get on two wheels. Our favorite biking spots in South Florida follow.

If you're interested in agrotourism, check out the Redland Trail (www.red landtrail.com). This 'trail' (more of an itinerary) is a collection of some of the weirder roadside attractions, locally sourced dining and general quirkiness of the outdoors in southern Dade County – essentially anything from the entrance to Everglades National Park to South Miami.

BIKES, BOATS & BEACHES BIKING

FLORIDA OUTDOORS

Miami

» Promenade (p51) The South Beach promenade is the quintessential spot to break out a beach cruiser.

» Oleta River State Park (p54) Four miles of novice, 3 miles of paved and 10 miles (!) of mountain-biking trail.

» Arch Creek Park (p54) The bike trails are particularly kid-friendly if you're traveling as a family.

» Bill Baggs Cape Florida State Park (p66) Has a 1.5-mile long paved path, plus a network of unpaved paths.

» Crandon Park (p65) Bike trails spread through this beachfront park.

» Haulover Beach Park (p54) An excellent spot for biking in North Miami Beach.

» Matheson Hammock Park (p76) Way down in South Miami you'll find some very fine biking trails.

The Everglades

» Shark Valley Tram Road Trail (p119) Pierces the Everglades' gator-infested saw-grass river.

The Keys

» Florida Keys Overseas Heritage Trail (p142) Cycle in paradise on a trail that mirrors the Keys Highway for 70 noncontiguous miles.

» Key West (p153) Cycling around the historic half of Key West is simply one of Florida's great pleasures.

For a comprehensive list of outdoor activities in South Florida, from everything we've mentioned above to horseback riding and hunting, plus links to local outdoors organizations, check out www.florida-outdoors.com.

Fishing

The world may contain seven seas, but there's only one Fishing Capital of the World: Florida. No, this isn't typically overwrought Floridian hype. Fishing here is the best the US offers, and for variety and abundance, nowhere else on the globe can claim an indisputable advantage. With that said, water pollution has shrunk Florida's recreational fisheries, and the quality of the angling in the state will rise and fall based on Florida's environmental conditions.

In the Keys, Bahia Honda (p150) and Old Seven Mile Bridge (p147) offer shore-fishing par excellence. Other good sites:

» Oleta River State Park (p54) The shores of the park front the Intracoastal Waterway; plus, there's a popular local fishing pier.

» Bill Baggs Cape Florida State Park (p66) Off-shore fishers here pull in some truly huge hauls.

» Matheson Hammock Park (p76) Drop a line here or just have a walk around the lovely manmade atoll.

Florida mystery writer Randy Wayne White has created an angler's delight with the *Ultimate Tarpon Book* (2010), a celebration of Florida's legendary big-game fish, with 'contributions' from Hemingway, Teddy Roosevelt, Zane Grey and more.

As 'Papa' Hemingway would tell you, the real fishing is offshore, where majestic sailfish leap and thrash. That's part of the reason the man moved to Key West, after all. Bluefish, marlin and mahimahi (known locally as dolphin, although it is not, in any way, the marine mammal) are other popular deep-water fish. See our Miami (p77) and Keys (p147) chapters for more information. The best strategy is to walk the harbor, talking with captains, till you find one who speaks to your experience and interests.

Sailing

If you prefer the wind in your sails, Florida is your place. Miami (p79) is a sailing sweet spot, with plenty of marinas for renting or berthing your own boat – Key Biscayne (p65) is a particular gem. In Key West (p159), sail on a schooner with real cannons, though tour operators are plentiful throughout the Keys.

Golf

Fun fact: With over 1250 courses (and counting), Florida has the most golf courses of any state. Whether or not this is related to Florida's high number of wealthy retirees isn't known, but one thing is certain: if you want to tee up, you won't have to look far. By far your best golfing options are in Miami, specifically in Coral Gables, Miami Beach and Key Biscayne; see p77 for more information. For a comprehensive list of Florida courses, see **Florida Golf** (www.fgolf.com).

Swamp Thing

Naturalist Marjory Stoneman Douglas called Florida 'a long pointed spoon' that is as 'familiar as the map of North America itself'. On that map, the shapely Floridian peninsula represents one of the most unique, ecologically diverse regions in the world.

It all began when, over millions of years, a thick layer of limestone was created as shells and bones drifted to the bottom of an ancient sea. As the Earth's tectonic plates shifted, North America rose up, slipped away from Africa, and left an ocean between them. The bit of limestone that would become Florida settled just north of the Tropic of Cancer, and this confluence of porous rock and climate gave rise to a watery world of uncommon abundance, one that is threatened to be undone by human hands in the geological blink of an eye.

The Land

Florida is many things, but it's also flat as a pancake, or as Douglas says, like a spoon of freshwater resting delicately in a bowl of saltwater – a spongy brick of limestone hugged by the Atlantic Ocean and the Gulf of Mexico. The highest point, the Panhandle's Britton Hill, has to stretch to reach 350ft, which isn't half as tall as downtown Miami. This makes Florida officially the nation's flattest state, despite being 22nd in total area with 58,560 sq miles.

However, over 4000 of those square miles are water; lakes pepper the map like bullet holes in a road sign. That shotgun-size hole in the south is Lake Okeechobee, the seventh-largest freshwater lake in the US. Sounds impressive, but the bottom of the lake is only a few feet above sea level, and it's so shallow you can practically wade across.

Lake Okeechobee ever so gently floods the southern tip of the peninsula (or it wants to; canals divert much of the flow). From here, the land inclines about 6in every 6 miles until finally Florida can't keep its head above water anymore, petering out into the 10,000 Islands and the Florida Keys, which end with a flourish in the Gulf of Mexico. Key West, the last in the chain, is the southernmost point in the continental US.

What really sets Florida apart, though, is that it occupies a subtropical transition zone between northern temperate and southern tropical climates. This is key to the coast's florid coral-reef system, the largest in North America, and to Florida's attention-getting collection of surreal swamps, botanical oddities, and monstrous critters. The Everglades gets the most press, and as an International Biosphere, World Heritage Site, and National Park, the 'river of grass' deserves it.

But the Keys are a crucially important, vital and unique treasure as well. To explore these islands is to enter genuine jungle while still technically within the Lower 48 (admittedly, as low as you can get in that Lower 48, but still). The teal and blue waterways that separate the Keys are as fascinating as the islands themselves; here the water gets so shallow, you can sometimes wade from Key to Key. Couple this shallow shelf with the rich sunlight of South Florida and you get one of the world's most productive aquatic biomes.

Wildlife

Get outside Miami's concrete jungle and you'd be forgiven for thinking you'd entered a real one. Alligators prowl the swamps, the USA's only crocodiles nest in the Keys, birds that resemble pteranadons flap over it all, and underneath rolls that gentle giant, the manatee.

Animals

Birds

Nearly 500 avian species have been documented in Florida, including some of the world's most magnificent migratory water birds: ibis, egrets, great blue herons, white pelicans and whooping cranes. This makes Florida the ultimate birder's paradise.

Nearly 350 species spend time in the Everglades, the prime birding spot in Florida. In fact, much of the initial attention to conservation that first popped up here was related to the illegal poaching of Everglades' wading birds; the beautiful beasts were being killed so their plumage could decorate fashionable women's hats in the early 20th century.

Songbirds and raptors fill Florida skies, too. The state has over 1000 mated pairs of bald eagles, the most in the southern US, and peregrine falcons, who can dive up to 150mph, migrate through in spring and fall.

The Everglades aren't the only place to bird-watch around here. Completed in 2006, the **Great Florida Birding Trail** (http://floridabirdingtrail .com) runs 2000 miles across the entirety of the state and includes nearly 500 bird-watching sites, including many South Florida stops outside the Glades. Other good spots for birding in the region:

» Oleta River State Park (p54)

» Arch Creek Park (p54)

» Haulover Beach Park (p54)

» Bill Baggs Cape Florida State Park (p66)

» Crandon Park (p65)

» Indian Key State Historic Sight (p143)

» Lignumvitae Key State Botanical Site (p143)

» Curry Hammock State Park (p145)

» Crane Point Museum (p147)

» Bahia Honda State Park (p150)

As well, we'd be remiss not mention the Florida Keys Wild Bird Rehabilitation Center in the Upper Keys (p140), where injured birds are nursed back to health by a lovely team of volunteers. Guests are welcome to walk the paths that meander past the hurt birdlife.

Land Mammals

Florida's most endangered mammal is the Florida panther. Before European contact, perhaps 1500 roamed the state. The first panther bounty ($5 a scalp) was passed in 1832, and over the next 130 years they were hunted relentlessly. Though hunting was stopped in 1958, it was too late for panthers to survive on their own. Without a captive breeding program, begun in 1991, the Florida panther would now be extinct, and with only some 120 known to exist (for more, see p131), they're not out of the swamp yet.

Easy to find, white-tailed deer are an all-too-common species that troubles landscaping everywhere. Endemic to the Keys are Key deer, a

Great Nature Guides

» *The Living Gulf Coast* (2011), Charles Sobczak

» *Priceless Florida* (2004), Ellie Whitney, D Bruce Means & Anne Rudloe

» *Seashore Plants of South Florida & the Caribbean* (1994), David W Nellis

Naturalist Doug Alderson helped create the Big Bend Paddling Trail, and in *Waters Less Traveled* (2005) he describes his adventures: dodging pygmy rattlesnakes, meeting Shitty Bill, discussing Kemp's ridley turtles and pondering manatee farts.

Honey-I-Shrunk-the-Ungulate subspecies: less than 3ft tall and lightweight, they live mostly on Big Pine Key (p150).

Marine Mammals

Florida's coastal waters are home to 21 species of dolphins and whales. By far the most common is the bottlenose dolphin, which is highly social, extremely intelligent and frequently encountered around the entire peninsula. Bottlenose dolphins are the species most often seen in captivity.

Winter is also the season for manatees, who seek out Florida's warmwater springs and power-plant discharge canals beginning in November. These lovable, lumbering creatures are another iconic Florida species whose conservation both galvanizes and divides state residents.

Reptiles & Amphibians

Boasting an estimated 184 species, Florida has the nation's largest collection of reptiles and amphibians, and it's growing. Uninvited guests add to the total regularly, many establishing themselves after being released by pet owners. Some of the more dangerous, problematic invasive species include Burmese pythons, black and green iguanas and Nile monitor lizards.

The American alligator is Florida's poster species, and they are ubiquitous in Central and South Florida.

South Florida is also home to the only North American population of American crocodile. Florida's crocs number around 1500; they prefer saltwater, and to distinguish them from gators, check their smile (actually, don't get that close) – a croc's snout is more tapered and its teeth stick out.

Turtles, frogs and snakes love Florida, and nothing is cuter than watching bright skinks, lizards and anoles skittering over porches and sidewalks. Cute doesn't always describe the state's 44 species of snakes – though Floridian promoters emphasize that only six species are poisonous, and only four of those are common. Feel better? Of the

FLORIDA'S MANATEES

It's hard to believe Florida's West Indian manatees were ever mistaken for mermaids, but it's easy to see their attraction: these gentle, curious, colossal mammals are as sweetly lovable as 10ft, 1000lb teddy bears. Solitary and playful, they have been known to 'surf' waves, and every winter, from November to March, they migrate into the warmer waters of Florida's freshwater estuaries, rivers and springs. Like humans, manatees will die if trapped in 62°F water for 24 hours, and in winter Florida's eternally 72°F springs are balmy spas.

Florida residents for over 45 million years, these shy herbivores have absolutely no defenses except their size (they can reach 13ft and 3000lb), and they don't do much, spending most of each day resting and eating 10% of their body weight. Rarely moving faster than a languid saunter, manatees even reproduce slowly; females birth one calf every two to five years. The exception to their docility? Mating. Males are notorious for their aggressive sex drive.

Once hunted for their meat, Florida's manatees have been under some form of protection since 1893, and they were included in the first federal endangered species list in 1967. Today manatee collisions with boats are a leading cause of death, accounting for over 20% annually. Further, propeller scars are so ubiquitous among the living they are the chief identifying tool of scientists.

Population counts are notoriously difficult and unreliable. Yet recent numbers are encouraging. A particularly cold 2010 winter yielded an all-time-high count of 5060 manatees, exceeding the previous high by 1200.

KEEPERS OF THE EVERGLADES

Anyone who has ever dipped a paddle among the saw grass and hardwood hammocks of Everglades National Park wouldn't quibble with the American alligator's Florida sobriquet, 'Keepers of the Everglades.' With snout, eyeballs, and pebbled back so still they hardly ripple the water's surface, alligators have watched over the Glades for over 200 million years.

It's impossible to count Florida's wild alligators, but estimates are that 1.5 million lumber among the state's lakes, rivers and golf courses. No longer officially endangered, they remain protected because they resemble the still-endangered American crocodile. Alligator served in restaurants typically comes from licensed alligator farms, though since 1988 Florida has conducted an annual alligator harvest, open to nonresidents, that allows two alligators per person, as long you get a permit from the Fish and Wildlife Commission. See http://myfwc.com/wildlifehabitats/managed/alligator/alligator -harvest/ for more information.

Alligators are alpha predators who keep the rest of the food chain in check, and their 'gator holes' become vital water cups in dry season and during droughts, aiding the entire wetlands ecosystem. Alligators, who live about 30 years, can grow up to 14ft long and weigh 1000lb.

A vocal courtship begins in April, and mating takes place in May and June. By late June, females lay nests of 30 to 45 eggs, which incubate for two months before hatching. On average, only four alligators per nest survive to adulthood.

Alligators hunt in water, often close to shore; typically, they run on land to flee, not to chase. In Florida, an estimated 15 to 20 nonfatal attacks on humans occur each year, and there have been 22 fatal attacks since 1948.

baddies, three are rattlesnakes (diamondback, pygmy, canebrake), plus copperheads, cottonmouths, and coral snakes. The diamondback is the biggest (up to 7ft), most aggressive and most dangerous. But rest assured, while cottonmouths live in and around water, *most* Florida water snakes are *not* cottonmouths.

If you're not daunted by the prospect of playing with some of South Florida's scaliest citizens, head to the delightful Skunk Ape Research Headquarters in the Everglades (p125). The zoo out back has to be one of the finest amateur reptile collections anywhere, and as a bonus, you may just spot the eponymous Skunk Ape, the American South's version of Bigfoot/Yeti (actual chances: slim to none).

Sea Turtles

Most sea-turtle nesting in the continental US occurs in Florida. Predominantly three species create over 80,000 nests annually, mostly on southern Atlantic Coast beaches but extending to all Gulf Coast beaches. Most are loggerhead, then far fewer green and leatherback, and historically hawksbill and Kemp's ridley as well; all five species are endangered or threatened. The leatherback is the largest, attaining 10ft and 2000lb.

During the May-to-October nesting season, sea turtles deposit from 80 to 120 eggs in each nest. The eggs incubate for about two months, and then the hatchlings emerge all at once and make for the ocean. Contrary to myth, hatchlings don't need the moon to find their way.

However, they can become hopelessly confused by artificial lights and noisy human audiences. For the best, least-disruptive experience, join a sanctioned turtle watch; for a list, visit http://myfwc.com/seaturtle, then click on 'Educational Information' and 'Where to View Sea Turtles.'

The Keys contain their very own Turtle Hospital (p147), a sanctuary for sick and injured gentle shelled giants. They're keen on visitors, so if you're rolling through Marathon, drop by.

AUDUBON OF FLORIDA

Audubon of Florida (www.audubonofflorida.org) is perhaps Florida's leading conservation organization. It has tons of birding and ecological information, and it publishes *Florida Naturalist* magazine.

POISSONS DE POISON

If we have learned anything about travel and the environment, one of the more obvious lessons is: if you find a dangerously poisonous fish in the tropics, don't release it in non-native waters.

Sadly, someone in Florida did not get this memo. To be fair, experts don't believe someone intentionally released the striped, spiny, venomous lionfish into Florida waters on purpose. The theory is some aquarium lionfish were swept into the water after Hurricane Andrew in 1992. The problem? Lionfish are eating machines with no natural predators, and they are disconcertingly adapt at A) breeding and B) poisoning native fish to death faster than you can say 'Finding Nemo'. In the two decades since they've invaded these waters, they've spread like a striped plague across the Atlantic and Caribbean.

Lionfish are detrimental for several reasons. Their environmental impact is, first and foremost, enormous; they can lay 30,000 eggs at a time and spawn as frequently as every four days, according to a 2010 *New York Times* article. That's a fairly huge break in the fragile Florida food chain. Also, their stings hurt – a lot. While rarely fatal, a lionfish sting is pretty painful, and while the fish are shy, there's so many floating about these days folks are bound to feel the wrath of their fins every now and then. With that said, the victims of stings are usually fisherfolk; the few Keys beaches are shallow and swimmers are rarely at risk of coming into contact with lionfish.

The response of the fishing-crazy inhabitants of the Keys to these stinging swimmers? Sting back. With spears, bait, line and tackle. The **Florida Keys National Marine Sanctuary** has been holding lionfish derbies since 2010, and the response from local fisherfolk has been enthusiastic; commercial fisherfolk, after all, stand to lose their livelihood if lionfish overwhelm the Keys. The spiny critters can be cooked (and taste pretty good – they've a light, delicate flavor that's not terribly fishy) and are increasingly popping up on Keys menus. So if you're down this way, push some culinary frontiers, have a lionfish fillet – and help the local environment out all at once.

Plants

The diversity of the peninsula's flora, including over 4000 species of plants, is unmatched in the continental US. Florida, especially South Florida, contains the southern extent of temperate ecosystems and the northern extent of tropical ones, which blend and merge in a bewildering, fluid taxonomy of environments. Interestingly, most of the world at this latitude is a desert, which Florida definitely is not.

Wetlands & Swamps

It takes special kinds of plants to thrive in the humid, waterlogged, sometimes salty marshes, sloughs, swales, seeps, basins, marl prairies and swamps of Florida. Much of the Everglades is dominated by vast expanses of saw grass, which is actually a sedge with fine toothlike edges that can reach 10ft high. South Florida is a symphony of sedges, grasses and rushes. These hardy water-tolerant species provide abundant seeds to feed birds and animals, protect fish in shallow water, and pad wetlands for birds and alligators.

The strangest plants are the submerged and immersed species that grow in, under and out of the water. Free-floating species include bladderwort and coontail, a species that lives, flowers and is pollinated entirely underwater. Florida's swamps are abundant with rooted plants with floating leaves, like the pretty American lotus, water lilies and spatterdock (if you love names, you'll love Florida botany!). Another common immersed plant, bur marigold, can paint whole prairies yellow.

NATIVE PLANTS

Visit the Florida Native Plant Society (www.fnps .org), a nonprofit conservation organization, for updates on preservation issues and invasive species and for a nice overview of Florida's native plants and ecosystems.

A dramatic, beautiful tree in Florida's swamps is the bald cypress, which is the most flood-tolerant tree. It can grow 150ft tall, with buttressed, wide trunks and roots with 'knees' that poke above the drenched soil.

Forests, Scrubs & Flatwoods

The forests of the mainland, such as they are, are mainly to be found in the Everglades, where small changes in elevation and substrate are the difference between prairie and massive 'domes' of Bald Cypress and towering pine trees. Cypress domes are a particular kind of swamp when a watery depression occurs in a pine flatwood.

Scrubs are found throughout Florida; they are typically old dunes with well-drained sandy soil. Scrubs often blend into sandy pine flatwoods, which typically have a sparse longleaf or slash-pine overstory and an understory of grasses and/or saw palmetto. Saw palmetto is a vital Florida plant: its fruit is an important food for bears and deer (and an herbal medicine that's believed to help prevent cancer), it provides shelter for panthers and snakes, and its flower is an important source of honey. It's named for its sharp saw-toothed leaf stems.

Formed by the interplay of tides, coral and mangroves, the Florida Keys contain the best (and in many cases, only) examples of tropical and subtropical hardwood 'hammock,' or forest, in the continental USA. The Crane Point Museum (p147) is an excellent starting point for learning about this extremely niche ecosystem.

Mangroves & Coastal Dunes

Where not shaved smooth by sand, South Florida's coastline is often covered with a three-day stubble of mangroves. Mangroves are not a single species; the name refers to all tropical trees and shrubs that have adapted to loose wet soil, saltwater, and periodic root submergence. Mangroves also develop 'live birth,' germinating their seeds while they're still attached to the parent tree. Of the over 50 species of mangroves worldwide, only three predominate in Florida: red, black and white. For more, see p148.

Mangroves play a vital role on the peninsula, and their destruction usually sets off a domino effect of ecological damage. Mangroves 'stabilize' coastal land, trapping sand, silt and sediment. As this builds up, new land is created, which ironically strangles the mangroves themselves. Mangroves mitigate the storm surge and damaging winds of hurricanes, and they anchor tidal and estuary communities, providing vital wildlife habitats.

Coastal dunes are typically home to grasses and shrubs, saw palmetto and occasionally pines and cabbage palm (or sabal palm, the Florida state tree). Sea oats, with large plumes that trap wind-blown sand, are important for stabilizing dunes, while coastal hammocks welcome the wiggly gumbo-limbo tree, whose red peeling bark has earned it the nickname of 'tourist tree.'

National, State & Regional Parks

About 26% of Florida's land lies in public hands, which breaks down to three national forests, 11 national parks, 28 national wildlife refuges (including the first, Pelican Island), and 160 state parks. Overall, attendance is up, with over 20 million folks visiting state parks annually. Florida's state parks have twice been voted the nation's best.

Florida's parks are easy to explore. For more information on what to do and where, see Bikes, Boats & Beaches (p197), as well as listings throughout this guide. For specific park information, the main organizations follow.

In Florida, even the plants bite: the Panhandle has the most species of carnivorous plants in the US, the result of its nutrient-poor sandy soil.

CARNIVOROUS PLANTS

SWAMP THING NATIONAL, STATE & REGIONAL PARKS

The Florida chapter of the Nature Conservancy (www.nature .org) has been instrumental in the Florida Forever legislation. Check the web for updates and conservation issues.

GHOST HUNTERS

Florida has more species of orchids than any other state in the US, and orchids are themselves the largest family of flowering plants in the world, with perhaps 25,000 species. On the dial of botanical fascination, orchids go well past 11, and the Florida species that inspires the most intense devotion is the extremely rare ghost orchid.

This bizarre epiphytic flower has no leaves and usually only one bloom, which is of course deathly white with two long thin drooping petals that curl like a handlebar mustache. The ghost orchid is pollinated by the giant sphinx moth, which is the only insect with a proboscis long enough to reach down the ghost orchid's 5in-long nectar spur and who arrives in the dead of night.

The exact locations of ghost orchids are usually kept secret for fear of poachers, who, as Susan Orlean's book *The Orchid Thief* made clear, are a real threat to their survival. But the flower's general whereabouts are common knowledge: South Florida's approximately 2000 ghost orchids are almost all in Big Cypress National Preserve (p124) and Fakahatchee Strand Preserve State Park (p128). Of course, these parks are home to a great many other wild orchids, as is Everglades National Park (p119).

To learn more, visit **Florida's Native Orchids** (www.flnativeorchids.com) and **Ghost Orchid.info** (www.ghostorchid.info).

Florida State Parks (www.floridastateparks.org)
National Forests, Florida (www.fs.usda.gov/florida)
National Park Service (NPS; www.nps.gov)
National Wildlife Refuges, Florida (NWR; www.fws.gov/southeast/maps /fl.html)
Recreation.gov (www.recreation.gov) National lands campground reservations.

The **Florida Fish & Wildlife Commission** (http://myfwc.com) manages Florida's mostly undeveloped Wildlife Management Areas (WMA). The website is an excellent resource for wildlife-viewing, as well as boating, hunting, fishing and permits.

Environmental Issues

Florida's environmental problems are the inevitable result of its century-long love affair with land development, population growth and tourism, and addressing them is especially urgent given Florida's uniquely diverse natural world. These complex, intertwined environmental impacts include erosion of wetlands, depletion of the aquifer, rampant pollution (particularly of waters), invasive species, endangered species, and widespread habitat destruction. There is nary an acre of Florida that escapes concern.

In the last decade, Florida has enacted several significant conservation efforts. In 2000, the state passed the **Florida Forever Act** (www.support floridaforever.org), a 10-year, $3 billion conservation program that in 2008 was renewed for another 10 years. It also passed the multibillion-dollar **Comprehensive Everglades Restoration Plan** (CERP; www.everglades plan.org). For more on Everglades restoration, see p123.

The Everglades once stretched over some 11,000 square miles, but today, the wetlands are less than half the size they were a century ago.

Signs of progress can be encouraging. For instance, phosphorous levels in the Everglades have been seriously reduced, and in 2010, the state completed a purchase of 300 sq miles of Lake Okeechobee sugarcane fields from US Sugar, intending to convert them back to swamp. Along with plans to bridge 6.5 miles of the Tamiami Trail, the lake may once again water the Glades.

And yet, these efforts alone are insufficient to fix the sins of the past, and money tends to dry up faster than an afternoon rainstorm in August. For instance, Governor Scott and his government cut Florida Forever's 2010 funding entirely, and the program's future viability is now in question.

Lake Okeechobee, source of the Everglades, has been imprisoned by Hoover Dike since 1928. It is now full of toxic sludge, which gets stirred up during hurricanes and causes 'red tides,' or algae blooms that kill fish. Red tides occur naturally, but they are also sparked by pollution and unnatural water flows.

Studies have found that half of the state's lakes and waterways are too polluted for fishing. Though industrial pollution has been curtailed, pollution from residential development (sewage, fertilizer runoff) more than compensates. This is distressing Florida's freshwater springs, which can turn murky with algae. Plus, as the groundwater gets pumped out to slake homeowners' thirsts, the springs are shrinking and the drying limestone honeycomb underfoot sometimes collapses, causing sinkholes that swallow cars and homes.

And residential development continues almost unabated. The Miami–Fort Lauderdale–West Palm Beach corridor (the USA's sixth-largest urban area) is, as developers say, 'built out'. Every day, Miami and Homestead's urban (and in the case of Homestead, agricultural) footprint grows deeper into the west, on the edge of the Everglades. While conservation laws protect the national park itself, the run-off and by-product of such a huge urban area inevitably has its impact in the incredibly fragile Glades.

Then there's the coming apocalypse: rising seas due to global warming. Here, the low-lying Florida Keys are a 'canary in a coalmine' that's

A KINDER, GENTLER WILDERNESS ENCOUNTER

While yesterday's glass-bottom boats and alligator wrestling have evolved into today's swamp-buggy rides and manatee encounters, the question remains: just because you *can* do something, does it mean you *should*? In Florida, everyone has an obligation to consider the best ways to experience nature without harming it in the process.

For most activities, there isn't a single right answer; specific impacts are often debated. However, there *are* a few clear guidelines.

» **Airboats and swamp buggies** While airboats have a much lighter 'footprint' than big-wheeled buggies, both are motorized (and loud) and have far larger impacts than canoes for exploring wetlands. As a rule, nonmotorized activities are the least damaging.

» **Dolphin encounters** Captive dolphins are typically rescued animals already acclimated to humans. For a consideration of dolphin swims, see p146. However, when encountering wild dolphins in the ocean, federal law makes it illegal to feed, pursue, or touch them. Habituating any wild animal to humans can lead to the animal's death, since approaching humans often leads to conflicts and accidents (as with boats).

» **Manatee swims** When swimming near manatees, a federally protected endangered species, look but don't touch. 'Passive observation' is the standard. Harassment is a rampant problem that may lead to stricter 'no touch' legislation.

» **Feeding wild animals** In a word, don't. Kind animals like deer and manatees may come to rely on human food (to their detriment), while feeding bears and alligators just encourages them to... *hunt you*.

» **Sea-turtle nesting sites** It's a federal crime to approach nesting sea turtles or hatchling runs. Most nesting beaches have warning signs and a nighttime 'lights out' policy. If you encounter turtles on the beach, keep your distance and no flash photos.

» **Coral-reef etiquette** Never touch the coral reef. It's that simple. Coral polyps are living organisms. Touching or breaking coral creates openings for infection and disease.

being watched worldwide for impacts. In another century, some quip, South Florida's coastline could be a modern-day Atlantis, with its most expensive real estate underwater.

On the subject of real estate, the Keys happen to be governed by a labyrinthine set of zoning regulations. Getting permission to build on the land that remains is an arduous process, although many Keys law firms are solely dedicated to navigating this paper trail; as such, the Keys are not immune to overdevelopment, but are also better protected than much of the rest of Florida.

Art-Deco Miami

Showing Off in Style

For years now, south Miami Beach – also known as 'South Beach' for those who may have been in a cave – has been 'hot,' in the shrieking, Paris Hilton–induced awe-of-celebrity sense of the word, and it owes this cachet to two words: art deco. It was deco that first made Miami Beach distinctive, and when the celebs find a new spot to act sexy, it will (hopefully) be deco that remains: the signature, sleek face of the American Riviera.

Deco, Design & Dreams

The early-20th-century school of design was the aesthetic backbone of old South Beach, and the driving force of its 1980s resurrection. A sustained campaign to preserve the wonderful deco hotels of Miami Beach provided what tons of tourism brochures could never create: brand. Sun, sand, surf: a lot of cities can lay claim to them.

The end of WWI in 1918 ushered in an era of increased interest in the romance and glamour of travel, which lasted well into the 1930s. There was a giddy fascination with speed and cars, ocean liners, trains and planes. Not coincidentally, the US postindustrial revolution, concerned with mass production, kicked into high gear. New materials such as aluminum, polished bronze and stainless steel were utilized in new and exciting ways. Americans began looking to the future, and they wanted to be on the cutting edge.

Meanwhile, in Europe, at a 1925 Paris design fair officially called the *Exposition Internationale des Arts Décoratifs et Industriels Modernes* (and eventually abbreviated to Arts Deco), decorative arts were highlighted, but the US had nothing to contribute. Europeans were experimenting with repeating patterns in Cubism and were influenced by ancient cultures (King Tut's tomb was discovered in 1921), and Americans had to play catch-up.

The deco district is bounded by Dade Blvd to the north, 6th St to the south, the Atlantic Ocean to the east and Lenox Ave to the west. The 1-sq-mile district feels like a small village, albeit a village inhabited by freaks, geeks and the gorgeous. Which is pretty cool.

THE DECO DISTRICT

CLASSIC TROPICAL DECO

There are some unifying themes to classical deco structures that are easy enough to spot with a discerning eye. Perhaps most noticeable is a sense of streamlined movement, exemplified by rounded walls, racing stripe details and 'eyebrows,' rounded buttresses that provided shade and visual eye candy to passersby. Porthole windows evoke cruise liners, while lamps and other home wares represent long-past idealizations of a space-age future. Call it 'ray-gun chic'. An intimate (some say cramped) sense of space is offset by terrazzo flooring, often imprinted with the fossils of sea animals, and open verandas, which would naturally cool building inhabitants in pre-air-conditioning days. The idea was to venerate technology while seizing on the natural features of the landscape (sea breezes and golden sunlight), adding a dash of organic aesthetic to the overall structure.

ADDRESSES

Back in the States, a mere year later, a devastating hurricane blew through Miami Beach, leaving few buildings standing. The wealthy folks who were living here before the hurricane chose to decamp. The second blow of a one-two punch for Miami's economy was delivered by the Great Depression. But in this dark time, opportunity soon came knocking. In Miami real estate, everything was up for grabs. The clean slate of the South Florida coastline was practically begging for experimentation.

Hotel rebuilding began in Miami Beach at the rate of about 100 per year during the 1930s. Many architects had 40 to 50 buildings in production at any one time until the inception of WWII. This overlapped with a surge in middle-class tourism between 1936 and 1941, when visitors started coming for a month at a time.

The post-Depression era was an optimistic time, with hopes and dreams pinned on scientific and technological revolutions. Reverence for machines took on almost spiritual dimensions, and found its aesthetic expression in both symbolic and functional ways.

What does all this have to do with architecture? Everything. The principles of efficiency and streamlining translated into mass-produced, modest buildings without superfluous ornamentation – at least in the Northeast USA.

Romance, Relief & Rhythms

In Miami Beach, cross streets are determined by building number. Two zeroes after the first number means the building is at the base of the block. So 700 Ocean Dr is at 7th St and Ocean, while 1420 Ocean Dr is at 14th St & Ocean, just north of the intersection.

Miami Beach, a more romantic and glamorous resort, developed what came to be known as tropical deco architecture. It organically reflected the natural world around it. For example, glass architectural blocks let bright Florida light in but kept sweltering heat out. They also served a geometric or cubist aesthetic. Floral reliefs, popular during the art nouveau period, appeared here, too. Friezes on facades or etched into glass reflected native flora and fauna such as palm trees, pelicans and flamingos. Friezes also took their cues from the uniquely American jazz movement, harmonious and lyrical. Surrounded by water, Miami Beach deco also developed a rhythmic language, with scalloped waves and fountains.

Creating a Miami Look

Whereas Northeast deco buildings had socialist overtones, the clean lines of Miami Beach architecture still made room for joyful, playful,

CLASSICAL DECO SOUTH BEACH STRUCTURES

» **Cardozo Hotel** (p87) This lovely building and the Carlyle Hotel were the first buildings rescued by the original Miami Beach preservation league when developers threatened to raze South Beach's deco buildings in the 1980s. Owned by Gloria Estefan.

» **Essex House Hotel** (p85) Porthole windows lend the feel of a grand cruise ship, while its spire looks like a rocket ship, recalling deco's roots as an aesthetic complement to modernism and industrialism. Beautiful terrazzo floors also cool the lobby.

» **Deco lifeguard stations on South Beach** Besides being cubist-inspired exemplars of the classical Deco movement, with their sharp, pleasing geometric lines, these stations are painted in dazzling colors. Found all along the beach from 1st St to 17th St.

» **Carlyle Hotel** (1250 Ocean Dr) Comes with futuristic styling, triple parapets, a *Jetsons* sort of vibe and some cinematic cachet: *The Birdcage* was filmed here.

» **Jerry's Famous Deli** (p95) Housed in the Hoffman Cafeteria Building, this spacious 1939 gem has a front that resembles the prow of a *Buck Rogers*–inspired ship. The carved owls on the roof scare off pigeons (and their poo).

DECO ELEMENTS & EMBELLISHMENTS

» **Waldorf Towers Hotel** (860 Ocean Dr) Deco guru L Murray Dixon designed the tower of this hotel to resemble a lighthouse, surely meant to shine the way home for drunken Ocean Drive revels.

» **Colony Hotel** (736 Ocean Dr) The Colony is the oldest deco hotel in Miami Beach. It was the first hotel in Miami, and perhaps America, to incorporate its sign (a zigzaggy neon wonder) as part of its overall design. Inside the lobby are excellent examples of space-age interiors, including Saturn-shaped lamps and Flash Gordon elevators.

» **Cavalier Hotel** (p88) The step-pyramid sides and geometric carvings that grace the front of this classic are some of the best examples of the 'Aztec/Maya temple-as-hotel' school of design.

» **Wolfsonian-FIU** (p42) The lobby of this museum contains a phenomenally theatrical example of a 'frozen fountain'. The gold-leaf fountain, formerly gracing a movie-theater lobby (you can bet it wasn't a multiplex!), shoots vertically up and flows symmetrically downward.

» **Crescent Hotel** (1420 Ocean Dr) Besides having one of Miami Beach's most recognizable neon facades, the Crescent's signage attracts the eye down into its lobby (the better to pack guests in), rather than up to its roof.

hopeful characteristics. Forward thinking and dreaming about the future took hold. Space travel was explored through design: buildings began to loosely resemble rockets, and rooflines embodied fantasies about traveling the universe. Geometric and abstract zigzag (or ziggurat) patterns not only reflected Aztec and Egyptian cultures, they also symbolized lightning bolts of electricity. Sun rays, more imagery borrowed from an ancient culture, were employed as life-affirming elements to counter the dark days of the Depression.

Since all hotels were built on the same size lots, South Beach architects began distinguishing themselves from their next-door neighbors through decorative finials and parapets. Neon signage also helped individualize buildings. Miami Beach deco relied on 'stepped-back' facades that disrupted the harsh, flat light and contributed to the rhythmical feel. Cantilevered 'eyebrows' jutted out above windows to protect interiors from unrelenting sun. Canopy porches gave hotel patrons a cool place to sit. To reflect the heat, buildings were originally painted white, with animated accent colors highlighting smaller elements. (It was only later, during the 1980s, that interior designer Leonard Horowitz decreed the pastel palette that became the standard. We're kinda happy he did).

With the effects of the Depression lingering, ornamentation was limited to the facades; interiors were stripped down. Labor was cheap and readily available.

Miami Beach needed a large number of rooms, most of which ended up being built small. With no expectation that they remain standing this long, most hotels were built with inexpensive concrete and mortar that had too much sand in it. Stucco exteriors prevailed, but locally quarried native keystone (an indigenous limestone) was also used. Except for the keystone, none of this would withstand the test of time with grace, which is one reason the district fell into such a state of disrepair and neglect. It's also why the district remains under a constant state of renovation.

Restoring the Deco District

South Beach's heart is its Art Deco Historic District, one of the largest in the USA on the National Register of Historic Places. In fact, the area's rejuvenation and rebirth as a major tourist destination results directly

Terrazzo is a popular construction medium in Florida. Italians were first hired to create terrazzo floors. They'd lay out a patterned grid and pour various colors of terrazzo – crushed stones, shells, marble chips or granite, mixed with concrete – into the grid and then polish it. It's a remarkable marriage of form and function, since terrazzo also cools the feet.

'NEW' DECO HOTELS

» **Delano Hotel** (p88) The top tower evokes old-school deco rocket-ship fantasies, but the theater-set-on-acid interior is a flight of pure modern fancy. The enormous backyard pool mixes jazz-era elegance with pure Miami muscular opulence.

» **Hotel Victor** (p84) Forward-thinking management (who give a nod to the past) has done an excellent job of turning this L Murray Dixon original into an undersea wonderland of jellyfish lamps and sea-green terrazzo floors.

» **Tides** (p88) The biggest deco structure of its day was a temple to the deco movement. Today, the lobby feels like Poseidon's audience chamber, while rooms exemplify modern boutique aesthetics.

» **Royal Palm Hotel** (p89)There's no better place to feel a sense of seaborne movement than the *Titanic*-esque, ocean-liner back lobby of this massive, beautifully restored hotel. The mezzanine floor has modern dimensions in its enormity mixed with classic deco styling.

» **Surfcomber** (p89) One of the best deco renovations on the beach is offset by sleek, transit lounge lines in the lobby and a lovely series of rounded eyebrows.

from its protection as a historic place in 1979. The National Register designation prevents developers from razing significant portions of what was, in the 1980s, a crime-ridden collection of crumbling eyesores populated primarily by both criminals and society's dispossessed – the elderly, the mentally ill and the destitute. It's a far cry from that now. Today, hotel and apartment facades are decidedly colorful, with pastel architectural details. Depending on your perspective, the bright buildings catapult you back to the Roaring Twenties or on a wacky tour of American kitsch.

The National Register listing was fought for and pushed through by the Miami Design Preservation League (MDPL), founded by Barbara Baer Capitman in 1976. She was appalled when she heard of plans by the city of Miami to bulldoze several historic buildings in what is now the Omni Center. And she acted, forcefully.

MDPL cofounder Leonard Horowitz played a pivotal role in putting South Beach back on the map, painting the then-drab deco buildings in shocking pink, lavender and turquoise. When his restoration of Friedman's Pharmacy made the cover of *Progressive Architecture* in 1982, the would-be Hollywood producers of *Miami Vice* saw something they liked, and the rest is history.

One of the best things about the 1000 or so buildings in the deco district is their scale: most are no taller than the palm trees. And while the architecture is by no means uniform – you'll see Streamline Moderne, Mediterranean revival and tropical art-deco designs – it's all quite harmonious.

Interestingly, the value of these Miami Beach deco buildings is based more on the sheer number of structures with protected status from the National Register of Historic Places. Individually, the inexpensively constructed houses would be worth far less.

With over 400 registered historic landmarks, you can follow the Beach boom phases through the district: from the 1930s when 5th St through mid-Beach was developed; to the late '30s to early '40s up toward 27th St; and heading north into the '50s, the era of resorts, hotels and condominiums.

Why We Love Deco Design

So what, you may ask, is the big deal about art deco? The term certainly gets thrown around enough in Miami. Given the way this architectural style is whispered about by hotel marketing types, you'd be forgiven for thinking art deco was the pièce de résistance, 'Well, the so-and-so resort has a lovely deco facade'; 'Our boutique properties incorporate deco porches'; 'Did you notice the deco columns in our lounge?' And so on.

One of life's little ironies is this: deco was supposed to make its contemporary viewers contemplate tomorrow. Today, it puts modern viewers in mind of yesterday.

PORTHOLES

But to be fair, deco has been a sort of renaissance for Miami Beach. It was art deco that made these buildings unique, that caught the eye of Hollywood, which saw something romantically American in the optimism and innovation of a style that blends cubism, futurism, modernism and, most of all, a sense of movement. Beyond that was a nod to, and sometimes even reverence for, the elaborate embellishment of Old World decor. In art deco, we see the link between the lavish design aesthetic of the 19th century and the stripped-down efficiency of the 20th. Unlike a skyscraper, a deco hotel is modern yet accessible, even friendly, with its frescoed walls and shady window eyebrows.

But what's truly great about Deco Miami is the example it sets. The Art Deco Historic District of South Beach, one of the hottest tourist destinations in the word, is a reminder to city fathers that preserving historic neighborhoods is not just a matter of slavish loyalty to aesthetics, but sometimes the economically practical and innovative way forward. In a city built on fast real estate, it's a bit delicious that the heart of the sexiest neighborhood is the child of preservation and smart planning.

Post-Deco, Miami Modern & Beyond

The tale of Miami architecture is defined by more than deco. As in all cities, Miami's architecture reflects the tastes and attitudes of its inhabitants, who tend to adhere to the aesthetic philosophy espoused by Miami Beach's favorite architect, Morris Lapidus: 'Too much is never enough'. The earliest examples of this homegrown over-embellishment are the Mediterranean-revival mansions of Coral Gables (p71) and the Fabergé egg fantasy of the Vizcaya (p68). These residential wedding cakes established Miami's identity as a city of fantasies and dreams, outside the boundaries of conventional tastes, where experimentation was smiled upon as long as it was done with flash. They also spoke to a distinct Miami attitude that is enshrined in city tastes to this day: If you've got it, flaunt it, then shove it back in their faces for a second serving.

This penchant for imaginative, decorative flair overlaid the muscular postwar hotels and condos of the 1950s, giving birth to Miami Modernism (or Mimo). Mimo drew off the sleek lines and powerful presence of International Modernism, but led by Lapidus, it also eschewed austerity for grand, theatrical staging. Lapidus himself described his most famous structure, the Fontainebleau (p90), as influenced by the most popular mass media of its time: Hollywood and cinema. The glamour Lapidus captured in his buildings would go on to define Miami's aesthetic outlook; Versace incorporated it into his clothes and Ian Schrager has decked out his hotels with this sense of fairy-tale possibility. Which makes sense: the word 'glamour' originally meant a kind of spell that causes people to see things differently from what they really are, which makes it an appropriate inspiration for the buildings of the 'Magic City.'

The deco movement came about in the early 20th century, when affordable travel became a reality for the developed world. Sea journeys represented the height of luxury, and many deco buildings are decorated with nautical porthole windows.

Although art deco was inspired by stripped-down modernist aesthetics, it partly rebelled against utilitarianism with fantastically embellished bas-relief and frieze work, noticeable on the exterior of many South Beach hotels.

QUIRKY DECO DELIGHTS

» **Berkeley Shore Hotel** (1610 Collins Ave) One of the older hotels in South Beach, the Berkeley Shore has a lovely exterior set off by a cylindrical 'prow' rising out of candy-colored shade-providing 'eyebrows', plus elegant exterior friezes.

» **Avalon Hotel** (700 Ocean Dr) The exterior of the Avalon is a fantastic example of classical art-deco architecture – clean lines, old-school signage font lit up by tropical-green deco, fronted by a vintage 1950s Oldsmobile.

» **11th Street Diner** (p94) It doesn't get much more deco than dining in a classical Pullman train car. Many buildings on Miami Beach evoke planes, trains and automobiles – this diner is actually located in one.

THE CONCH CASTLES OF KEY WEST

Miami this, Miami that; yes, the flashy overstatement of the Magic City's architecture sure is beautiful. But what about Key West? Plenty of gorgeous historical buildings are packed into an easily walkable space and happen to be located on one of the prettiest islands in America. What are we waiting for?

Traditional Keys homes are known as 'Conch Houses' for the conch shell that was used as a building material to supplement what were traditionally low amounts of stone and wood; today the nickname also references Keys natives, known as Conchs. Conch Houses are perhaps the finest example of Caribbean Colonial architecture in the US outside of New Orleans. They're elegant, recognizably European homes, and while no two dwellings are exactly identical, there are some commonalities across the board. Shuttered windows, wraparound verandas, sloped roofs and structures built on raised piers – these are all elements that maximized shade and airflow in an era that preceded air-conditioning.

Many Conch Houses had fallen into states of total disrepair in the early 20th century, but as in South Beach, a community of artists, gays and lesbians established themselves here, refurbished the neighborhood and saved a bit of American heritage, all the while giving Key West the distinctive aesthetic profile that adds so much to its tourism appeal. You can see plenty of Conch Houses in the Key West historic district (the west end of the island); to see a particularly fine assortment in a small space, walk the four blocks along Eaton St from Eaton and William to Eaton and Whitehead.

A fun way to conduct an art-deco walking tour is to seek out certain design trends, such as Meso American temple flourishes, cruise-liner-modeled buildings, specific space-age structures and the like. There are certain Miami buildings that are exemplars of one or more themes.

There are excellent deco renovations all along Miami Beach which manage to combine modern aesthetic tastes with classical deco details. But in a sense, the modern South Beach school of design is just the natural evolution of principles laid down by deco in the early 20th century. Hoteliers such as Ian Schrager combine a faith in technology – in this case flat-screen TVs, Lucite 'ghost chairs' and computer-controlled lobby displays – with a general air of fantastical glamour. Conceptions of the future (a fantasy of the best the future can be), plus a deep bow to the best of historical decorative arts, still drives the design on Miami Beach. Newer hotels like the W (p88) and Ganservoort South (p88) have also expanded the architectural sense of proportion, integrating deco style into Miami Modern (which is to say, enormous) proportions. Whereas in the past deco hotels occupied a lot on a block, the mega-hotels of Miami Beach's future now stretch for an entire block.

Survival Guide

Directory A–Z

Accommodations

Our reviews (and rates) use the following room types:
» single occupancy (s)
» double occupancy (d)
» room (r), same rate for one or two people
» dorm bed (dm)
» suite (ste)
» apartment (apt)

Unless otherwise noted, rates do not include breakfast, bathrooms are private and all lodging is open year-round.

Rates don't include taxes, which vary considerably between towns; in fact, hotels almost never include taxes and fees in their rate quotes, so always ask for the *total rate with tax*. Florida's sales tax is 6%, and some communities tack on more. States, cities and towns also usually levy taxes on hotel rooms, which can increase the final bill by 10% to 12%.

Throughout the book, quoted rates are usually 'high season' rates, unless rates are distinguished as winter/summer or high/low season. Note that 'high season' can mean summer *or* winter depending on the region; see

destination chapters, and for general advice, see p14.

Our hotel price indicators rate is for standard double rooms:
» $ = under $100
» $$ = $100 to $200
» $$$ = over $200

These price indicators are guidelines only. Many places have certain rooms that cost above or below their standard rates, and seasonal/holiday fluctuations can see rates rise and fall dramatically, especially in Miami and tourist beach towns. Specific advice for the best rates varies by region, and is included throughout: on the one hand, booking in advance for high season tourist hot spots (like Miami and beaches towns) can be essential to ensure the room you want. On the other, inquiring at the last minute, or even same-day, can yield amazing discounts on any rooms still available.

Icons in reviews indicate the following:
» ℗ parking available; used only when parking is an issue
» ❄ air-conditioning
» @ internet terminal for guest use

» 🛜 wi-fi access in rooms
» 🌊 swimming pool
» 👪 family-friendly, when particularly notable
» 🐾 pet-friendly

For discounted rooms and last-minute deals, check the following websites:
» www.expedia.com
» www.hotels.com
» www.hotwire.com
» www.orbitz.com
» www.priceline.com
» www.travelocity.com
» www.roomsavers.com

B&Bs & Inns

These accommodations vary from small, comfy houses with shared bathrooms (least expensive) to romantic, antique-filled historic homes and opulent mansions with private baths (most expensive). Those accommodations focusing on upscale romance may discourage children. Also, inns and B&Bs often require a minimum stay of two or three days on weekends and advance reservations. Always call ahead to confirm policies (regarding kids, pets, smoking) and bathroom arrangements.

Camping

Three types of campsites are available: undeveloped ($10 per night), public ($15 to $20) and privately owned ($25 and up). In general, Florida campgrounds are quite safe. Undeveloped campgrounds are just that (undeveloped), while most public campgrounds have toilets, showers and drinking water. Reserve state park sites by calling ☎800-326-3521 or visiting www.reserveamerica.com.

Most privately owned campgrounds are geared to RVs (motor homes) but will also have a small section available for tent campers. Expect tons of amenities, like swimming pools, laundry facilities, convenience stores and bars. **Kampgrounds of America** (KOA; ☎406-

BOOK YOUR STAY ONLINE

For more accommodations reviews by Lonely Planet authors, check out hotels.lonelyplanet.com/florida. You'll find independent reviews, as well as recommendations on the best places to stay. Best of all, you can book online.

248-7444; www.koa.com) is a national network of private campgrounds; its Kamping Kabins have air-con and kitchens.

Hostels

In most hostels, group dorms are segregated by sex and you'll be sharing a bathroom; occasionally alcohol is banned. About half the hostels throughout Florida are affiliated with Hostelling International USA (HI-USA; ☑301-495-1240; www.hiusa .org). You don't have to be a member to stay, but you pay a slightly higher rate; you can join HI by phone, online or at most youth hostels. From the US, you can book many HI hostels through its toll-free reservations service (☑888-464-4872).

Florida has many independent hostels (www.hostels .com); most have comparable rates and conditions to HI hostels, and some are better.

Hotels

We have tried to highlight independently owned hotels in this guide. South Florida is a region rich in independent accommodation options, but in some towns, like Homestead, chain hotels are the best and sometimes the only option. In addition, if you're looking to spend less than $100 a night on a room in Miami, chain hotels are a decent option.

The calling-card of chain hotels is reliability: acceptable cleanliness, unremarkable yet inoffensive decor, and a comfortable bed. A TV, phone, air-conditioning, mini-refrigerator, microwave, hair dryer and safe are standard amenities in mid-range chains. A recent trend, most evident in Miami, is chain-owned hotels striving for upscale boutique-style uniqueness in decor and feel. High-end hotels – Ritz-Carlton in particular – overwhelm guests with services: valet parking, room service, newspaper delivery, dry cleaning, laundry, pools, health clubs, bars and other niceties. You'll find plenty of boutique and specialty hotels in places like South Beach and Key West. While all large chain hotels have toll-free reservation numbers, you may find better savings by calling the hotel directly.

Chain-owned hotels include the following:

Hilton (☑800-445-8667; www.hilton.com)
Holiday Inn (☑888-465-4329; www.holidayinn.com)
Marriott (☑888-236-2427; www.marriott.com)
Radisson (☑888-201-1718; www.radisson.com)
Ritz-Carlton (☑800-542-8680; www.ritzcarlton.com)
Sheraton (☑800-325-3535; www.starwoodhotels.com/sheraton)

Business Hours

Unless otherwise noted the standard business hours in this guide are as follows:
Banks 8:30am to 4:30pm Monday to Thursday, to 5:30pm Friday; sometimes 9am-12:30pm Saturday.
Drinking In Miami, most bars 5pm to 3am, in Miami Beach 24 hours, but most bars close for a few hours at 5am, in Key West 5pm to 4am, elsewhere 5pm to 2am. In all places, some bars close earlier if business is slow.

PRACTICALITIES

» South Florida has a number of major daily newspapers: *Miami Herald* (in Spanish, *El Nuevo Herald*), the *Miami New Times* and the *Key West Citizen* are the main newspapers covering the regions reviewed in this book.

» Florida receives all the major US TV and cable networks. Florida Smart (http://floridasmart.com/news) lists them all by region.

» Video systems use the NTSC color TV standard, not compatible with the PAL system.

» Electrical voltage is 110/120V, 60 cycles.

» Distances are measured in feet, yards and miles; weights are tallied in ounces, pounds and tons.

» Florida bans smoking in all enclosed workplaces, including restaurants and shops, but excluding 'standalone' bars (that don't emphasize food) and designated hotel smoking rooms.

» South Florida is in the US eastern time zone: noon in Miami equals 9am in San Francisco and 5pm in London. During daylight-saving time, clocks 'spring forward' one hour in March and 'fall back' one hour in November.

Businesses 9am to 7pm Monday to Friday.

Eating Breakfast 7am to 10:30am Monday to Friday, brunch 9am to 2pm Saturday and Sunday; lunch 11:30am to 2:30pm Monday to Friday; dinner 5pm to 10pm, later Friday and Saturday.

Post offices 9am to 5pm Monday to Friday; sometimes 9am to noon Saturday.

Shopping 10am-6pm Monday to Saturday, noon to 5pm Sunday; shopping malls keep extended hours.

Discount Cards

In Miami, check out the **Go Miami** card (www.smartdestinations.com). In Key West, there's **Gold Card Key West** (www.goldcardkeywest.com). In the rest of the Keys:

Keys Coupons (www.keyscoupons.com)

Keys Kash (www.fla-keys.com/keyskash)

Mile Marker Discounts (www.milemarkerdiscounts.com)

South Florida is a *very* competitive tourist destination, so persistence usually pays dividends.

Being a member of certain groups also gives access to discounts, usually about 10%, at many hotels, museums and sights. Simply carry the appropriate ID.

Auto-club membership See the Transportation chapter (p232)

Students Any student ID is typically honored; international students might consider an **International Student Identity Card** (ISIC; www.isiccard.com).

Seniors Generally refers to those 65 and older, but sometimes those 60 and older. Join the **American Association of Retired Persons** (AARP; ☑888-687-2277; www.aarp.org) for more travel bargains.

Electricity

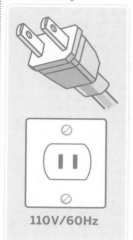

110V/60Hz

110V/60Hz

Food & Drink

In this book, price indicators apply to the typical dinner main:

» $ = $15 or less
» $$ = $15 to $30
» $$$ = $30 or more.

Outside of Miami, you can drop this range by $5 for each budget category.

As a rule, tip 15% to 20% of the total bill; you should only tip below this, or not tip at all (the latter is a pretty drastic move in American restaurants) if the service was bad.

You're expected to tip in bars as well, but the rules here are a little less defined. In general, you should definitely tip every time a bartender mixes you a complicated cocktail. But you'll be expected to tip for beer as well, which understandably doesn't go down well with a lot of foreigners. In this situation, you can tip a few dollars ($2 to $5 depending on the size of the round) on your first batch of beers. For every hour you stay at the bar, it's polite to tip a few more bucks. If you follow this approach, you don't have to tip a buck every time a bartender pops a cap off a bottle.

Gay & Lesbian Travelers

Miami, the Keys and Key West are out areas, where homosexuality is practiced openly year-round. Events like the White Party and Fantasy Fest are major dates in the North American gay calendar (see p20). Smaller towns in the Everglades region may be more culturally conservative, but even here gay travelers won't cause much of a stir. In Miami, the gay scene is so integrated it can be difficult to separate from the straight one; popular hot spots include South Beach (p104), North Beach (p105), and Wynwood and the Design District (p106). Check out our LGBT guides to Key West on p165).

Good gay and lesbian resources:

Damron (https://damron.com) Publishes popular national guidebooks, including *Women's Traveller, Men's Travel Guide,* and *Damron Accommodations.*

Gay Key West (www.gaykeywestfl.com)

Gay Yellow Network (www .gayyellow.com) City-based yellow-page listings include six Florida cities.

Key West Gay (www.key westgay.com)

Miami Gay Travel (www .miamigaytravel.com)

Miami-Dade Gay & Lesbian Chamber of Commerce (www.gogay miami.com)

Out Traveler (www.out traveler.com) Travel magazine specializing in gay travel.

Purple Roofs (www.purple roofs.com) Lists queer accommodations, travel agencies and tours worldwide.

Health

Florida, and the USA generally, has a high level of hygiene, so infectious diseases are not generally a significant concern for most travelers. There are no required vaccines, and tap water is safe to drink. Despite Florida's plethora of intimidating wildlife, the main concerns for travelers are sunburn and mosquito bites – as well as arriving with adequate health insurance in case of accidents. For hospital listings, see our respective chapters in Miami (p115) and Key West (p166). If you experience a major medical emergency in the Everglades, chances are you will end up in Miami. Most of the major islands in the Keys, including Marathon, Islamorada and Key Largo, have emergency medical facilities.

Internet Resources

There is a vast wealth of travel health advice on the internet. Two good sources:

MD Travel Health (www .mdtravelhealth.com) Provides complete, updated and free travel-health recommendations for every country.

World Health Organization (www.who.int/ith) The superb book International

Travel and Health is available free online.

Also, consult your government's travel-health website before departure, if one is available:

Australia (www.smartraveller .gov.au)

Canada (www.hc-sc.gc.ca /index-eng.php)

UK (www.fco.gov.uk/en/travel -and-living-abroad)

United States (wwwnc.cdc .gov/travel)

Health Insurance

The United States offers possibly the finest health care in the world. The problem is that it can be prohibitively expensive. It's essential to purchase travel-health insurance if your policy doesn't cover you when you're abroad.

If your health insurance does not cover you for medical expenses abroad, consider obtaining supplemental health or travel insurance. Find out in advance whether your insurance plan will make payments directly to the providers or if it will reimburse you later for any overseas health expenditures.

Health Care

In general, if you have a medical emergency, go to the emergency room of the nearest hospital.If you need any kind of emergency assistance, such as police, ambulance or firefighters, call 🚨911. This is a free call from any phone.

If the problem isn't urgent, call a nearby hospital and ask for a referral to a local physician; this is usually cheaper than a trip to the emergency room. Stand-alone, for-profit urgent-care centers provide good service, but can be the most expensive option.

Medications

Bring any medications you may need in their original containers, clearly labeled. A signed, dated letter from your physician that describes all of your medical conditions

and medications (including generic names) is also a good idea.

Pharmacies are abundantly supplied. However, some medications that are available over the counter in other countries require a prescription in the US. If you don't have insurance to cover the cost of prescriptions, these can be shockingly expensive.

Infectious Diseases

In addition to more-common ailments, there are several infectious diseases that are unknown or uncommon outside North America. Most are acquired by mosquito or tick bites.

Giardiasis Also known as traveler's diarrhea. A parasitic infection of the small intestines, typically contracted by drinking feces-contaminated freshwater. Never drink untreated stream, lake or pond water. Easily treated with antibiotics.

HIV/AIDS As do all sexually transmitted diseases, HIV infection occurs in the US. Use a condom for all sexual encounters.

Lyme Disease Though more common in the US northeast than Florida, Lyme disease occurs here. It is transmitted by infected deer ticks, and is signaled by a bull's-eye rash at the bite and flulike symptoms. Treat promptly with antibiotics. Removing ticks within 36 hours can avoid infection.

Rabies Though rare, the rabies virus can be contracted from the bite of any infected animal; bats are most common, and their bites are not always obvious. If bitten by any animal, consult with a doctor, since rabies is fatal if untreated.

West Nile Virus Extremely rare in Florida, West Nile virus is transmitted by culex mosquitoes. Most infections are mild or asymptomatic, but serious symptoms and even death can occur. There is no treatment for West Nile virus. For the latest update on affected areas, see the **US Geological Survey disease maps** (http://disease maps.usgs.gov).

Animal & Spider Bites

Florida's critters can be cute, but they can also bite and sting. Here are a few to watch out for.

Alligators and snakes Neither attacks humans unless startled or threatened. If you encounter them, simply back away. Florida has several venomous snakes, so always immediately seek treatment if bitten.

Jellyfish and stingrays Florida beaches can see both; avoid swimming when they're present (lifeguards often post warnings). Treat stings immediately; they hurt but aren't dangerous.

Spiders Florida is home to two dangerously venomous spiders – the black widow and the brown recluse. Seek immediate treatment if bitten by any spider; bites can cause major illness, and even death.

Insurance

It's expensive to get sick, crash a car or have things stolen from you in the US. Make sure to have adequate coverage before arriving. For car insurance see p232. To insure yourself for items that may be stolen from your car, consult your homeowner's (or renter's) insurance policy or consider investing in travel insurance.

Worldwide travel insurance is available at www .lonelyplanet.com/travel _services. You can buy, extend and claim online anytime – even if you're already on the road.

Internet Access

The USA and Florida are wired. Nearly every hotel and many restaurants and businesses offer high-speed internet access. In hotel listings, @indicates a guest internet terminal and 🛜indicates in-room wi-fi. With few exceptions, all hotels offer in-room plug-in and wi-fi in the lobby. Always ask about connection rates.

Most cafés offer inexpensive internet access, and most transportation stations and city parks are wi-fi hotspots. Public libraries provide free internet terminals, though sometimes you must get a temporary nonresident library card ($10). See Destination chapters, Information sections.

For a list of wi-fi hotspots (plus tech and access info), visit **Wi-Fi Alliance** (www.wi -fi.org) and **Wi-Fi Free Spot** (www.wififreespot.com). If you bring a laptop from outside the USA, invest in a universal AC and plug adapter. Also, confirm that your modem card will work.

Legal Matters

In everyday matters, if you are stopped by the police, note that there is no system for paying traffic tickets or other fines on the spot. The patrol officer will explain your options to you; there is usually a 30-day period to pay fines by mail.

If you're arrested, you are allowed to remain silent, though never walk away from an officer; you are entitled to have access to an attorney. The legal system presumes you're innocent until proven guilty. All persons who are arrested have the right to make one phone call. If you don't have a lawyer or family member to help you, call your embassy or consulate. The police will give you the number on request.

Drinking & Driving

Despite what you sometimes see, it's illegal to walk with an open alcoholic drink on the street. More importantly, don't drive with an 'open container'; any liquor in a car must be unopened or else stored in the trunk. If you're stopped while driving with an open container, police will treat you as if you were drinking and driving. Refusing a breathalyzer, urine or blood test is treated as if you'd taken the test and failed. A DUI (driving under the influence) conviction is a serious offense, subject to stiff fines and even imprisonment.

To purchase alcohol, you need to present a photo ID to prove your age.

Money

Prices quoted in this book are in US dollars ($). See Need to Know (p15) for exchange rates. Exchange foreign currency at international airports and most large banks in Miami, Orlando, Tampa and other Florida cities.

There is ease and availability of ATMs. Most ATM withdrawals using out-of-state cards incur surcharges of $2 or so.

Major credit cards are widely accepted, and they are required for car rentals.

ATMs have largely negated the need for traveler's checks. However, traveler's checks in US dollars are accepted like cash at most midrange and top-end businesses (but rarely at budget places). Personal checks not drawn on US banks are generally not accepted.

Tipping

Tipping is standard practice across America. In restaurants, for satisfactory to excellent service, tipping 15–20% of the bill is expected; less is okay at informal diners. Bartenders expect $1 per drink; cafe baristas a little change in the jar. Taxi drivers and hairdressers expect 10–15%. Skycaps at airports and porters at nice hotels expect $1 a bag or so. If you spend several nights in a hotel, it's

INTERNATIONAL VISITORS

Entering the Region

A passport is required for all foreign citizens. Unless eligible under the Visa Waiver Program (see below), foreign travelers must also have a tourist visa. To rent or drive a car, travelers from non-English-speaking countries should obtain an International Drivers Permit before arriving.

Travelers entering under the Visa Waiver Program must register with the US government's ESTA program (https://esta.cbp.dhs.gov) at least three days before arriving; earlier is better, since if denied, travelers must get a visa. Registration is valid for two years.

Upon arriving in the US, all foreign visitors must register in the US-Visit program, which entails having two index fingers scanned and a digital photo taken. For information on US-Visit, see the Department of Homeland Security (www.dhs.gov/us-visit).

Visas

All visitors should reconfirm entry requirements and visa guidelines before arriving. You can get visa information through www.usa.gov, but the US State Department (www.travel.state.gov) maintains the most comprehensive visa information, with lists of consulates and downloadable application forms. US Citizenship & Immigration Services (www.uscis.gov) mainly serves immigrants, not temporary visitors.

The Visa Waiver Program allows citizens of three dozen countries to enter the USA for stays of 90 days or less without first obtaining a US visa. See the ESTA website above for a current list. Under this program you must have a nonrefundable return ticket and 'e-passport' with digital chip. Passports issued/renewed before October 26, 2006, must be machine-readable.

Visitors who don't qualify for the Visa Waiver Program need a visa. Basic requirements are a valid passport, recent photo, travel details and often proof of financial stability. Students and adult males also must fill out supplemental travel documents.

The validity period for a US visitor visa depends on your home country. The length of time you'll be allowed to stay in the USA is determined by US officials at the port of entry. To stay longer than the date stamped on your passport, visit a local USCIS (☎800-375-5283; www.uscis.gov) office.

Customs

For a complete, up-to-date list of customs regulations, visit the website of US Customs & Border Protection (www.cbp.gov). Each visitor is allowed to bring into the US duty-free 1L of liquor (if you're 21 or older) and 200 cigarettes (if you're 18 or older) and up to $100 in gifts and purchases.

Embassies & Consulates

To find a US embassy in another country, visit the US Department of State website (www.usembassy.gov). Most foreign embassies in the US have their main consulates in Washington, DC, but some have representation in Miami. All are in Miami, except Italy.

Australia (☎305-858-7633; http://australia.visahq.com; 2103 Coral Way, Suite 108)

Brazil (☎305-285-6200; www.brazilmiami.org; 80 SW 8th St, Suite 2600)

Canada (☎305-579-1600; www.canadainternational.gc.ca/miami; 200 S Biscayne Blvd, Suite 1600)

France (☎305-403-4150; www.consulfrance-miami.org; 1395 Brickell Ave, Suite 1050)

Germany (☎305-358-0290; www.germany.info; 100 N Biscayne Blvd, Suite 2200)

Italy (☎305-374-6322; www.consmiami.esteri.it/Consolato_Miami; 4000 Ponce de León, Suite 590, Coral Gables)

Mexico (☎786-268-4900; http://consulmex.sre.gob.mx/miami; 5975 SW 72nd St, Suite 302)

Netherlands (☎877-388-2443; http://miami.the-netherlands.org; 701 Brickell Ave, Suite 500)

UK (☎305-374-3500; http://ukinusa.fco.gov.uk/florida; 1001 Brickell Bay Dr, Suite 2800)

polite to leave a few dollars for the cleaning staff.

Photography

All camera supplies (print and slide film, digital memory, camera batteries) are readily available in local drug-stores, which also usually provide inexpensive film developing (including one-hour service) and burning photo CDs and DVDs.

Don't pack unprocessed film (including the roll in your camera) into checked luggage because exposure to high-powered X-ray equipment will cause it to fog. As an added precaution, 'hand check' film separately from carry-on bags at airport security checkpoints.

When photographing people, politeness is usually all that's needed (though street performers appreciate a tip).

For a primer on taking good shots, consult Lonely Planet's *Travel Photography*.

Post

The **US Postal Service** (USPS; ☎800-275-8777; www .usps.com) is reliable and inexpensive. For 1st-class mail sent and delivered within the USA, postage rates are 44¢ for letters up to 1oz (20¢ for each additional ounce) and 29¢ for standard-size postcards. International airmail rates for postcards and letters up to 1oz are 80¢ to Canada and Mexico, and 98¢ to other countries.

You can have mail sent to you c/o General Delivery at most big post offices (it's usually held for 30 days). Most hotels will also hold mail for incoming guests.

Public Holidays

For festivals and events, see Month by Month (p20). On the following national public holidays, banks, schools and government offices (including post offices) are closed, and transportation, museums and other services operate on a Sunday schedule. Many stores, however, maintain regular business hours. Holidays falling on a weekend are usually observed the following Monday.

New Year's Day January 1

Martin Luther King Jr Day Third Monday in January

Presidents Day Third Monday in February

Easter March or April

Memorial Day Last Monday in May

Independence Day July 4

Labor Day First Monday in September

Columbus Day Second Monday in October

Veterans Day November 11

Thanksgiving Fourth Thursday in November

Christmas Day December 25

Safe Travel

Parts of Miami proper, including Little Haiti and nightlife hotspots like Overtown (just north of Downtown), experience high crime rates. You should be careful in these areas, and as a rule of thumb, avoid hanging out too much in Downtown after dark. Miami Beach on the other hand is safe from a crime perspective, although drunk driving seems depressingly common.

If you need any kind of emergency assistance, such as police, ambulance or firefighters, call ☎911. This is a free call from any phone. For health matters see p223.

Hurricanes

Florida hurricane season extends from June through November, but the peak is September and October. Relatively speaking, very few Atlantic Ocean and Gulf of Mexico storms become hurricanes, and fewer still are accurate enough to hit Florida, but the devastation

they wreak when they do can be enormous. Travelers should take all hurricane alerts, warnings and evacuation orders seriously.

Hurricanes are generally sighted well in advance, allowing time to prepare. When a hurricane threatens, listen to radio and TV news reports. For more information on storms and preparedness, contact the following:

Florida Division of Emergency Management (www .floridadisaster.org) Hurricane preparedness.

Florida Emergency Hotline (☎800-342-3557)

Miami Hurricane Hotline (☎305-468-5400)

National Weather Service (www.nws.noaa.gov)

Telephone

Always dial '1' before toll-free (☎800, 888 etc) and domestic long-distance numbers. Some toll-free numbers only work within the US. For local directory assistance, dial ☎411.

To make international calls from the US, dial ☎011 + country code + area code + number. For international operator assistance, dial ☎0. To call the US from abroad, the international country code for the USA is ☎1.

Pay phones are readily found in major cities, but are becoming rarer. Local calls cost 50¢. Private prepaid phone cards are available from convenience stores, supermarkets and pharmacies.

Most of the USA's mobile-phone systems are incompatible with the GSM 900/1800 standard used throughout Europe and Asia. Check with your service provider about using your phone in the US. In terms of coverage, Verizon has the most extensive network, but AT&T, Sprint and T-Mobile are decent. Cellular coverage is generally excellent, except in the Everglades and parts of rural northern Florida.

The area codes in Miami and the Keys are ☑305 and ☑786; in the Everglades ☑239.

Tourist Information

There are plenty of chambers of commerce and visitor centers in the region itching to help you make the most of your trip and pass out veritable libraries of pamphlets and coupons.

To order a packet of Florida information prior to coming, contact **Visit Florida** (www.visitflorida.com), and also see the list of websites in Need to Know (p15).

In Miami:

Coconut Grove Chamber of Commerce (☑305-444-7270; www.coconutgrovechamber.com; 2820 McFarlane Rd, Coconut Grove; ☺9am-5pm Mon-Fri)

Coral Gables Chamber of Commerce (☑305-446-1657; www.coralgableschamber.org; 224 Catalonia Ave, Coral Gables; ☺9am-5pm Mon-Fri)

Downtown Miami Welcome Center (☑786-472-5930; www.downtownmiami.com; 900 S Miami Ave; ☺9am-5pm Mon-Fri) Provides maps, brochures and tour information for the downtown area.

Greater Miami & the Beaches Convention & Visitor's Bureau (☑305-539-3000, 800-933-8448; www.miamiandbeaches.com;

701 Brickell Ave; ☺8:30am-5pm Mon-Fri) Located in an oddly intimidating high-rise building.

Miami Beach Chamber of Commerce (☑305-672-1300; www.miamibeachchamber.com; 1920 Meridian Ave, South Beach; ☺9am-5pm Mon-Fri)

In the Everglades:

Everglades City Area Chamber of Commerce (☑239-695-3941; cnr US Hwy 41 & Hwy 29; ☺9am-4pm)

Homestead Chamber of Commerce (☑305-247-2332; www.chamberinaction.com; 455 N Flagler Ave, Homestead; ☺9am-noon & 1-5pm Mon-Fri)

Ernest Coe Visitor Center (☑305-242-7700; www.nps.gov/ever; 40001 State Rd 9336; ☺8am-5pm)

Shark Valley Visitor Center (☑305-221-8776; www.nps.gov/ever/planyourvisit/svdirections; per car/bicycle $10/5; ☺8:30am-6pm)

Big Cypress Natural Preserve Visitor Center (☑239-695-4758; 33000 Tamiami Trail E; ☺8:30am-4:30pm)

In the Keys:

Key West Chamber of Commerce (☑305-294-2587; www.keywestchamber.org; 510 Greene St; ☺8:30am-6:30pm Mon-Sat, to 6pm Sun)

Lower Keys Chamber of Commerce (☑305-872-2411; www.lowerkeyschamber.com; MM 31 oceanside; ☺9am-5pm Mon-Fri, 9am-3pm Sat)

Marathon Visitors Center Chamber of Commerce (☑305-743-5417, 800-262-7284; www.floridakeysmarathon.com; MM 53.5 bayside; ☺9am-5pm)

Islamorada Chamber of Commerce (☑305-664-4503, 800-322-5397; www.islamoradachamber.com; MM 83.2 bayside; ☺9am-5pm Mon-Fri, 10am-3pm Sat & Sun)

Key Largo Chamber of Commerce (☑305-451-1414, 800-822-1088; www.keylargo.org; MM 106 bayside; ☺9am-6pm)

Travelers with Disabilities

Because of the high number of senior residents in Florida, most public buildings are wheelchair accessible and have appropriate restroom facilities. Transportation services are generally accessible to all, and telephone companies provide relay operators for the hearing impaired. Many banks provide ATM instructions in Braille, curb ramps are common and many busy intersections have audible crossing signals.

A number of organizations specialize in the needs of disabled travelers:

Access-Able Travel Source (www.access-able.com) An excellent website with many links.

Flying Wheels Travel (☑507-451-5005; http://flyingwheelstravel.com) A full-service travel agency specializing in disabled travel.

Mobility International USA (www.miusa.org) Advises disabled travelers on mobility issues and runs an educational exchange program.

Travelin' Talk Network (www.travelintalk.net) Run by the same people as Access-Able Travel Source; a global network of service providers.

Volunteering

Volunteering can be a great way to break up a long trip, and it provides memorable opportunities to interact with locals and the land in ways you never would when just passing through. Any of the animal sanctuaries and small parks listed in our chapters are always on the lookout for short-term volunteer help.

Miami Habitat for Humanity (☑305-634-3628; www.miamihabitat.org; 3800 NW 22nd Ave) Does a ton of work in Florida, building homes and helping the homeless.

Shake a Leg Miami (☎305-858-5500; www.shakealeg miami.org; 2620 S Bayshore Dr) A community watersports complex in Coconut Grove that aims to serve economically and physically disadvantaged children.

Florida Keys National Marine Center (☎305-292-0311; floridakeys.noaa.gov/vol unteer_opportunities/welcome) Can hook folks up with a plethora of environment-focused volunteer programs across the Keys.

Everglades National Park (☎305-242-7752; www.nps .gov/ever/supportyourpark /volunteer) Active volunteer program recruits both individuals and groups.

Volunteer Florida (www .volunteerflorida.org) The primary state-run organization; coordinates volunteer centers across the state. Though it's aimed at Floridians, casual visitors can find situations that match their time and interests.

Florida's state parks would not function without volunteers. Each park coordinates its own volunteers, and most also have the support of an all-volunteer 'friends' organization (officially called Citizen Support Organizations). Links and contact information are on the main **state park website** (http:// floridastateparks.org/getin volved/volunteer.cfm).

Women Travelers

Women traveling by themselves or in a group should encounter no particular problems unique to Florida. Indeed, there are a number of excellent resources to help traveling women.

The community website www.journeywoman.com facilitates women exchanging travel tips, with links to resources. The Canadian government (www.voyage.gc.ca) also publishes the useful, free, downloadable booklet 'Her Own Way'; online, look under 'Publications.'

These two national advocacy groups might also be helpful:

National Organization for Women (NOW; ☎202-628-8669; www.now.org)

Planned Parenthood (☎800-230-7526; www.planned parenthood.org) Offers referrals to medical clinics throughout the country.

In terms of safety issues, single women need to exhibit the same street smarts as any solo traveler, but they are sometimes more often the target of unwanted attention or harassment. Some women like to carry a whistle, mace or cayenne-pepper spray in case of assault. These sprays are legal to carry and use in Florida, but only in self-defense. Federal law prohibits them being carried on planes.

If you are assaulted, it may be better to call a rape-crisis hotline before calling the **police** (☎911); telephone books have listings of local organizations, or contact the 24-hour **National Sexual Assault Hotline** (☎800-656-4673; www .rainn.org). Or, go straight to a hospital. Police can sometimes be insensitive with assault victims, while a rape-crisis center or hospital will advocate on behalf of survivors and act as a link to other services, including the police.

Work

Seasonal service jobs in tourist beach towns and theme parks are common and often easy to get, if low-paying.

If you are a foreigner in the USA with a standard nonimmigrant visitors visa, you are forbidden to take paid work in the USA and will be deported if you're caught working illegally. In addition, employers are required to establish the bona fides of their employees or face fines. In particular, South Florida is notorious for large numbers of foreigners working illegally, and immigration officers are vigilant.

To work legally, foreigners need to apply for a work visa before leaving home. Student exchange visitors need a J1 visa, which the following organizations will help arrange:

American Institute for Foreign Study (AIFS;☎866-906-2437; www.aifs.com)

BUNAC (☎020-7251-3472; www.bunac.org)

Camp America (☎020-7581-7373; www.campamerica.co.uk)

Council on International Educational Exchange (CIEE; ☎800-407-8839; www .ciee.org)

InterExchange (☎212-924-0446; www.interexchange.org) Camp and au-pair programs.

International Exchange Programs (IEP) Australia (☎1300-300-912; www.iep.org .au); New Zealand (☎0800-443-769; www.iep.org.nz)

For nonstudent jobs, temporary or permanent, you need to be sponsored by a US employer (who will arrange an H-category visa). These aren't easy to obtain.

Transportation

GETTING THERE & AWAY

Nearly all international travelers come to South Florida by air, while most US travelers prefer air or car. Getting to South Florida by bus is a distant third option and by train an even more distant fourth. Miami is a major international airline hub, particularly for American Airlines, and it's the first port of call for many flights from Latin America and the Caribbean. Most flights come into Miami International Airport (MIA), although many are also directed to Fort Lauderdale-Hollywood International Airport (FLL). Seeing as it is located at the tip of the USA, Greater Mi-

ami is more of a termination of highways and rail lines, rather than a major land-transit interchange area.

Flights, tours and rail tickets can be booked online at www.lonelyplanet.com/bookings.

Air

Unless you live in or near Florida, flying to the region and then renting a car is the most time-efficient option.

Airports & Airlines

Miami International Airport (MIA; www.miami-airport.com) One of the state's two busiest airports, and one of the nation's most important international gateways.

Key West International Airport (EYW; www.monroecounty-fl.gov) A much quieter airport, located off S Roosevelt Blvd on the east side of the island.

Fort Lauderdale-Hollywood International Airport (FLL; www.broward.org/airport) A decent alternative gateway airport to the region, located 21 miles north of Downtown Miami.

Air service to Miami is frequent and direct. Flights come from all over the USA, Europe, Latin America and the Caribbean; Key West is served far less often, and often indirectly. The following international airlines service South Florida:

Aerolineas Argentinas (www.aerolineas.com)

AeroMexico (www.aeromexico.com)

Air Canada (www.aircanada.com)

Air France (www.airfrance.com)

Air Jamaica (www.airjamaica.com)

Air New Zealand (www.airnewzealand.com)

Alitalia (www.alitalia.com)

Bahamas Air (www.bahamasair.com)

British Airways (www.britishairways.com)

Cayman Airways (www.caymanairways.com)

El Al (www.elal.com)

Iberia (www.iberia.com)

KLM (www.klm.com)

Lan (www.lan.com)

CLIMATE CHANGE & TRAVEL

Every form of transportation that relies on carbon-based fuel generates CO_2, the main cause of human-induced climate change. Modern travel is dependent on airplanes, which might use less fuel per kilometer per person than most cars but travel much greater distances. The altitude at which aircraft emit gases (including CO_2) and particles also contributes to their climate-change impact. Many websites offer 'carbon calculators' that allow people to estimate the carbon emissions generated by their journey and, for those who wish to do so, to offset the impact of the greenhouse gases emitted with contributions to portfolios of climate-friendly initiatives throughout the world. Lonely Planet offsets the carbon footprint of all staff and author travel.

Lufthansa (www.lufthansa.com)

Qantas (www.qantas.com)

Swiss International Airlines (www.swiss.com)

Varig Brazilian Airlines (www.varig.com)

Virgin Atlantic (www.virgin-atlantic.com)

Land

Bus

For bus trips, **Greyhound** (☎800-231-2222; www.greyhound.com) is the main long-distance operator in the US. It serves Florida from most major cities. It also has the only scheduled statewide service (for more, see Getting Around).

Standard long-distance fares can be relatively high: bargain airfares can undercut buses on long-distance routes; on shorter routes, renting a car can be cheaper. Nonetheless, discounted (even half-price) long-distance bus trips are often available by purchasing tickets online seven to 14 days in advance. Then, once in Florida, you can rent a car to get around. Inquire about multiday passes.

Sample one-way fares (advance-purchase/standard fares) between Miami and some major US cities:

CITY	FARE	TIME	DAILY
Atlanta	$79/144	16-18hr	5-6
New Orleans	$136/149	23-24hr	3-4
New York City	$156/172	33-35hr	5-6
Washington, DC	$149/164	27-29hr	5-6

Car & Motorcycle

Driving to Florida is easy; there are no international borders or entry issues. Incorporating Florida into a larger USA road trip is very common, and having a car while in Florida is often a necessity.

Sample distances and times from various points in the US to Miami:

CITY	ROAD DISTANCE	TIME
Atlanta	660 miles	10½hr
Chicago	1380 miles	23hr
Los Angeles	2750 miles	44hr
New York City	1280 miles	22hr
Washington, DC	1050 miles	17hr

Train

If you're coming from the East Coast, **Amtrak** (☎800-872-7245; www.amtrak.com) makes a comfortable, affordable option for getting here. Amtrak's *Silver Service* (which includes *Silver Meteor* and *Silver Star* trains) runs between New York and Miami, with services that include major and small Florida towns in between. Unfortunately, there is no longer any direct service to Florida from Los Angeles, New Orleans, Chicago or the Midwest. Trains from these destinations connect to the *Silver Service* route, but the transfer adds a day or so to your travel time.

Book tickets in advance. Children, seniors and military personnel receive discounts.

FROM	TO	FARE	TIME
New York	Jacksonville	$125-210	18-20hr
New York	Miami	$125-215	28-31hr
New York	Orlando	$125-210	22-23hr
New York	Tampa	$125-210	26hr

Sea

Florida is nearly completely surrounded by the ocean, and it's a major cruise-ship port. If you arrive in Miami via a cruise ship, you'll likely arrive via the **Port of Miami** (☎305-347-4800; www.miamidade.gov/portofmiami), which received nearly four million passengers in 2003 and is known as the 'cruise capital of the world'. You can boat from Miami to the Keys on the **Key West Express** (☎888-539-2628; www.seakeywestexpress.com), which departs from Fort Myers Beach daily at 8:30am and does a 3½-hour cruise to Key West. Returning boats depart the seaport at 6pm. You'll want to show up 1½ hours before your boat departs. During winter and fall the Express also leaves from Marco Island.

GETTING AROUND

Once you reach South Florida, traveling by car is the best way of getting around – it allows you to reach areas not otherwise served by public transportation.

Air

The US airline industry is reliable, safe and serves Florida extremely well, both from the rest of the country and within Florida. However, the industry's continuing financial troubles have resulted in a series of high-profile mergers in recent years: Midwest joining Frontier, Orlando-based Air Tran merging into Southwest, and biggest of all, Continental merging with United.

In general, this has led to fewer flights, fuller airplanes, less perks, more fees and higher rates. Airport security screening procedures also keep evolving; allow extra time.

Airlines in Florida

Main domestic airlines operating in South Florida:

American (AA; ☎800-433-7300; www.aa.com) Has

Miami hub and service to and between major Florida cities.

Cape Air (9K; ☑866-227-3247; www.flycapeair.com) Convenient between Fort Myers and Key West.

Delta (DL; ☑800-221-1212; www.delta.com) International carrier to main Florida cities, plus flights from Miami to Orlando and Tampa.

Spirit (NK; ☑800-772-7117; www.spiritair.com) Florida-based discount carrier serves Florida cities from East Coast US, Caribbean, and Central and South America.

United (UA; ☑800-864-8331; www.united.com) International flights to Orlando and Miami, plus domestic flights to and between main Florida cities.

US Airways (US;☑800-428-4322; www.usairways.com) Serves Florida from most of US.

Air Passes

International travelers who plan on doing a lot of flying, both in and out of the region, might consider buying an air pass. Air passes are available only to non-US citizens, and they must be purchased in conjunction with an international ticket. Conditions and cost structures can be complicated, but all include a certain number of domestic flights (from three to 10) that must be used within 60 days. Sometimes you must plan your itinerary in advance, but sometimes dates (and even destinations) can be left open. Talk with a travel agent to determine if an air pass would save you money based on your plans.

The two main airline alliances are the **Star Alliance** (www.staralliance.com) and **One World** (www.oneworld .com).

Bicycle

Regional bicycle touring is very popular. Flat topo-graphy, ocean breezes on the Overseas Highway and increasing bicycle infrastructure in Miami and Miami Beach make for great itineraries. Just be wary of your surroundings, especially if you go biking near the north of Downtown. A few blocks north of that area are especially tense. You may want to target winter to spring; summer is unbearably hot and humid for long-distance biking.

Renting a bicycle is easy in South Florida. Try the Everglades International Hostel if you want to cycle in the Glades (p129). In Key West there's a plethora of options located on the main drags of Truman Ave and Simonton St; bicycle is probably the easiest way to get around flat Key West. Don't forget that a bike-share program now makes cycling in Miami Beach especially easy. For more information on the bike-share program, rental agencies and routes in greater Miami, see p116 and p76.

Some other things to keep in mind:

Helmet laws Helmets are required for anyone age 16 and younger. Adults are not required to wear helmets, but should.

Road rules Bikes must obey auto rules; ride on the right-hand side of the road, with traffic, not on sidewalks.

Transporting your bike to Florida Bikes are considered checked luggage and often must be boxed and fees can be high (over $200).

Theft Bring and use a sturdy lock (U-type is best). Especially in Miami Beach, theft is common.

For more information and assistance, visit these organizations:

League of American Bicyclists (www.bikeleague .org) General advice, plus lists of local bike clubs and repair shops.

International Bicycle Fund (www.ibike.org) Comprehensive overview of bike regulations by airline and lots of advice.

Better World Club (www .betterworldclub.com) Offers a bicycle roadside assistance program.

Boat

Florida is a huge destination and departure point for cruises of all kind. The **Port of Miami** (www.miamidade.gov /portofmiami) likes to brag that it's the 'cruise capital of the world' with good reason: this is the largest cruise-ship port on Earth. **Port Everglades** (www.porteverglades.net, www.fort-lauderdale-cruises .com), located near Fort Lauderdale, is also a potential gateway port to the Miami region.

For specials on other multi-night and multiday cruises, see the following:

» www.cruise.com
» www.cruiseweb.com
» www.vacationstogo.com
» www.cruisesonly.com

Major cruise companies:
Carnival Cruise Lines (☑800-764-7419; www.carnival .com)
Norwegian Cruise Line (☑866-234-7350; www2.ncl .com)
Royal Caribbean (☑866-562-7625; www.royalcaribbean .com)

Bus

Greyhound (☑800-231-2222; www.greyhound.com) is the major carrier in and out of Miami. There are four major terminals: **Airport terminal** (☑305-871-1810; 4111 NW 27th St); **Main Downtown terminal** (Map p56; ☑305-374-6160; 1012 NW 1st Ave); **North Miami terminal** (Map p52; ☑305-945-0801; 16560 NE 6th Ave); and the **Southern Miami terminal** (☑305-296-9072;

GREEN TRAVEL

» **Biking** Good exercise, no gas, fresh air – what's not to love?

» **Metromover** A free way of getting around downtown, but only serves Miami (not Miami Beach).

» **Tri-rail** Cheap, fast links between Miami and its outer suburbs.

» **Gables Trolley** Fun, nostalgic public transportation through Coral Gables.

» **Walking!** Especially in South Beach, which is barely 2 miles (2.8km) long.

Cutler Ridge Mall, 20,505 S Dixie Hwy).

Car & Motorcycle

The easiest and most popular way to travel around South Florida is by car. While it's possible to avoid using a car on single-destination trips to Miami or Key West, relying on public transit is inconvenient for even limited regional touring. Motorcycles are also popular in Florida, given the flat roads and warm weather (summer rain excepted). In addition, you practically must have motorized transport to explore the Everglades. Greyhound buses run through the Keys, but you can't pull over and smell the roses by the side of the Overseas Highway, which is 90% of the fun.

Roads are well-kept and maintained, with the exception of the occasional pothole and construction site in Miami, and the muddy Loop Rd in the Everglades (which was being improved at the time of writing).

Admittedly, driving in Miami can be its own special... experience (read: hell). For more information, see p116.

Automobile Associations

The **American Automobile Association** (AAA; ☎800-874-7532; www.aaa.com) has reciprocal agreements with several international auto clubs (check with AAA and bring your membership card). For members, AAA offers travel insurance, tour books, diagnostic centers for used-car buyers and a greater number of regional offices, and it advocates politically for the auto industry.

An ecofriendly alternative is the **Better World Club** (☎866-238-1137; www .betterworldclub.com), which donates 1% of earnings to assist environmental cleanup, offers ecologically sensitive choices for services and advocates politically for environmental causes. Better World also has a roadside assistance program for bicycles.

In both organizations, the central member benefit is 24-hour emergency roadside assistance anywhere in the USA. Both clubs also offer trip planning and free maps, travel agency services, car insurance and a range of discounts (car rentals, hotels etc).

Driver's License

Foreign visitors can legally drive in the USA for up to 12 months with their home driver's license. However, getting an International Driving Permit (IDP) is recommended; this will have more credibility with US traffic police, especially if your home license doesn't have a photo or is in a foreign language. Your automobile association at home can issue an IDP, valid for one year, for a small fee. You must carry your home license together with the IDP. To drive a motorcycle, you need either a valid US state motorcycle license or an IDP specially endorsed for motorcycles.

Insurance

Don't put the key into the ignition if you don't have insurance, which is legally required, or else you risk financial ruin if there's an accident. If you already have auto insurance (even overseas), or if you buy travel insurance, make sure that the policy has adequate liability coverage for a rental car in Florida; it probably does, but check.

Rental-car companies will provide liability insurance, but most charge extra. Always ask. Rental companies almost never include collision damage insurance for the vehicle. Instead, they offer optional Collision Damage Waiver (CDW) or Loss Damage Waiver (LDW), usually with an initial deductible of $100 to $500. For an extra premium, you can usually get this deductible covered as well. However, most credit cards now offer collision damage coverage for rental cars if you rent for 15 days or less and charge the total rental to your card. This is a good way to avoid paying extra fees to the rental company, but note that if there's an accident, you sometimes must pay the rental-car company first and then seek reimbursement from the credit-card company. Check your credit card policy. Paying extra for some or all of this insurance increases the cost of a rental car by as much as $10 to $30 a day.

Parking

Parking in Miami is pretty straightforward. Regulations are well signed and meters and street parking is plentiful, with the exception of Downtown by day (and the area by Brickell at almost anytime) and South Beach by night. Downtown, near Bayside Marketplace, parking is cheap but confusing: you must find a place in the head-on parking lots, buy a ticket from a central machine, and display it in your windshield.

Miami Beach Parking (☑305-673-7275; www .miamibeachfl.gov/parking) does a good job of maintaining a series of extremely convenient garages across Miami Beach (and cheap, at $1 per hour, although there is a $15 flat rate from 8pm to 5am on Friday, Saturday and Sunday). Look for giant blue 'P' signs at Collins Ave at 7th St, Collins Ave at 14th St, Washington Ave at 12th St, Washington Ave at 16th St, and 17th St across from the Jackie Gleason Theater of the Performing Arts (perfect if you're headed to Lincoln Rd). If you park illegally or if the meter runs out, parking fines are about $25 to $34, but a tow could cost a lot more. Other useful parking garages can be found in Coral Gables and Coconut Grove.

Street meters in Miami Beach south of 23rd street are $1.50 per hour and need to be fed from 9am to 3am! North of 23rd St meters cost $1 per hour and operate from 8am to 6pm. Most meters allow you to pay for up to three hours, although some have increased that range. Many meter machines include a credit card option; failing that, you may want to purchase a Meter Card, available from the **Miami Beach City Hall** (Map p44; 1st fl, 1700 Convention Center Dr); the **Miami Beach Chamber of Commerce** (Map p44; 1920 Meridian Ave); any municipal parking lot or any Publix grocery store. Denominations come in $10, $20 and $25 (and meters cost $1 per hour).

Rental
CAR
Car rental is a very competitive business. Most rental companies require that you have a major credit card, that you be at least 25 years old and that you have a valid driver's license (your home license will do but an IDP

is recommended). Some national companies may rent to drivers between the ages of 21 and 24 for an additional charge. Those under 21 are usually not permitted to rent at all.

Good independent agencies are listed in this guide and by **Car Rental Express** (www.carrentalexpress.com), which rates and compares independent agencies in US cities; it's particularly useful for searching out cheaper long-term rentals.

National car-rental companies include the following:
Alamo (www.alamo.com)
Avis (www.avis.com)
Budget (www.budget.com)
Dollar (www.dollar.com)
Enterprise (www.enterprise .com)
Hertz (www.hertz.com)
National (www.nationalcar .com)
Rent-a-Wreck (www.renta wreck.com)
Thrifty (www.thrifty.com)

Rental cars are readily available at all airport locations and many downtown city locations. With advance reservations for a small car, the daily rate with unlimited mileage is about $35 to $55, while typical weekly rates are $200 to $400, plus a myriad of taxes and fees. If you rent from a nonairport location, you save the exorbitant airport fees.

An alternative in Miami is **Zipcar** (www.zipcar.com), a car-sharing service that charges hourly/daily rental fees with free gas, insurance and limited mileage included; prepayment is required.

MOTORCYCLE
To straddle a Harley across Florida, contact **EagleRider** (☑888-900-9901; www.eagle rider.com), which has offices in Miami. It offers a wide range of models, which start at $150 a day, plus liability insurance. Adult riders (over 21) are not required by Florida law to wear a helmet, but you should.

MOTORHOME (RV)
Forget hotels. Drive your own. Touring Florida by recreational vehicle can be as low-key or as over-the-top as you wish.

After settling on the vehicle's size, consider the impact of gas prices, gas mileage, additional mileage costs, insurance and refundable deposits; these can add up quickly. Typically, RVs don't come with unlimited mileage, so estimate your mileage up front to calculate the true rental cost.
CruiseAmerica (☑800-671-8042; www.cruiseamerica .com) The largest national RV-rental firm has offices across South Florida.
Adventures on Wheels (☑800-943-3579; www.adven turesonwheels.com) Office in Miami.
Recreational Vehicle Rental Association (www.rvra.org) Good resource for RV information and advice, and helps find rental locations.

Road Rules
If you're new to Florida or US roads, here are some basics:

» The maximum speed limit on interstates is 75mph, but that drops to 65mph and 55mph in urban areas. Pay attention to the posted signs. City street speed limits vary between 15mph and 45mph.

» Florida police officers are strict with speed-limit enforcement, and speeding tickets are expensive. If caught going over the speed limit by 10mph, the fine is $155.

» All passengers in a car must wear seat belts; the fine for not wearing a seat belt is $30. All children under three must be in a child safety seat.

» As in the rest of the US, drive on the right-hand side of the road. On highways, pass in the left-hand lane, but anxious drivers often pass wherever space allows.

» Unless otherwise signed, you can turn right at a red

light as long as you come to a stop first. At four-way stop signs, the car that reaches the intersection first has right of way. In a tie, the car on the right has right of way.

Hitchhiking

Hitchhiking is never entirely safe in any country, and we don't recommend it. Travelers who decide to hitch should understand that they are taking a small but serious risk. You may not be able to identify the local rapist or murderer before you get into the vehicle. People who do choose to hitch will be safer if they go in pairs and let someone know where they are planning to go. Be sure to ask the driver where he or she is going rather than telling the person where you want to go.

Local Transportation

Bus

MIAMI

Miami's local bus system is called **Metrobus** (☑305-891-3131; www.miamidade.gov/transit) and, though it has an extensive route system, service is pretty spotty. Each bus route has a different schedule and routes generally run from about 5:30am to about 11pm, though some are 24 hours. Rides cost $2 and must be paid in exact change with a token, coins or a combination of a dollar bill and coins (most locals use the monthly Metropass). An easy-to-read route map is available online.

In South Beach, an excellent option is the **South Beach Local Circulator** (☑305-891-3131), a looping shuttle bus with disabled-rider access that operates along Washington between South Pointe Dr and 17th St and loops back around on Alton Rd on the west side of the beach. Rides cost only 25¢ and come along every 10 to

15 minutes between 7:45am and 1am Monday to Saturday and 10am to 1am Sunday and holidays. Look for official bus stops, every couple of blocks, marked by posts with colorful Electrowave signs.

Coral Gables has its own new shuttle in the form of a hybrid-electric bus disguised as a trolley. It's free, but only really good for getting around the Gables (also, you may have to put up with some cutesy barbershop quartet – we guess this makes the whole experience more old timey). The north–south route runs along Ponce de León Blvd from the Douglas Metrorail Station to SW 8th St (between 6:30am and 8pm Monday to Thursday, and 6:30am and 10pm Friday).

KEY WEST

Key West Transit (☑305-809-3910; www.kwtransit.com; single fare $2) operates a local bus service on Key West. The bus line connects the western, historical half of the island to the residential units and strip malls of eastern Key West. This is primarily a utility service for island residents who work on the west half of Key West and do not have the means to drive the way.

If you're a tourist, KW Transit's more useful service is the **Lower Keys Shuttle**; see www.keywestcity.com and look under departments, then Department of Transportation. This commuter bus service runs between Key West and Marathon nine times a day; fare is just $3. From Marathon you can connect to the **301 Dade-Monroe Express** ($2.35), operated by Dade County, which connects Marathon to Florida City six times a day; see www.miamidade.gov/transit for a detailed schedule. This route works in the opposite direction as well, which means you can feasibly take public buses from Florida City all the way to Key West. Just plan on a

long day; for example, if you left from Key West airport at 12:21pm, you'd reach Mile Marker 50 in Marathon at 2pm. Then you'd have to wait till the 301 leaves from MM 50 at 3:45pm, landing you in Florida City at 6pm.

Metro

In Miami, the driverless **Metromover** (www.miami dade.gov/transit/mover) circles downtown and connects with **Metrorail** (www.miamidade.gov/transit/rail). It is a 21-mile-long heavy rail system that has one elevated line running from Hialeah through downtown Miami and south to Kendall/Dadeland. Trains run every five to 15 minutes from 6am to midnight. The fare is $2, or $1 with a Metromover transfer. As of this writing, plans had already started on an extension of the Metrorail from Miami proper to the airport.

The regional **Tri-Rail** (☑800-874-7245; www.tri-rail.com) train connects Dade, Broward and Palm Beach counties. Fares are calculated on a zone basis, and the route spans six zones. No tickets are sold on the train, so allow time to make your purchase before boarding. All trains and stations are accessible to riders with disabilities. For a list of stations, log on to the Tri-Rail website.

Taxi

Outside MIA, South Beach and the Port of Miami, where taxis buzz around like bees at a hive, you'll likely use a phone to hail a cab. Try **Metro** (☑305-888-8888), **Sunshine** (☑305-445-3333) or **Yellow** (☑305-444-4444) for a ride.

Taxis in Miami have flat and metered rates. You will not have to pay extra for luggage or for extra people in the cab, though you are expected to tip an additional 10% to 15%. Add about 10% to normal taxi fares (or a dollar, whichever is greater). If you have a bad experience, get the driver's chauffeur license number, name and license plate number and contact the **Taxi Complaints Line** (☑305-375-2460).

In Key West, pick up a metered pink taxi from **Key West Taxis** (☑305-296-6666).

Train

Amtrak (☑800-872-7245; www.amtrak.com) trains run between a number of Florida cities. As a way to get around Florida, Amtrak offers extremely limited service, and yet for certain specific trips their trains can be very easy

and inexpensive. In essence, daily trains run between Jacksonville, Orlando and Miami, with one line branching off to Tampa. In addition, thruway motorcoach (or bus) service gets Amtrak passengers to Daytona Beach, St Petersburg and Fort Myers.

behind the scenes

SEND US YOUR FEEDBACK

We love to hear from travelers – your comments keep us on our toes and help make our books better. Our well-traveled team reads every word on what you loved or loathed about this book. Although we cannot reply individually to postal submissions, we always guarantee that your feedback goes straight to the appropriate authors, in time for the next edition. Each person who sends us information is thanked in the next edition – and the most useful submissions are rewarded with a free book.

Visit **lonelyplanet.com/contact** to submit your updates and suggestions or to ask for help. Our award-winning website also features inspirational travel stories, news and discussions.

Note: We may edit, reproduce and incorporate your comments in Lonely Planet products such as guidebooks, websites and digital products, so let us know if you don't want your comments reproduced or your name acknowledged. For a copy of our privacy policy visit lonelyplanet.com/privacy.

OUR READERS

Many thanks to the travelers who used the last edition and wrote to us with helpful hints, useful advice and interesting anecdotes:

Lars Andersson, Jorge Azcarate, Chris Brown, Jeff Buckley, Ray Dunn, Judy Gawelek, Stefan Girsberger, Catherine Larkman, Samuel Martin, Christianne Oosterbaan, Samuela Poncia, Priya Sharma, Ben Singer

AUTHOR THANKS

Adam Karlin

Thanks: Anna Whitlow, Paula Nino, Jordan Melnick, Megan Harmon, the Paquet family, my Keys crew and every other Floridian who hooked it up. Big thanks to the Lonely Planet crew: Alison, Jennye Garibaldi, Jeff, Jennifer and Emily. Thanks to my grandmother, Rhoda Brickman, for getting me down to Florida in the first place, to my parents who always give me a place to write, and to Rachel for being Rachel.

ACKNOWLEDGMENTS

Climate map data adapted from Peel MC, Finlayson BL & McMahon TA (2007) 'Updated World Map of the Köppen-Geiger Climate Classification', *Hydrology and Earth System Sciences,* 11, 163344.

Cover photograph: Modern version of art-deco-style building, South Beach, Miami, Cosmo Condina / Getty Images ©

Many of the images in this guide are available for licensing from Lonely Planet Images: www.lonelyplanetimages.com.

THIS BOOK

This 6th edition of Lonely Planet's *Miami & the Keys* guidebook was written by Adam Karlin, who also wrote the previous edition. Earlier editions were written by Beth Greenfield, Kim Grant, Nick Selby and Corinna Selby. This guidebook was commissioned in Lonely Planet's Oakland office, and produced by the following:

Commissioning Editor Jennye Garibaldi

Coordinating Editor Charlotte Orr

Coordinating Layout Designer Wibowo Rusli

Managing Editor Brigitte Ellemor

Senior Editor Susan Paterson

Managing Cartographer Shahara Ahmed

Managing Layout Designers Chris Girdler, Jane Hart

Assisting Editors Alice Barker, Jackey Coyle, Briohny Hooper, Anne Mulvaney

Assisting Cartographers Anita Banh, Valeska Canas, Xavier Di Toro

Cover Research Naomi Parker

Internal Image Research Sabrina Dalbesio

Thanks to Sasha Baskett, Ryan Evans, Heather Howard, Trent Paton, Raphael Richards, Gerard Walker

NOTES

index

how to use this book

These symbols will help you find the listings you want:

⊙	Sights	☞	Tours	♟	Drinking
🏖	Beaches	🎎	Festivals & Events	☆	Entertainment
🏃	Activities	🛏	Sleeping	🔒	Shopping
🐾	Courses	✕	Eating	ℹ	Information/Transport

Look out for these icons:

TOP CHOICE	Our author's recommendation
FREE	No payment required
🌱	A green or sustainable option

Our authors have nominated these places as demonstrating a strong commitment to sustainability – for example by supporting local communities and producers, operating in an environmentally friendly way, or supporting conservation projects.

These symbols give you the vital information for each listing:

☎	Telephone Numbers	☎	Wi-Fi Access	🚌	Bus
⊙	Opening Hours	🏊	Swimming Pool	Ⓜ	Metro
Ⓟ	Parking	🥗	Vegetarian Selection	Ⓢ	Subway
⊖	Nonsmoking	📖	English-Language Menu	⊖	London Tube
✳	Air-Conditioning	👪	Family-Friendly	🚋	Tram
@	Internet Access	🐾	Pet-Friendly	🚆	Train

Reviews are organised by author preference.

Map Legend

Sights
- 🏖 Beach
- ⚑ Buddhist
- 🏰 Castle
- ✚ Christian
- 🕉 Hindu
- ☪ Islamic
- ✡ Jewish
- ❶ Monument
- 🏛 Museum/Gallery
- ⊗ Ruin
- 🍷 Winery/Vineyard
- 🐾 Zoo
- ◉ Other Sight

Activities, Courses & Tours
- 🤿 Diving/Snorkelling
- 🛶 Canoeing/Kayaking
- ⛷ Skiing
- 🏄 Surfing
- 🏊 Swimming/Pool
- 🚶 Walking
- 🏄 Windsurfing
- ✚ Other Activity/Course/Tour

Sleeping
- 🛏 Sleeping
- ⛺ Camping

Eating
- ✕ Eating

Drinking
- ♟ Drinking
- ☕ Cafe

Entertainment
- ✪ Entertainment

Shopping
- 🛍 Shopping

Information
- ✉ Post Office
- ℹ Tourist Information

Transport
- ✈ Airport
- ⊗ Border Crossing
- 🚌 Bus
- 🚠 Cable Car/Funicular
- 🚲 Cycling
- ⛴ Ferry
- Ⓜ Metro
- 🚝 Monorail
- Ⓟ Parking
- Ⓢ S-Bahn
- 🚕 Taxi
- 🚆 Train/Railway
- 🚋 Tram
- ⊖ Tube Station
- Ⓤ U-Bahn
- ● Other Transport

Routes
- Tollway
- Freeway
- Primary
- Secondary
- Tertiary
- Lane
- Unsealed Road
- Plaza/Mall
- Steps
-)=(Tunnel
- Pedestrian Overpass
- Walking Tour
- Walking Tour Detour
- Path

Boundaries
- International
- State/Province
- Disputed
- Regional/Suburb
- Marine Park
- Cliff
- Wall

Population
- ✪ Capital (National)
- ◉ Capital (State/Province)
- ● City/Large Town
- ● Town/Village

Geographic
- 🏠 Hut/Shelter
- 🔦 Lighthouse
- 👁 Lookout
- ▲ Mountain/Volcano
- 🌴 Oasis
- 🌳 Park
-)(Pass
- 🌲 Picnic Area
- 💧 Waterfall

Hydrography
- River/Creek
- Intermittent River
- Swamp/Mangrove
- Reef
- Canal
- Water
- Dry/Salt/Intermittent Lake
- Glacier

Areas
- Beach/Desert
- +++ Cemetery (Christian)
- ××× Cemetery (Other)
- Park/Forest
- Sportsground
- Sight (Building)
- Top Sight (Building)

OUR STORY

A beat-up old car, a few dollars in the pocket and a sense of adventure. In 1972 that's all Tony and Maureen Wheeler needed for the trip of a lifetime – across Europe and Asia overland to Australia. It took several months, and at the end – broke but inspired – they sat at their kitchen table writing and stapling together their first travel guide, *Across Asia on the Cheap*. Within a week they'd sold 1500 copies. Lonely Planet was born.

Today, Lonely Planet has offices in Melbourne, London and Oakland, with more than 600 staff and writers. We share Tony's belief that 'a great guidebook should do three things: inform, educate and amuse'.

OUR WRITERS

Adam Karlin

Coordinating Author Adam grew up, as so many Americans do, with grand-parents in Florida, and fondly remembers many a December snowbirding in West Palm Beach. Later in life he worked as a reporter for the *Key West Citizen*. What followed was a period of writing on trailer-park evictions, mosquito-eating guppies, melodramatic local government hearings (is there any other kind?) and Cuban boat people, plus short stints working as a radio DJ and bouncer in the Keys. Eventually he was hired by Lonely Planet to cover South Florida in all her myriad weirdness. Since then he's written or contributed to over two dozen guidebooks for the company, almost always in tropical places: the Southern USA, Caribbean, Africa and Southeast Asia. It's a living. Follow Adam at www.walkonfine.com.

Read more about Adam at:
lonelyplanet.com/members/adamkarlin

Published by Lonely Planet Publications Pty Ltd
ABN 36 005 607 983
6th edition – Jan 2012
ISBN 978 1 74179 577 6
© Lonely Planet 2012   Photographs © as indicated 2012
10 9 8 7 6 5 4 3 2 1
Printed in China